Nelson's Fleet at Trafalgar

BRIAN LAVERY

NAVAL INSTITUTE PRESS
ANNAPOLIS, MARYLAND

ACKNOWLEDGEMENTS

I would like to thank the following for their help in writing this book:

Colin White, Robert Gardiner, Alan Pearsall, Tom Wareham, Roger Knight,
Roger Morriss, Chris Ware, Pat Crimmin, Clive Wilkinson, Daniel Baugh,
Gillian Hughes, David Syrett, Andrew Lambert, Nicholas Rodger,
and the late David Lyon.

The staff and students of Maddingley Hall, Cambridge, and the
Open Museum at the National Maritime Museum.

The staff of the Library and Manuscripts Department of the National Maritime
Museum, including Jill Davies, Daphne Knott, Kiri Ross-Jones, Hellen Pethers,
Janny Harris and Liza Verity. At the Royal Naval Museum, Portsmouth,
Campbell McMurray and Matthew Sheldon.
Thanks also to the staff of the British Library, National Archive (known as the Public
Record Office while this research was done) and London Library.

Thanks also to Rachel Giles, Fiona Renkin and Eleanor Dryden
of the National Maritime Museum Publishing Department.

First published in 2004 by the
National Maritime Museum, Greenwich, London, SE10 9NF.
www.nmm.ac.uk

Published and distributed in the United States of America
and Canada by Naval Institute Press, 291 Wood Road,
Annapolis, Maryland 21402-5034

Library of Congress Control No 2003111378

ISBN 1 59114 610 0

Designed by The Book Group
Cover design by Mousemat Design Ltd
Printed and bound in Slovenia

Contents

Picture Acknowledgements 4

Chapter 1: Mobilization 5

Chapter 2: The *Victory* 14

Chapter 3: The Threat From Boulogne 26

Chapter 4: The *Bellerophon* 41

Chapter 5: The Crews 46

Chapter 6: The *Defence* 56

Chapter 7: The Mediterranean Fleet 61

Chapter 8: The *Mars* 73

Chapter 9: The Chase 77

Chapter 10: The *Euryalus* 87

Chapter 11: Barham at the Admiralty 91

Chapter 12: Cadiz 99

Chapter 13: The *Revenge* 107

Chapter 14: Officers 116

Chapter 15: Collingwood and the Stick 127

Chapter 16: The Fleet 134

Chapter 17: Into Battle 147

Chapter 18: The First Round 158

Chapter 19: The Later Battle 168

Chapter 20: The Storm 181

Chapter 21: The Aftermath 192

Notes 200

Index 205

Picture Acknowledgements

Page *9* Portsmouth City Museum, reference 15_92
Page *28* (bottom) Musée national de la Marine
Page *34* Courtesy of the Director, National Army Museum, London (71849)
Page *35* Courtesy of the Director, National Army Museum, London (71843)
Page *71* Portsmouth Historic Dockyard
Page *77* Private family collection
Page *99* © Bridgman Art Library 2004
Page *101* By permission of the British Library, London (C2929_02)
Page *102* Museo Naval, Madrid (PB-72)
Page *104* Museo Naval, Madrid (top 341 and bottom 342)
Page *159* Museo Naval, Madrid (923)

Maps and diagrams on pages *7, 61,* © National Maritime Museum, London.
Page *81, 140* © Conway Maritime Press
Page *145* From *The Mariner's Mirror*, by permission of the Society of Nautical Research
Page *185* with kind permission of Kluwer Academic Publishers. (*Climatic Change,* 48, P. 361- 385, f.6d.)

The following are NMM photographic references. Pictures may be ordered from the Picture Library, National Maritime Museum, Greenwich, London, SE10 9NF (tel. 00 44 20 8312 6600). All © National Maritime Museum, London.

Cover: D3481_3, D3481_7; (back) BHC2887, Greenwich Hospital Collection

CHAPTER 1
Page *5* PU8960; *8* BHC3001; *10* PU0958; *11* PY9712.

CHAPTER 2
Page *14* 219; *16* and *17* BHC1782, Greenwich Hospital Collection; *18* BHC2901; *19* BHC2736; *20* D8132_4; *21* D7689_5; *22* BHC3016; *23* PY8032; *24* BHC2352.

CHAPTER 3
Page *27* F2138-2; *28* (top) PY2265; *29* PY2262; *30* A929; *32* D9041; *36* F2122; *38* PU8229.

CHAPTER 4
Page *41* 240; *42* F2132; *44* F2124; *45* PU3562.

CHAPTER 5
Page *47* PW3760; *48* PW3853; *49* D4647; *51* D7689_3; *52* 3646.

CHAPTER 6
Page *57* (top) PX6492; *53* (bottom) B3858; *58* PW3515.

CHAPTER 7
Page *62* PY7846; *63* D8132_1; *65* F2125; *66* PW0028.

CHAPTER 8
Page *73* A1665; *74* PY5889.

CHAPTER 9
Page *79* PW7991 (x82); *80* PU8522; *83* PW8416; *85* F2127.

CHAPTER 10
Page *87* PW1024; *88* A9598; *89* PW3548.

CHAPTER 11
Page *91* BHC2529; *92* PU1390; *93* PU1358; *94* B9068; *95* B7603-1; *97* 8252-A.

CHAPTER 12
Page *100* PU1662; *105* PU8208.

CHAPTER 13
Page *107* PW8005; *109* F2130; *110* PW4163; *112* PW5043; *114* 6660; *115* PU0177.

CHAPTER 14
Page *116* PU4726; *118* PU4722; *120* PU4723; *122* PW5857; *124* D7562; *126* PW4971.

CHAPTER 15
Page *127* BHC2625, Greenwich Hospital Collection; *129* PU4701; *132* 1008 (details).

CHAPTER 16
Page *134* BHC2892, Greenwich Hospital Collection; *135* PU1071; *137* (top) PY5197, (bottom) ZAZ0357; *139* PU4050.

CHAPTER 17
Page *148* PW7977; *149* F2129; *150* D9880-1; *154* B9701-2; *155* PW4746; *156* F2128.

CHAPTER 18
Page *161* PU5707; *163* PU5750; *164* BHC0548; *166* 218; *167* BHC0552.

CHAPTER 19
Page *170* PU8487; *171* PU8484; *172* BHC2894, Greenwich Hospital Collection; *174* PW4730; *177* BHC0549; *179* PU5709.

CHAPTER 20
Page *182* PU5717; *186* PW5883; *187* PW4732; *190* D2575.

CHAPTER 21
Page *192* B2582; *193* PW3850; *195* PX6706; *198* PU3917.

CHAPTER I

Mobilization

Once the name Trafalgar was familiar only to seamen, as the northern entrance to the Strait of Gibraltar. The Royal Navy knew it well, for it was a major landmark on the passage between Cadiz, where they blockaded the Spanish fleet, and their base at Gibraltar. In a sense it was the extreme point of the Mediterranean, though 25 miles out into the Atlantic. According to the pilot book it was 'low, uneven and projecting, with a watch tower towards the extremity.' After passing it ships would turn on to a more easterly course and head for the Rock. But in passing they were wary, for there was a sandbank 4 miles offshore with only a depth of 18 feet of water at its shallowest point, and the average ship of the line needed 24 feet. Two miles further on was the shoal of Aceytera, even more dangerous, with a chain of rocks a mile long, some only 9 feet underwater. There was a passage between the rocks and the banks, but it included an area where, pilots were told, 'you will observe a boiling in the water … but this should occasion no uneasiness, for it is only the effect of the counter currents, and is called by the people of the country the Risa (the laughter) of the Cape.' The passage required careful navigation and was avoided by most British ships, especially when Spain was hostile. 'When there is a heavy swell, and the wind is unsteady, vessels of considerable draught ought not to attempt this passage, as the sea rolls deep; and should the wind fail, you will be obliged to come to anchor perhaps in bad ground and in an exposed situation.'[1] Most preferred to stay 5 miles offshore.

Today the name suggests a city square surrounded by cars, buses and vans heading in all directions, a place that seems very far from the sea. Since English speakers emphasize at least one syllable above the others, the name is pronounced Tra*fal*gar, not Trafalgar. To most of its citizens and visitors, Trafalgar Square signifies the centre of London more than any other famous location in this multi-cultural, pluralistic city. It is overlooked by the National Gallery and has views towards Buckingham Palace, Whitehall, the Houses of Parliament, and down the Strand in the direction of Fleet Street and the City of London. As if to remind us of the glories of the British Empire, it has the Canadian High Commission on one side and the South African on the other. To the native British the square is best known as a venue for demonstrations, often for causes that the admiral at the top of the column which lies at its centre would not have approved of.

Cape Trafalgar from the sea, drawn by Justine Percy, c. 1850.

There are many factors that caused this transformation of a simple name, but the most important events took place in the autumn of 1805, among seventy-three ships and more than 50,000 seamen of the British, French and Spanish navies. The British do not often name their major sites after battles. The other great victories of the age of sail – St James Day, Quiberon Bay, the Saintes and the Nile – are largely uncommemmorated. There is Waterloo Station to mark the great British land victory of the age, but that was built by private enterprise. What was so special about the Battle of Trafalgar, to make it remembered above all others?

The name of Horatio Nelson is indelibly associated with Trafalgar, in the square as elsewhere. He stands at the top of a 170-foot column, with his great battles represented in relief on panels round the base. Nelson was vital to the Battle of Trafalgar, in the way that the presence of his great adversary Napoleon could affect a land battle. Our memory of the battle is deeply coloured with the events surrounding Nelson's death. Yet Nelson was only one of 19,000 British sailors there, led by about 200 commissioned officers and headed by thirty-three captains and three admirals. Even after two centuries we can hear the voices of some of them through official accounts and private papers.

* * *

For many of the seamen who fought that day, the story began two and a half years earlier. They did not know it at the time, but on 8 March 1803 King George III, prompted by his Prime Minister, Henry Addington, sent a message to Parliament.

> … as very considerable military preparations are carrying on in the ports of France and Holland, he has judged it expedient to adopt additional measures for precaution for the security of his dominions…[2]

The French claimed that they were fitting out ships to regain their colonies in the West Indies, lost to slave revolts in the aftermath of the Revolution, but King George and his government did not believe this. The French dictator, or 'First Consul' as he called himself, was not to be trusted. Napoleon Bonaparte had first appeared as a young artillery officer who drove the British and their allies out of Toulon in 1794. In 1796–97 he led the victorious armies in Italy, and then, realizing that an invasion of England was impracticable, he led a force for the invasion of Egypt, as the simplest route to British India. In the first setback to his career, the French fleet was destroyed by Nelson at the Battle of the Nile. The army was stranded but Bonaparte made his way home, to assume power as First Consul in 1799. He was a great general, a great political organizer, a man of great energy and charm, but little moral sense. His ambition no longer threatened the stability of France alone, but the whole of Europe. In 1803 he already controlled the Netherlands, so he was in a good position to launch an invasion of Britain.

The parallels with Britain in 1939–40 are striking. The country was run by a weak government, determined on peace but driven to war by exasperation and fear. War aims were vague and unstated, and largely defensive. Apart from expeditions to the West Indies, on the periphery of the war, the government of 1803 had no plans at all except to defeat a French invasion when it happened. The war was the second phase of a world struggle which had already lasted more than a decade. It was to be fought against a dictator who was vilified in the British Parliament and press but who was revered by the majority of people in his own (adopted) country, where he had brought a measure of stability and glory.

The Admiralty was headed by Winston Churchill in 1939, and in 1803 it was led by another of the most forceful characters in naval history, Admiral Sir John Jervis, Earl of St Vincent. Jervis was born in 1735, and at the age of fourteen he hid aboard a ship, partly to avoid following his father as a lawyer. In acknowledgement, his family had him entered in the *Gloucester* early in 1749. He was a lieutenant by the age of twenty. He distinguished himself at the capture of Quebec in 1759. The following year Jervis was a captain at the age of twenty-five. In the war with the American colonists he saw action several times in command of a ship of the line. In the French Revolutionary War he led the naval forces in the capture of the valuable West Indian islands of Martinique and Guadeloupe in 1794.

He gained his greatest fame and notoriety as commander of the Mediterranean Fleet in 1795–99, and of the Channel Fleet in 1800–03. In the first post he defeated the Spanish at the Battle of St Vincent and took the title of his earldom from the site off the coast of Portugal.

As other fleets mutinied at Spithead and the Nore in 1797 he maintained discipline with an iron hand. He was equally demanding of his officers, causing them to share the hardships of the men and to maintain the dignity of their position. When he went to the Channel Fleet, it was reported, officers toasted: 'May the discipline of the Mediterranean Fleet never be applied in the Channel Fleet.' But St Vincent soon had the ships operating a 'close blockade' off the French port of Brest, rather than an 'open blockade' in which they had spent most of their time in harbour.

When the government of William Pitt fell in 1801 he was offered the political post of First Lord of the Admiralty. It was not unusual for a naval officer to hold the position, but St Vincent was no great politician and he had accepted his masters' belief that the truce with France was permanent. By 1803 he had begun to reform the Royal Dockyards, which he believed were sinks of inefficiency, laziness and corruption. Reform was clearly necessary, but St Vincent was too impatient and destroyed much that was useful.[3] When war was seen as necessary, St Vincent threw himself into the preparations with characteristic energy and total ruthlessness.

Europe in 1805, showing the extent of French power.

Admiral the Earl of St Vincent, painted by Sir William Beechey.

In one sense the Addington government was not as pacific or inept as commonly believed. It had kept a substantial force of warships in commission throughout the peace, manned by 50,000 men compared with a normal peacetime force of 20,000. Most of the active ships were in the Mediterranean or further afield, where disputes with the French might flare up before a fleet had time to get there from the home ports; but substantial numbers were in commission in and around the dockyards at Portsmouth, Plymouth, the Thames and Chatham. The crews of these ships, and the men of the Royal Marines, would form the nucleus of the new naval mobilization.

On the evening of 9 March 1803, while the general population was still unaware of the King's message, more than 600 men left the warships in Portsmouth harbour, organized into press gangs, each led by an officer. By law they could take only experienced seamen for the fleet, and indeed they had little use for unskilled landsmen. They headed for the coal ships awaiting unloading, and took out every man they could find, even though some may have been visiting landsmen, and certainly the captains, chief mates and carpenters were protected from impressment. They would resolve this issue later, but in the meantime the men were imprisoned, either on board ship or in a marine guardhouse near the Dockyard. For days the town was paralyzed. The boatmen of the Gosport ferry had been pressed or had fled, and none of the merchant ships in port could move until their key men came back.

At Plymouth, the Admiralty messenger arrived at 4.00 a.m. on the 9th, after a fast journey. The gates of the marine barracks at Stonehouse were closed immediately, and all communication with the outside world was stopped. At 7.00 p.m. the gates re-opened. Parties of twelve or fourteen armed marines left the barracks, each headed by a naval and marine officer. Some went towards the New Quay, where tiers of colliers were moored, and began to board them. Until this point the marines had no idea of what they were to do, but now they were ordered to take out every man on board, and they escorted them towards the flagship, *Culloden*. Other gangs went out by boat to merchant ships anchored at Cattewater and Sutton Pool, while yet more toured the gin shops of the port, taking landsmen as well as seamen. One gang went to the Dock Theatre and cleared out all the men in the gallery. The town, as the *Naval Chronicle* reported, 'looked as if in a state of siege' but more than 400 useful men were found for the navy.

A stream of orders poured out from London. Merchant ships were forbidden to leave port until further notice. Seamen serving with foreign ships were recalled, and others were prevented from seeking work. Seamen and landsmen who volunteered for the navy were offered cash bounties. The militia, the part-time national defence force, was to be mobilized. The Royal Dockyards were to work evening and Sunday overtime.[4] Captains were appointed to ships, and officers were sent to head the press gangs round the coast. Lieutenant William Dillon was devastated to be offered an appointment to the press gang at Hull. 'None, generally speaking, but worn-out lieutenants were employed in that service.' At the Admiralty, where the Second Secretary reassured him that St Vincent had selected him personally – he 'had changed the whole system relating to the Impress Service by nominating young and active officers to it instead of old ones' – Dillon had no choice but to comply.[5]

In Edinburgh, on the fringes of the press gang's power, there was a night of 'general impress' on 10 March. The gangs in the Forth raised seventeen able seamen, eleven ordinary seaman and one landsman who was presumably a volunteer – a total of twenty-nine, compared with several hundred in the dockyard ports.[6] At Shields in north-east England, John Wetherell, a merchant seaman, heard an early rumour of a frigate pressing men at the mouth of the Thames. Anxious to get to London, he obtained a forged protection for a ship's carpenter, which should have made him exempt from the press gang, and set sail in a collier. On 19 March the ship was boarded by several boats and a naval officer said to her captain, 'Where is your carpenter?' On being told that he was at the helm, the officer ordered, 'Relieve him and put his things in the boat.'

'Why Sir he is protected.'

'That is the reason we want him in our carpenter's crew. Come, make haste. Coxswain,

bundle his things in the boat.' Thus Wetherell became a seaman in the frigate *Hussar*.

He soon became involved in the press gangs himself. On 1 April boats from the *Hussar* and two other ships landed at Harwich to begin a 'man plunder'.

> The Market house was to be their prison, where a lieutenant was station'd with a guard of Marines and before daylight next morning their prison was full of all denominations, from the Parish Priest to the farmer in his frock and wooden Shoes. Even the poor Blacksmith cobler taylor barber baker fisherman and doctor were all dragg'd from their homes that night ...

The people of Harwich gathered round the market house. '… their business was quickly made known. Wives demanded their husbands, children their Fathers, and aged parents their Son perhaps their only support.' A nervous lieutenant tried to pacify them.

> My good people, you no doubt feel alarmed at this unexpected visit we have paid your town and its vicinity, a visit to you verry rare and to us verry unpleasant but as our orders are from the Admiralty we dare not refuse to obey their command. However, good people, I give you my word and honour that by this day noon your husbands, Fathers and Children shall be restored to your arms again, only such as are entitled to serve their king owing to being able Seamen or gain their living by the Salt water such as Fishermen &c. Every other will be liberated as soon as my brother Officers can all meet here, which I know must be shortly.

Eventually the other gangs arrived and the men who were deemed to be seamen were marched down to the boats in parties of twelve or fifteen, guarded by the armed marines. One fishermen managed to leap from the boat as it left the shore and ran swiftly up the beach, dodging the fire of the marines. The rest were taken on board the ships.[7]

In the Dockyards, there was feverish activity to get ships ready for the men. In peacetime most were laid up 'in ordinary', without upper masts, sails, rigging, guns or stores. Some were in the middle of large repairs in dry-docks, but a swift mobilization had to concentrate on those that would be made ready in a hurry. After St Vincent's half-completed reforms, Chatham yard was 176 shipwrights short of its complement of 644 and there were not enough seamen to row the boats that carried material and stores out to the ships in the river.[8]

Pressing men at Portsmouth. Although conventionally dated from 1798, this shows marines engaged in the activity, as happened in 1803.

The port of Harwich, drawn by William Daniell in 1822, showing the lighthouses which formed leading marks into the port.

Leaving aside the squalor of the recruitment process, there was great romance in the fitting of a ship. George Canning, a friend of Pitt and Nelson and soon to become Treasurer of the Navy, visited the ships laid up at Plymouth twenty years later and was inspired to oratory.

… one of these stupendous masses, now reposing on their shadows in perfect stillness, would upon any call of patriotism or of necessity, assume the likeness of an animated thing, instinct with life and motion: how soon it would ruffle, as it were its swelling plumage, how quickly it would put forth all its beauty and its bravery, collect its scattered elements of strength and waken its dormant thunder … Such is England herself; while apparently passive and motionless, she silently concentrates the power to be put forth on an adequate occasion.[9]

By 1 April 1803 the correspondent of the *Naval Chronicle* was moved, 'at the setting sun, to see Britannia's bulwarks, so lately commissioned, towering in all their native pride'. Five ships of the line, including *Spartiate*, *Tonnant* and *Mars*, were, to use the rigger's phrase, complete all *tanto*, that is, all the lower and upper masts up, capped, rigged over-head, and all the standing and running rigging set up. These ships are nearly provisioned and stored; and if men come round soon, they will be in Cawsand Bay in ten days.

His colleague at Plymouth was equally excited by the preparations; on 13 April he reported: 'Cawsand Bay and Plymouth look as gay as in the height of war; there being in the former nine men of war, and in the latter two men of war, and six East Indiamen.' The East Indiamen mentioned had arrived off the Eddystone Lighthouse the day before, and found the wind unfavourable to go up the Channel. Their crews were totally unaware of the mobilization until a naval frigate came up to them and took off 300 prime seamen. It was a heartbreaking experience for men who were almost in sight of home after a round trip of a year.

Officers viewed the prospect of war very differently from the seamen, for they had hopes of promotion and prize money. Lieutenant Frederick Hoffman was thoroughly bored with peacetime life with his mother in London and Surrey, in which time passed 'as monotonously as that of a clock in an old-maid's sitting room.' He solicited an appointment from the Admiralty but was less pleased when he found his new ship, the 74-gun *Minotaur*, laid up in the Medway without masts, stores or guns. Things got worse when he learned that he and his fellow officers had to pay their own expenses in the Tap Inn at Sheerness, or 'Shurnasty'. 'We drank elevation to the noble Secretary of the Admiralty, for, owing to his ignorance, we had been obliged to spend seven shillings daily more than our pay.'[10] Hoffman found himself in charge in the absence of the captain. He had no crew and relied on dockyard riggers and disabled naval pensioners from Greenwich Hospital.

The captain finally arrived and commented, 'Hulloa, how is this? I expected to find the ship masted. I will thank you to desire the boatswain to turn the hands up to hear my commission read, and quarter-master, go down and tell the officers I am on board.' He was told that the 'quartermaster' was actually a dockyard workman and not a member of the crew. 'So, this is the manner King's ships are to be fitted out. Why, it will take us a month of Sundays before the lower masts are rigged. What the devil did they send these old codgers with their wooden legs here for?' He lobbied the port admiral, who sent more officers, including two who were senior to Hoffman, and then a company of marines under their officers. One day a barge crashed heavily alongside the *Minotaur*, carrying fifteen prisoners sent by the magistrates of Maidstone. Her skipper told Hoffman, 'They be all of them tolerable good men, except five, who have been condemned to be transported, and two to be hung, but as they be contrabanders like, the Government have sent orders for 'em to be sent on board your ship.' The smugglers were quite welcome, being skilled seamen with none of the anti-social tendencies of those convicted of violence or robbery. Some time later 200 more conventional recruits were sent down from the press gangs at Chatham. A month after commissioning the ship had most of her rigging complete, but only half her crew of 640 men, and only about forty of these were experienced, fit seamen who could work aloft. It was decided to head for Plymouth in the hope of finding men there. On the way the admiral at the Nore provided fifty more good seamen, and the ship made a fast passage of two days to Plymouth Sound.

On arrival, Hoffman and his captain went on board the flagship, the ex-Spanish *Salvador Del Mundo*, where the victims of the press gang were being held until they could be allocated to ships. They were too late. The remaining men were lined up with their toes on the 'seam'

Ships fitting out at Chatham Dockyard in 1793, by Richard Paton, Pierre Canot, Richard Mortimer and John Hamilton.

of tar between two planks – 'toeing the line', as close to military discipline as seamen could be expected to get. The captain told Hoffman,

> 'You help me look at these fellow's phizes … I am to take thirty of them; they are queer-looking chaps, and I do not much like the cut of their jib. … But mind, don't take any one that has not a large quid of tobacco in his cheek.'

> I went up to the second man, who had a double allowance of Virginia or some other weed in his gill, the captain following me. 'Well, my man,' said I, 'How long have you been to sea?' 'Four months,' was the reply. 'Why, you d—d rascal,' said our skipper – for observe, reader, he never swore – 'what the devil business have you with such a quantity of tobacco in your mouth? I though you were an old sailor.' 'No sir,' answered the man, 'my trade is a tailor, but I have chawed bacca from my infancy.' 'Question another,' was my order. I interrogated the next, who was a short, slight, pale-faced man. 'And pray,' said I, 'what part of the play have you been performing: were you ever at sea?' 'No, sir,' said he; 'I am a hairdresser, and was pressed a week ago.' 'D—n these fellows!' said my captain: 'they are all tailors, barbers or grass-combers. I want seamen.' [11]

Eventually he settled for the tailor and twenty other men, though they were 'bad enough, as they were the worst set I ever saw grouped. Their appearance and dress were wretched in the extreme.'

There was continuous activity in the naval ports throughout April. During the week of the 12th the *Russell* and *Aurora* sent gangs ashore at Portsmouth every night, but found only six or seven men each time. On the 17th there was another hot press in Plymouth when several 'holiday folks' in the area were found to be liable to serve in the navy. But three days later the work on fitting out ships began to slow down, and the riggers from London began the journey home. Two ships, including the 98-gun *Prince*, were left to their own devices but it was commented, 'they are so forward in their rigging, that their own ships' companies can finish both ships with the greatest ease, and at considerably less expense.' On Portsmouth on the 21st it was reported,

> The preparations in fitting out the ships, &c. seem, within these few days, to be very much relaxed. The orders which have been received are not so urgent, and indeed every department is comparatively passive. There have been no gangs from the ships of war this week parading the streets to pick up men.[12]

Later in the month gangs were sent out from ships at sea to the Devon ports of Dartmouth, Paignton, Brixham, Torquay and Teignmouth with orders to ignore protections, except those guaranteed by act of Parliament, or for ships on voyages of direct use to the navy. This was not a great success. Several shipwrights, a sail-maker, fishmonger, coal-factor, grocer, cooper, watchmaker, ostler, waggoner, labourer, shoemaker, constable and a basket-maker had to be let go, along with a man who appeared to be dumb. Only ten eligible men were found. Efforts revived at Plymouth on 9 May, with another hot press and a picket of fifty marines to keep order.[13]

For all the great efforts to mobilize the ships, there was not much for them to do. The Mediterranean Fleet had been kept up to considerable strength during the peace, so most of the newly commissioned ships went to the Channel or the North Sea Fleets. By 1 May the Channel Fleet had ten ships of the line in service and a month later it had grown to sixteen of the line and eight smaller vessels, while the North Sea Fleet had thirty-four vessels of all kinds. But, as yet, the French, surprised by the suddenness of the British mobilization, had no plans to attack Britain, while the British had no offensive plans against France, except in the West Indian colonies.

The main British naval force under Admiral Sir William Cornwallis was concentrating in

Torbay in Devon, where a large fleet could anchor, protected from westerly winds, but be ready to sail across the English Channel when the winds permitted. By 6 May there were ten ships of the line in the bay, or on the way there, including the *Dreadnought* and *Neptune* of 98 guns and the *Thunderer* and *Minotaur* of 74. The *Tonnant* of 80 guns and *Mars* and *Spartiate* of 74 guns were still at Cawsand Bay with two other ships, waiting to go round, while three frigates, including the 38-gun *Naiad*, were on their way to Torbay. Many of the ships were not well manned. The *Thunderer* was short of forty-six seamen and ten marines out of a complement of 590. Furthermore, 'her men of all descriptions appear to be weak, and a very moderate crew, she having ten more ordinary and fifty-one more landmen than the scheme allows, and only 101 petty [officers] and able [seamen].'

War began formally on 18 May 1803. The great mobilization was a success in that the 10,000 men voted by Parliament were soon raised, but in the long term naval recruitment remained very slow. Parliament voted for a navy of 100,000 men early in 1804, but only 84,431 had actually been recruited. In the following year it voted for 120,000, but only 109,205 were found.[14] However efficient the mobilization, it was chiefly remembered for the ruthlessness with which it was carried out. Many of the legends of the press gang were created by the clearing of the gallery of a theatre at Plymouth, the 'man plunder' at Harwich and the disregard of legitimate protections. The gangs often exceeded their authority in seizing men of all trades for the navy. In a few cases, such as the hairdresser in the *Salvador Del Mundo*, they seem to have kept them, though they were of very little use.

There were also cases when impressed landsmen were kept on out of spite. When pressed into the *Hero* later in 1803 John Parr made the mistake of trying to swim ashore and was flogged for it. He tried to keep this news from his mother and wrote nonchalantly to tell her that he was 'very Happy at my Situation at present' and asking her to send on 'my Box and Dixionary and some wrigthing Papper.' But to his brother he revealed the true depth of his misery. In January 1804 he was still under confinement and had not been able to take off his clothes more than six times since he was pressed.

> Brother I Ham sorrey to Hear of my Mother Taken it so Much to Heart a Bou it but Make her as Comfortabel as Posibel and I Hope I shal injoy her Once a gain Brother I shal by Much a Oblige to you if you will send me a few Nessereys for have got Nothin but What I stand huprite in for I have had but One Shirt on since that Fatal Job Happined.[15]

Even seamen who were pressed legitimately were not necessarily happy with their lot. Benjamin Stevenson used the alias of Thomson, perhaps to evade the press gangs, but nevertheless he was taken in the spring of 1803 and found himself on board the *Victory*. In August he wrote to his brother at Gateshead. Several men from the ship were able to get their release by paying others to serve in their places. His brother would need to find two men at £2 each, but 'I think if you can get two for twice as much I would not begrudge the money for to be got clear of this prison.' He was just as unhappy in May 1804 and wrote, 'I shall live in hope of God to set me clear of this wicked wooden world. This one long twelve-months I have lived in this wicked state of life.'[16]

CHAPTER 2

The Victory

On 26 March 1803, as the press gangs combed the coastal towns of England, Horatio Nelson still did not know his immediate future. 'War or Peace? Every person has a different opinion. I fear perhaps the former, as I hope so much the latter.' He already knew that in the event of war he would be recalled to service as commander-in-chief of the Mediterranean Fleet, and he had chosen his secretary for the coming campaign. John Scott, a former purser, received a letter 'acquainting me that Lord Nelson had accepted my services as Secretary in the event of war, and said that I must be ready at 48 hours notice.' [1] Nelson also knew that his flagship would be the 100-gun *Victory*. Thus began an association of names of great historic resonance.

The *Victory* was already more than forty years old, a great age for a wooden warship on active service. She was first ordered in December 1758. The Seven Years War was at its height, the French fleet was strong and undefeated, and Parliament voted money for twelve new ships of the line, headed by a 100-gun first-rate, the largest ever built for the Royal Navy. Like all ships of her size at that time she would be built in a dry-dock and floated out, rather than launched from a building slip. No private shipyard had the capacity for such a

Victory at sea, published by R. Dodd in 1807.

leviathan, so she would be built in the Royal Dockyard at Chatham, still the largest in the country, as soon as they had finished with their 74-gun ship, the *Valiant*.

British ship design was recovering its stride after a long depression, which lasted most of the first half of the century. In 1755 Lord Anson, First Lord of the Admiralty, picked out the shipwright Thomas Slade and made him Surveyor of the Navy. Slade produced new classes of ship – the 74 and the frigate – influenced by French practice but not direct copies. He used a method of drawing the lines of the ship, known technically as the 'diagonal of floor ribbands' system, which produced a particularly smooth hull, suitable for all the conditions of wind, weather and sea in which a sailing warship might find herself. The first of his new ships, the 74s of the *Dublin* class and the frigates of the *Southampton* class, were already entering service and Slade was approaching his maturity as a designer.

In June 1759 the shipwrights of Chatham were ready to cut the first timbers of the new ship. Her keel was laid in Number 1 Dock in August but construction began to slow down. The French fleet was defeated decisively at Quiberon Bay in November and the great new first-rate was no longer so urgent. In October 1760 she was given the name *Victory*, the fifth to take the name in the Royal Navy.

The war ended in 1763 with a complete British victory and the need for the new first-rate further diminished. The *Victory*'s long period on the stocks was to her ultimate advantage, for it allowed the timbers a good deal of time to season. When she was finally floated out into the Medway on 7 May 1765, there was still no immediate need for her – the navy had been reduced from 70,000 men in wartime to 16,000 in peace and it was impossible to man such a large ship for any length of time. She was eventually rigged and went to sea for trials in 1769, but was soon laid up again, to remain in the Medway for the next nine years. Meanwhile a revolt of American colonists intensified into the War of Independence. In February 1778 the French joined the war against Britain and large ships were needed again. Almost immediately, work began to make the *Victory* ready for service and in May she sailed as flagship of Admiral Augustus Kepple of the Channel Fleet. She first saw battle in an inconclusive engagement off Ushant that year. She led Admiral Lord Howe's relief of Gibraltar in 1782 and was paid off when the war ended in the following year.

She was re-commissioned during passing threats of war in 1790 and 1791. In 1793, when the war began with Revolutionary France, she became the flagship of the Mediterranean Fleet. She saw a succession of admirals, including Sir John Jervis. It was under his flag that she led the defeat of the Spanish Fleet off Cape St Vincent in February 1797, in which Commodore Nelson of the *Captain* played a distinguished part.

By now the *Victory* was more than thirty years old and Earl St Vincent shifted his flag to the new first-rate *Ville de Paris*. The *Victory* was eventually sent home. When she arrived at Chatham that November, it seemed like the end of a long and honourable career. She was to become a hospital ship for the Frenchmen, Dutchmen and Spaniards held as prisoners of war on the River Medway.

The *Victory*'s fortunes changed early in 1800 when the Admiralty ordered her to be repaired. On 11 April she was put into Number 4 Dock at Chatham, just 250 yards from where she was built nearly forty years earlier. It was intended that she should have a 'middling repair'. The Chatham Yard officers completed their survey of the ship and sent it to the Navy Board on 19 July. They estimated that repairs would cost £48,817 and take fifteen months. On the 30th, the Navy Board sent a reply to Chatham – they were to go ahead with the repair, taking care not to exceed the estimate. By August it had been upgraded from a 'middling' to a 'large repair'.[2]

This meant in practice that all the planks would be stripped from her hull and the majority of timbers that formed her frame would be replaced, but her fine hull shape would be retained. It also gave the builders a chance to incorporate the latest improvements in design. The Admiralty was keen to restrict the amount of decorative work undertaken on ships, to cut costs and prevent shipbuilders from glorifying themselves. In November the Admiralty produced plans for decorations on the *Victory*'s head and quarter and sent them to Chatham by coach.

Chatham was one of six Royal Dockyards, probably the largest industrial undertakings of the age anywhere in the world. Even in peacetime they employed 9000 men, and that figure might rise to 15,000 in war. The yard was set on the bank of the River Medway, 11 miles from where it met the Thames estuary at Sheerness. It occupied 1500 yards of river frontage, which formed three areas. The southern end was dominated by the great ropery building, 1135 feet long so that it could make the longest ropes, the anchor cables of 720 feet. In the centre were four building slips where ships (all but the very largest) were constructed, and between them were four dry-docks used mainly for ship repair, including the 'large repair' of the *Victory*. Behind them were offices and houses for the dockyard officers, while to the north was a series of industrial buildings, including a smithy for making anchors, the mast house and the boat house. The whole site was surrounded by a high and forbidding wall to prevent theft or sabotage, and beyond that were defenses against enemy invasion. Outside the dockyard proper were some of the other buildings necessary to support a navy – an armament depot, a marine barracks and a small victualling yard.

On 26 March 1803, according to *The Times*, 'The *Victory* having had a most complete repair, she is ordered to be fitted for a flag. She will be out of dock in a few days.' The 'large repair' had cost £70,933, more than the cost of the original ship. With the imminent threat of war, she was quickly prepared for sea. On 18 April *The Times* reported, 'Such has been the

Chatham Dockyard from the air, painted by Joseph Farringdon in the 1790s. In the long buildings to the right are the anchor wharf storehouses with the ropery behind. To the left of that, ships are under construction and repair.

expedition used on the *Victory*, that her topgallant masts are up, and nearly all her stores are on board.'

The painter, John Constable, saw her soon after her launch. On 23 May he noted, 'At Chatham I hired a boat to see the men of war, which are there in great numbers. I sketched the *Victory* in three views. She was the flower of the flock, a three-decker of 112 guns. She looked very beautiful, fresh out of dock and newly painted. When I saw her they were bending her sails; which circumstance, added to a very fine evening, made a charming effect.' [3]

*   *   *

Horatio Nelson was born on 29 September 1758, just over two months before his famous flagship was ordered. The son of a country parson, he joined his first ship in 1771 under the patronage of his uncle, Captain Maurice Suckling. His apparently delicate constitution concealed a very tough body and an iron determination. Peacetime service in the River Medway did not appeal to him, so he enrolled in a merchant ship for a voyage to the West Indies, where he learned much about seamanship. Back in the Medway, he took charge of one of the ship's boats and learned about small boat seamanship. In 1773 he volunteered for Arctic exploration in the *Carcass*, and then found his true métier in the frigate *Seahorse* in the

Nelson as a young man, painted by Francis Rigaud. In the background is the fort in Nicaragua where he became ill in 1782.

Indian Ocean until illness caused him to be sent home in 1776.

War had broken out with the American colonies and Nelson was promoted lieutenant at the age of eighteen. He soon showed his remarkable gifts for leadership, seamanship and decision-making in many adventures, and after two years he became captain of the tiny brig *Badger*. In July 1779, at the age of twenty, he became a post-captain, eligible to command any ship in the navy. He led the naval side of an expedition into the Spanish colony of Nicaragua. His health broke down again and he was sent home in 1780. He returned to the war in the West Indies in 1782 only to lead a small landing operation in the Bahamas before the war ended in 1783.

In 1784 Nelson took up his first peacetime command, of the frigate *Boreas*, and returned to the West Indies, where a much-reduced British force was attempting to enforce the Navigation Acts, which prevented direct trade between the British islands and the newly independent American states. Nelson, in characteristic style, threw himself into the task. But it was a lost cause, for hardly anyone wanted to enforce the Acts. One pleasant consequence was contact with Frances Nisbet, a young widow and niece of the President of the Council on the island of Nevis, one of the few officials to offer Nelson any comfort. Nelson was also supported by Prince William Henry, later the Duke of Clarence, third son of King George III, in command of the frigate *Pegasus*. When Nelson married Frances on Nevis in March 1787, Prince William gave the bride away. But Nelson had upset too many people. He returned home and was not employed again for more than five years.

Finally in 1793, after war had broken out with Revolutionary France, Nelson was given command of the 64-gun ship of the line, *Agamemnon*. Nelson was overjoyed with her good sailing qualities and his release from rural boredom in Norfolk. He sailed for the Mediterranean, the sea that was to shape his destiny for the next seven years. He was engaged in the siege of Calvi in Corsica, where he lost the sight of his right eye.

Nelson had never faced what most regarded as the supreme test of a naval officer – a general battle between two fleets. His chance almost came in March 1795, in the *Agamemnon* under Admiral Sir William Hotham. The French Fleet was encountered off Corsica by the Mediterranean Fleet and Nelson captured two stragglers, but the Admiral made no attempt to chase the rest. Nelson went on board the flagship in a towering, insubordinate rage, urging the Admiral to pursue. Hotham replied, to Nelson's disgust. 'We must be contented. We have done very well.' Nelson wrote to Frances, 'had we taken ten sail, and allowed the 11th to escape when it had been possible to have got at her, I could never call it well done.' It was a manifesto for Nelson's future conduct in battle.

At the end of the year Admiral Sir John Jervis took command of the Mediterranean Fleet and he and Nelson soon developed a great affinity. After Spain entered the war against Britain in 1796, Jervis withdrew his ships from the Mediterranean to concentrate on blockading the Spanish port of Cadiz. When the Spanish Fleet came out in February 1797, Nelson, now in command of the 74-gun *Captain*, had his first chance of fame. Jervis's approach to battle was too slow and Nelson broke the line to follow a quicker route to the enemy, supported by Cuthbert Collingwood in the *Excellent*. Nelson led a boarding party to storm the Spanish *San Nicolas* of 80 guns, then passed over her to take the *San Josef* of 114 guns – 'Nelson's patent bridge for boarding First Rates'. He became a national hero.

Five months later, promoted rear-admiral, Nelson led an attack on the Spanish island of Tenerife. The attack failed, and Nelson lost his right arm. In the spring of 1798 he was given command of a force to re-enter the Mediterranean. Napoleon Bonaparte was fitting out a mysterious expedition at Toulon and Nelson was to find out its purpose. His squadron was reinforced to thirteen 74-gun ships, though his own flagship, the *Vanguard*, was badly damaged by storm. Nelson eventually surmised that Bonaparte was on his way to invade Egypt. He narrowly missed him twice, but on 1 August 1798 he found the French Mediterranean Fleet anchored in Aboukir Bay near Alexandria. The battle that followed led to the blowing up of the French flagship, *L'Orient*, and to Nelson being wounded in the head. Eleven enemy sail of the line out of thirteen were captured or destroyed.

Jubilant but exhausted, Nelson went to Naples where he developed an affair with Emma

Hamilton, the wife of the British ambassador, who had been a servant girl, and possibly a prostitute, before her marriage. To some he cut an absurd figure during these years. He was disappointed that he was only created a baron after the great victory at the Nile. He became too involved in Neapolitian politics, and supported the savage repression of a republican rebellion. When St Vincent retired in 1799, Admiral George Keith was given command of the Mediterranean Fleet and Nelson struck his flag. He travelled home through central Europe with Sir William and Lady Hamilton.

Nelson arrived at Great Yarmouth in November 1800 to find that he was loved by the common people but distrusted by high society because of his relationship with Lady Hamilton. His marriage ended very publically and he went to live with Sir William and Lady Hamilton at Merton, south of London. His career seemed to be in serious decline.

He was rescued in January 1801 when he was recalled to service under Admiral Sir Hyde Parker. In April he led the attack against the anchored Danish Fleet at Copenhagen. Famously he ignored Parker's signal to retreat, putting his telescope to his blind eye and remarking, 'I have only one eye – I have a right to be blind sometimes.' He went on to negotiate a truce with the Danes. Back in home waters, he raided the French invasion port of Boulogne in August 1801, but suffered substantial losses and achieved nothing. The war ended soon afterwards and Nelson returned to Merton.

Nelson had several qualities that would shape his life. In the first instance his immense charm was noticed by many people and often contrasted with his undistinguished appearance. In 1798, Lady Spencer, wife of the then First Lord of the Admiralty, initially saw him as 'a most uncouth creature' with the appearance 'of an idiot', but once in conversation, 'his wonderful mind broke forth.' [4] Second was his amazing tactical skill, based on a thorough understanding of seamanship, which allowed him to spot any weakness in the enemy deployment, or a slight advantage to be gained by a change in the direction of the wind. He had shown this by his action at the Battle of Cape St Vincent. Thirdly, Nelson's great zeal and courage was shown in the same battle, when he led the boarding of two great Spanish ships, much to his wife's horror. Any naval seaman had to be brave in those days, for death was never far away even without the risks of battle. Fourth was his confidence in his subordinates, in an age when centralization was still the rule in naval tactics. At the Nile he allowed Captain Thomas Foley, at the head of the line in the *Goliath*, to decide the main element in the tactics used. He knew about the high fighting spirit in the British fleet, that any captain (with a very few exceptions) could be relied to put his ship alongside the enemy in the most effective way possible.

Lady Emma Hamilton in her youth, painted by George Romney.

* * *

At her completion at Chatham in March 1803 the *Victory* was commanded by Samuel Sutton, who had served under Nelson at Copenhagen. Nelson had already decided that his old friend, Thomas Masterman Hardy, should be his flag captain, but Hardy was still in the frigate *Amphion*, which would sail with the *Victory*. The first lieutenant was John Quillam, a Manxman who had been born in 1771. One legend in his home island suggests that he was originally pressed into the navy. This does not bear examination, as he first appears in the navy records in 1791, in time of peace; but there is no doubt that he came up the hard way. He may have taken up the sea to escape trouble at home, for his father was arraigned in church for fornication. He enjoyed some support from a fellow Manxman in the ship, Peter Heywood, who had been sentenced to death for a part in the famous *Bounty* mutiny of 1789 and then reprieved. In October 1794, at the age of twenty-three, he went to the 74-gun *Triumph* under his old captain, Erasmus Gower, with Peter Heywood on the quarterdeck. The expanding wartime navy had need for new officers and Quillam was soon promoted to master's mate, senior to a midshipman. In this capacity he fought at the Battle of Camperdown in 1797 and by 1798 he was acting lieutenant in the 98-gun *Neptune*. On 6 June 1798 he was examined at the Navy Board and became a full lieutenant.

Quillam became the senior surviving lieutenant in the frigate *Amazon* when her captain was killed at Copenhagen. Samuel Sutton took over the ship, and it seems likely that he was

The attack at the Battle of the Nile, by Cooper Willyams. The main French line is clearly distinguishable, with the frigates nearer the foreground. The British fleet is just about to round their line, headed by Thomas Foley in the Goliath.

impressed by Quillam's abilities. When he was recalled from the Isle of Man during the mobilization of 1803, it was to be a lieutenant in the *Victory*.[5] As a lower-deck entrant to the navy, Quillam brought certain advantages to Nelson. He had no well-connected relatives to press for his promotion to commander, and he was rather older than the average lieutenant who had entered more conventionally. He could bring experience, stability and maturity to the job of first lieutenant.

The other lieutenants included George Bligh (no relation to the captain of *Bounty* fame), son of a well-known admiral. Now nineteen, he had served under his father early in the last war and had endured six months' captivity in Brest when his father's ship was taken. He had been a lieutenant since 1801.[6] John Yule was twenty-five and less well-connected. He had been a lieutenant in the *Alexander* at the Battle of the Nile five years previously under Nelson's old friend, Alexander Ball, but for some reason he was not promoted at that time.[7] Instead he was recommended to Nelson, and he followed him from ship to ship during the Copenhagen campaign, then to the *Victory*.[8]

Nelson took a good deal of interest in the appointment of officers to the *Victory*, although he did become distracted when his great friend, Sir William Hamilton, became gravely ill and died on 6 April. Nelson had enough influence at the Admiralty to get what he wanted. He sent a list of six lieutenants, out of a complement of eight, 'which will be enough to begin with.' By 17 April, when the youngest son of a distinguished admiral applied for a post as lieutenant, he was too late. Nelson told the Duke of Clarence, his royal patron,

> I agree with your Royal Highness most entirely, that the son of a Rodney ought to be the protégé of every person in the Kingdom, and particularly of the Sea-Officers: had I known that there had been this claimant, some of my own Lieutenants must have given way to such a name, and he should have been placed in the *Victory* – she is full, and I have twenty on my list.

Meanwhile the ship was manned, largely by transferring men from the receiving ship *Utrecht*.

One of the key figures in any ship was the master. Thomas Atkinson was from the village of West Gilling near Richmond in Yorkshire, born around 1768 and almost certainly a merchant seaman by training. He first entered the navy in 1787, probably pressed from a merchantman during a mobilization of the fleet, but war was averted and he was discharged after three months. In June 1793, early in the war with Revolutionary France, he was attracted by the bounty of £5 and volunteered for the frigate *Blonde*. Within two months he was rated as master's mate. Two years later, after a voyage to the West Indies, he passed an examination by the Brethren of Trinity House as master of a sloop and was appointed to the *Rattler*. Within six months he had passed another examination and took up a post in the fifth-rate *Emerald*.

The master of a ship of the line in 1812, drawn by Reverend Edward Mangin.

The duties of the master included the navigation of the ship, in the broadest sense – handling the ship in confined situations as well as finding her position and setting courses. He was responsible for the supply of charts and nautical instruments, usually purchased out of his own pocket. He supervised the trim of the ship, which was largely controlled by the ballast and the stowage of the hold. Though he was socially inferior to the lieutenants, and had far less prospect of promotion to captain, he was better paid than most of them, had a better cabin in the wardroom, and a greater role in running the ship than everyone except the captain and first lieutenant.

In 1797 Atkinson was appointed master of the third-rate, 74-gun *Theseus* captained by Ralph Miller and carrying the flag of the newly promoted Rear-Admiral Nelson. He helped Nelson and Miller restore order among a disgruntled crew, and in July that year he was with the ship when Nelson lost his right arm at Tenerife. At the Battle of the Nile the *Theseus* was the fourth ship to round the head of the enemy line. In May 1799 an accidental explosion on board killed Miller and Atkinson was slightly wounded.

He married Sarah Hornby of Lancashire in a church in Blackfriars Road, London. About the same time he was appointed master of the Spanish prize, *San Josef*, now flying Nelson's flag as vice-admiral. Early in 1801 Nelson shifted his flag to the three-decker *St George* and took Atkinson with him to Copenhagen. Atkinson was one of the masters employed in finding a passage through the shoals. He went out in the sloop *Ranger*, buoying channels for the fleet to approach. The *St George* was too large to lead the attack so Nelson transferred to the 74-gun *Elephant*, leaving Atkinson to witness the battle from afar. He was now established in Nelson's estimation as 'one of the best Masters I have seen in the Royal Navy.' He was appointed to the *Victory* when war resumed.

As yet the rank of master had no uniform; the first one would be approved in August 1805. Atkinson, then at sea with Nelson, wrote to his tailor from off Cadiz,

> Will you have the goodness to make enquiry whether the Masters New Uniform is made known and I wish you to find out as soon as possible and when you have got the plan of the pattern of it to make a coat compleat. I mean coat, waistcoat and breeches and then send them out to me as soon as they are done by the first Man of War that comes out to us…

William Adair was the captain of marines, in charge of a force of sea soldiers, which, in theory, included three lieutenants, four sergeants, four corporals, two drummers and 131 'private centinels'. He was a twenty-seven-year-old Irishman from County Antrim who had nominally been an officer since the age of six. The marines tended to be a family business and his father was a lieutenant-colonel in the corps, while his younger brother had been an officer since the age of eleven.[9]

John Scott, the Admiral's secretary, came on board at Portsmouth, after missing the ship at Chatham. He was from the north of Scotland, and his mother was still a tenant of the Duke of Gordon – Scott worried about her infirmity, and had to give up his claim to the farm in 1805, regretting the loss of ties with his 'native spot'. He had been a purser since 1789 and in 1800–03 he had been in the 100-gun *Royal Sovereign*, where he had shared the

Reverend Alexander John Scott by Siegfried Bendixen. The picture behind shows his ship being struck by lightning.

wardroom with John Quillam, now first lieutenant of the *Victory*.[10] He had a wife, Charlotte, and three 'dear boys' in London, and was grieved to be leaving them. Upon arriving on board he was pleased to find his quarters 'very comfortable. I shall be able to get my drawers etc fixed at once in their proper place instead of being kicked about from ship to ship, which would have been the case had I come out in the *Amphion*.' [11]

His near namesake, Alexander John Scott, was appointed as the *Victory*'s chaplain, who was also to operate as Nelson's interpreter and diplomatic secretary. Born in 1768 in Rotherhithe near London, he studied at Cambridge, but his obvious brilliance did not fit in with the system there. In 1791 he was ordained in the Church of England and soon afterwards he was appointed chaplain of the 74-gun *Berwick*. In 1801 he served at Copenhagen, and demonstrated his remarkable flair for languages. On the way to the Baltic he learned Danish and Russian from textbooks, and Nelson used him in negotiating the armistice with Denmark after the battle.

Later in that year he was struck by lightning while in his hammock in Jamaica. Some gunpowder exploded nearby and knocked out two teeth, and he fell to the deck. In 1803 he felt that the climate of the Mediterranean might help restore him – like most people he expected a short campaign. Nelson was pleased to get his services, for he was determined to have a chaplain on board, and Scott's linguistic abilities would be invaluable in the Mediterranean. Scott, Nelson wrote, had 'abilities of a very superior cast.' [12] He collected books in many languages, but nothing of 'what the world calls *management*', according to his daughter.[13] He was described as 'pale, thin and tall in person, very romantic and enthusiastic. … his forehead was singularly fine and intellectual, and the benevolent expression of his countenance and eyes, did justice to the universal kindness of his feelings.' [14]

He came on board the *Victory* on 20 May 1803 and dined with the Admiral. He had feared that Nelson would be 'distant and haughty' after his successes, but it was 'quite the reverse' and he soon found himself 'very happily situated with Lord Nelson.' He then transferred to the *Amphion*, which was to take him out to the Mediterranean.[15]

George Magrath, the surgeon of the *Victory*, was, according to Nelson, 'by far the most able medical man I have ever seen.' He had been born in County Tyrone, Ireland, and trained as a surgeon. Nelson worried about losing men like him to the army, which for the moment offered better pay and conditions.[16] His concern was not without reason, for at a later date Magrath and his medical colleagues would give Nelson a rather wordy petition complaining of 'the invidious disparity of encouragement existing between the Army and Naval Medical Establishments.'

> … in the life of the naval surgeon, there are no seductions! Nothing as it now stands can induce a young man to enter into this service but a want of that necessary education which fits him for such a responsible and important profession, and the total want of friends.[17]

William Bunce was the carpenter of the *Victory*, charged with the maintenance of the hull of the ship and all her wooden parts, and had a team of fourteen men – the carpenter's crew – under him. He had served briefly under Nelson in the *San Josef* in 1801 when the ship was being fitted out, very slowly, by the dockyard workers at Plymouth. He may well have made an impression of the Admiral then, for he was transferred to the *Victory* in March 1803. Nelson was to write of Bunce in January 1805 that he was a man 'for whose abilities and good conduct I would pledge my head.'[18] In 1803 the boatswain was Mr Jones, until he was sent to work at Gibraltar in November 1804, and replaced by William Willmot.

In theory the gap between the 'wardroom' warrant officers, such as the master and the surgeon, and the 'standing' officers, such as the boatswain and the carpenter, was not an easy one to bridge. Surgeons and masters were gentlemen, albeit on sufferance, and had the right to take their recreation on the quarterdeck with the captain and lieutenants. Carpenters, gunners and boatswains were tradesmen. But William Rivers, the gunner of the *Victory*, seems to have crossed the gap quite casually in both directions.

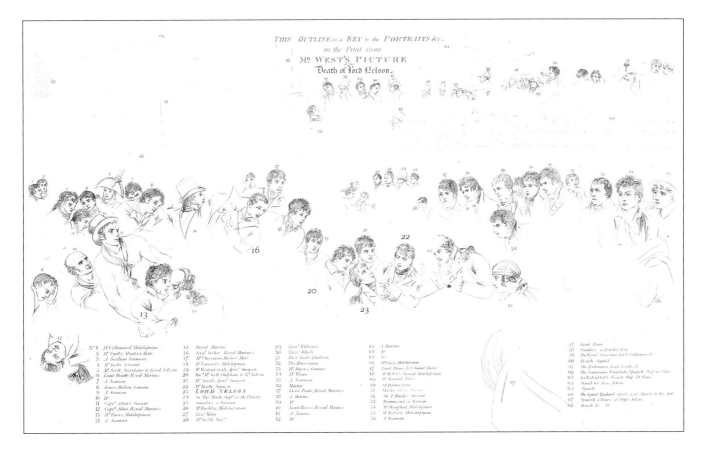

He first entered the Royal Navy in 1778 at the age of twenty-three. A native of Bermondsey, London, he was married to Ann Elphinstone of Wapping, just across the River Thames. He had almost certainly spent some time in the merchant service and he was quickly rated master's mate in the 74-gun *Triumph*, with good prospects of promotion to lieutenant after three years in the navy. Apparently the opportunities for promotion were not sufficient, or perhaps a leg wound in battle in the West Indies in May 1780 affected his health, but early in 1781 he moved sideways to become the gunner of the ship. As such, he was mainly responsible for the maintenance of the guns, their carriages, tackle, gunpowder and shot, as the actual firing was supervised by the captain and lieutenants. Rivers later moved to the 90-gun *Barfleur* and then to the first-rate *Victory* in 1790. This was as high as a gunner was likely to go.

He was responsible for the three magazines of the *Victory* and the safety of their contents. He had a team of four mates, an armourer and two mates, two yeomen of the powder room as storekeepers and twenty-five quarter-gunners to help him.

His notebooks suggest that he was better educated than the average gunner. His handwriting was good when he was not in a hurry, he could spell reasonably well and he kept meticulous tables on such matters as slow match, the composition of fuses, gun carriages, powder allowed for service and salutes, ranges and flights of guns, and even the making of rockets.

Standing officers were so called because they stayed with the ship until promoted to a higher rate; Rivers was already in a first-rate by the age of thirty-five and was to remain gunner of the *Victory* for more than twenty years. He went ashore when the British fleet took Toulon in 1794 and helped to defend it against the young Napoleon Bonaparte. He took part in the invasion of Corsica and fought at the sieges of Bastia and Calvi, alongside Captain Nelson.

If Gunner Rivers had apparently spurned the quarterdeck, this was not the case with his family. All three of his daughters who survived infancy married naval lieutenants. Rivers's

Details from a drawing of the death of Nelson (23), showing Midshipman Rivers (13), Sergeant Secker (16), Reverend Scott (20) and Surgeon Beatty (22).

Captain Thomas Hardy by Domenico Pellegrini.

son, also William, had first been entered at the age of six, in 1794, under his father's 'care and protection'. The captain rated him midshipman in consideration of his father's 'large family and long services in His Majesty's Navy.' He was in the *Victory* when Nelson captured two French ships at Hotham's Action in 1795, and when she was Jervis's flagship at the Battle of Cape St Vincent. Late in 1797, as the ship was laid up at Chatham, his father wrote to the Admiralty that the boy was now aged nine and a half and had been on board for three-and-a-half years. Gunner Rivers asked if his son could be sent to school for two or three years to get a normal education, rather than turned over to another ship.[19]

Midshipmen were young men who had already, in theory, served at least three years at sea and were training to become lieutenants. Besides Midshipman Rivers, their berth on *Victory* included some young men who had already accrued considerable experience. William Chaseman, a twenty-one-year-old from Plymouth, had taken part in the capture of five French ships in 1801. Henry Cary, an eighteen-year-old from Portarlington in Ireland had survived the wreck of the *Resistance* off Cape St Vincent a few weeks previously. John Carslake was the brother-in-law of the fourth lieutenant, John Yule.[20]

For Nelson, the possession of his flagship was not secure in May 1803. The Mediterranean Fleet had a vital role in neutralizing the French Fleet at Toulon, and in preventing French movements in the area; but it had to take third place to the North Sea Fleet and the Channel Fleet, which would protect Britain against invasion. The North Sea Fleet had less need of great ships like the *Victory*, but early in May St Vincent made a casual remark about her remaining in England for some time, while Nelson had heard that Admiral Lord Keith of the North Sea Fleet wanted her. This was enough to distress Nelson, who pointed out that 'all my things, servants, wines etc, etc, are ordered to be sent to her, be where she will – even my sheep, poultry, hay, corn and every comfort are ordered to her. But if Lord Keith, or any other man is to have her, I must un-order all these things.'[21] Fortunately this did not happen.

Throughout April the *Victory* was fitted out at Chatham. Samuel Sutton then took the *Victory* round to Portsmouth and Nelson arrived there early in the afternoon of 18 May, the same day as war was declared with France. He was rowed out to her and at 3.30 p.m. his flag was hoisted at the foremast. The next day he wrote to St Vincent, 'If the Devil stands at the door, the *Victory* shall sail tomorrow forenoon.' But if a ship was sent on foreign service without paying her crew first, there was a grave risk of mutiny. The payment began at 8.00 a.m. on the 19th and took several hours. It was early in the afternoon of Saturday the 20th when she raised anchor and sailed eastwards down the Solent to St Helens, then out to sea in company with the frigate *Amphion*.

Still Nelson was not at ease. His orders were to find Admiral Sir William Cornwallis with the Channel Fleet off Brest, and then turn the *Victory* over to him if he needed her to reinforce his own command. He was off Brest two days later, but there was no sign of the Fleet. Nelson stayed there for more than a day, 'not in a little fret.' His opinion on what to do next was perhaps not entirely unbiased.

> In this case, I have my choice to take the *Victory* or Frigate. I am decidedly of opinion that I ought, under all the circumstances of the case, to proceed in the *Victory*; for either Admiral Cornwallis has found the French Fleet ready for sea so insignificant, that it was not an object to block up Brest very close, in which case he would not want a First-rate, which would remove the objection of the Admiralty to my taking the *Victory*; or, the Admiral has judged it proper to go off the Coast, in which case I do not think I ought to leave the Victory.[22]

But he thought better of this and transferred his most urgent personal goods to the *Amphion*, sailing at 6.30 p.m. on the 23rd and leaving a message for Cornwallis. 'If you have no commands for the *Victory* I trust you will order her to join me without a moment's notice.' It was an unfortunate choice, for Cornwallis arrived at noon on the 25th. He did not need the *Victory* and sent her on with all dispatch; but she sailed much slower than the *Amphion*, and for the next two months Nelson had to live in the cramped quarters of a frigate, rather than the *Victory*'s great cabin.

Finally, on 30 July, Nelson's goods were transferred back to the *Victory* and he wrote, 'a few days will put us in order.' Captain Hardy came with him, and took command of the *Victory*. Sutton went into the *Amphion*, for a frigate command was ideal for a young man of twenty-six.

Captain Thomas Masterman Hardy was eleven years younger than Nelson, and entered the navy in 1781 under the patronage of his Dorset neighbours. Like Nelson he spent some time in the merchant service as a young man, and in 1790 he was taken up by Captain Alexander Hood, another Dorset man and member of a powerful naval family. He first met Nelson in 1795, when he was a lieutenant in the frigate *Meleager*. Late that year he was transferred to the *Minerve*, under Nelson as commodore. They captured a Spanish frigate and Hardy took charge of the prize crew, but enemy reinforcements arrived and he was captured. After an exchange of prisoners, the *Minerve* was pursued by a superior Spanish force, when a man fell overboard. Hardy set out in the jolly boat to rescue him and was in danger of being swept away to renewed captivity causing Nelson to call out, 'By God, I'll not lose Hardy; back the mizzen topsail.' As the British frigate stopped in the water the Spanish took it as a sign of confidence and retreated.

Hardy served in the Battle of Cape St Vincent, and in the Nile campaign he commanded the smallest British ship, the brig *Mutine*, which he had captured from the French. He became Nelson's flag captain in the *Vanguard* during his time in Naples, although he disapproved of his liaison with Lady Hamilton. He was Nelson's flag captain again at Copenhagen, and he spent the night before the battle in a boat taking soundings in the channel to the city – so close that he rowed round one of the enemy ships.[23]

Hardy was a very tall man, in contrast to Nelson. His cheerfulness and optimism tended to carry Nelson through his bouts of depression. 'I never knew Hardy wrong upon any professional subject,' wrote the Admiral, 'he seems imbued with an intuitive right judgement.' He was, of course, an excellent seaman, and a strict disciplinarian – there were 380 punishments during just over two years in the *Victory*, more than in any other ship of the fleet.[24]

Hardy brought a few followers, including some well-connected midshipmen. George Augustus Westphal was the son of an aristocratic German family and his career was supported by the Duke of Kent. Festing Horatio Grindall's father was already captain of a ship of the line. Many of these men joined the flagship with the hope of immediate action and quick promotion to the next rank, as did the lieutenants, but most were to be disappointed.

CHAPTER 3

The Threat from Boulogne

Napoleon Bonaparte was surprised by the declaration of war in 1803. In his opinion it was the British who had failed to observe the terms of the Peace of Amiens (1801) by refusing to leave Malta. He was engaged in far-reaching reforms of French law and administration and had no wish to be interrupted. His first reaction was to intern all British subjects visiting France – an unprecedented action that merely confirmed the British belief in his barbarism. He could launch no immediate attack on Britain, and war on her trade or colonies would take time and resources. Instead, he contented himself with an invasion of King George's other dominion, Hanover. The small state was invaded and conquered two weeks after the declaration of war. This did nothing to harm the British people, but dealt a severe blow to their King. But Bonaparte, with a vast army and the whole coast of Europe from the Pyrenees to the Frisian Islands under his command, did not hesitate in making plans to strike directly at his enemy.

On 18 May 1803, the same day as war was declared, the first fifty-seven craft of an invasion fleet were ordered. Seven hundred were on order by the end of the week and more than 1400 by July. Their design was ambitious to say the least. They were intended to be rowed as well as they could be sailed, and each was armed with a small number of heavy guns, with the hope that in combination they would be able to take bigger warships. The barges were to be of several types. The largest were *prames* or '*bateux de grande espace*'. Despite the title they were small by warship standards, 110 feet long, carrying thirty-eight sailors and 120 soldiers with an armament of twelve 24-pounder guns. They were an unhappy compromise, too narrow to carry sail on a cross wind, but too big to be rowed. The next group, also of the '*premier espace*' were the *chaloupes cannonieres*, 76 or 80 feet long and with three 24-pounders. Their hulls, it was found, were too light to withstand the effects of rough seas, or to support the guns they were to carry.

Next were the second-class vessels, the *bateaux cannoniers*, 60 feet long and intended to be rowed rather than sailed. They had three guns of various types and could carry 100 soldiers. They, too, would find manoeuvring very difficult in a rough sea. The third-class vessels, the *peniches* or barges, were of similar length and even narrower, and of lighter construction. In reality they were enlarged rowing boats, carrying sixty-six soldiers. Clearly Bonaparte's plans depended on a landsman's optimism, good weather, a short passage and minimal intervention by British forces. Even the smallest warship would be able to sink a *prame* with ease, not to mention the smaller vessels.

But the programme pressed ahead, and every shipyard on the north and west coasts of France, and in Flanders and Holland, was pressed into service. By the end of August 1803 there were forty-three *prames* under construction, with 241 *chaloupes*, 392 *bateaux* and 393 *peniches*. Fourteen hundred and two fishing boats had also been requisitioned.

The coastal geography of the English Channel had a profound effect on the wars between Britain and France. On the English side there are great natural harbours at Falmouth, Plymouth and Portsmouth, and large anchorages at Plymouth Sound, Cawsand Bay, Torbay, Portland, Spithead, St Helens, Dungeness and the Downs where a fleet can assemble. The

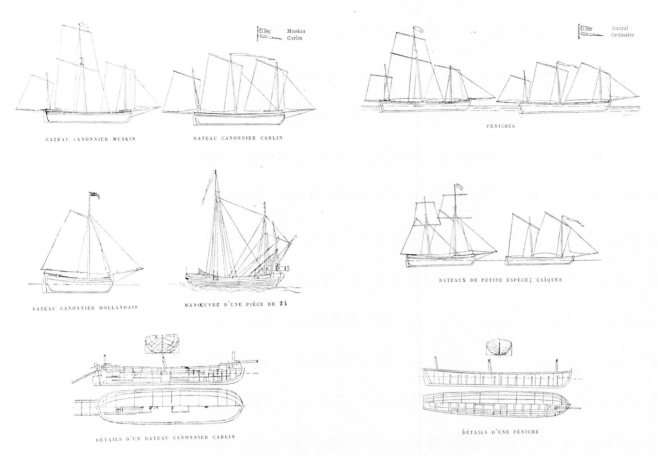

BATEAUX DE 2ᵉ ESPÈCE

BATEAUX DE 3ᵉ ESPÈCE

Muskin
Carlin

Amiral
Ordinaire

BATEAU CANONNIER MUSKIN

BATEAU CANONNIER CARLIN

PÉNICHES

BATEAU CANONNIER HOLLANDAIS

MANŒUVRE D'UNE PIÈCE DE 24

BATEAUX DE PETITE ESPÈCE; CAÏQUES

DÉTAILS D'UN BATEAU CANONNIER CARLIN

DÉTAILS D'UNE PÉNICHE

Types of craft designed for the invasion of England.

French side had none of these facilities. Only at Brest, on the extreme western tip of France, was there a large natural harbour with anchorages around it. In the days before steam power was available to aid dredging, to power cranes and diggers and to transport materials by sea and by land, any improvement would involve massive manpower and risk.

For the French it was necessary to find ports in the invasion area that satisfied several criteria. The ports had to be large enough to hold a sufficient number of craft; these vessels had to be able to get out all on a single tide; or alternatively, they needed protected anchorages outside the ports, where they could assemble safe from enemy attack. By July 1803, two months after the start of the war, Bonaparte had formulated his initial plan. Three hundred boats would depart from Flushing in the Netherlands. From the Flanders coast, 300 more would leave the ports between Ostend and Nieuport with 30,000 men. In the centre of the force, 300 more would leave Dunkirk, Gravelines and Calais with 6000 horses. But the main force, 100,000 men, 3000 horses and 125 pieces of artillery, would sail from the ports closest to the English shore, those of Boulogne, Wissant, Ambleteuse and Etaples.

Bonaparte clearly decided that the sea journey was too long from the Dutch and Flemish ports for the light and fragile invasion craft. The larger types were based there in some numbers. Calais was marginally closer to the English coast than Boulogne, but only to the well-defended area of the Downs and the unassailable town of Dover, not to the more vulnerable areas to the west. Furthermore, Calais was relatively open to attack, whereas Boulogne had a sandbank, the *Bassure de Basse*, a mile offshore. The water over it was only a few feet deep and offered protection from British frigates and sloops. The bank created an

Boulogne in 1800 at low tide, with the old town and castle on top of the hill to the right.

anchorage where an invasion fleet could assemble.

However, the port of Boulogne itself was far too small to mount an invasion. It was based on the River Liane whose channel was only about 30 metres wide opposite the town; it was 3.7 metres deep at the harbour mouth. There were two small jetties to protect the harbour and some quays and a customs house on the east bank, but otherwise the harbour was primitive. The biggest problem of all was the tides, for no craft could enter or leave against them. Boats could begin to get out an hour before high tide and could continue until low water seven hours later, with perhaps more time available for rowing craft.

Bonaparte was approaching the height of his glory and power. He was not religious in the conventional sense, but he believed in a fate which controlled individual destinies and certainly favoured his. It had elevated a young soldier from an obscure family to become the most powerful man in the world. Was it too much to expect it to give him three days of calm weather in the English Channel to complete his design?

Major warships – ships of the line, frigates and sloops – were designed to operate in all conditions of wind and weather. They had quite broad hulls which enabled them to carry sail

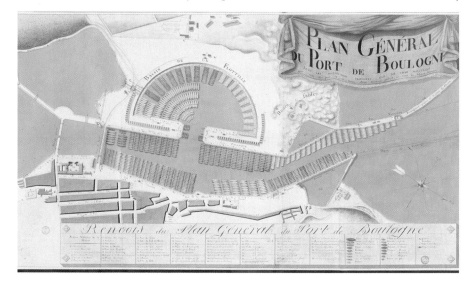

Map of Boulogne showing the Bassin Napoleon where the invasion craft were assembled.

when the wind was coming from the side or a little way ahead. They could store provisions for three to six months in their holds, to feed their large crews. Many sloops could be rowed if necessary, but it was rarely done, for their bulky hulls were difficult to move through the water, and it was not easy to find places for the oars low down in the structure without weakening it. Such ships would make very little progress by rowing in a calm, and none against the wind. The crew would quickly become exhausted. If it was absolutely necessary to move a ship in a chase or to escape from rocks, then it was better to kedge it – to row an anchor out ahead, drop it and then haul the ship up to it. If the water was too deep for that, then it was best to row the ship's boats, towing the ship through the water. But at best, it was a slow and exhausting process, only to be used for short distances. The flotilla craft of Boulogne were very different. They had large crews for rowing, but only carried provisions for a few days. They had light, narrow hulls with low sides where it was much easier to mount oars.

Bonaparte had dismissed Boulogne in 1798 claiming, 'It would be useless to carry out long works and banks at the port of Boulogne to enable it to contain a large number of boats as they could not get out in a single tide.'[1] He either forgot or disregarded this in 1803, and ordered massive works to make the port usable. The channel would be dredged and widened and a canal would be constructed south of the town. A semi-circular dock 78 metres in diameter was to be cut out on the west bank opposite the town. Forts were to be built in rocks to the east and west of the river mouth. Fort de la Creche and Fort de l'Heurt would protect the entrances to the anchorage against British attacks, while numerous batteries elsewhere on the rocks, and on the cliffs above, would offer more cover.

But the works were almost impossible with the civil engineering resources and techniques of the time, and soon fell behind schedule. In August 1803 a British intelligence report described the situation.

They are making amazing works, upwards of 3,000 hands employed besides the soldiers. … The fort buildings at low-water mark are to be finished in three months,

Fort Rouge on the beach near Boulogne, drawn by Clarkson Stanfield in 1817.

The British squadrons off Boulogne c. *1805, with French craft drawn up nearer the shore.*

but five weeks are elapsed and only an eighth finished. The opening for the harbour to admit frigates is an immense undertaking, and it is thought cannot succeed; it is Bonaparte's order and must be attempted.[2]

The other ports in the area were even less suitable than Boulogne. Etaples at the mouth of the River Canche had slightly deeper water on the bar, but no harbour facilities of any kind. At Ambleteuse, several projects had been suggested over the previous ten years and in September 1803 Bonaparte ordered the planning of a basin to hold up to 100 vessels. A similar scheme was proposed for Wimereaux just along the coast.

While the building works went on, Napoleon, who crowned himself Emperor of France in May 1804, assembled his 'Army of England' in a camp on the cliffs above Boulogne. In July 1804 he made his famous plea, 'Let us be masters of the Channel for six hours, and we shall be masters of the world.' This was doubly optimistic. Six hours were not enough to get more than a fraction of the invasion craft out of Boulogne, far less to send them across the channel; and in any case, how were even six hours to be gained, against the vigilance of the Royal Navy?

* * *

Across the Channel, all this preparation produced an enormous reaction. Great Britain was more united than ever before. The Jacobite threat had long since receded; unlike the American War of Independence, there was no large body of opinion that opposed the war aims of the government. Middle-class support for the French Revolution had evaporated and the working-class opposition movement had not yet arisen. Napoleon's rise to First Consul and then Emperor had discredited the Revolution in the eyes of all radicals. As E. P. Thompson wrote, 'France appeared to many now simply in the guise of a commercial and imperial rival, the oppressor of Spanish and Italian peoples.'[3]

For Britain, the war started as a purely defensive one. The French fleet was less threatening since Nelson had showed up its weakness at the Nile in 1798. It had about forty ships of the line in 1803. No doubt French privateers would launch a campaign against British commerce, but that threat had been faced many times before. Attacks might be made on British colonies, but these, too, could be contained. The only serious threat was that of an invasion of England, and it seemed very real at the time. As Admiral Lord Keith of the North Sea Fleet told the Prime Minister in 1804, 'This is a war unlike any previous and must be differently treated, defence and security in the first instance is the first duty.'[4]

The defence of Britain was multi-layered, the outer one of which extended many hundreds of miles from the shores of Britain. Two great naval forces, the Channel and Mediterranean Fleets, kept up patrols off the main French ports of Brest and Toulon respectively. The defence of the English Channel was more immediate to the threat of invasion, and in a sense it was the key to the whole campaign. Captain Sir Edward Pellew summed up the strategy when he told the House of Commons of

… a triple naval bulwark, composed of one fleet acting on the enemy's coast, of another consisting of heavier ships stationed in the Downs, ready to act at a moment's notice, a third close to the beach, capable of destroying any part of the enemy's flotilla that should escape the vigilance of the other two branches of our defence.[5]

In October 1803 the Admiralty made plans for defence during the winter.

1. That of having an active force on the enemy's coast for the purpose of keeping a vigilant and constant lookout on their proceedings and preventing … any considerable number of boats or craft from leaving the ports unmolested.

2. To fix such stations on our coast as may be best calculated to operate against the enemy in case they should elude the vigilance of our cruisers on their coast, and put to sea in such force as to render the light cruisers incapable of making any effectual resistance against them.[6]

In May 1803 Admiral George Elphinstone, Viscount Keith was appointed commander-in-chief of the North Sea Fleet, with responsibility for all the British coast between Beachy Head, not far from Portsmouth, and the Shetland Islands, and for enemy coasts from Le Havre to the Dutch borders. For most of the time he flew the flag on shore from his headquarters at Ramsgate in Kent, and he controlled a considerable and vitally important force.

The French had to move their flotilla craft out of their ports of building to the ports of assembly, and that gave the Royal Navy its best opportunity for aggressive action. In May 1804 Commodore Sir Sidney Smith saw fifty-nine craft coming out of Flushing to make their way to Boulogne. They hoped to get some protection from the complex sandbanks of the area, but Smith attacked with his frigates and sloops. The French boats went inshore and some went aground, protected by the shore batteries, but their sortie failed. The French also kept some of the flotilla craft in the road off Boulogne, to provide a constant threat to the British. In July 1804 Captain E. W. C. R. Owen, one of the greatest of the British frigate captains, spotted that a strong wind from the east-north-east was causing some distress to nearly ninety craft in the roads. Three of his ships raided them and drove most of them inshore, again stranding several on the beach. There were countless actions of this kind all along the French coast, but Keith had to urge caution and ordered captains 'not to suffer themselves to be drawn under the enemy's batteries on the coast, unless with a fair prospect of deriving some advantage correspondent to the risk.'[7]

In theory invasion might come anywhere on the eastern and southern coasts of Britain, and Keith was urged to defend the Firth of Forth, although he was sceptical about the chance of attack in that area. 'Where is the expedition to come from?' The Dutch ports were carefully blockaded and in any case they would soon be frozen up for the winter.[8] However,

The Strait of Dover in 1816, showing the Downs and the sandbanks.

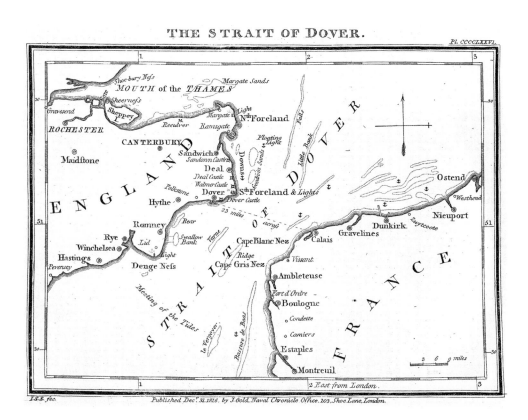

THE STRAIT OF DOVER.

he agreed that all angles had to be covered. In practice it was accepted that the south-east coast was a far more probable target. As General Dundas wrote in 1804, 'the line of coast and country the nearest to the enemy's preparations, apparently the most exposed to his attack, and certainly the most important to defend, is that which extends near 60 miles between Folkestone signal house and Beachy Head.'[9]

Keith, with his eye for land and sea topography, soon saw the difficulty of an invasion from Boulogne and in October 1803 he wrote in a report, 'there is not above five hours of tide out of twelve to depart with and the troops must be seen embarking.' He thought Le Havre was much more likely, 'the quarter from which I should most expect an embarkation for England to come, because any number of vessels can be assembled there without being subject to our view, and because they can quit the river in a fair wind at any time of tide and the troops can be embarked unperceived.' But a month later in November 1803 his intelligence reports showed that Bonaparte did indeed favour Boulogne. There were 379 boats and 32,000 troops there, compared with 196 boats and 22,000 men at Ostend, the next largest, and eighty-eight boats and 5500 men at Dunkirk. Apart from Calais and St Omer near Boulogne, no other port had more than 100 boats or 3000 men. Le Havre had ninety-three boats but only 1400 men.[10] It was clear that Bonaparte, no seaman, had decided on the shortest route across the Channel.

The Downs Squadron, as a result of this intelligence, became the key to British defence. Keith had three other forces under his command, based at Leith for the defence of the northern parts of the kingdom, at Yarmouth for guarding the Dutch coast, and at Sheerness to protect the Thames estuary. But the most important was based in the anchorage at the Downs, between the Kentish coast and the Goodwin Sands. The ships of this squadron spent a good deal of time at anchor off Boulogne – in June 1805 there were ten frigates and sloops there, with two bomb-vessels and fifteen small gunboats, backed up with a force of ten more ships across the Channel in the Downs. The anchorage outside the sandbanks was described by Captain Francis Austen.

There is no danger whatever in approaching the anchorage usually occupied by the

English Squadron employed at the blockade of Boulogne, as the water is deep and the soundings are regular. There is a bank called the 'Basse de Basse' which is about a mile off Ambleteuse, extending in a direction nearly parallel to the shore but rather diverging outwards.[11]

The most obvious difference between 1803 and 1940 was the number of resources available to the participants – guns had short ranges in the days of Napoleon, there were no submarines and aircraft, and ships were powered by sail or oar rather than steam. Yet all these ideas were considered and sometimes tried in the years of crisis from 1803 to 1805. The steamboat *Charlotte Dundas*, named after a cousin of Lord Melville, who was to become First Lord of the Admiralty in 1804, had already sailed on the Forth and Clyde Canal, and that year a Mr Thomson of Kirkintilloch wrote to the First Lord suggesting that steamboats could be used as fireships against Boulogne. Another Scot, Donald Campbell of Edinburgh, claimed he had 'invented a rocket to run under the surface of water, which when it struck the bottom of a ship would explode and blow her to shivers.'[12] The American inventor, Robert Fulton, tried to sell plans for a submarine to both sides. A prototype was evidently built at Lymington in Hampshire in 1804, but never launched. Another American called Mumford got the support of St Vincent for a plan to block up the invasion ports by sinking ships loaded with stones, but that failed. Floating mines got rather further and were first used in October 1804 in an attack on Boulogne; but according to an eyewitness they produced 'nothing but a grand and expensive *feu de joie*.'[13] A plan for aerial bombardment of Boulogne was rather more far-fetched. It involved a balloon which would float over the port where a clockwork mechanism would cause it to lose height. Then, in the words of its inventor, 'the fuse explodes the rockets and lights the fuse of the shells, which drop by means of the clockwork. The last ignition to the gas by means of the matches annihilates all.'[14] This was never tried, but rockets designed by William Congreve were actually used, after Trafalgar.

As a last line of defence afloat, the Admiralty revived the Sea Fencibles, a kind of maritime home guard. The force was open to local sailors, such as ferrymen and fishermen, who were not liable for impressment, though it sometimes served as a refuge for men who wanted to evade naval service. First formed in 1798 and disbanded at the Peace of Amiens, it took its title from land-based Fencibles, or 'defensible men', a semi-obsolete form of volunteer force. In 1803 it was planned to raise 25,000 men, but that target was not approached until 1810, and only by including men from Ireland and Western England, well away from the invasion areas. But in 1803 there was much interest in Kent, Sussex and Essex. At the end of the year there were nearly 3000 men between Beachy Head and Harwich, mustering about 120 armed boats. They were put under the command of regular naval captains and lieutenants and expected to drill regularly with cannon or pike. They might well have been an effective force in a real action, but as Captain Schomberg said of the Dungeness force: 'Notwithstanding the number of men who volunteered to go afloat, it is inconceivable the difficulty I find when the time arrives to persuade them to embark. … The people, who are mostly smugglers or wreckers, object to go on board the Revenue Cutters.'[15]

Communication was obviously important. The first stage was to warn the forces at home if the enemy attempted to get out of Boulogne. According to Keith's orders of October 1803,

The commanders of His Majesty's ships and vessels that may be cruising on the enemy's coast and who shall observe that the enemy are making preparation to embark, or that they are embarked and have sailed, are to dispatch a fast sailing vessel (or row boat if the weather will admit) to the nearest port, anchorage or signal station to give notice of the same, directing such vessel to keep abroad the signal expressive of the enemy's movements till she reaches the shore, that the information may be made as general as possible …[16]

The 10th Light Dragoons arriving at camp near Brighton in 1803.

There were two forms of communication operated by the Admiralty. Coastal signal stations were set up on important headlands and cliffs round the coast, and gave warning of enemy movements – not just an attempted invasion, but attacks by privateers and warships on merchant and naval shipping. Each station was manned by a naval lieutenant, a midshipman and two men. The Admiralty Telegraph was a chain of signal stations placed on inland hills, linking the Admiralty in London with the naval ports of Chatham, Sheerness, Deal and Portsmouth. In clear weather a message could be passed either way in a few minutes, compared with several hours by mounted messenger.

* * *

Apart from old-fashioned groups like the yeomanry and the fencibles, there were three main levels of service in the British army – regulars, militia and volunteers. The regular army was the only force to be mobilized in peacetime; it had 9429 cavalry and 17,984 infantry at home in April 1803, just before war was declared. These were spread around the country, with about an eighth of the force in south-east England, where an invasion was expected to land, and only 523 men in East Anglia. By August the regular forces had been augmented to 10,559 cavalry and 24,895 infantry, and the militia had been called out, adding 46,695 infantry. Of these, 16,498 were in the Eastern District and 19,596 in the Southern, so more than half the force was concentrated in the most likely invasion areas.[17]

Compared with the navy, the British army had few successes to look back on in the last war, apart from the campaign in Egypt at the very end. It had failed in the Netherlands and suffered heavy losses from disease in the West Indies. It was fully conscious of its inferiority to the French, who seemed to sweep all before them. At the root of the problem was the suspicion in which the army was held by Parliament and people. A navy could not be used to repress a population, an army could, and had done so in the days of Oliver Cromwell a century and a half before. The navy was clearly the main defence of the country and St Vincent did not see the need for an army at all. As a measure of control, the Mutiny Act, which enforced discipline on the army, had to be passed annually by Parliament. The Articles of War, which did the same job for the navy, were permanent.

There was no conscription for the regular army and service in the ranks had very low prestige, so the standard of recruit tended to be low – 'the scum of the earth' as the Duke of Wellington famously called them. The army suffered from a complicated administrative system with control divided between four independent bodies. The Secretary of State for War and the Colonies was a cabinet minister and the political head. The Secretary at War was more junior. He supervised army pay and various details of its movements. The Commander-in-Chief – appointed only in wartime – commanded the troops at home; and the Ordnance Board supervised the artillery and engineers and provided weapons and other stores.

The officer's uniform was glamorous and service in the commissioned ranks was highly valued by the upper and middle classes. 'I cried for two days together when Colonel Millar's regiment went away. I thought I should have broke my heart', says Mrs Bennet in *Pride and Prejudice*. In most cases, especially in peacetime, an officer had to pay a substantial sum for his commission and for each step in rank up to colonel. This, of course, meant that merit was not necessarily recognized, and there was a proportion of dilettante officers on home service, more interested in the social than the military duties of their rank. Furthermore, the army had fought no sustained European campaign for many years. About half of it was devoted to home defence and the other half was deployed throughout the empire, attacking enemy colonies and defending British ones. This brought much active service, but in conditions very different from those to be expected in Europe. All these problems would be addressed and largely solved in the next ten years, but at the beginning of the nineteenth century the army's military prestige was low.

The more traditional squires and gentry were particularly fearful of the regular army, for their folk-memory extended back to the days of Cromwell. They much preferred the militia, which was raised within the counties and was largely under the control of the local gentry. In peace it was a part-time force, so it was much less expensive. It was recruited by drawing lots among local people, so in theory it included a cross-section of the population; though in practice those with some money could buy their way out by paying a substitute, or even take out an insurance policy against being conscripted. The militia was for home defence only, although many of its members would later volunteer for transfer to the regular army. The first act on the threat of war was for the King to 'embody' the militia, as was done on 12 March 1803. The units marched to their war stations, along routes carefully monitored by the Secretary at War. Most went south to man castles and batteries on the coasts, but some stayed close to home for local defence.

In another striking parallel with 1940, volunteer units for local defence were formed in

The Staffordshire Militia on parade in front of Windsor Castle in 1804.

The Dover area from a map of 1801, the forerunner of the Ordnance Survey.

all parts of the country. West of London, for example, there was 'a numerous and respectable meeting of the inhabitants the Parish of Ealing' in the vestry of the local church. It agreed unanimously 'with the utmost readiness and alacrity [to] give our assistance to repel the common enemy.' A recruiting poster was issued claiming that Bonaparte had told his troops, 'The spoil must be immense – their wives and daughters will fall within our power – and every French soldier may have an Englishman for his slave.' The corps adopted 'a uniform scarlet regulation jacket, blue cuffs and collar, no lapels, uniform buttons and lace – blue pantaloons ornamented with scarlet worsted in front, and buttons at the ankle – black cloth full gaiters, edged on the top with scarlet.' Banners were blessed by the vicar. 'In the Temple of God, whose altar is menaced by an unprincipled infidel, I shall have the honour to deliver these banners into your hands. Rather die! and let these colours precede you to your grave, than surrender them to an atheist and a regicide.' By January 1804 the corps could parade 326 men under a major, five captains and ten subalterns, and there were 250 more on the list.[18]

In 1804 it was estimated that 385,000 men were serving with the various volunteer corps.[19] At army headquarters there was concern about the unevenness of the volunteer forces, for it was impossible to plan a campaign when nothing was known about the reliability of the different units. Some were enlisted to fight in their local areas, some within the country, some in a wider area. Some men were drilled by ex-soldiers and presumably conformed to army practice, others did not. Inspectors were appointed for the various districts, 'to be continuously employed in visiting and superintending the drill and field exercises of the several corps of yeomanry and volunteers.'[20] But the volunteers never saw action and remained an unknown quantity.

As Commander-in-Chief, the Duke of York issued detailed orders on what to do if the enemy landed. Troops were to 'drive the country' – removing all horses and cattle – ahead of an enemy advance. Corps of local guides and pioneers were to be formed. As the enemy was worn down by losses, it was expected that 'the more irregular troops' would become important. Such units were to be kept small so that all the men would know each other without the opportunity to exercise together. Their main object was to 'Harass, Alarm and Fatigue' the French. The word 'guerrilla' would enter the English language a few years later, but already there was some understanding of its meaning.[21]

In 1803 there were already some fixed defences on the south and east coasts of England. Three old castles from the time of Henry VIII defended the coast at the Downs, but no more was needed as there were always warships at anchor there. Dover was not a likely site for a landing, but its subsequent capture would give the enemy a harbour to bring in reinforcements and supplies. It was defended by a medieval castle, recently modernized. A new fortress was constructed on the Western Heights on the other side of the town and completed in 1805. The fort at Tilbury protected the Thames and one at Landguard protected the entrance to the River Stour at Harwich. The Royal Dockyards at Plymouth, Portsmouth and Chatham had strong defensive works, and those in the Chatham area would also help to stop an enemy from crossing the River Medway and advancing on London.

In addition, it was proposed to defend the most vulnerable landing places by means of 'Martello Towers' based on the design of one at Mortella, Corsica, which had held out against British forces in 1794. Seventy-four towers were built on the south coast between Folkestone and Eastbourne, with a concentration around the vulnerable area of Romney Marsh; their purpose was to delay the enemy and allow time for the sluices to be opened to flood the area. Twenty-seven more were built along the east coast, between Clacton and Aldeborough, against the threat from Holland. As a further defence of Romney Marsh, the Royal Military Canal was cut to separate the area from the mainland. Its projectors suggested that 'it would not be totally unproductive and be of use for commercial and Husbandry purposes,' but its main aim was to 'bar the entry into the Country out of Romney Marsh.'[22] None of these defensive works were ready until after the threat of invasion had passed, and besides which their value was controversial. The towers would only have worked if they had been manned by determined men who would hold out when isolated by enormous enemy forces, but the question of where to find these men was never resolved. As for the canal, it is difficult to see how it would have had much effect on a force that had already succeeded in crossing the English Channel against the force of the Royal Navy.

The government knew far more about the country and its people than ever before. The Ordnance Survey had begun in 1791 and by 1803 it had surveyed most of the south coast of England. This was augmented by numerous reports from naval and military officers on the state of the coastline, and the problems in defending it. The émigré French general, Charles Francois Dumouriez, shared some of his inside knowledge.

> The most important, best-thought-out and most dangerous plan was the old one for a descent on the roadstead of Romney, and simultaneously on that of new Romney, thus embracing Dungeness on its two flanks. … Seeing that this plan belongs to the sphere of high tactics and is decisive for every war between England and France, I have worked at it with care, and at the time I made detailed notes on it that have impressed it on my memory.

> The plan is still quite new, and its execution is made easier owing (1) to the kind of craft the French have just adopted for their attempts against England; (2) to the proximity of Holland, Flanders and Picardy, whence their army is to start; (3) to the facility with which such small craft can be collected even in the least spacious tidal harbours … ; (4) to the swifter and surer passage of these row-boats and the possibility of beaching them on the very strand; (5) to the facility of making the landing at any point, even on cliff-bound shores, with little tidal rise or fall; (6) to the speed of embarkation and landing.[23]

From a naval point of view, Keith did not neglect the possibilities of an invasion of Ireland or the west of England, though these areas were outside his command. Of the south coast of England he wrote,

> The landing places along this coast are – All the beach near Brighton in certain winds. Seaford Bay very good in east winds. The east side of Beachy in Pevensey

Viscount Melville as First Lord of the Admiralty.

Bay and Rye Bay with westerly winds. The west side of Dungeness with easterly winds. The opposite side and all Hythe Bay with westerly winds. A small part of Wear Bay near Folkestone. I think that the Downs are secure, unless the enemy be superior at sea …[24]

Keith was aware of the possibility of an invasion from Dutch waters, especially from Flushing, which he regarded as 'by far the most considerable port on that side.' He was particularly concerned about Essex and the Thames Estuary. On the south side of the Thames, Thanet (no longer an island since medieval times) could almost be ruled out, being surrounded by high cliffs. The shore east of that was vulnerable. 'The coast from Bishoptown to Whitstable is good for landing upon but the water is shallow. Boats of small draught may in good weather land at half flood …' Sheppey and Grain were still real islands and the enemy was unlikely to land on them and risk being cut off, but the dockyard at Sheerness on Sheppey had to be defended.

Across the estuary, the extensive sands at Maplin and Buxey would probably secure these areas, for crossing them, even in small boats, was 'attended with great danger.' The entrances to the Essex rivers were 'intricate and easily defended'. But the coast around Clacton was far more vulnerable, despite a sandbank parallel to the coast – 'the whole of the Wallet is a harbour and most of its coast is fit to land upon, but the water is so deep as to admit of ships sailing near the shore all over it. The accesses to it are pretty well defended.' Harwich harbour was defended by Landguard Fort, but there were several good beaches to the north of it, perhaps too exposed for a landing.[25]

Meanwhile the local officers in charge of the Sea Fencibles sent in their own reports, on how the coast could be defended and the people better mobilized. They showed Britain in all its diversity, especially in the remote maritime districts. At Dungeness, according to Captain Austen,

> The religion of the inhabitants (if they have any) is that of the established Church of England; the government, the same as the rest of the British dominions; the disposition to make money without being very scrupulous about the means, seems to have its full influence in the neighbourhood, and the language in common use is a dialect of the English.

> As there is no harbour here, there can of course be no shipping belonging to the place, nor any craft longer than what may be hove up out the beach, of which there are very few. The only trade carried on is smuggling, which I have reason to believe is carried on to a very considerable extent.[26]

Austen had a reputation in some quarters for humourlessness, but perhaps he shared the irony of his sister, Jane.

The Thames Estuary was a key area for an invasion, and Captain William Bligh of *Bounty* fame did a more technical survey. After describing the hydrographic features he commented,

> Dungeness is perhaps the most extraordinary accumulated mass of pebbles ever seen, over which it is so difficult to pass, that it is like a barrier to the country for full two miles. The beaches are steep, and a heavy sea rolls on them in bad weather, but landing can generally be effected on one side or the other of Ness Point.

Income tax had first been introduced by William Pitt in 1798 and the new Addington government re-established it to pay for the war. The Census of 1801 had enumerated the British population for the first time, and found there were 8,893,000 people in England and Wales and 1,608,000 in Scotland. The Irish, still being reluctantly absorbed into the United Kingdom, remained uncounted but were estimated at 5 million. At a much lower level, numerous lists were made of local populations and resources to help with raising the militia and 'driving the country'. Thus it was found that Pevensey Rape, a district on the vulnerable coast of Sussex, had 5213 oxen, 2334 other cattle, 95,696 sheep, eleven goats and 12,064 pigs. It had 4430 horses, 1572 wagons and 2505 carts, as well as twenty-nine watermills and twenty windmills, and thirty-eight barges on the River Ouse.[27]

Colonel Crawfurd MP was sceptical about the possibilities of invasion and in August 1803 he told the House of Commons,

> The distance is considerable. The management of a fleet of three or four hundred vessels is extremely difficult, even without being disturbed by an enemy. To such a fleet, crowded with landsmen, the mere chances of a sea would be formidable. A long calm would be a great distress; a gale of wind might be fatal. The wind must not only be favourable, but moderate. A short passage would be essential to success; but then it must blow fresh, which would bring them on a lee shore, where they would find such a surf, as a great fleet so filled could not encounter without very considerable risk.[28]

With his inside knowledge of French plans, General Dumouriez was just as sanguine.

> However numerous the means of transport the French are now collecting in the various ports of France and Holland, it is easily conceivable that were this flotilla massed at one starting point capable of holding it, a small part only of the English naval forces would amply suffice to prevent it from landing on English soil an army corps of such dimensions as to endanger the British empire. The greater the number of craft in any one roadstead at the time of departure, the more thorough the havoc wrought by the English stationary squadrons adequately strengthened … The great armament would bear the semblance of a gigantic wreck or a bloody sea-fight; and the few vessels that escaped in scattered disorder would seek the refuge of the smaller harbours on the French coast.[29]

St Vincent is quoted as saying, 'I do not say they cannot come, only that they cannot come by sea.' British naval commanders were not usually as complacent as that, for they were constantly aware of the difficulties presented by wind and weather. On the French side, Bonaparte had rejected an invasion plan in 1798 on the grounds that 'To perform a descent on England without being master of the seas is a very daring operation and very difficult to put into effect',[30] but now he seemed confident that it could succeed. From his point of view, it appeared to be possible. Britain was headed by an inexpert government whose peace treaty, followed by a declaration of war eighteen months later, only showed its lack of judgement. In the last war large elements of the British people had supported radical movements sympathetic to the French Revolution, the Irish had revolted and even the navy had mutinied. There was no reason to believe that the Addington government would be able to lead the people against the might of the French army.

Henry Addington, the Prime Minister at the start of the war, had been a very successful Speaker of the House of Commons. In January 1801 William Pitt, Prime Minister for the previous seventeen years, had a serious constitutional dispute with the King. Faced with the threat of rebellion in Ireland, Pitt had advocated Roman Catholic emancipation, including voting rights. But this would have led to a Catholic majority in the Irish Parliament and it was decided to merge with the British Parliament in London. That measure was pushed through with great difficulty, partly relieved by bribery. The new Parliament met, the British flag was changed to incorporate St Patrick's cross of Ireland, but the King declared that Roman Catholic emancipation would be a contradiction of his coronation oath to defend the Church of England. Pitt could not agree to drop the measure and resigned in protest. The King approached Addington as a man who might be acceptable to all important shades of public opinion. He accepted, but most of the leading figures of Pitt's administration refused to support him, leaving him with a cabinet woefully lacking in political experience. According to his biographer, he had three main disadvantages. 'He was not an aristocrat, he was not an orator and he was not William Pitt.'[31] The greatest blow to his historic reputation came with William Canning's jibe that 'Pitt is to Addington as London is to Paddington', comparing the city of nearly a million people with a village just outside.

Addington, a lawyer himself and the son of a doctor, was the first middle-class prime minister, and he was despised by the aristocracy but liked by 'country' backbenchers who had seen too much of men of genius. His performances in the House of Commons were uninspired; he had no administrative experience and little political skill. The credibility of the government was undermined by the failure of the peace, and diminished as the war dragged on with no land contact between the fighting forces, and no clear strategy. At first Pitt refused to attack the government out of loyalty to the crown. When he finally did so in the spring of 1804, it quickly collapsed and Pitt was invited to form a ministry early in May.

To the position of First Lord of the Admiralty Pitt appointed his most powerful political associate, Lord Melville. Trained as a lawyer in Edinburgh, he had first entered Parliament in 1774 as Henry Dundas and within a few years he had built up an unparalleled power base in Scotland. Manipulating an electoral system, which was even more archaic and ramshackle than that of England, he controlled elections in most of the Scottish burghs, with thirty-six out of forty-five members under his influence at his peak in 1796. He was more than a political boss; in 1798, for example, while Nelson was searching the Mediterranean for Bonaparte's expeditionary force, Dundas was the first in Britain to guess they were going to Egypt, although it was too late to get a message to Nelson.

Dundas's control of the Scottish electorate was sustained by his ability to deliver jobs for the sons and nephews of the voters. One field for this was the East India Company, of which he was Chairman from 1793 to 1801. As Reverend Sydney Smith put it: 'As long as he is in office the Scotch may beget younger sons with the most perfect impunity. He sends them by loads to the East Indies, and all over the world.'[32] For all that, Dundas had many enemies in Scotland, because he led the repression of the radicals in the aftermath of the French Revolution. His influence in naval affairs began in 1782 when he became Treasurer of the Navy. He was generally believed to be keen to advance young Scotsmen – a reputation he tried to live down. Dundas was created Viscount Melville in 1802.

He tackled his new job as First Lord with great energy and determination. He won the respect of naval officers, including Captain Hardy who conceded grudgingly that 'it was much his wish to befriend the navy in spite of his being a Scotchman.'[33] Sir Charles Middleton, admittedly a supporter of the Dundas family but not an easy man to please, wrote that 'I never remember so many judicious measures brought forward for the benefit of the navy, nor anything like [the] energy with which they are carrying into execution at present.'[34]

But the Addington government had left a time bomb, which was soon to explode under the new one. Forced on by Melville's predecessor, St Vincent, it had set up a series of enquiries into naval abuses. St Vincent had no doubt been sincere in his desire to root out corruption, but such campaigns usually become political sooner or later. The Tenth Report of the Commissioners appeared in March 1805 and dealt with the office of the Treasurer of the Navy, held by Melville for most of Pitt's first administration. He clearly had something to fear, for when his first copy arrived while he was talking to William Wilberforce about the slave trade, he seized it and looked intensely through its uncut pages. Melville found he was accused of 'malversation of public funds'. It was largely a technical offence, for it had been common to transfer interest in government funds into private accounts until he himself had reformed the system some years previously; but a motion against him was debated in the House of Commons on 8 April 1805 and carried with the Speaker's casting vote, to opposition cries of 'view hollo' and 'We have killed the fox'. Melville was forced to resign. Pitt was in tears and regarded it as a political disaster, as important as losing a major battle.

CHAPTER 4

The Bellerophon

One ship that was very little affected by the hot press of 1803 was the *Bellerophon*. She was already on service in Jamaica and her crew must have been horrified to hear that their time in the navy was likely to be prolonged yet again, after they had missed the demobilization of 1801.

The *Bellerophon* (known as the *Billy Ruffian* to the lower deck, who had not had the advantage of classical education) was fitted out at Portsmouth in the summer of 1801, and she was already quite an old ship. Built in 1786, she was a good example of the classic 74-gun, two-decker, ship of the line. The type was very much influenced by French design, in particular with the capture of the French 74, *Invincible*, in 1747; but it was not a slavish copy, for the British ships had a different gun arrangement, different underwater lines and a rather stronger structure. Compared with the *Victory* of 100 guns, the most obvious difference was that the 74 only had two instead of three complete decks of guns. Apart from that, the two types did not differ radically in size. The *Victory* was 186 feet long on the gundeck and the *Bellerophon* was 168 feet long, but some of the later 74s were only 4 feet shorter than the *Victory*. The 74 was the most common type of ship of the line in most of the larger navies, for it represented a very successful compromise between gun power and speed. Three-deckers were considerably more powerful, but were not expected to compete with two-deckers in a chase. Seventy-fours could sail as well as they could fight.

The Bellerophon *in later life, with Napoleon boarding her to go into exile.*

The lower and orlop decks of the 74-gun Achille, *similar in layout to the* Bellerophon.

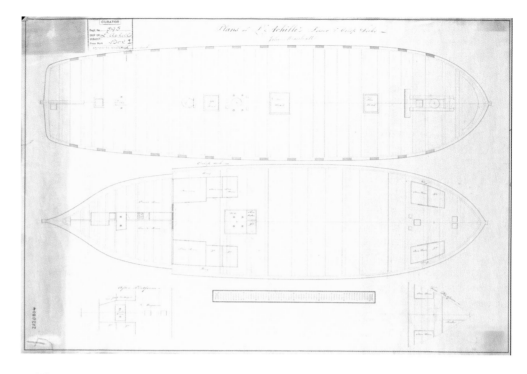

The *Bellerophon* had fought at the 'Glorious First of June' and the Nile. She went into dock for a 'middling repair' and was re-floated on 22 June 1801, the work having cost £33,206. She was needed for the Channel Fleet, and at the Admiralty St Vincent was impatient. Men were found by taking them from other ships. A draft of about three dozen men came from the *Royal William*, the flagship of the port admiral, and was largely made up of experienced petty officers and able seamen who would form the nucleus of the crew, and many of them were sent on to other ships afterwards.[1] The Admiralty ordered the port admiral to discharge men from other ships, such as the 74-gun *Goliath* and the 18-gun sloop *Swallow*. On 9 August they ordered that half the larboard watch of the 74-gun *Defiance*, then coming out of service after being used as a flagship at the Battle of Copenhagen, should be lent to help fit out the *Bellerophon*, and the other half should help with the 98-gun *Dreadnought*, and a race developed between the two ships to see which would be ready first. The *Bellerophon* won, and was needed so urgently that this transfer became permanent, and yet more men were brought over from the *Defiance*. On 24 August the ship set sail to join the fleet off Ushant – so fast that one suspects it was done before the seamen had any chance to protest.[2]

Though most of the men from the *Defiance* and other ships had already spent some years in the navy, they were far less skilled than the *Royal William* draft. Many of them had come into the navy as a result of the Quota Acts of 1795. These had demanded that each county and seaport town in Britain should provide a certain number of men for the navy, with one seaman counting for two landsmen. London, for example, produced 1371 able and ordinary seamen, equivalent to 2742 landsmen, and 2522 landsmen, making a total of 5264. The government claimed that the scheme was a success, and certainly it increased the numbers of the navy in a time of crisis. There was much criticism of the quality of many of the landsmen, who were often lured by bounties paid by the local authorities, and it was suggested that their presence undermined the stability of ship life, contributing to the mutinies of 1797.

The landsmen who joined the *Bellerophon* in August 1801 reflected the unemployment caused by agricultural and industrial change. Henry Beaver of Reading, Robert Benny from Fife and Hugh Cairns of Belfast were all handloom weavers who had been displaced by the power loom. James Dunman of Somerset and John Lee of Crediton, Devon, were both shoemakers, while George Housden of St Neots had doubled, rather bizarrely, as a shoemaker and an apothecary. There were farm labourers, former tenant farmers, stocking weavers, mercers, plasterers, ostlers and barbers. Their prospects were bleak in the navy, for only a few would find outlets for their skills aboard ship. Richard Bovett, a wheelwright from Sidmouth in Devon, used his woodworking craft as a member of the carpenter's crew. The rest had mostly risen from landsmen to ordinary seamen after five or six years of service; but even in 1805, after nine or ten years in the navy, Robert Benny, the Fife weaver, and Hugh Cairns from Belfast were still rated as 'landsmen' at the ages of thirty-five and thirty.

On 20 October 1801 Admiral Cornwallis, commander-in-chief of the Channel Fleet, received nine-day-old orders from the Admiralty 'directing me immediately to abstain from all acts of hostility against the possessions and citizens of the French Republic and its allies.'[3] The Peace of Amiens had been signed and the war was over. The *Bellerophon* was at anchor in Torbay by the beginning of November, while most of the ships of the navy were paid off in peacetime.

Not so for the *Bellerophon*. The government decided to increase the naval strength in the West Indies in response to a French build-up in the area. This was intended to regain control of the colony of St Domingue (later Haiti) after a slave revolt led by Toussaint L'Ouverture, but there was no guarantee that it would not be used against the British islands. Early in March 1802, under the command of Captain John Loring, the *Bellerophon* set sail for Jamaica in company with five other ships of the line. There is no sign that the crew revolted against their fate, or even protested – there were no courts martial or mass floggings for mutiny, and no petition appears in the Admiralty records; but it is not likely that they were happy.

Loring reacted to the restart of war by pressing men from any merchant ships he came across and on 29 June 1803, after escorting a convoy some way from Jamaica, the ship's boats were hoisted out and used to press fourteen men from the ships of the convoy.[4] The newly-pressed men were generally very experienced and many were soon promoted to petty officer. Richard Nicholson was thirty-five years old, a shipwright from Blyth in Northumberland. He had already spent thirteen years in the Royal Navy and six in the merchant service and bore scars from his tools, on the thumb and middle finger of his left hand. He became a member of the carpenter's crew and was eventually promoted to warrant officer in 1807. Samuel Lindley was twenty-four, from Lenham in Suffolk, with three years' experience in the merchant service. Despite his pale, thin face he was considered 'well looking'. John Hillock from Dundee had first gone to sea in 1787 at the age of eleven, and since then his time had been divided equally between the merchant and Royal navies. Isaac Harrison of Norwich had spent thirty-two of his forty-five years at sea. He was 'bald, a little deaf, thick set and strong made' and was soon given a job as a quarter-gunner.[5]

The *Bellerophon* and other ships were employed against the French in St Domingue – a complicated operation, as the French on shore were themselves besieged by the black rebels. In July 1803, with the 74-gun *Vanguard* and several other ships, she helped capture the French 74, *Duquesne*, which was attempting to escape from Cape François. In November Captain Loring of the *Bellerophon* was in command of the naval force off Cape François that accepted the surrender of French General Rochambeau, with two fine frigates and numerous other prizes.

During peacetime the health of the *Bellerophon*'s crew had been quite good according to her surgeon, Alexander Whyte. Like many naval surgeons, he tended to believe that contact with the shore was the worst thing for naval health, and the ship had had little of that. But now large parties were sent on board the captured French ships. Those who went on board the *Duquesne* soon caught fevers from the crew. In January 1804 about half the *Bellerophon*'s men were sent to work on the prize ships in Port Royal Harbour, Jamaica, while others manned boats for communication between the ships, and to row guard round the ships holding the French prisoners. After a while, they complained 'their labour and duty was so severe that they sometimes dropped down in the execution of it.' No less than 212 men were put on the sick list for fevers, of whom 101 were sent to hospital, seventeen died on board ship and about forty in hospital. The sick list also included many men with fluxes and ulcers, and thirty-one with scurvy. The situation was not aided, the surgeon claimed, by 'the excess which success always paves the way among seamen', leading to large-scale drunkenness. Whyte was pleased when the ship was ordered to sea, after which 'the attacks became much less frequent and more mild.'

The ship sailed from Jamaica on 17 June 1804 on the way back to the war in Europe, but the medical problems were not over. Although the change in climate had less effect than might have been expected, the West Indies had left another mark on the crew. In Port Royal they had been given a certain amount of leave to go on shore by turns. There were sixty-seven cases of venereal disease, in many cases concealed by the victims for fear that their shore leave would be stopped. They came to light gradually during the course of the voyage across the Atlantic. The case of Charles Atkinson was only discovered late in November in Portsmouth, six months after he had contracted it.[6]

After her return from the West Indies, the *Bellerophon* saw much hard service in the blockades of Brest, Cartagena and Cadiz. In November 1804 William Pryce Cumby arrived to become first lieutenant of the ship. He came from a family that was struggling hard to climb the naval ladder. His grandfather had been a master, his father a captain and two of his mother's brothers were lieutenants. Born in Dover, he entered the service at the age of thirteen, and, like Nelson, in peacetime he made voyages as a merchant seaman 'for the purpose of improving himself in nautical science.' During the Spanish Armament of 1789 he attracted the notice of Lord Mulgrave, a powerful admiral who had served on the Board of Admiralty. In 1792 he had mixed fortunes. He passed for lieutenant at the age of twenty-one, but his patron died. The new Lord Mulgrave took some interest in him, but not as much as his father had done.

In 1795 Cumby was appointed to the frigate *Astrea* under Lord Harry Paulet, who had been his shipmate in the 50-gun *Assistance*, and followed him into the *Thalia*, in which they fought in an action off Lorient in June 1795, before transfer to the Mediterranean Fleet. Cumby, a 'Merry, clever little fellow' and an 'excellent officer', produced a biblical satire on St Vincent's style of leadership. Copies were made and circulated in the wardrooms of the fleet, until it came to his lordship's notice. He found out who the author was and summoned Cumby to his cabin. He surprised him with a copy of the parody and forced him to read it out to the assembled captains, much to Cumby's horror and their amusement. Then St Vincent, who was not lacking in a rather cruel humour, gravely pronounced a verdict.

Lieutenant Cumby, you are unanimously found guilty, *and without a court martial, Sir*, of parodying the Holy Writ, and that too for the purpose of bringing your commander-in-chief into ridicule. … The sentence, therefore, upon you, *without a trial*, I do adjudge, – that for this your offence you have my permission of three months leave of absence in England.[7]

CAPTAIN FRANKLIN, R.N.

John Franklin in later life.

Cumby resumed his service in the *Excellent* under Cuthbert Collingwood, but his career was patchy for the next five years. He was flag lieutenant to a port admiral, commander of a cutter in the North Sea and an officer of the Norfolk Sea Fencibles, until Captain Loring applied for him to be his first lieutenant in the *Bellerophon*. At thirty-three he must have felt that promotion was passing him by, unless he could distinguish himself in action.[8]

In August 1804 Midshipman John Franklin, later to become famous as the tragic Arctic explorer, joined the ship. Born in 1786 in inland Lincolnshire as the ninth child of twelve in a rising middle-class family, he joined the 64-gun *Polyphemus* in 1801, just in time to fight under Nelson at Copenhagen. He then sailed with his cousin, Matthew Flinders, in the *Investigator*, surveying the coast of Australia and demonstrating remarkable navigational skill. He was shipwrecked and sent home in the East Indiaman *Earl Camden*, in which he still could not avoid action. The East India fleet was threatened by the French Admiral Linois, and the Indiamen posed as warships to scare them off. Franklin took charge of the signals.

The British seaman was an un-military figure, who resisted all attempts at drill and uniform. The Description Book of the *Bellerophon* shows him in all his diversity. Some would have been considered unfit for any modern navy. John Millikan was an 'amaciated thing'. Henry McGee was blind in one eye and Thomas Jewell had lost his right one. James Robinson was a 'stupid fellow' in his officers' estimation, John Sullivan was 'very old looking', and Michael Carvel was 'not a good character but very strong.'

Not all were young, for the *Bellerophon* had been in continuous commission throughout the peace and had some men with quite long service. Out of 264 men on board who were not officers, marines or boys, more than a fifth were over forty. James Marshall was the oldest at fifty-six, while James Gill, aged fifty-one with twenty-seven years' service in merchant ships and thirteen in the Royal Navy since the age of eleven, was a quartermaster and a 'good old seaman'. Eighty-seven more of the crew were in their thirties, fifty-seven in their late twenties and sixty-four were between twenty and twenty-five. They were not particularly tall. Jack Allen, a Negro from Grenada, was the tallest at 5 feet 11 inches. Some were remarkably short, such as Edward Ford of Sunderland, who was under 5 feet, but made up for it by being 'thick set, strong made'. John Cook, formerly a watch motion maker of Cripplegate in London, was only 4 feet 11 inches. He worked in the hold, where small stature was an advantage.

They came from all corners of the United Kingdom, which included Ireland from 1801. Nearly seventy of them came from that island, with forty-seven more from Scotland. There were foreigners from Germany and Sweden and a few Negroes, of varying abilities. Jack Allen was 'very infirm' at forty-three, and 'good for nothing'. The grades of coloration produced by racial mixing in the West Indies were meticulously recorded. Samuel Marlow of Jamaica, described as a 'Sambo', one quarter white, was a wardroom steward. David Young and Evans Lyon were both 'mustees', one eighth black, from Antigua.[9]

In April 1805 Captain Loring was replaced by John Cooke, the forty-two-year-old son of an Admiralty cashier, who had served throughout the War of Independence and commanded a succession of frigates in this war and the last. Franklin observed that he was, 'Very gentlemanly and active. I like his appearance much.'[10] To Midshipman Robert Patton he was 'an excellent officer and strict disciplinarian.'[11] Lieutenant Cumby, though a Loring follower, stayed on under the new captain.

After a brief cruise with the Channel Fleet off Brest, the *Bellerophon* received new orders. She sailed from Cawsand Bay near Plymouth on 19 May 1805, and anchored off Cadiz to join the blockade of that port on 10 June.

CHAPTER 5

The Crews

The target of the great mobilization of 1803, the object of all the impressment effort, was the able seaman, young and fit enough to climb the mast in a storm, but experienced enough to carry out the hundreds of jobs that he might be called upon to do. The navy had virtually no mechanism for training these men, and relied almost totally on the merchant fleet for its recruits. Yet they were not made easily. John Nicol of Edinburgh had spent eight years in the navy during the Revolutionary War and fought at the Battles of Cape St Vincent and the Nile. From 1803 he had to work in a quarry rather than at his trade as a cooper, where he would have attracted the notice of the press gang. Although the quarry ruined his health, he preferred it to the navy, but he took a perverse pride in his value to the state. When mocked by his friends about his need to hide, he replied, 'Could the government make perfect seamen as easily as they could soldiers, there would be no such thing as the pressing of seamen, and I was happy to be of more value than them all put together, for they would not impress any of them, they were of so little value compared with me.'[1] As Captain Hardy put it early in 1805, 'How fortunate it is for us that he [Napoleon] cannot cast sailors in a mould.'[2]

What made the seaman so valuable? He was not, in contemporary terms, a skilled artisan, for he had probably not served an apprenticeship and was not a member of a guild or corporation. Yet his skills were considerable. A sailing ship of the age had perhaps 40 miles of rope rigging and a good seaman was expected to know it intimately, to find the right line in the dark, in the rain, or in a storm. He could tie twenty or thirty different knots without hesitation, and perform various kinds of splices. He could prepare ropes by worming, parcelling and serving. He knew about seizings, mouses, points, gaskets, mats, Turks' heads and a dozen other ways of using rope. He could run 100 feet up the ratlines on the orders of his officer, and then out to the end of a yardarm with only an inch of footrope between him and death. He could spend half his working life up there, as the ship swayed with the motion of the sea. He could grapple with a wind-filled sail, helping to furl or reef it as a storm threatened. On coming down from the rigging he could swab the decks, push at the capstan bars, row the ship's boats, rig all kinds of tackle for hoisting weights or raising or lowering the anchor. He had to be able to tolerate hardship, while the ship spent days in a storm and the pumps had to be manned continuously, or ran short of victuals on a long voyage. In action he helped to serve the guns, loading and running them out by muscle power alone.

That was enough experience to make an ordinary seaman, but an able seaman needed more. He had to be able to read a compass and to take over as main helmsman to keep the ship on course and with her sails filled; to stand in the main chains which projected from the side of the ship and heave the lead line so that the navigator could know the depth of water underneath; and to carry out these tasks with utmost reliability, for the entire safety of the ship might depend on him alone. Yet the most important men of a ship were probably not there by choice according to Admiral Philip Patton.

> … by far the larger portion of a ship's company are there against their will. Many are

Sailors reefing topsails in a gale. The lighter spar, the studding sail boom, had been lashed up to keep it out of the way.

impressed and forcibly brought. Others enter because if they do not, they will be impressed and although they are cheerful and apparently contented, there is still that difference between them and the officers; the latter are there by choice.[3]

An early start was the key to a maritime career. Most boys came from seafaring families or at least lived in port towns where ships were familiar. It was doubtless family custom, rather than economic advantage, which caused boys to go to sea. As Adam Smith put it in 1776,

> The lottery of the sea is not altogether so disadvantageous as that of the army. The son of a creditable labourer or artificer may frequently go to sea with his father's consent; but if he enlists as a soldier, it is always without it. … Common sailors, therefore, more frequently get some fortune and preferment than common soldiers; and the hope of these prizes is what principally recommends the trade. Though their skill and dexterity are much superior to that of almost any artificers, and though their whole life is one continual scene of danger and hardship, yet for all the skill, for all the hardships and dangers, while they remain in the condition of common sailors, they receive scarce any other recompense than the pleasure of exercising the one and of surmounting the other. Their wages are not greater than those of common labourers at the port which regulates the rate of seaman's wages.[4]

Most started at the age of twelve or thirteen and were 'bred to the sea', as a universal expression of the time puts it. As Admiral Collingwood found, boys of fourteen to sixteen years were at an ideal age, strong enough to begin to work hard, but young enough to learn. 'Such

The popular view of the sailor ashore, in a cartoon of 1819 by S. W. Fores.

A SAILORS MARRIAGE.

boys soon become good seamen: landsmen very rarely do, for they are confirmed in other habits.'[5]

For seamanship is rather like a language. Learning it at the right age is not considered particularly clever, but to become fluent in later life is very difficult. Appropriately enough, the seaman had developed his own vocabulary, because of his separation from shore life and the many technical terms of his trade. A thousand broadsheets, pamphlets, novels and cartoons parodied his style of conversation. 'He ran foul of me on my larboard side as I was steering through Wapping so I hove him a gentle topper and knocked him down', says a sailor in a cartoon, accused of assault.[6] 'Tell him he may go on deck if he likes', says another, temporarily rich from prize money, hiring a whole stagecoach for himself, 'and I hope he'll look after you, and see you are steady at the helm, and don't sarve us the same as one of your land-lubbers did about three years ago, when he run foul of one of the landmarks, and pitched us all overboard.'[7]

The seaman had his own style of dress, created by personal taste, practicality and what was available over the course of a long voyage. His short jacket and loose trousers contrasted with the long coat and breeches of the landsman. There was no uniform, although on long voyages seamen were dependent on the ship's purser for supplies, so they might take on a certain similarity in their appearance. The clothes belonged to the seaman himself, but many captains regulated a minimum amount of clothing that had to be in their possession. Captain George Duff of the *Mars* demanded two 'outside' and two 'inside' jackets, four shirts, one 'frock' or loose shirt, two pairs of breeches or drawers, three pairs of white trousers and one of blue, two pairs of shoes and three of stockings, two hats and a back silk handkerchief. The men were mustered every Sunday morning and their officers checked that the clothes were clean.[8] Andrew Sack, a Swiss who served as a petty officer in *Victory*, was in possession of a sea chest, at least nine pairs of trousers, nine shirts, six frocks, four handkerchiefs, two pairs of shoes and one pair of boots and two jackets in 1805. Most items could be bought from the purser, at a cost of £0.7.2 (36p) for a jacket, £0.4.7 (23p) for a shirt and £0.4.0 (20p) for a pair of woollen trousers.[9] Men coming on board were allowed the credit of only two months wages to buy clothes. When John Mason joined *Africa* in 1805 after a row with his brother, he was 'indifferent in regard to clothes, being so little time on board here and receiving no wages as yet neither shall we at present.'[10] Above all, seamanship was an attitude of mind. Seamen lived constantly with danger and had to make light of its presence. They had to live for the moment, without any thought for the future.

The ordinary and able seamen lived alongside the marines, the skilled artisans such as coopers and armourers, the officers' servants, the unskilled landsmen and the ship's boys. Collectively they were known as the lower deck, because that was where they ate and slept in a major warship. In a frigate or a sloop this deck carried no guns because it was very close to the waterline of the ship. In a ship of the line, the lower deck carried the main armament, usually 32-pounder guns, and the seamen had to share the space with them. In partial compensation, the gunports allowed much better lighting and ventilation in good weather.

As well as a place of battle, with gun batteries powerful enough to rival most major fortresses on land, the lower deck of a 74-gun ship was the dormitory and dining room for about 500 men. Its usable area was about 115 feet long and about 40 feet broad at its widest. At night the sailors slung their hammocks there, from hooks or rails fixed to the beams of the deck above. The situation of each hammock was carefully controlled by the first lieutenant, usually dictated by the teams in which the men worked. By St Vincent's orders of the previous decade, the marines were berthed separately from the seamen, in the aftermost part of the ship. Other groups, including the gunners, carpenters and sail-makers, lived a deck below among the ship's cables. This was regarded as a privilege, despite the lack of ventilation, for the men were less likely to be disturbed in the night. [11]

Each man was allowed 14 inches of width for his hammock, somewhat mitigated by the fact that one watch was likely to be on duty at sea, giving 28 inches; the men were carefully interspersed, a port watch man next to a starboard watch man, and so on. But against this, watchkeepers, the majority of the crew, often had only four hours' sleep at a time. William Robinson of the *Revenge* describes the ship's night.

The hammocks on the lower deck of the 74-gun Bedford, *c. 1800. Marines are in red, and the tiller and its sweep can be seen at the stern, with the outlines of some officers' cabins.*

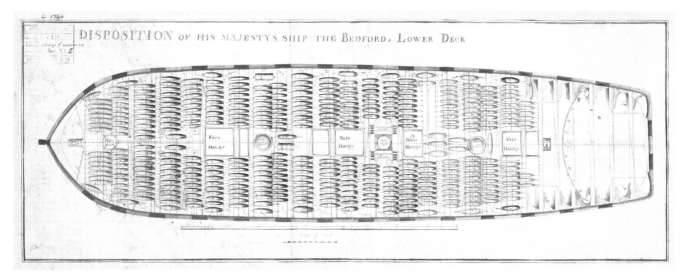

Our crew were divided into two watches, starboard and larboard. When one was on deck the other was below; for instance the starboard watch would come on at eight o'clock at night, which is called eight bells; at half-past is called one bell, and so on; every half hour is a bell, as the hour glass is turned, and the messenger sent to strike the bell, which is generally affixed near the fore-hatchway. It now becomes the duty of the officer on the deck to see that the log-line is run out, to ascertain how many knots the ship goes an hour, which is entered in the log-book, with any other occurrence which may take place during the watch. At twelve o'clock, or eight bells in the first watch, the boatswain's mate calls out lustily, '*Larboard watch, a-hoy.*' This is called the middle watch, and when on deck, the other watch go below to their hammocks, till eight bells, which is four o'clock in the morning.

Captain Thomas Bladen Capel, in command of the frigate *Phoebe* at Trafalgar, was unusually strict in ordering that 'men are not allowed out of their hammocks during the night on any pretext but going to the head,' but his order that 'No-one is to piss on the main deck' was addressing a real concern.[12]

In general there was no problem about cold at night. Some years later Chaplain Edward Mangin referred to the heat in the 'cavern' of the lower deck, 'so entirely filled with human bodies', as 'overpowering'; though this refers to the North Sea in Spring, when the ports were usually kept closed.[13]

The ship was relatively quiet during the night hours, from 8.00 p.m. to 4.00 a.m., unless some immediate danger threatened. Officers of the watch tried to avoid calling all hands, and if the ship had to be tacked on a long passage they would try to do it at 4.00 a.m. as the watches changed. The duty watch had a fairly easy time, and in warm climates the men who were not immediately needed might be allowed to nap on deck, although some captains expressly forbade this.

The ship's day began at 4.00 a.m. when the new watch came on deck. According to Robinson,

They then come on deck again, pull off their shoes and stockings, turn up their trowsers to above their knees and commence *holy-stoning* the deck, as it is termed. … here the men suffer from being obliged to kneel down on the wetted deck, and a gravelly sort of sand strewed over it. To perform this work with their bare knees, rubbing the deck with a stone and the sand, the grit of which is often very injurious. In this manner the watch continues till about four bells, of six o'clock; they then begin to wash and swab the decks till seven bells, and at eight bells the boatswain's mate pipes to breakfast.[14]

In the morning, perhaps at 7.00, the hammocks were taken down and each was rolled in a tight cylinder with the man's bedding. They were taken up to the decks above, where they were stowed in rails along the sides, in a rather optimistic attempt to protect the decks from shot in action. The lower deck of each ship of the line was then converted into a dining room for perhaps 500 men. The common picture, supported by drawings and prints of the period, is of a group of men sitting round a table between a pair of guns. It is necessary to modify this picture, for it would be physically impossible to seat all the men in this way. Some men sat at tables down the centre line of the ship and others perhaps had their messes below on the orlop deck. Even so there must have been more than eight men at each table and often several messes had to share, making it extremely crowded.[15]

Captain Capel of the *Phoebe* was typical when he decreed, 'The ship's company are not to be interrupted during meal times excepting in any urgent cases of service, and on no account whatever are boats to be sent from the ship during that period on private occasions.' He allowed the men an hour for midday dinner and half an hour for breakfast, but some captains allowed an hour and a half for dinner.[16]

Most seamen could not choose whether they joined the navy or not. Once there, they had little choice about which ship they served in, or the duties they did on board. Their only real choice was of their messmates, their companions for eating, drinking and in all their leisure activities. According to Captain A. J. Griffiths, 'the privilege the seamen and marines had of changing their messes the first of the month if they thought fit was their Magna Carta.'

While in command, my crew ever messed as they liked. The berth was allotted to the number it was calculated to hold and if one, two or three messes were in it, that rested with themselves. … So satisfied was I with the misery of obliging men to mess together that among my punishments was a drunken, dirty, a blackguard and a thieves mess.

The wardroom of HMS Gloucester, 1812. Drawn by Edward Mangin.

Instead of being numbered, they were called by these names at the grog tub, the cook's coppers, etc. Experience showed me that a decree placing a man in one of these messes for a given time on account of misconduct had more effect than corporal punishment.[17]

This mess-deck culture came to dominate the seaman's life. The most experienced men would tend to congregate together, perhaps taking a few newcomers under their wing. They might spend years together. The messes of more experienced men would be the leading groups of the ship's company, and their word would spread throughout the ship. According to Admiral Phillip Patten, 'They know that the safety, nay the existence of the whole machine depends on sailors and they see that in cases which require exertion and activity, one good seaman can do more than ten men who have not been bred to active labour on the masts and rigging.'[18]

Robinson resumes his description of the ship's day with breakfast.

The meal consists of burgoo, made of course oatmeal and water; others will have Scotch coffee, which is burnt bread boiled in some water, and sweetened with sugar. This is generally cooked in a hook-pot near the galley, where there is a range. Nearly all the crew have one of these pots, a spoon, and a knife; for these are things indispensable: there are also basons, plates &c. which are kept in each mess, which generally consists of eight persons, whose berth is between two of the guns on the lower deck, where there is a board placed, which swings with the rolling of the ship, and answers for a table.[19]

After breakfast, both watches were on duty for the rest of the morning, carrying out maintenance in the hull or rigging, or taking part in sailing exercises or drill with the guns. In contrast to the dark overcrowding of the lower deck, the masts and rigging of the ship were airy, open, and even lonely on occasion – a midshipman might be 'mastheaded' as a punishment – sent to spend hours in an isolated spot up there. The seamen were more likely to work in teams, spending a large part of their waking lives aloft, maintaining the miles of rope rigging and handling the various sails. It was the skill of these men that determined the prowess of the ship. If a captain knew that his men could take a topsail in less than ten minutes as a gale blew up, he would be able to carry full sail in a chase. If he knew that his men

could tack the ship, or drop the anchor without hesitation or risk of mistake, he could sail close to the wind or go inshore among hazards. Although the 'true-bred' seaman was a professional who would do his job in any ship he found himself, such men needed to be led not driven to achieve their best. Their internal motivation was more important than any pressure from above. The crew was divided into teams according to the part of ship where they worked. In the *Spartiate* in 1805, Lieutenant John McKerlie placed fifty-eight men on the forecastle, twenty-nine from each watch. There were forty-eight fore topmen, who worked aloft, and the same number of main topmen, followed by thirty-four men on the smallest mast, the mizzen. There were 130 waisters, the lowest skilled group in the ship, and seventy from the afterguard. The 'idlers', mostly skilled craftsmen who did not have to keep watch during the night, numbered eighteen.

After any punishments were carried out, the boatswain's mate piped to dinner, 'the pleasantest part of the day' according to Robinson.

> … at one bell the fifer is called to play 'Nancy Dawson' or some other lively tune, a well known signal that the grog is ready to be served out. It is the duty of the cook from each mess to fetch and serve it out to his messmates, of which every man and boy is allowed a pint, that is one gill of rum and three of water, to which is added lemon acid, sweetened with sugar.

After dinner one watch was allowed to rest while the other was on duty. Robinson continues,

> … At two bells in the afternoon, or at one o'clock, the starboard watch goes on deck, and remains working the ship, pointing the ropes, or doing any duty that may be required until the eight-bells strike, when the boatswain's mate pipes to supper. This consists of half a pint of wine, or a pint of grog to each man, with biscuit and cheese, or butter. At one bell, or half-past four, which is called one bell in *the first dog-watch*, the larboard watch comes on duty, and remains until six o'clock, when that is relieved by the starboard watch, which is called the *second dog-watch*, which lasts till eight o'clock.[20]

The reason for two watches in this four-hour period was to ensure that they alternated from day to day – that the men who had the midnight to 4.00 a.m. watch one day would not have it the following day.

The hammocks were taken down in the evening, perhaps at 7.00. Sometimes this could lead to farce. One evening in May 1804 while the *Victory* was blockading Toulon, Nelson spotted something under the foresail and went to the side to investigate. At the same moment the boatswain piped hammocks. 'One of the main topmen who had hauled his hammock out of the netting swinging it over his shoulder came in contact with his lordship's head and laid him prostrate on the deck.' With great dexterity the seaman restored the Admiral to his feet and apologized profusely, protesting he was not aware of anyone behind him. Nelson replied, 'My man, it was not your fault, it was my own. I ought to have known better than to stand in your way.'[21]

*   *   *

Seamen had two ways of resisting the power of the navy and protesting about their lot. Collectively or in small groups they could mutiny; individually they could desert. The great wave of naval mutiny had reached its peak at Spithead and the Nore in 1797. In the first, a seaman's strike caused many concessions, including the first pay rise for nearly 150 years. In the second the demands were more extreme; the revolt was eventually crushed, and fifty-nine men were sentenced to death. There were no mutinies on that scale again, and even the smaller revolts became less common. There were twelve courts-martial for mutiny of 1805, including two officers. A boatswain was dismissed from the service and a captain's clerk was awarded 150 lashes for expressing republican views. The only incident that approached mass disobedience was when eleven men were found guilty of using mutinous language and given 50 to 200 lashes. A seaman who refused to strip for punishment was given 500 lashes, while a man who proposed to throw a midshipman overboard was given the supreme penalty, death.[22] There is evidence that captains had learned something from 1797, and were showing greater humanity in their treatment of the crews. Admiral Patton, who served on the Board of Admiralty during the Trafalgar Campaign, wrote,

> ... Although seamen may have been regarded (by certain characters who have unfortunately had power and who were ignorant of their dispositions) as a species of mankind deficient in the nicer feelings of humanity, whose attachments might be sacrificed, their friendships disregarded and even their healths ruined or destroyed upon the most frivolous occasions; yet they are very far from being inferior to other men, either in generous or in elevated sentiments.[23]

There was no let up in the seamen's tendency to desert at the first opportunity. Patton calculated that more than 12,000 men – about a tenth of the fleet – took their leave in this way in just over a year up to June 1805.[24] Dr Thomas Trotter, naval physician and medical author, wrote that a newly-pressed man would show a 'sulkiness of disposition, which is gradually overcome, when he recollects that he only resigns his liberty for a season, to become a champion for that of his country. It, however, often preserves a determination to watch every opportunity for effecting his escape ...'[25]

It was impossible to keep the men on board in all circumstances, especially on foreign stations where ships often had to find their own resources. At anchor in the Gulf of Palma, Captain Henry William Bayntum of the *Leviathan* had to send men ashore for many duties, including cutting wood to make brooms to beat out fires. John Kean, a landsman, was sent with one of these parties but it was soon discovered that he had taken his bag with all his goods with him, as well as the clothes of several other men, and was planning to desert. A midshipman was sent to bring him back but Kean escaped. Meanwhile four other men, oarsmen in the ship's pinnace that had taken the broomers ashore, also ran. All five men were apprehended by the local authorities and taken on board under escort. Captain Bayntum applied for a court martial.[26]

There was little of hope of tracing a man after he had disappeared, but captains kept 'description books' of the crew just in case. Seven crew members – two marines and five boys – disappeared from the *Defence* between May and July 1805 and Captain George Johnstone

Hope sent their details to the Admiralty. The boys, all aged thirteen to fifteen, deserted on 22 and 23 June. Three were from London, one from Kent and one from Bristol. Thomas Neal was an able seaman from Carlow in Ireland who had joined the ship on 1 April 1804 and deserted thirteen months later. He was 5 feet 11 inches tall, of sallow complexion, with a 'short forefinger on the left hand'. Michael Knox of Berwick went on the same day. He was 5 feet 3½ inches, of ruddy complexion with short red hair. They would have made an interesting contrast if seen together, but there was little hope of finding them.[27]

Even if a seaman was loyal to his ship and his captain, he did not always manage to stay out of trouble. James Powel or Polphie (a large number of seamen used aliases for one reason or another) was transferred from the *Victorious* to the *Euryalus* in 1804, after seven years' service. He told Captain Henry Blackwood that he had been separated from his family at Dover for most of that time, and since the ship was based in the Downs, it was not too difficult to give him a short leave of absence. On shore, Powel was 'seized with the effects of a violent liver complaint.' He sent word to Blackwood, but the ship had moved on and the message did not reach him. The letter 'R', signifying 'Run' or deserted, was placed against his name in the ship's books, which were sent on to the Admiralty. When Powel recovered, he enrolled in the Dover Sea Fencibles, 'hoping again to join the *Euryalus*, as Captain Blackwood had behaved generously to him.' He was sent out on an exercise which took him near the guardship at the Nore, where he was pressed into the navy, then drafted into the depot ship *Glatton*. He managed to contact Blackwood, who wrote to the Admiralty to have the R removed, and Powel was paid the five years wages due to him.[28]

The average seaman had no great ambition. He might become a petty officer, but that rate was at the whim of the captain of the ship and might often be lost on transfer to another. The best-known petty officers were the boatswain's mates – their duties included flogging, which gave them a peculiar relationship with the rest of the ship's company. They ought to be

> … very select men as the leaders of the ship's company. They should be very perfect seamen, and as having an irksome, unpopular part to perform, they ought to be circumspect and determined in their conduct. … The situation must be countenanced and supported, as no man otherwise would feel spirit sufficient to enforce the orders he delivers, and obedience to his commands.[29]

Gunners mates and quarter-gunners were assistants to the gunner and spent much of their time on maintenance work on guns and their tackles and ammunition. Since there was one quarter-gunner to every four guns they were quite numerous, and tended to be used as an elite division of seamen. The quartermasters were among the most skilled seamen of all, mainly used in supervising the steering of the ship. The job was 'frequently a retreat for old seamen.' The petty officer was rewarded by slightly higher pay and a larger slice of the prize money. He was allowed a position round the sides of the deck to sling his hammock and had 28 instead of 14 inches hammock space – they 'should not be pinched', according to a document of 1796.[30] Captains of various parts of the ship – the forecastle, waist, quarterdeck (or afterguard) and the three masts, were only rated and paid as able seamen.

Other men were essentially petty officers but appointed by warrant by the Admiralty and therefore protected from dis-rating by the captain. Some were highly skilled men, employed on maintenance, who could only enter through a long apprenticeship – coopers, ropemakers, sail-makers and carpenter's crew for example. The position of master-at-arms was theoretically open to seamen, although some suggested it was better to employ an ex-soldier. His main roles were to train the seamen in small arms firing, and to act as head of the ship's police. His assistants were the ships' corporals, who patrolled the decks at night.

Many officers acknowledged their debts to the petty officers in running the ships. Admiral Patten wrote, 'These are confidential situations, nor is any king's ship perfectly safe if all these offices be not filled by real practical seamen, well affected, and desirous of continuing in, and attaining promotion in the navy.'[31] Most agreed that they were underpaid and under-recognized for the work they did. Promotion could be very fast for an experienced man. In the *Africa*, John Mason wrote, 'I was appointed quartermaster of the ship on my first joining her and have every reason to believe that I am both respected by officers and men in the ship.'[32]

There was no real career structure for men below warrant officer, and the hope of promotion was not what drove them on. What really inspired the seaman, apart from prize money and patriotism, was the need for the esteem of his fellows. This was an incredibly powerful force in the enclosed world of a sailing warship, and it inspired men to great feats of endurance and heroism. For all his discontents and disadvantages, the British seaman was probably his country's greatest single asset.

CHAPTER 6

The Defence

Thomas Huskisson made a very late start to his naval career, joining his first ship just days short of his sixteenth birthday. His father had died when Thomas was five, leaving a deeply divided family. The four sons of his first wife were estranged from the five children, including Thomas, of his second. The eldest son of the first marriage was William Huskisson, later famous as President of the Board of Trade, tariff reformer and the first man to die in a railway accident. He inherited the family estate near Wolverhampton, leaving the younger children with £1100 each – enough to give a young man pretensions to the gentry, but not enough to support him in any style.

In 1798 young Thomas was at boarding school in Wolverhampton. One of his friends, (either Thomas Seymour or John G. Taylor) had already entered the navy and was killed in Nelson's *Vanguard* at the Battle of the Nile. This tragic news, combined with the triumphalism following the victory, was enough to interest Thomas. His half-brother, William, was now an M.P. and Under-Secretary at War, and he was beginning to heal the family rift. He had been forced to sell the family estate to enter public life, but he procured a commission for Thomas's brother, John, in the 51st Regiment in Ceylon. He also married Elizabeth, youngest daughter of Admiral Mark Milbanke, the commander-in-chief at Portsmouth. This was an obvious route of entry to the navy for his half-brother and, despite his rather advanced age, Thomas travelled south in July 1800 to Portsmouth, having 'but a very indistinct notion of what a ship-of-war could be like.'

He was to enter the tiny sloop *Beaver* as an able seaman – a common way for potential officers to get their first experience of the sea before becoming midshipmen. Since the *Beaver* was at sea when he arrived at Portsmouth, he spent his time at Admiral Milbanke's house and on board his flagship, the *Royal William*, of 84 guns. This giant ship, cut down from a three-decker of 100 guns launched more than eighty years earlier, gave Huskisson a rather misleading impression of naval life. A week or ten days later the *Beaver* arrived and he was shocked.

> Until I went on board *Beaver*, the only ship I had ever had my foot in was the 'Old Billy', and the contrast between the cleanness of the guardship and that of the sloop-of-war was the first thing that struck me, impressing me with a high opinion of the former compared with the latter. It made me once more regret that the *Beaver* was not a seventy-four.

He was no more satisfied with the captain, Christopher Basset Jones, 'a tyrannical martinet'. The other officers were as unhappy as Huskisson. There were constant quarrels among them; the first lieutenant, surgeon and purser were court martialled. Huskisson began to fear that all ships were like this. 'These scenes were enough in themselves to disgust any young lad; but I had made my own election and embarked fully in the service, and however much I may have regretted my choice I could not recede.' He was rescued by Milbanke, who transferred him to the *Romney* of 50 guns, then fitting out at Sheerness under the command of Sir Home

Popham, one of the great captains of the age and a friend of his half-brother, William.

Huskisson served very happily all through the peace of 1801–03 in the Red Sea. Captain Popham had a thorough method of training his young men. He tended to call all the candidates for commissions 'midshipmen', even though, strictly speaking, those with less than three years' service were Volunteers First Class. He divided them into three groups.

> 1st, Those who have been upwards of four years at sea, and appear to have employed their time properly; 2d, Those that have been from two to four years; 3dly, All under two years. It should be noticed, that the greatest mark of disgrace, is placing a Midshipman in a class lower than the one to which he is entitled, from the length of his servitude; and that, during the period he is so disgraced, he is never to dine with the Captain, or in the Ward-room, nor is he to be suffered to go on shore. A mark of distinction for the three Classes, will be settled by the Captain.[1]

Captain Sir Home Popham in 1807, by Anthony Cardon.

Popham favoured training by example. Perhaps he had the relatively old Huskisson in mind when he wrote,

> It is very difficult to prescribe rules for the guidance of the Midshipmen and young Gentlemen of the Quarter-deck, because they are of various ages, and different standing in the service, from their first day of their coming to sea, to a servitude beyond the necessary time to qualify them for Lieutenants; but, speaking in general terms, it is particularly recommended to the elder Midshipmen to set a good moral example to the youngsters; to let every action be marked with integrity; and to check every dissolute and immoral propensity. If, however, in despight of these virtuous efforts, such propensity should be very prominent in any one Gentleman, then it becomes the duty incumbent on them to represent such a character to the Commanding Officer. This conduct will always recommend them in the strongest view to their superiors, will tend most materially to render them respectable in the eyes of the Ship's Company, and make them happy in each other's society. In regard to their military duty, they have every thing to learn; they should therefore be attentive to all the various duties of the ship, and endeavour to vie with each other in the quickest attainment of any particular branch; this will recommend them to their Superiors, and they will be ultimately rewarded for such exemplary conduct.[2]

The *Romney* arrived back in England just as the fleet was being mobilized for war, and

Defence, while serving in the East Indies in the 1780s, with a cutter under her stern to receive orders.

Captain Sir George Johnstone Hope in 1833.

Popham told Huskisson that he 'had entered the service rather late in life than was usual, and that I ought not to lose a single day.' Using his influence, Popham had him appointed directly to the 74-gun ship, *Defence*, fitting out at Chatham.

No ship had seen more active service than the *Defence*. She had been launched at Plymouth Dockyard in 1763 too late for the Seven Years War. She did not see active service until the American War broke out, and in 1780 she was with Admiral Rodney at the relief of Gibraltar and helped capture a rich Spanish convoy a few days before engaging the Spanish Fleet in a Moonlight Battle. She had the highest casualties of any British ship, and conducted the captured Spanish flagship to Gibraltar. She then went to the Indian Ocean where she fought in a battle off Pondicherry in 1783, though a peace treaty had already been signed in Europe by that time.

She saw some peacetime service as a flagship and with the declaration of war in 1793 she became part of Admiral Lord Howe's fleet in the English Channel. Under the command of Captain James Gambier, she fought in the 'Glorious First of June' in 1794. She was the first ship to break the enemy line, suffering heavy damage to her masts and rigging. A year later, under a different captain, she took part in Hotham's indecisive action in the Mediterranean and witnessed Nelson fight for the first time in a fleet engagement. She missed the Battle of Cape St Vincent and her crew took part in two mutinies in 1797, but in 1798 she was with Nelson again when he encountered the French at Aboukir Bay and destroyed them in the Battle of the Nile. After seeing action again off Brest in 1799, she was once again with Nelson at Copenhagen in 1801, although she was unable to get into the action in time.

The *Defence* was antiquated and in poor condition, though her forty-five-year-old design had never been improved upon. Huskisson soon found her an excellent sailer. 'Neither up to this time nor subsequently did we ever meet with a ship of any class that sailed as well as the Defence, and I have no doubt that she was one of the fastest ships in the service on all points of sailing.' [3]

Her captain, George Johnstone Hope, was a great-grandson of the First Earl of Hopetoun of Hopetoun House, designed by Robert Adam and perhaps the grandest house in Scotland. Despite being born in Finchley near London, Hope's roots gave him a strong Scottish identity. He was well connected with the Dundas family. According to his colleagues: 'His manners were of the true seaman-like appearance and the frankness which is so peculiarly the characteristic of the gallant defenders of the country was combined with the manners of the perfect gentleman.'[4] Huskisson would not have disagreed with that.

Two master's mates and eight seamen went with Huskisson into the Defence, and they turned out to be almost the only good seamen on board, 'the rest, being composed partly of impressed men from the neighbourhood of the Tower [of London], jail birds and the like.' The Captain was anxious to get to sea, believing that the first stage of the war was the best time to pick up prizes. He was disappointed, because he was sent to the North Sea where opportunities were rare. However, he did take the chance to improve the quality of his crew. Anchored in Hollesley Bay off the coast of Suffolk, his boats boarded hundreds of Newcastle colliers taking their cargoes to London, and took off the best men.

> ... Either by volunteering or by impressment, we procured upwards of a hundred able seamen, all of whom proved not only excellent sailors but a very orderly, well-behaved crew. When we took more men from any vessel than she could spare consistently with her safety, we generally sent an equal number of men, 'long shore fellows', on board to assist in navigating her. They were called 'ticket men' from being supplied with a ticket requiring them to join the first man-of-war they met with after reaching the ship's destination. I do not recollect that any of them ever found their way back to the *Defence*. The ticket was indeed virtually a discharge, and so, I suppose, they considered it. They were, of course, not worth looking after, and were probably 'dead' tired of a man-of-war.[5]

Thus the dregs of the hot press of March 1803 were disposed of.

Huskisson was promoted midshipman soon after joining the *Defence*. It did not take long to notice the accents of most of his fellows. Captain Hope shared the Scottish tendency to fill a ship with his countrymen, but unlike Captain Duff of the *Mars*, he had excellent relations with English and other officers. Huskisson wrote of the midshipmen's quarters,

> My messmates were most of them from Scotland – good-humoured, pleasant young men amongst whom I scarcely recollect anything like discord. We had at first starting one very black sheep amongst us, a native of Sheerness, who was received from the guardship of the Nore, but we got rid of him at the end of our third cruise – after he had robbed almost everyone in the gunroom. I believe he has long since been transported to Botany Bay.

The four masters' mates were the senior members of the mess, promoted after some experience as midshipmen. The most senior was Huskisson's friend, Richard Marks, who had a scrape ashore with Huskisson. One of their messmates loaded a pebble into a gun and fired it, expecting that it would shatter on leaving the gun. Instead it went through Marks's hat and grazed his scalp. He considered his survival miraculous, and later left the navy to take up evangelical preaching. The next master's mate was William Buchanan, who had already been invalided out of the navy in 1796 at the age of nineteen, but returned three years later to begin a slow climb that would eventually take him to captain. Thomas Skead was Scottish, as was Adam Greive of Leith. The latter had entered directly as a master's mate in 1797 at the age of twenty-seven, suggesting that he had served as a mate in the merchant service before being pressed into the navy.

The midshipmen were an equally mixed bunch. Charles Hope Watson, from Edinburgh, was a nephew of Rear-Admiral the Earl of Northesk.[6] William Dumbreck, on the other hand, ran away from home in Edinburgh at the age of thirteen in 1803 and entered the flagship *Gorgon* off Leith. He served as a boy in the *Alonzo* sloop and several other ships, until family influence eventually came into play. He was transferred to the *Ruby* under Admiral Edward Thornborough. He was sent into the mizzen top as a trainee seaman and then to the quarterdeck as a potential officer. Thornborough then had him transferred to the *Defence* where Hope, a fellow Scot in spirit if not birth, could be relied on to look after him. William Robertson was also from Leith, while W. J. Napier of Merchiston was the son of Lord Napier, an unusual example of an eldest son who went to sea. The other midshipmen mostly came from the south-east of England – two from London, one from Surrey and one from Sussex.[7]

Accommodation was cramped because the *Defence*, unlike other ships of the line, did not have separate berths on the lowest deck, the orlop, for the midshipmen. Instead, they lived in a much more open space in the gunroom aft on the lower deck, with the ship's clerks and the Volunteers First Class who had not yet served long enough to become midshipmen. There were no racks for cups and plates. As Huskisson comments,

> The want of proper accommodation for the disposal of our mess utensils soon reduced our 'establishment' of crockery ... Many of us were obliged to drink our tea out of soup plates, the few tea cups remaining being always appropriated by the first that could get hold of them – and as to glass, there was scarcely an article left after the first gale of wind.

Undeterred, Huskisson began to run a ship's newspaper, the *Orlopian Gazette*, a practice he had started in the *Romney*.

> As I had taken a leading part in the business I was dubbed editor. That not only entailed upon me the duty of writing a large proportion of the articles, but also of making two entire copies weekly of the paper itself, one for each [midshipmen's] berth.

It was written on a sheet of foolscap and always chock full. I adopted for its motto

QUI CAPIT, ILLE FACIT

Or, in other words,

IF THE CAP FITS
WEAR IT

The paper appeared every Saturday evening and was often seen by the lieutenants of the wardroom, causing the contributors to 'keep on the right side of decorum'. One of the most prolific contributors was Richard Marks.[8]

After completing her crew off the east coast of England in 1803, the *Defence* was sent to join the blockade of the main Dutch naval base at the Texel. The men, such as Huskisson, who had come from the *Romney* suffered terribly in the English winter, after the heat of the Red Sea.

> My feet were quite in ulcers from chilblains for some length of time and one of my old shipmates was found dead in his hammock on the lower deck, which was probably due to the sudden change of climate to which he was then exposed. He was one of the men we got at Jiddah from the crew of the *Forte* and had been in the East Indies upwards of ten years. To me, who had only been three preceding winters in a hot climate, the cold was scarcely supportable; but to the men whom we received from *Forte* and who had joined *Defence* when *Romney* was paid off it was cruelly distressing.

After almost a year of this, the *Defence* went to the Medway for repairs in October 1804. In November she sailed south, to join Admiral Sir John Orde in the blockade of the Spanish Fleet at Cadiz, for Spain was about to declare war on Britain. The fleet was in a very exposed situation during the winter gales and the ancient mainmast of the *Defence* was found to be damaged. She went to Gibraltar for repairs, but plague was raging on the Rock. They had to communicate by means of letters passed down at the end of a boathook. A different mast was found and fitted, though it was not new. Then a gust of wind carried away the mizzen-mast, which had been badly secured, and that, too, had to be replaced. The *Defence* sailed over to Tetuan on the coast of Morocco early in January 1805 to replenish her water, and then re-joined the blockade.

In March 1805 Captain Hope complained that the *Defence* had a leak near the bows, which was badly decayed. It caused the water to rise 5 inches in the hold even in moderate weather, and 13 inches in rough seas. The pumps had to be kept in constant use to keep the ship afloat, a labour that caused true hardship for the men.

> Few officers of any experience must not have known the difficulty with which men are almost drove to return to the pumps of leaking ships, when obliged to keep them constantly going. It strains their loins, affects the muscular parts of their arms like violent rheumatic pains, and galls their hands.[9]

In addition, several of the beams of the orlop deck needed inspection. The ship, in general, needed caulking and some of her old timbers were rotten. The main and mizzen masts, taken from old stocks at Gibraltar three months earlier, were in poor state – according to Hope they 'complain much in carrying sail'. Even the hand pumps were in poor repair and the galley needed some work. She was sent back to Portsmouth for repair 'to stop leaks'. When she emerged from the dock at the beginning of June, £1485 had been spent on her hull, £1298 on her masts and £2898 on her rigging and stores.[10]

Huskisson, like his late schoolmate, was now to serve under the same Admiral Nelson who had first inspired his interest in the navy. He had every hope of fighting in a great battle, though presumably he did not wish to follow his friend in death.

CHAPTER 7

The Mediterranean Fleet

In many ways Nelson's Mediterranean command was the best in the Royal Navy. The Channel Fleet had a comparable number of large ships and, theoretically, equal prospects of fleet action and glory. The Mediterranean command's main attraction was that it was the largest, and closest to home of the overseas fleets. In the Channel or North Sea Fleets the admiral was always under the eye of the Admiralty, and he did not have the right to promote his subordinates; the commander-in-chief of the Mediterranean Fleet could promote officers up to the rank of captain to fill vacancies as they occurred, whether by death or illness, or by the capture of enemy ships.

The other overseas commands, in the East and West Indies for example, were even freer

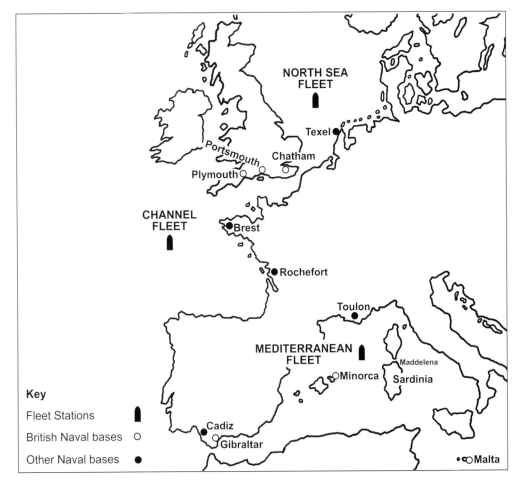

Europe in 1803–5.

from Admiralty interference, and the West Indies also offered excellent opportunities for prize money. But the fleets on these stations were much smaller. The prospect of a great sea battle was much reduced, and the ultimate honour could not be won without one. Two of the five battles of the previous conflict (Camperdown and Copenhagen) had been fought by forces in the North Sea; one (the 'Glorious First of June') by the Channel Fleet and the other two (St Vincent and the Nile) by the Mediterranean Fleet.

The Mediterranean Fleet was the third most important instrument in British naval policy. It was behind the Channel Fleet, which protected the entrance to the Channel and blockaded the main French base at Brest, and the North Sea Fleet, which was the main defence against invasion. Why was it so important? Britain had bases in the area at Gibraltar and Malta, but these were a means to an end. There were no colonies in the sense of India and the West Indian islands, which were vastly profitable. In contrast the Rock of Gibraltar was just as unproductive as its name suggests, while Malta could barely support its own population.

The Fleet had three main aims; to destroy enemy trade, to support Britain's allies and potential allies and to neutralize the French fleet in the area. Nelson's orders of 18 May 1803 also mentioned some specific points. He was to

> … proceed off Toulon, with such part of the squadron under your command as you may judge to be adequate to the service, and take up such a position as may, in your Lordship's opinion, be most proper for enabling you to sink, burn or otherwise destroy, any Ships and Vessels belonging to France, or the Citizens of that Republic, and also for detaining and sending into Port any ships or Vessels belonging to the Batavian Republic, or the citizens therof that you may happen to fall in with.

In view of events in the last war, Nelson was to gather intelligence from the ports of France and Italy, in case the French should mount another expedition to Egypt or elsewhere

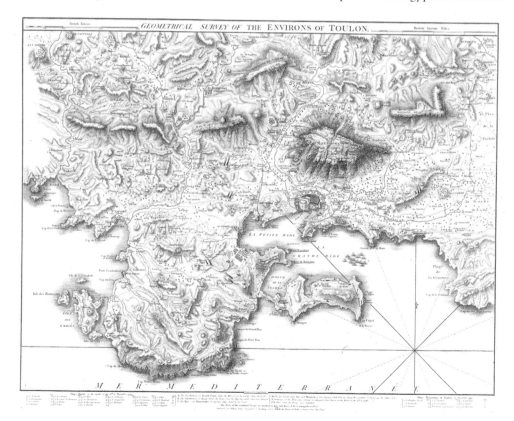

Toulon in 1793, with the small anchorage, petite rade, *and the large anchorage,* grande rade, *near the centre.*

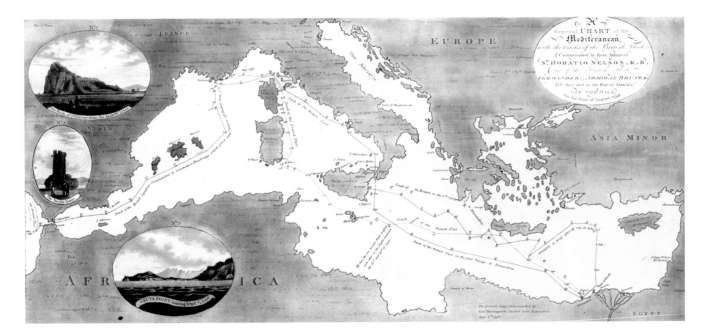

in the Turkish dominions. He was also to monitor the movements at the ports of Spain in case she became hostile, and to look out for any French ships returning to Europe from an expedition to the West Indies. [1]

Nelson visited Malta in the middle of June 1803 and was met by the governor, Captain Alexander Ball, who had been one of his most important officers in the Nile campaign. Chaplain Scott also went ashore and found much to interest him, as one of Ball's officers took him on a tour of the Arsenal. 'We found it really a beautiful sight. The white arms of very many grand masters, officers, and soldiers; muskets after the modern fashion, and many arms after the ancient.' Outside he found a bookshop where he bought an illustrated work on Malta and thirty volumes of Buffon's philosophy to add to his extensive 'floating library'.[2] This was to be Nelson's last trip ashore for two years; the fleet sailed after two days.

Arriving off Toulon on 8 July, Nelson stationed his fleet to the westward of Cap Sicie, 'to answer two important purposes.' In the event of Spain joining the war, this would help prevent the two enemy fleets linking up; and in a westerly gale it would allow him to take shelter behind the islands and headlands of the area.[3] St Vincent's extremely close blockade of Cadiz in the Revolutionary War had been like a cork in a bottle. Nelson's more distant blockade of Toulon was, rather, like a cat waiting outside a mouse hole.

In his heart Nelson wanted a brief and decisive fleet battle, not the wearing and expensive strategic advantage that might be gained by blockade. He wrote of his 'intention to try every possible means to induce the French Fleet at Toulon to put to sea.' As part of that strategy, the blockade must not be too tight. The main fleet was out of sight of the port, with frigates watching it. Captain John Whitby, who commanded the *Belleisle* for a short time in the fleet, was critical of Nelson's system.

> First, then, he does not cruise upon his rendezvous; second, I have consequently repeatedly known him from a week to three weeks, and even a month, unfound by ships sent to reconnoitre … thirdly, he is occasionally obliged to take the whole squadron in to water, a great distance from Toulon.

When he was off station Nelson left at least two frigates off Toulon, one to follow the enemy if he came out, the other to report to him. On 24 October 1803, for example, he issued orders to Captain Ross Donnelly of the *Narcissus* to 'remain off Toulon, and occasionally on

The Mediterranean, showing the routes used by Nelson in his chase of the French in 1798, by Cooper Willyams.

the Rendezvous, till my return, taking every care in your power that the French Fleet do not put to sea without your knowing it.'[4]

Other British interests in the Mediterranean Sea had to be covered. On 21 June 1804, for example, the main Fleet was off Toulon as usual with eight of the line and seven smaller vessels under Nelson's direct control. Two frigates were just outside the Strait of Gibraltar, 'for the protection of our Trade bound into the Mediterranean, and the destruction of the Enemy's Privateers and Cruisers.' Two more ships were just inside the Strait with similar aims, and to help the garrison of Gibraltar when needed. Five ships were patrolling to keep the Adriatic open to trade and prevent an attack on Greece. The frigate *Juno* was off Barcelona to pick up any intelligence about a Spanish declaration of war. Other ships were in transit to Malta or Gibraltar for minor repairs, or to rendezvous with supply ships.[5]

Maintenance facilities in the Mediterranean were sparse, and there was no dry-dock outside the French port of Toulon. Because the fleet had been kept up to strength in peace-time, and because of the need to send ships home for major repairs, its strength did not increase greatly during the next few years. When Nelson arrived at the end of July 1803 there were already ten third-rate ships of the 74 or 80 guns, to be augmented by the 100-gun *Victory*; nine frigates, six sloops and seven other vessels. By the end of the year this had risen to one first-rate and twelve third-rates, ten frigates and ten sloops. By March 1804, with the arrival of the 100-gun *Royal Sovereign*, Nelson had fourteen ships of the line, a figure that declined until he had only twelve by the end of that year. During the same period he usually had ten to twelve frigates and nine to thirteen sloops to work with the fleet, escort convoys and patrol all parts of the Mediterranean.[6]

Nelson did not feel he could reduce his numbers by sending ships away in turn to replenish, for that was risking defeat for the reduced force. Nor did he want to have convoys of storeships searching for the fleet off Toulon and risking capture. The only alternative was to take the whole fleet away from time to time to take on food, water and all the other stores needed to keep a great fleet and its men alive and operational. For this he needed bases, as close as possible to the enemy position at Toulon, and preferably on islands the French army could not reach.

Gibraltar, in British possession for a century, had serious limitations as a naval base. It was constantly under the eye of the Spanish, who might become enemies at any moment. It had not much of a harbour, it could provide no supplies of its own and it was more than 700 miles from Toulon. It was useful as a staging post on the way into the Mediterranean, but it could not serve as a main base for Nelson's fleet.

Though in a sense it was the cause of the re-start of the war in 1803, Nelson could see little use for Malta in the present circumstances. He recognized that the island might be useful as a post on the route to India, which would 'ever give us great influence in the Levant and indeed all the southern parts of Italy.' Nevertheless it was 600 miles or, he claimed, three weeks sailing, from Toulon, and he could not afford to take the fleet on such a journey and leave the French fleet uncovered for so long.[7] 'As to Malta, it is a perfectly useless place for Great Britain; and as a Naval Port to refit in, I would much sooner undertake to answer for the Toulon Fleet from St Helens [Isle of Wight], than from Malta.'[8]

Back in 1802, Captain George Ryves of the *Agincourt* had surveyed among the Maddalena Islands to the north of Sardinia, and produced a chart which showed three routes through the rocky islands, and several possible spots where ships of the line could anchor, including one which he named Agincourt Sound. Nelson took the fleet there at the end of October 1803 to get water and 'some refreshments for our crews, who have now been upwards of five months at sea.' Nelson was impressed, both with the accuracy of Ryves's chart, and the quality of the anchorage. It was 'absolutely one of the finest harbours I have seen.' It was a sheltered area for transferring stores from transports, and it was easy to get in and out of in most winds. Nelson returned there many times during the course of the next two years.[9]

Nelson also needed an anchorage further south, where he could rendezvous with transports from Malta. In December 1803 he headed for the anchorage behind the island of San Pietro off the south-west corner of Sardinia, where he had repaired the wounded *Vanguard* in desperate circumstances in 1798. He found it impossible to enter in bad weather, so he headed round the island of San Antioco, where he found an 'excellent and commodious bay' in the Gulf of Palma. It was 'without exception the finest open Roadstead I ever saw.'[10]

From August 1804 Nelson also used the anchorage in Pula Bay in the south of Sardinia, near the capital, Cagliari. Diplomatically this was more difficult than the isolated Maddelena Islands, and Captain William Parker of the *Amazon* had to do much negotiation.

> I was obliged to take a very active part to obtain pratique [the right to communicate with the shore] for the Fleet and ourselves, which was at first refused; but at last gaining our point, I waited on the Viceroy (the King of Sardinia's brother). I was received in great state by His Royal Highness, who keeps up the parade and pomp of a great nation, though their government and situation is miserably wretched.[11]

The island was ruled, corruptly and ineptly according to Nelson, by a count under the authority of the King of Piedmont. It had 'no money, no troops, no means of defence.' According to Nelson's intelligence, the town of Alghero in the north east was 'fortified with seventy large cannon, and containing 10 or 12,000 inhabitants. It has forty soldiers and a Governor, not one of whom has been paid any wages for more than three years.'[12] The island was only 10 miles by sea from French Corsica, and Nelson worried constantly that the French might invade, or at least apply pressure to stop the British anchoring there. The Sardinians had no force, either military or naval, strong enough to prevent a fleet of a dozen ships of the line anchoring off their shores.

For all its faults, Malta had the advantage that it could always be held by a strong naval power. As Lord Keith reported,

Nelson's anchorage at Maddelena showing the rocks and islands, and the routes through them.

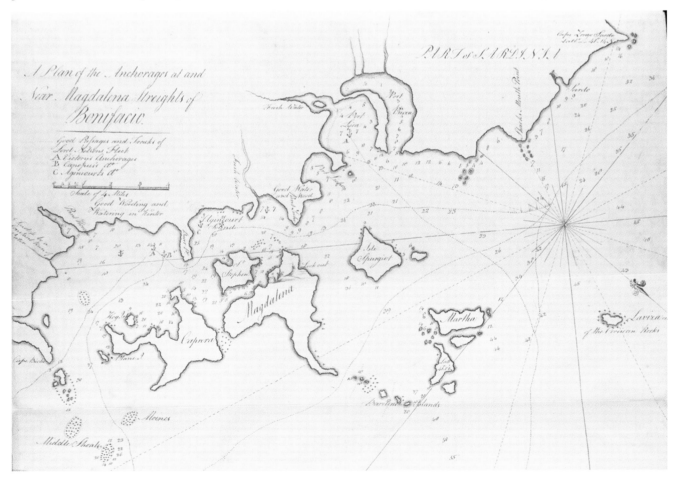

Cagliari in Sardinia, by Lieutenant William Pocock.

Malta has the advantage over all other ports that I have mentioned, that the whole harbour is covered by its wonderful fortifications, and that in the hands of great Britain no enemy would presume to land upon it, because the number of men required to besiege it could not be maintained by the island; and on the appearance of a superior fleet, that besieging army would find itself obliged to surrender to the besieged or starve.[13]

Despite it not being suitable as a fleet anchorage in the circumstances, it was a secure rearward base. Stores could be collected there from other parts of the Mediterranean, and sent in convoys to the fleet. Men could be recruited to the Royal Marines from all over the region, for the Admiralty had to acknowledge that 'it has been found impossible to complete the Royal Marines to the number voted by Parliament', and Nelson appointed his friend, Captain Adair, the inspecting officer of recruits, 'the subjects of any Country excepting France, who may be disposed to enter'.[14] A recruiting station was opened on Malta in 1805.

In December 1803 Nelson was shocked to find that although Malta had been retained specifically as a naval station, there were no plans for a hospital there.[15] One was soon opened on the peninsula of Bighi, where the men could be kept secure from infection and desertion.

There was no dry-dock at Malta, but repairs to smaller ships could be carried out, and late in 1804 the frigate *Amazon* had a refit and had her copper repaired.[16] Nelson was always concerned about the condition of his ships. In December 1803 his 'crazy fleet' was in 'a very indifferent state', though he refused to take them to Malta for the winter.[17] The same month he complained,

> Every bit of twice-laid stuff [re-used rope] belonging to the Canopus is condemned, and all the running rigging in the Fleet, except the Victory's. We have fitted the Excellent with new main and mizzen rigging; it was shameful for the Dock-yard to send a Ship to sea with such rigging. The Kent is gone to Malta, fit only for a summer's passage.[18]

Though the *Victory*'s rigging was comparatively sound, her hull above the waterline was not, for it had not been properly caulked to keep the water out. It took 'great exertion' to carry the work out at sea.[19]

Because of the long supply lines any losses of equipment could cause difficulty. When the *Belleisle* lost her anchor and cable at Maddelena Nelson ordered Captain Whitby to drag the bottom to retrieve it as it was 'of great importance'.[20] Due to the lack of full repair facilities for large ships, many had to be sent to dockyards at home.

> I approve most fully of the Gibraltar's being sent home. She ought to have gone a year ago. The Kent is in a miserable state. Superb cannot keep the sea this winter. Renown and Triumph ought also to go home; it would be saving five ships instead of destroying them.[21]

The turnover in ships was quite high. Of Nelson's eleven ships of the line in the spring of 1805, only the *Victory*, *Donegal* and *Belleisle* had been with him all the time. The *Canopus* had joined later in 1803, the *Royal Sovereign* had come out in February 1804, and was now in urgent need of re-coppering. The *Leviathan* had joined in April 1804, the *Spencer* later that year, and the *Conqueror* in 1805.[22]

In contrast, the situation within the confines of the individual ships, including the Victory, was unusually stable. Certainly Nelson had power, as commander–in–chief in the Mediterranean, to promote officers, but that depended on suitable vacancies, which in turn depended on prizes, and these were rare. In August 1803 he had to apologize for his failure to promote the young son of Admiral Bligh. 'It would give me great pleasure to do it, but I see no prospect unless we capture the whole French fleet at Toulon.'[23] It was a constant refrain, and in June 1804 he referred to the good health of the fleet and the favourable climate as another reason for the lack of vacancies – 'nobody will die or go home'.[24] In an extreme case, Midshipman Benjamin Baynton served in the flagship for a period in 1803, before transferring to the *Amphion*. He was not confirmed as a lieutenant until 1810, and had to wait thirty-two years for the next step to commander.[25] In the short term the *Victory* was not to prove a springboard to quick promotion, as most flagships did. Many of the officers and men on board would still be there in 1805, creating a stable if slightly discontented team.

However, a few new officers did join the *Victory* over the months. Lieutenant Alexander Hills joined in January 1805. A native of Portsea near Portsmouth, he had been appointed lieutenant of the *Conqueror* in November 1804 and transferred to the *Victory*, where he was noted for his meticulous attention to detail.[26] William Ram, a depressive twenty-one-year-old midshipman from Wexford in Ireland, arrived in April 1804. As he wrote to his sister, 'I frequently think myself unhappy.'[27]

Most people still expected a short war, and Nelson was no exception. Soon after he joined the *Victory* off Toulon at the end of July 1803 he wrote to Emma, 'I do not think it can be a long war; and, I believe, it will be much shorter than people think.' In May 1804, as Napoleon crowned himself Emperor of France, Nelson wrote 'either the Invasion will take place, or we shall have Peace.'[28] He heard the French firing a *feu de joie* to celebrate the coronation and wrote, 'What a capricious Nation those French must be! However I think it must, in a way, be advantageous for England. There ends, for a century, all Republics! By Vessels from Marseilles, the French think it will be a peace … I earnestly pray that it may be so.'[29]

The other way to bring an end to the campaign was for the French to come out and be defeated. There was no reason to assume that they would behave so suicidally, and indeed Napoleon's mind was concentrated on the English Channel until early in 1805, so there was no pressure for them to do anything except tie down Nelson's forces. Again Nelson lived in constant hope. In September 1803 some of them did indeed come out, but they 'took wit in their danger, and returned again.' In January 1804 he wrote, 'I think they cannot remain much longer in port. If they do, they might as well have no fleet.'[30] Two months later, he was even more expectant.

> Day by day, my dear friend, I am expecting the French Fleet to put to sea – every day, every hour, and moment: and you may rely that if it is within the power of man to get at them, it shall be done; and, I am sure, all my brethren look to that day as the finish of our laborious cruise.[31]

In April 1804 the French did briefly leave again while Nelson was on his way back to his station, but did not stay out for long. The lower deck was becoming contemptuous of the enemy and Quartermaster Benjamin Stevenson of the *Victory* though that '...they are very much afraid of Nelson for if ever they see a small boat they say it is the English Fleet.'[32]

For the moment Nelson had to play the long game, and maintain his own and the fleet's morale as weeks turned into months. He wrote in October 1803 that 'Our days pass so much alike that, having described one, you have them all.' In spite of everything mood in the fleet remained high, and there was only one instance of disaffection, when a shot was thrown at the lieutenant commanding the brig *Spider*. Nelson, however, did not approve of the lieutenant's reaction in flogging the whole crew one by one until he found the name of the man responsible. It was 'a measure so foreign to the rules of good discipline and the accustomed practice of His Majesty's Navy.'[33]

Naval food has always been a subject of propaganda and jokes. In 1761 a former employee of the Victualling Board had published a pamphlet claiming that

> the bread so full of black-headed maggots that the men have so nauseated the thoughts of it as to be obliged to shut their eyes to confine that sense from being offended before they could bring their minds to a resolution of consuming it.

These images lingered on, and no doubt there was a certain amount of corruption and waste in the Victualling Office; but the writers of such articles knew very little about how much the admirals cared about feeding their men, and how proud they were when their crews were healthy. On 19 August 1805, at anchor at Spithead after two years of gruelling service, Nelson wrote that 'Neither the *Victory*, or the *Superb*, have on board even an object for the hospital.' In May 1804 he was of the opinion that 'the health of this Fleet cannot be exceeded.' In August 1805 it was calculated that the fleet had suffered only 110 deaths in two years.[34]

The general health of the fleet depended very much on co-operation between the Admiral and the Physician of the Fleet. Dr Leonard Gillespie acknowledged this and gave several reasons for the good health of the Mediterranean Fleet. Nelson made sure that 'good and wholesome wine' was supplied instead of spirits, that fresh beef was procured as often as possible, the same for fresh fruit and vegetables. He restricted the practice of constantly washing the lower decks, and so helped cut down on cases of rheumatism. The fleet rarely stood still for long, and the men were not exposed to 'the consequences of the idleness and intemperance which too often take place on board of ships lying in harbour.' Since the ships were never in port, it was impossible for the men to get hold of illegal spirits to increase their tendency to drunkenness. Nelson and his captains looked after the morale of the men, encouraging 'music, dancing and theatrical entertainments.' Following the example of St Vincent in the last war, sick bays in ships were now sited under the forecastle where they could be heated or ventilated as required, and the sick were given priority for the most wholesome food, such as livestock, vegetables, fruit, soft bread, macaroni and other articles of diet. Finally, Nelson ordered that 'Peruvian bark', from the cinchona tree, be mixed with rum for men who went on shore for wooding and watering, for

> It is well known to experienced officers in the Navy that on foreign stations sickness

very often finds its entrance to ships from the wooding and watering parties being first attacked by fevers in consequence of fatigue and exposure, which fevers often spread among the ship's company and become a formidable and epidemic disease.[35]

Nelson had to rely on finding regular supplies of fresh food locally, which took considerable effort. Lemon juice was essential in the fight against scurvy and Nelson bought it in the Maddelena Islands, finding it 'much better than we procure from England.'[36] While Spain remained neutral he was able to purchase onions and live oxen and bullocks from Rosas near Barcelona and sent frigates there to carry as much as they could. In January 1804 he planned to go to Rosas Bay with his fleet to intimidate the Spanish governors into giving him supplies, but was diverted by a report that the French were out.[37]

Often he had to substitute well-tried foodstuffs for more exotic provisions. He felt that rice and sugar were 'poor substitutes' for butter and cheese and tried to buy cocoa and sugar instead.[38] He was in favour of macaroni, however, as 'a light, wholesome and nourishing food' for 'restoring the health of the sick and convalescent seamen.'[39]

Scurvy was under control, but not completely eliminated, and old cases might recur. In May 1804 Nelson found that thirty-seven men of one of his ships were inflicted with 'an inveterate scurvy' and the Physician of the Fleet informed him that they needed 'six ounces of lemon juice, and two ounces of sugar, daily, in addition to the present quantity issued by the Purser, for the space of twelve days.'

Nelson was perpetually hampered by the cumbersome administrative system, for ships carried no large quantities of money. Instead, they relied on British consuls, or on bills payable at the Victualling Office in London. Neither of these carried much weight in the wilds of Sardinia, and in November 1803 Captain Hardy had to lend money from his own pocket for bullocks and sheep at the Maddelena Islands.[40] The situation gradually improved as local agents were appointed in different territories.

Naples, which Nelson had made his spiritual home in 1798–1800, now had an uneasy neutrality under threat of French invasion, but Nelson was able to get supplies of food and clothing from there from time to time. Much of the meat and water supply came from North Africa and Nelson knew how necessary it was to keep good rapport with the states there, despite cultural and religious differences and their habit of raiding European commerce and holding white slaves. Tunisia and Tripoli were both friendly, but relations were strained with the Dey of Algiers.[41] When Nelson arrived on station in the middle of 1803 the Dey had already expelled the British Consul, John Falcon, for allegedly entertaining Arab women in his rooms. The circumstances of the expulsion were regarded as extremely insulting and Nelson wanted a full apology. He sent his close friend, Captain Richard Keats, in the *Superb* to demand it. On 17 January 1804 Keats arrived off Algiers with a fleet to enforce it, but 'the Dey is violent, and will yield not one point. I have no further business here. Time and opportunity will make him repent.'[42] The diplomatic issue was settled by the end of the year, but in the meantime the Dey had seized a British merchant ship, the *Ape*, and was holding her crew. A new Consul, Richard Cartwright, was able to resolve the issue and relations were resumed.[43]

Chaplain Scott began to develop his own intelligence network and spent considerable time ashore in various ports. He was aided by his flair for languages but he also found his membership of the freemasons useful.[44] Though apparently heterosexual himself, he sometimes excited passion in others of his own sex. He entered into a 'romantic friendship' with Francois Paul Magnon, a Sardinian soldier, philosopher and poet who was in charge of a watch tower near the Maddelena Islands, and used him as a spy on the French across the straits in Corsica. Scott visited a monastery in Sicily and a young monk tried to persuade him to join the order. Scott replied that 'he intended to return to England to marry, and settle in domestic life.' The monk was contemptuous of this, and 'proceeded to unfold such a system of depravity and hypocrisy, as utterly confounded and horrified his hearer.'[45] Scott himself conceived an affection for Nelson which went well beyond the normal relations between an admiral and his chaplain – he became his 'beloved and adored friend.'[46]

In December 1804 the Spanish finally declared war, two months after British frigates captured the Spanish treasure fleet in the Atlantic. Nelson had been in poor health in August 1804, and perhaps the Admiralty thought it was relieving him of some of the pressure when it divided his command. He was mortified when Admiral Sir John Orde was appointed to take charge of the forces off Cadiz, traditionally part of the Mediterranean Fleet. It was not just the personality of the Admiral that aggrieved him. Orde, slightly senior to Nelson, had been a dog in the manger for some years, as when he protested when St Vincent gave Nelson the command of the force that eventually fought the Battle of the Nile. More importantly, the forces off Cadiz had excellent chances to make prize money, unlike those in the Mediterranean. Nelson complained that Orde was 'sent off Cadiz to reap the golden harvest.'[47]

Orde did not arrive in any spirit of co-operation with Nelson, who complained in December that he had been three weeks off Cadiz without attempting to communicate. Indeed Orde issued strict orders to his cruisers to stop Nelson's ships operating in what he regarded as his territory. When Captain Parker was sent with dispatches to Lisbon, he was chased by Orde's ships. He complained, 'Everybody is astonished that Nelson has been so ill used. … after his Lordship has fagged and persevered in keeping the sea 18 months, at the very time he might expect to reap the advantage of a Spanish war …'.[48]

Despite numerous precautions a fire broke out in the *Victory* on at least one occasion. Midshipman John Carslake played a key role in putting it out, and was congratulated by Lieutenant John Pasco. 'The fire caused such panic on board the 'Victory' that many jumped overboard and were not restored to a sense of their duty but by the drummer beating to quarters and by you. It was your coolness and self command that got the fire under, by causing wet hammocks to smother the blaze and it was generally thought at the time that had you been qualified Lord Nelson would have promoted you on the instant'.[49]

Another danger was of men falling overboard, especially from working in the rigging. Chaplain Scott reports one case that took place 'One bright morning, when the ship was moving about four knots an hour through a smooth sea.' Midshipman Flinn was sketching on deck when he saw his own servant, a non-swimmer, in the water. The Captain of Marines threw the man a wardroom chair while Flinn dived in and rescued him. The midshipmen and crew cheered and Nelson witnessed it from the quarterdeck, but he offered nothing more material than praise.

> Stop, young gentlemen! Mr. Flinn has done a gallant thing to-day – and he has done many gallant things before – for which he has got his reward, but mind! I'll have no more making lieutenants for servants falling overboard![50]

In contrast to the Nile campaign some years previously, Nelson had a congenial and competent staff around him, although at the end of 1804 he lost Surgeon Magrath to the naval hospital at Gibraltar. Nelson always found comfort in religion and Chaplain Scott described him as 'a thorough clergyman's son' who 'never went to bed or got up without kneeling down to say his prayers.' Scott conducted a service every Sunday when the weather was suitable, and Nelson often commented on it – either giving his approval, or perhaps saying that it was over the heads of the seamen. If the lifestyle seemed civilized, Nelson was unwell and unhappy. In November 1804 he wrote to Emma, 'My cough is very bad; and my side, where I was struck on the 14th of February, is very much swelled; at times a lump as large as my fist, brought on occasionally by violent coughing; but I hope and believe my lungs are safe.'[51]

Dr Gillespie, the Physician of the Fleet, arrived on board on 2 January 1805. In 1791 he had left the sloop *Racehorse*

> … without regret, rather rejoicing that my military bondage and my narrow confinement within a sloop's wretched gunroom had expired, and sincerely wishing that I might never more be necessitated to serve on board a ship of war when, alas, indolence, intemperance, spleen, envy etc too often infect the crew and spread unhappiness and discord.[52]

The spacious quarters of the *Victory* were far more congenial, as was the company. Gillespie painted a very rosy picture of life on board the flagship early in 1805, and one might suspect that he was painting a gloss on things over for his sister. Yet his admiration of Nelson seems sincere. His 'noble frankness of manner, freedom from vain personal formality and pomp (so necessary to the decoration of empty little men), can only be equalled by the unexampled glory of his naval career and the watchful and persevering diligence with which he commands the fleet.' Gillespie found that his duties were light, because health was so good. Only one man out of 840 in the ship was confined to bed due to sickness and the other ships of the fleet, also part of Gillespie's medical practice, were in equally good condition. Nelson and the other officers did not appear to have been overworked either, at least in good weather.

At Six o'clock my servant brings a light and informs me of the hour, wind, weather and course of the ship, when I immediately dress and repair on the deck, the dawn of the day at this season and latitude being apparent at about half or three-quarters of an hour past six.

Breakfast is announced in the Admiral's cabin, where Lord Nelson, Rear-Admiral Murray, the Captain of the Fleet, Captain Hardy, Commander of the *Victory*, the Chaplain, the secretary, one or two officers of the ship, and your humble servant assemble and breakfast on tea, hot rolls, cold tongue etc., after which, when finished, we repair upon deck to enjoy the majestic sight of the rising sun (scarcely ever obscured by clouds in this fine climate) surmounting the smooth and placid waves of the Mediterranean which supports the lofty and tremendous bulwarks of Britain, following in regular train their Admiral in the *Victory*.

Between the hours of seven and two there is plenty of time for business, study, writing and exercise, which different occupations, together with that of occasionally visiting the hospital of the ship when required by the surgeon, I endeavour to vary in such a manner as to afford me sufficient employment.

At two o'clock a band of music plays till a quarter to three, when the drum beats the tune called 'The Roast Beef of Old England', to announce the Admiral's dinner, which is served at exactly three o'clock, and which generally consists of three courses and a dessert of the choicest fruit, together with three or four of the best wines, champagne and claret not excepted; and what exceeds the relish of the best viands and most exquisite wines, if a person does not feel himself perfectly at ease it must be his own fault, such is the urbanity and hospitality which reign here, notwithstanding the four orders of Knighthood worn by Lord Nelson and the well-earned laurels which he has acquired.

Coffee and liqueurs close the dinner about half past four or five o'clock, after which the company generally walk the deck, where a band of music plays for nearly an hour.[53]

At six o'clock tea is announced, when the company then assemble in the Admiral's cabin, where tea is served up before seven o'clock, and as we are inclined, the party continue to converse with his lordship, who at this time generally unbends himself, though he is at all times as free from stiffness and pomp as a regard to proper dignity will admit, and is very communicative.

At eight o'clock a rummer of punch, with cake or biscuit, is served up, soon after which we wish the Admiral a good night, who is generally in bed before nine o'clock.

For my own part, not having been accustomed to go to bed quite so early, I generally read an hour, or spend one with the officers of the ship, several of whom are old acquaintances, or to whom I have been known by character.

Nelson's life was not as easy as Gillespie suggests. He was heavily engaged in diplomatic correspondence and spent a good deal of time with Chaplain Scott on his paperwork.

Day after day might be seen the admiral in his cabin, closely employed with his secretary over their interminable papers. They occupied two black leather armchairs, in the roomy pockets of which Scott, weary of translating, would occasionally stuff away a score or two of unopened letters.[54]

The year 1805 was to prove far more eventful than 1803 and 1804 had been. Bonaparte's original invasion plan was to have the flotilla sail across during a calm, foggy night during the winter of 1803–04, when the boats would use their guns to fight off any British warship that happened to be in their way – the Channel was 'a mere ditch, and will be crossed as soon as someone has the courage to attempt it.' In January 1804 he abandoned this idea, realizing that his main fleet would have to clear the way; the armed boats at Boulogne had been misconceived, for their armament was useless. In January 1805 Napoleon planned an invasion of Ireland, probably the weakest point in all the British domains, where a revolt had taken place as recently as 1798.

On 19 January 1805 the frigates *Active* and *Seahorse* arrived at Maddelena with the news that at last the French were out. Nelson was not to know that they were only at sea for a few hours before losing their nerve in a storm and returning to Toulon. With no positive evidence about the French being seen in the western Mediterranean or Italy, he set off for Egypt as he had done nearly seven years ago. Arriving at Alexandria, he found that 'Three Turkish frigates were in the Port, and not more than 300 bad troops in the Town; indeed nothing was less thought of than resistance.'[55] There was no sign of the French and he justified himself to Lord Melville.

Feeling as I do, that I am entirely responsible to my King and Country for the whole of my conduct, I find no difficulty at this moment, when I am so unhappy at not finding the French Fleet, nor having obtained the smallest information where they are, to lay before you the whole of the reasons which induced me to pursue the line of conduct I have done.[56]

He headed back, arriving back at Palma in a gale of wind on 8 March. 'So we have had a proper wild goose chase', wrote Able Seaman Thomas Pickering to his mother.[57] The Admiral wrote to Lady Hamilton, 'I do assure you, my dearest Emma, that nothing can be more miserable, or unhappy, than your poor Nelson.'[58]

Chapter 8

The Mars

The *Mars* had been on blockade service since the war began in May 1803, initially off Brest. She was a rare example of the British-built 'large class' of 74-gun ship, with 24-pounder instead of 18-pounder guns on her upper deck, giving her a broadside of 880 pounds (exclusive of carronades) compared with 781 pounds for the 'common class'. She was ordered during peacetime in 1788, just as the Royal Navy was becoming aware that French ships were larger and more powerful. She was designed by Sir John Henslow, a rather uninspired designer, who had taken office as Surveyor of the Navy in 1784. Priorities were low in peacetime and it was twenty-one months before her building began in the Royal Dockyard at Deptford. It took just over five years to complete her and she was launched on 25 October 1794, costing over £43,000 to build and £6730 to equip, compared with £36,000 for the hull of a standard 74. She was also expensive in manpower, for she was allocated fifty more men than a standard or 'common class' 74.[1]

The war with Revolutionary France had begun by this time and the *Mars* was quickly rushed into service under Captain Charles Cotton. In June 1795 she took part in Cornwallis's Retreat in the Channel, along with the *Royal Sovereign*. She was placed at the rear of the British line because, unlike the *Bellerophon* and *Brunswick*, which were badly

The 74-gun Mars.

Captain George Duff.

trimmed, she could stand the loss of a sail or two and still hope to escape. As a result she bore the brunt of the action, with twelve men wounded and her mainmast and much rigging damaged. Some of her guns were mounted in the stern galleries during the chase, and damaged the light structure there. A year later the Admiralty decided to adopt the 'closed gallery' of the form that can be seen today on *Victory*.

In May 1797 the men of the *Mars* played a leading part in the Spithead Mutiny. They were one of the few crews, in that relatively restrained protest, to turn the officers out of the ship. Delegates from the other ships in the fleet met on board the *Mars* and, according to one report, they tried Admiral Sir John Colpoys in his absence and convicted him of the murder of three seamen committed by men loyal to him in the act of resisting the mutiny. The *Mars* was one of the last ships to accept the government concessions that ended the mutiny.[2]

A year later the *Mars* chased the French 64-gun ship *Hercule* and the French captain decided to try to escape through the Passage du Raz. The currents proved too strong and *L'Hercule* anchored across the stream. The *Mars* anchored alongside the Frenchman and the two ships fought it out at exceptionally close range, unable even to run their guns out but instead being obliged to fire them from inside the ship. *L'Hercule* was seriously damaged by the British gunfire and forced to surrender after several hours of intense combat. The action made the *Mars* famous, and at least five different prints were published depicting the engagement.

She continued with the Channel Fleet, serving in 1799 to 1800 as the flagship of Admiral George Berkeley at the Blockade of Rochefort. In 1801 she became the flagship of Admiral Edward Thornborough at the Blockade of Brest and at the end of the war she sailed home to be laid up at Plymouth in 1802.

In May 1803 she was brought back into service again as war with France resumed. Her captain was John Sutton, a veteran of the Battle of Cape St Vincent. He became a rear-admiral in a general naval promotion in April 1804 and was replaced on a temporary basis by Samuel Pym, until Captain George Duff arrived a month later. He was one of four Scottish captains who would serve in Nelson's fleet in October 1805. As a youth he had been 'passionately fond of the sea, and was always to be found among the boats in Banff harbour, near his father's house. At the age of nine he managed to conceal himself on board a small merchant ship, and actually sailed to a neighbouring port.'[3] Less than 100 years after the Union with England in 1707, the Scots were a strong force in the Royal Navy. George's great-uncle, Robert Duff, one of the numerous relatives of the Earl of Fife, had been the first of the family to enter, in the 1730s. He was commissioned as a lieutenant in 1739 and promoted to commander in 1744, taking charge of the aptly-named bomb-vessel *Terror*, in which he helped suppress the 1745 rebellion on the east and west coasts of Scotland.

George Duff took up the family's naval mantle at the age of thirteen when he joined his great-uncle Robert in the *Panther* off Gibraltar in 1777. The War of Independence was at its height and young George was in action thirteen times throughout the next six years, culminating in the Battle of the Saintes in the West Indies in 1782. He was already a lieutenant, having been commissioned in 1779 at the age of sixteen, with less than three years' service. With the patronage of Henry Dundas as well as the Earl of Fife, he was promoted commander in peacetime in 1790. He sought further advancement in order to marry his childhood sweetheart, Sophie Dirom. His father wrote to the Earl,

> Miss Dirom's friends are most desirous to get George forward, with this view they have solicited the Duke and Duchess of Gordon who have wrote favourably of him, the Duke to Lord Chatham [First Lord of the Admiralty], the Duchess to Mr Dundas, the consequences will in time appear, but Im not sanguine, the young ladys friends are.[4]

The marriage took place in 1791 and Duff was promoted in 1793. The only son, Norwich, was born in 1792.

When he was appointed to the frigate *Glenmore* in 1795, she became perhaps the most Scottish ship ever in the Royal Navy. Her name apart, the ship was actually built from fir timber from the Great Glen, because shortage of English and Baltic oak had forced the

Navy to accept materials that it believed, with some justice, to be inferior. The Scottish captain had many countrymen appointed to his ship. An English Lieutenant, William Dillon, commented, 'the officers appeared a nice set of gentlemen, but, the captain being a Scot, they were all, nearly, from the same country, so I found myself a sort of lonely person among them.'[5]

Duff found it more difficult to fill the *Mars*'s wardroom and gunroom with Scots, because he had taken over a ship already in commission and in the short term he had to accept the appointments already made by Captain Sutton. Nevertheless his followers and relations began to join the ship over the months. His early appointments included his cousin, twenty-year-old Alexander Duff, who joined the ship in August 1804 and was promoted master's mate a month later. The second master was John Lindsay of Aberdeen. The other master's mates included James Horrie, aged twenty-two, and J. Wilkie, both from Scotland.

It was the 'young gentlemen' from the gunroom who approached the Captain early in November 1804, while the ship was at anchor in Torbay, with an idea for some amateur dramatics. They wanted to stage John Home's tragedy *Douglas*, which had first been performed in Edinburgh in 1756, to cries of 'Whaur's your Wullie Shakespeare noo?' and had enjoyed a long run. All was ready by 5.00 p.m. on 9 November, and the performance took place in relatively calm weather. Duff wrote, 'You cannot imagine how gay we are to be to-night.' The young men had of course assumed the female parts and improvised dresses from silk handkerchiefs and sheets – they were 'not very fine, but did credit to their invention.' The scenery was 'not badly painted.' After the 'tragedy' one of the sailors sang an Irish song and then there was a much lighter play, the pantomime *Harlequin and the Miller*. The whole evening concluded with a rendering of God Save the King at 8.45, for sailors did not keep late hours except when on watch.[6]

The *Mars* had been dry-docked at Plymouth in September 1804 and Duff was generally pleased with the result. However, he had only been allocated a complement of 590 men, the same as a ship of the 'common class' with 18-pounders on the upper deck. The *Mars* had 24-pounders and needed more men to operate them. But his request for more men went unheeded and he had to renew it six weeks later. In February 1805 the ship carried a total of 582 men, not 640 as originally planned.

Throughout his naval career Duff wrote daily to his beloved Sophie, although he often had to wait weeks to send the letters on by another ship. After his return from each voyage he insisted on destroying these letters, as the correspondence became very voluminous. It was only from his last voyage, beginning in October 1805, that the letters were preserved and later published. Duff reminisced about how he had known Sophie as a child. 'I frequently recollect with pleasure our playing together when at school, at my father's.' He lamented that he had spent so little time with her. 'This day 14 years was the first time I could claim you as my own, and we have had very little of one another's society since we have been married.' He hoped that the war would soon end and they would be reunited. 'I hope the Austrians and Russians will make quick work with Buonaparte, and let us get to our homes once more.' He was not to know that the Austrians would be defeated at Ulm less than three weeks after that letter, or that the wars would last for another decade. He hoped that his seniority would soon bring him promotion to rear-admiral, but he was sceptical. 'We have long been told that a promotion is to take place, but I will never believe it till I see it in the Gazette, as I cannot see how they can make one, when we have so many on the Admiral's list already.' His surviving letters say little about home matters, but he longed for home in Castle Street, Edinburgh. He was disappointed with his wife's new portrait, which she sent on to him. 'I think the one done by Smith was better.'

His son, Norwich Duff, 'had always shown a strong predilection for the sea.' In 1805 the boy, just short of his thirteenth birthday, sailed from Portsmouth in the frigate *Aurora* to join his father's ship off Cadiz. He had a good passage and was proud that he was not seasick, unlike most of the other boys. Duff took the boy to live in his own cabin until he was ready for the midshipmen's berth. Norwich was pleased to be in a large ship and wrote to his mother, 'Although I liked the *Aurora* very much, yet I like the *Mars* twenty times better.' His father wrote, 'He seems very pleased with his choice of profession.' With him arrived his fourteen-year-old cousin, Thomas, brother to Alexander and now rated a Volunteer First Class, and another Scot, William Dalrymple, from Closeburn in Dumfries, aged twenty, who soon became a midshipman. Given time, Duff would have filled the wardroom and gunroom with his countrymen.

Duff took good care of his son's education. He employed a Mr Dalrymple, as purser and instructor, and the latter wrote to the boy's mother,

> Norwich and all the young gentlemen are making proficiency. We have got an excellent globe which we shall study occasionally; every morning ... a certain number of words. Learn English grammar once a week, and in the evening read geography, history, etc, after having pored over their navigation, French, arithmetic, etc, the greater part of the day.

The Captain continued to support those bearing the family name, however distant their relationship, however humble their present station. In May 1805, William Duff, sometime sergeant in the 44th Regiment, wrote to him. The Sergeant's son had been serving as an apprentice in the merchant ship *Ganges* of Aberdeen and completed a voyage from Riga to Portsmouth. Oblivious to the dangers of a naval town, the boy went ashore and was taken up by a press gang under Mr Willard, the master of the *Pluto* sloop, although as an apprentice he should have been protected. The boy did not mind serving in the navy, where he was now the first lieutenant's servant, but after the war his master might reclaim him and force him to complete his time. Could Captain Duff have him discharged, or perhaps transferred to his own ship where, it was left unsaid, he might expect some patronage? Sergeant Duff was, by his own account, only a 'distant relation' who had met the Captain's father but had 'not the least acquaintance' with the Captain himself. Nevertheless Captain Duff sent the letter on to Viscount Garlies at the Admiralty, another Scot, with the comment that 'it seems a very hard case for the boy' and that he would be obliged if his lordship would look into it.[7]

Duff was not the only married officer to feel the strains of naval service. Many thought that family life was completely incompatible with a naval career, and when Nelson married in 1787 his friend, Captain Pringle, commented, 'the Navy lost yesterday its greatest ornament by Nelson's marriage. It's a national loss that such an officer should marry. Had it not been for that circumstance I foresee he would be the greatest officer in the service.' Of course this was very far from the truth, but it did highlight an essential dilemma. The current campaign was Captain Edward Codrington's first real separation from his wife Jane; they had married in December 1802, during the peace, and the Captain remained at home until May 1805 when he was appointed to the *Orion* of 74 guns. Off Cadiz in August he wrote of his children,

> Alas! I cannot look back to our little domestic enjoyments without feeling quite unmanned by the prospect of long, long absence from all hope of renewal of them. Surely Edward misses me, even if fat little William has lost all remembrance of my dandling him. His sweet laugh has, however, left such traces in my memory as will not be easily forgotten! But now I am distressing myself to such a degree that I must quit the subject altogether.

He summed it up when he wrote, 'On the quarterdeck I am the captain; in my cabin I am the husband and father, with a full sense of the blessing of being so.' But he realized that some of his fellow captains had far more cause for complaint. 'Hope has been fourteen months at home in these eight years; and Captain Rutherford told us yesterday, declaring that it was d—d foolish for a sailor to marry – that he had been in that happy state for nine years, one only of which had been with his wife.'[8]

CHAPTER 9

The Chase

Captain Francis Austen had mixed feelings as he climbed up the companionway of the 80-gun *Canopus* for the first time on 29 March 1805, while the ship was at anchor in the Bay of Palma, Sardinia. He had travelled out in the frigate *Ambuscade* with his admiral to replace Captain John Conn, and as his head reached the level of the quarterdeck the boatswain's mates began to pipe him aboard with their shrill whistles. Austen's orders from the Admiralty were read out to the assembled crew and he officially took command. The *Canopus* had been the French *Franklin*, captured by Nelson at the Nile and towed back to Plymouth to be repaired. British officers tended to be enthusiastic about the sailing qualities of French prizes and the Canopus was no exception. She could do 12½ knots in a fair wind, and 9 knots in a gale with most of her sails taken in. According to one report, 'Sails well on all points, but best with the wind abeam …'.[1] Eighty-gun ships such as the *Canopus* were not popular with the Admiralty, probably because they cost more than standard 74s, and the Royal Navy had to rely mainly on French prizes for such powerful ships. Compared with the 74, the 80's advantage was not just a matter of six extra guns. The 80 had 24-pounders on the upper deck while most 74s had 18-pounders, so the broadside weight, without carronades, was 947 pounds compared with 781 pounds. Almost any captain in the navy would be proud to command a ship like the *Canopus*. Not so Captain Austen – he longed for a frigate in which he could enrich himself with prize money.

Captain Francis Austen in 1806.

Austen came from a social background almost identical to Nelson's – the son of a country clergyman with a large family and a highly-placed relative in the naval administration. Like Nelson he had begun life as a spirited youth, as described by his admiring sister;

Fearless of danger and braving pain,
And threaten'd very oft in vain[2]

There were two essential differences. Frank Austen was not the genius of his family. This would prove to be his sister. Jane had already written three novels but she would publish nothing until 1811, and indeed her fame was almost entirely posthumous. Frank provided her with much naval background for her novels *Mansfield Park* and *Persuasion*.

The second difference was that Austen's talents lay in administration rather than leadership and tactics. Since his promotion to captain four and a half years earlier, he had served as flag captain to Admiral James Gambier, who was First Sea Lord on the Board of Admiralty by 1805; he had commanded the Kent Sea Fencibles, which had given him a chance to court Mary Gibson of Ramsgate. After that he was flag captain in the 50-gun *Leopard* under Rear-Admiral Thomas Louis, one of Nelson's Band of Brothers at the Nile, in the English Channel. Now transferred to the Mediterranean Fleet, he remained under Louis. Austen was a victim of his own administrative skills. The situation of flag captain carried some distinction, but it meant that Austen was always under the eye of the admiral.

Austen had more urgent reasons for wanting a change. He was aware that time was running out. Frigates were usually commanded by junior captains, and he was now almost too senior. Potential French and Spanish prizes were being swept from the seas, and for all he knew the war might end at any minute. Through Lord Moira, a retired general and family friend, he solicited Nelson for a transfer. Nelson was firm and Austen, an 'excellent young man', had to do his duty where he was most needed. 'I hope to see him alongside a French 80 gun ship and he cannot be better placed than in the *Canopus*, who was once a French adl.'s ship and struck to me.'[3]

The fleet was not in the Gulf of Parma for long. It sailed on 29 March for Pula Bay where watering was easier, and on 4 April the frigate *Phoebe* was sighted. She had met the sloop *Bittern*, which in turn had spoken to a cartel ship that had passed through a great fleet. This could only mean one thing. The *Victory* signalled, 'Enemy fleet at sea' and made preparations for a chase. One of the British frigates, it soon transpired, had tried to follow the French but had lost them during the night.

Napoleon had conceived a grand plan to culminate in the invasion of Britain. His separate fleets, and those of the Spanish, would escape from their blockaders and concentrate in the West Indies, to produce a huge and hopefully irresistible force. The British would be dispersed in fruitless chases of them, and the French would sail back across the Atlantic to take control of the English Channel. Admiral Villeneuve's fleet in Toulon was to be the first to move.

Nelson was more cautious than last time he heard the French were out, and told Governor Ball, 'I must not make more haste than good speed, and leave Sardinia, Sicily, or Naples for them to take, should I go either to the Eastward or Westward without knowing something more about them.'[4] His first concern was to stop them going east, where there was no other British fleet to stand in their way. To the Grand Vizier of Turkey he expressed the opinion that 'their destination may be either to the Morea or Egypt',[5] but that was probably to keep the Turks on their toes.

Nelson analyzed the information he had. The French fleet, reported as eleven ships of the line, seven frigates and two brigs, was roughly equal to his own in numbers, but almost certainly inferior in skill. It had last been seen 60 miles south of Toulon heading south-south-west with the wind behind them. The fleet was not heading directly for the Italian coast through the strait between Corsica and the mainland, nor was it heading for north-east Spain, but there were other options. Nelson took his fleet to a position between Sardinia and the coast of Tunisia to cover any move to the east. He sent one frigate to the Galite Isles off Tunisia, and one between the islands and the mainland to prevent the French coming along the North African coast. Another cruised off the same coast. Two more were sent off Toro, a tiny island off south-western Sardinia, to look for the enemy passing close inshore, and another went along the east side of Sardinia towards the Maddelena Islands. After two days with no news Nelson shifted his fleet to Ustica north of Sicily, where he could cover any move against Naples, or protect Sicily.

Nelson was elated that the French were finally out after two years, but anxious about the prospects of finding them before they could do any damage. To Lord Melville on 5 April he wrote, 'Although I feel comfortable that the French Fleet is out, yet I must have a natural, and I hope laudable anxiety of mind, until I have the happiness of seeing them.' To Ball at Malta he was a little more frank. 'I am, in truth, half dead; but what man can do to find them shall be done.' To Hugh Elliot in Naples he wrote, 'I am most unlucky, that my frigates should lose sight of them; but it is in vain to be angry, or repine.'[6] Captain William Parker of the *Amazon* began to doubt whether the French were still out. 'I hope we shall soon have it cleared up, for I cannot help thinking they have merely been as far as Minorca, thrown in succours and reinforcements, and then returned to Toulon.[7]

On 10 April Nelson met the *Tigre* under Captain Benjamin Hallowell and was told of a completely new factor. A great troop convoy was heading for the Mediterranean and seven Russian ships of the line were to join it. Nelson was shocked that he had not been told about this before. He did not know that the fall of Melville had caused paralysis at the Admiralty. It seemed highly likely that the French were sailing to intercept the convoy, but in fact this information was a red herring, as Villeneuve's force was not intended against them. Nelson began to head west, a long way behind the French, hindered by unfavourable winds. On the morning of 16 April the fleet met a ship which signalled 'that the French squadron of 16 ships (12 of the line) were seen by the stranger on the 7th inst off Cape Gatto [southern Spain] standing to the westward with a fresh breeze.'[8] The information was reliable, and it was now certain that the enemy was heading out of the Mediterranean.

The fleet made very slow progress towards Gibraltar. Nelson wrote to Ball, 'My good fortune seems flown away. I cannot get a fair wind, or even a side wind. Foul! – Dead Foul!'[9] On 1 May a corvette arrived from home with newspapers that were only a fortnight old announcing the rather disconcerting news that Melville, the First Lord of the Admiralty, had resigned but no successor was yet appointed.[10] Nelson wrote, 'I believe Lord Melville would have been a good friend to the Navy; and therefore I am sorry he is out.'[11] Parker of the *Amazon*, on the other hand, was a St Vincent protégé and was not sorry at Melville's demise.[12] It took three weeks to reach Tetuan Bay in Morocco, across the strait from Gibraltar. The fleet anchored there on 4 May and took on water.

The eleven French ships of the line had sailed to Cadiz and slipped through a gap in Admiral Orde's blockade. (He would be ordered to strike his flag, or give up his command, because of this.) They were joined by a stray French 74 and a squadron of five Spanish ships. On 9 April they had sailed to an unknown destination. Nelson already suspected that the enemy had gone to the West Indies and left instructions for Rear-Admiral Sir Richard Bickerton to take command of the Mediterranean in his absence. However he could not set off 'without something beyond mere surmise.'[13] A supply of bullocks was purchased and got ready on the beach for loading, but the wind suddenly became favourable and the fleet set sail. Nelson anchored again in Rosia Bay, Gibraltar to take on stores. He was shocked to find that Admiral Orde, in command just outside the Strait, had done nothing to seek out the enemy. However, he did get some information from Rear-Admiral George Campbell, a Briton in the neutral Portuguese service, which apparently confirmed his belief about the French destination.[14] On the day that many of the officers took the chance to take their linen ashore for washing, Nelson spotted that the wind was favourable. A gun was fired from the *Victory* and the Blue Peter hoisted at her masthead. All boats were recalled and the linen was left behind as the fleet sailed out into the Atlantic.[15]

Nelson headed for Lagos Bay, on the south coast of neutral Portugal, to meet Parker's frigate *Amazon*, which had been sent to Lisbon to make contact with British diplomats. First he met the *Amphion*, still commanded by his old friend, Samuel Sutton, but now under Orde's command. Sutton had seen or heard nothing of the enemy, but that news was interesting in itself, as it suggested he had not gone north. Nelson did not expect any intelligence from the south, where ships followed the one-way system created by the trade winds. No ships were

The Canopus *in later life, drawn by Thomas B. Horner in 1866.*

likely to sail back against them, so the absence of information was not necessarily significant.

Nelson met Parker on 10 May, and received several contradictory reports from Lisbon. The most important one, however, was the certainty that 'the enemy were not gone to the north.'[16] Thus the decision was made, on the balance of probabilities rather than any compelling piece of evidence. Nelson took the chance to replenish his ships. 'Here we are, my dear Campbell, clearing Sir John Orde's transports, which I found in Lagos Bay, completing ourselves to five months; and tomorrow I start for the West Indies.'[17] Just as the fleet was leaving, the troop convoy under Rear-Admiral John Knight arrived, eliminating one factor from the equation. Nelson allocated the *Royal Sovereign*, a powerful but slow 100-gun ship, to increase Knight's escort, and now he was free to leave the area if he thought it necessary. Nelson wrote his final letters to the Admiralty and the government.

> Under the most serious consideration which I can give from all I hear, I rather think the West Indies must be the destination of the Combined Squadrons. A trip to England would have been far more agreeable, and more necessary for my state of health; but I put myself out of the question upon these occasions.[18]

Nelson kept on the 74-gun *Superb* under his friend Richard Keats, although she, too, was in need of maintenance. He wrote to Keats,

> I am fearful that you may think the Superb does not go as fast as I could wish. However that may be (for if we all went ten knots, I should not think it fast enough,) yet I would have you be assured that I know and feel that the Superb does all which is possible for a ship to accomplish; and desire that you will not fret upon the occasion.[19]

Gibraltar from the south. The small breakwaters shown were almost the only harbour facilities.

In addition, Nelson had the *Canopus* under Rear-Admiral Louis and Captain Austen; a powerful and fast sailing ship by any standards; one more 80-gun ship, the *Tigre*, captured from the French ten years previously; seven additional 74s, and three frigates.

The officers knew that their squadron was numerically inferior to that of the enemy, by about three to two, and that they were about a month behind him, but they were confident both of

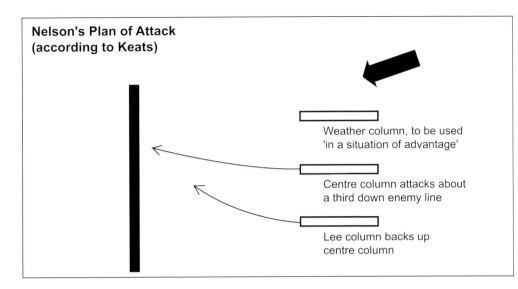

**Nelson's Plan of Attack
(according to Keats)**

Weather column, to be used
'in a situation of advantage'

Centre column attacks about
a third down enemy line

Lee column backs up
centre column

*Nelson's tactics, according to
Captain Richard Keats.*

catching him up, and defeating him. One day, as the fleet followed the trade winds across the Atlantic, Nelson and Hardy had the men of the *Victory* called to their quarters for a tour of inspection. The Admiral stopped on the lower deck and sat on the pump near the mainmast. He

> … made a short speech to the men, telling them that he expected and hoped to fall in with the French fleet before they reached Barbados. 'I have it from good authority that they have 15 sail of the line and we have only 13. I am very sure every ship will easily manage one each when there will be two left for us, and it be very harsh indeed if we are not able to give a very good account of them.'

After this 'pretty and laconic speech' the men gave him three cheers.[20]

During the passage, Nelson took the opportunity to develop his views on naval tactics. He was a practical rather than a theoretical tactician and there is no sign that he read the numerous books on naval tactics, mostly French, that were published in the age of sail. The one possible exception is the well-informed Scottish landsman, John Clerk of Eldin, for Hardy later wrote that he

> … read Mr Clerk's works with great attention and frequently expressed his approba-tion of them in the fullest manner; he also recommended all the captains to read them with attention, and said that many good hints might be taken from them.[21]

In any case, Nelson had produced his first-known writing on naval tactics by 15 May, when the fleet was approaching Madeira. Most authorities accept that it was the one printed in Nelson's letters, although there is some dispute about this.[22] The surviving memorandum began in typical Nelsonic style, with its emphasis on getting at the enemy and allowing full initiative to the individual captains and admirals.

> The business of an English Commander-in-Chief being first to bring an Enemy's Fleet to Battle, on the most advantageous terms to himself, (I mean that of laying his Ships close on board the Enemy, as expeditiously as possible;) and secondly, to continue them there, without separating, until the business is decided; I am sensible beyond this object it is not necessary that I should say a word, being fully assured that the Admirals and Captains of the Fleet I have the honour to command, will, knowing my precise object, that of a close and decisive Battle, supply any deficiency in my not making signals.

He went on to outline two possible means of attack starting from the conventional point where the two fleets would meet at sea and both seek battle. Once committed, each would steer as close as possible to the wind, hoping to gain the 'weather gage', to have the wind behind them and therefore control of the battle. Nelson might then decide to pass the leading enemy ship and stay to windward of his fleet, just out of range. Nelson's ships would then turn together towards the enemy and concentrate on his leading ships. A second possibility was for Nelson to decline the weather gage, go to windward of the enemy line and then break through it about the sixth ship from the van. The rear ships of the British fleet would then turn to engage the section that had been cut off. There was a third possibility: that the enemy would retreat, in which case the tactics would be simple and each ship would be on its own from the beginning, according to its sailing qualities.

> If the Enemy are running away, then the only signals necessary will be, to engage the Enemy as arriving up with them; and the other Ships to pass on for a second, third &c. giving, if possible, a close fire into the Enemy in passing, taking care to give our Ships engaged, notice of your intentions.[23]

Nelson called the *Amazon* to come alongside the flagship and ordered Captain Parker to distribute a set of instructions to each ship in turn. Parker developed his own technique for doing this with minimum interruption to the progress of the fleet. He set extra sails on the *Amazon* and drew ahead and to windward of the first ship. He let loose a boat so that it could drift easily on to the other ship and deliver the documents. The *Amazon* took in some sail and fell behind the other ship, on the leeward side, to pick up the boat and repeat the process with the next ship.[24]

In the *Canopus*, Captain Austen had difficulties with supplies. The ship had been hurried out to the Mediterranean from home service without the usual complement of supplies and there was a 'great deficiency of ordnance stores'. At anchor in Tetuan Bay the jolly boat disappeared with three members of the crew. As the voyage west progressed one sail after another was condemned as unfit, but the Canopus's fine sailing qualities were not affected. Austen's discipline seems to have been quite mild, though back on 11 April, Seaman George Smith was given a dozen lashes for 'telling a scandalous lie' – not an offence covered in the Articles of War, but perhaps reflecting the captain's religious background.[25]

To Lieutenant W. P. Green of the *Conqueror*, the voyage was 'uneventful'; perhaps he amused himself by working on his inventions and his study of electricity. Chaplain Scott had no intelligence work to undertake and used the time to read a few of the books he had collected.

> Read lately Herbert Marsh's History of Politics between Great Britain and France. Finished Robertson's History of Charles V.' Letters on Taste, Gorvani's Travels in Italy, Play of John Bull, and other comedies, Tears and Sighs of P. P. Gratitude is the memory of the heart.[26]

Austen kept himself occupied by navigation. He discovered that the log line, used to measure the speed of the ship, was 8 inches too long and applied that correction to the ship's position. He recorded the distance the ship ran each day, and found that progress varied even in the trade winds. One hundred and twenty-eight miles were covered on 15 May and 137 on the 16th, but by the 18th the distance covered had fallen to 80 miles, then a low of 59 the next day. After that speed picked up considerably and runs of up to 170 miles were recorded by the end of the month, as the ships neared Barbados. Austen used three different means to calculate the longitude of his own ship. Dead reckoning was done by calculating the movement of the ship since the last known position, and it was notoriously inaccurate over long distances. Lunars involved measuring the distance of the moon from a particular star at a particular time. It was accurate, but involved intricate calculations. The chronometer was generally regarded as the most accurate, though some ships, including the *Donegal*, did not carry one. Austen also compared the positions of other ships in the fleet, probably by hailing those within range. On

Bridgetown and Carlisle Bay in Barbados, drawn by Captain Edward Brenton.

the morning of 4 June, as Barbados was sighted in the distance, he had a chance to compare the different ships and methods. He found that the *Canopus*'s chronometer was the most accurate, putting the ship within about a mile of its true position.[27]

The island of Barbados was already in some turmoil. There had been an invasion scare in February, when a French squadron under Admiral Missiessy arrived at Martinique. Lord Seaforth, the Governor, was already at odds with the island's assembly. Following Nelson's example of twenty years ago, he was trying to stop illegal trade with the United States. Furthermore, he had offended the planters by trying to push through a law making it a felony to kill a slave. The island had never been invaded in 178 years of British rule, and the white population had a deep-rooted aversion to martial law. The militia could not be called out until the enemy was actually in sight. There was relief when Rear-Admiral Thomas Cochrane arrived in the area with a small fleet early in April.

There was a further alarm on 15 May, when news was received that Admiral Villeneuve had arrived in the region. The Governor issued a proclamation: 'The enemy are at Martinique at single anchor in very great force – We have the best intelligence of their intentions to attempt the capture of this colony.' But elections to the assembly were in progress, the militia act had expired, and the Governor had to exceed his powers in order to recall it. This infuriated his main political opponent, Thomas Williams, who was also colonel of the St Thomas Regiment of the militia. In the Governor's presence he 'harangued' his men about the actions of 'those who called themselves the King's Council.' Williams, a slave owner himself, asserted that the white population were 'hell-fire oppressed, they are hell-fire tyrannised over.'[28]

Nelson arrived a few days afterwards, with his ten ships of the line. According to Parker, Nelson was 'not a little elated at finding that he had taken the right road, by the information of the enemy having reached Martinico …'.[29] He found the 74-gun *Northumberland* under Rear-Admiral Cochrane, and the 74-gun *Spartiate* and incorporated them in his fleet. From Lieutenant-General Sir William Myers, in charge of the troops in the islands, he received information of enemy movements which originated from Brigadier-General Robert Brereton, the army commander in St Lucia. A large group of ships, presumed to be the Franco-Spanish fleet and its transports, had been seen heading south past the island. Nelson was anxious to get after them, but Myers offered to put 2000 troops with Nelson. The Admiral was sceptical about the value of such men afloat and resented the delay in embarking them, but he could not refuse 'such a handsome offer'.[30] He sailed in the morning of 5 June.

The fleet headed south in hourly expectation of battle. According to Parker, 'Every preparation was accordingly made for attacking them at anchor, and the greatest anxiety prevailed throughout the fleet, now apparently drawing to a crisis.'[31] This was increased when the brig *Curieux* signalled that she had received information from an American ship which had been boarded by one ship from a large fleet. Then a local schooner made a signal that was mistaken for one indicating that the enemy was at Trinidad. As the fleet approached the island they saw flames as guard posts were set on fire.[32] Nelson, according to his biographers, 'anticipated a second Aboukir in the Bay of Paria.'[33]

Trinidad had been alert since 23 May, when a letter arrived from Myers informing them that a large enemy force was at Martinique. Unlike his colleague at Barbados, the Governor had no difficulty in calling out the militia and imposing martial law. Trinidad had been taken from the Spanish as recently as 1795. Its militia was largely made up of men of mixed race who had fled from the effects of the French Revolution in other parts of the Caribbean. They had no wish to return to French rule and the Governor had nothing but praise for their 'solid and steady behaviour.'[34]

But Trinidad had not been invaded, and every piece of Nelson's information proved false. Brereton's report of the enemy heading south is rather mysterious, but a convoy may have been mistaken for the French and Spanish. The American's information to the *Curieux* was probably a lie; the signal from the schooner was a coincidence; and the Trinidadian guard posts were on fire because the troops mistook Nelson's fleet for the enemy. Nelson anchored the fleet overnight in the Gulf of Paria and next day, as they were leaving, an advice boat arrived from Barbados with news that the French fleet, far from attacking Trinidad, had taken the British-held outpost of Diamond Rock off Martinique, 100 miles north-west of Barbados. Nelson was devastated and wrote of 'the misery I am feeling, at hitherto having missed the French Fleet; and entirely owing to false information ...'[35]

In fact the combined squadron had begun to move north on 5 June, on the way home following the cyclical pattern of winds in the North Atlantic. Apart from capturing Diamond Rock, which had certainly been a thorn in the French side, and taking a convoy of fourteen ships off Antigua, it had done nothing to exploit its temporary local superiority in the West Indies.

Nelson was not far behind. His fleet followed them up the chain of islands that form the Lesser Antilles. On 12 June Nelson was off Monserrat where he got 'only vague and unsatisfactory intelligence' at first, but later heard that the French were pushing on past Antigua. He was off that island later in the day, when he 'received intelligence of importance.' He had heard that they had landed all the troops and stores they had taken on at Guadeloupe, and therefore were not intending to attack any of the West Indian islands. That and their course confirmed his growing belief that they were heading back to Europe. He wrote letters warning the Admiralty of this and sent them on in the brig *Curieux*, well known as a fast sailer.[36] He stopped briefly at Antigua to disembark Myers's troops, then set sail for Europe.

Nelson still had hopes of meeting the enemy in mid-Atlantic, although he did not intend to risk a headlong attack, for he knew that the French fleet had been augmented in the West Indies. He is said to have told one of his officers late in the voyage,

> All the way out he was getting stronger and I was getting weaker. All the way home I am getting stronger and he is getting weaker. If we fell in with him now and fought him, I don't doubt we should beat him, and it would be a great thing for my personal glory; but I think I should be doing my country a great wrong. I know that in a week's time I shall get reinforcements, and he will get none, and then I must annihilate him. [37]

Nelson was not to know that the fleets were following slightly different routes. He had concluded that the French were going back to the Mediterranean and turned east after reaching the latitude of about 35°N. In fact Villeneuve was heading for Brest and the English Channel and went a little further north before turning to sail east by north. On 19 June the *Curieux* spotted the enemy in the distance, still heading north. Captain George Bettesworth followed them for a while then decided to continue with his mission, rather than try to find Nelson with the news. At the beginning of July the French fleet passed just north of the Azores, the British

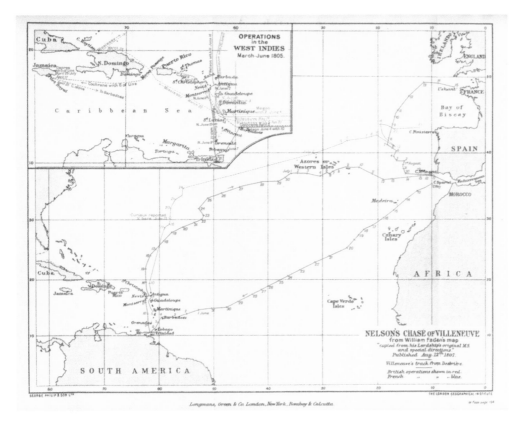

*The chase across the Atlantic,
from Sir Julian Corbett's*
Campaign of Trafalgar.

just south, only about 200 miles apart after a chase of three months; but they did not meet.

On 20 June a British brig was sighted heading for the West Indies and the *Amphion* made contact. She had no intelligence of the enemy, but a supply of British newspapers up to 3 May, reporting 'interesting debates' in Parliament. Captain Sutton signalled to the *Victory* and Nelson asked, 'Who is the First Lord of the Admiralty?' He was probably surprised with the answer 'Lord Barham'. Sir Charles Middleton had only taken the title on 27 April and it is not clear if Nelson knew who he was under his new name.[38]

In light winds Nelson occasionally took the opportunity to invite officers from the other ships on board. On 1 July he wrote to Admiral Louis, 'I think you may with great safety venture to dine on board the *Victory* today, for I too much fear that we shall not have a wind to move us faster than the boats can pass.'[39]

On 13 July, less than 600 miles from Cape St Vincent, Nelson sent a frigate ahead to Gibraltar to warn of his coming, and suggest that this news be kept as secret as possible. Water was running low, and the crews were put on short allowance of 5 pints per man per day.[40] By midday on 18 July Cape Spartel, on the African side of the Strait of Gibraltar, was in sight and Nelson was still unhappy. '… no French fleet, nor any information about them: how sorrowful this makes me, but I cannot help myself.'[41] At 7.30 next morning the Victory anchored at Gibraltar, with the rest of the fleet 'anchored as convenient'. On the 20th Nelson landed on the Rock, leaving the decks of the *Victory* for the first time in 'two years wanting ten days.'[42]

Although he had not got the fleet battle he had wanted, Nelson might have taken satisfaction from the way in which he had second guessed the enemy twice, had almost caught up with him after being a month behind, had prevented him from doing any serious damage in the West Indies and had given the Admiralty the information which allowed them to make new dispositions against Villeneuve's returning force; but he did not and he was still distressed at losing the enemy.

The health of the ships remained good after the long voyage, with only twenty-three cases of scurvy. Others were 'scorbutic' – slightly affected by the disease but not yet struck down by it. Of these, 160 were concentrated in the *Belleisle*, which had come directly from the Channel Fleet without any chance to adapt to Mediterranean practices.[43] It was, Hardy thought, 'a very pleasant passage.'[44]

Nelson remained at Gibraltar for four days, still in an agony of mind, which he did not hesitate to express to the Secretary of the Admiralty.

> I am, my dear Marsden, as completely miserable as my greatest enemy could wish me; but I neither blame fortune or my own judgement. Oh General Brereton! General Brereton! [45]

On 23 July the fleet headed across to Tetuan to water and Nelson heard a report that the enemy had been seen heading north, so he sailed towards Ushant near Brest. On 15 August he met Cornwallis's fleet and at last he was able to catch up with news of the war. He learned that Vice–Admiral Sir Robert Calder had met Villeneuve's fleet off Cape Finisterre in northern Spain and had forced them to retreat. Nelson shared in 'the joy of the event', although he was bewildered that 'John Bull was not content' with the scale of the victory.[46] He also received new orders for the Admiralty. The bulk of his ships were to be left to reinforce the Channel Fleet. The *Victory*, which had not been in a dockyard for more than two years, was to head for home with the worn-out *Superb*.

The medical men noted that the condition of the sick began to improve with 'the pleasing and exhilarating prospect of soon seeing England.'[47] Benjamin Stevenson, pressed into the *Victory* in May 1803, was no happier with his lot, despite promotion to quartermaster and the pleasure of nearing home.

> Thank God for it my Brother we have once more arrived in England and once more beg your friendship in getting me clear of this miserable situation … for this is one of the miserablest lives that ever a man led.[48]

Hardy was much happier as he could look forward to home leave, unlike the men on the lower deck,

> We are now standing in to Spithead and shall be at anchor in about an hour. I have applied to the Admiralty for leave of absence, therefore in all probability I shall have the pleasure of seeing my friends in Dorsetshire the latter part of this month.[49]

At 4.00 a.m. on 18 August the *Victory* and *Superb* anchored at Spithead in sight of Portsmouth. At 9.00 p.m. the following day Nelson's flag was hauled down from the foremast of the *Victory* and he was rowed ashore, to make way to his personal 'paradise' with Lady Hamilton at Merton.

CHAPTER 10

The Euryalus

If one wanted a contrast with the heavy industry and urban setting of Chatham Dockyard, Buckler's Hard in Hampshire was as good a place as any to find it – 3½ miles up the narrow Beaulieu River, 10 miles overland from the ancient port of Southampton and 17 miles by sea from Portsmouth Dockyard. The frigate *Euryalus* was almost ready for launch there by the end of May 1803. She did not quite dominate the site, for she was overshadowed by the frames of a much larger ship, the 74-gun *Swiftsure*. The village of Buckler's Hard was tiny and isolated, but it had an unexpected grandeur. Eighty years ago the Duke of Montagu had planned a port to handle trade from the Caribbean Island of St Lucia. The venture failed, and only one end of one of the planned streets was ever built. The houses were far too modern, regular and uniform for a typical village in rural Hampshire, and the street was wider than one would expect.

In the 1740s the village reverted to an older function, building ships for the Royal Navy. The river was only 250 yards wide at high water, but there was a convenient bend where ships could be launched. The banks were firm, there was suitable timber nearby and it was close enough to Portsmouth for the navy to keep a strict eye on what was going on. Apart from the relative grandeur of its architecture, Buckler's Hard was typical of dozens of sites on the Thames, Medway, Solent and Plymouth Sound where private shipbuilders supplemented the work of the Royal Dockyards in producing ships for the navy.

No one could have any doubt about the role of the village in 1803. Apart from the two ships under construction at the end of the only street, there were great piles of timber on each side of the road, often blocking the light from the houses. Some were rough logs, some were 'sided', that is, cut to shape on the flat sides ready to be selected and shaped as the

Buckler's Hard, painted by William Lionel Wyllie.

'futtocks' which would form the ribs of a ship, and some had already been made ready to be erected. Some piles were of curved timber for futtocks or knees, some were of straight wood for deck beams or planks. During the hours of daylight there was constant noise and bustle from the riverside, as teams of horses moved timber, joiners sawed, shipwrights trimmed, hammered and drilled, while caulkers boiled tar to fill the gaps between the planks of the ships. The house at the riverside end of the street was used by the present owners of the yard, Balthazar and Edward Adams. They were less fearsome than their father, who had taken over the yard fifty years before, but the old man was still very much alive and kept a watchful eye on progress from a cabin with semi-circular windows. During his career he had built three dozen ships for the navy, including Nelson's famous *Agamemnon*.[1]

The *Euryalus* was a typical 36-gun frigate. When the 'true' frigate was first introduced to British service in the 1750s, 32-gun ships with a main armament of 12-pounders had predominated. Since then, there had been an increasing tendency to build large and more powerful ships, mainly because the French opponents were getting larger. The 36-gun frigate, and the 38, which was slightly closer to French principles, had 18-pounders as their main guns, making them far more effective in action. By the 1790s orders for 18-pounder frigates predominated, and 32s were only built as cut-price versions, offering a form of economy which usually turned out to be false. The *Euryalus* was the last frigate to be ordered before the war ended in 1802. She was the third ship of the *Apollo* class, designed by Sir William Rule, Surveyor of the Navy, which was eventually to number twenty-six ships.

The frigate was designed round her sailing qualities rather than her gun armament, but she had to make a respectable show against enemy ships of similar type, for she often had to fight enemy frigates either in her role of fleet reconnaissance or in convoy escort. The main characteristic, as compared with the ship of the line, was that the lower deck was unarmed and had no gunports. The ship could carry her guns rather higher out of the water without losing stability, and could afford to heel rather more in a beam wind. Her lines were finer, and the ship was faster in light winds, though not in gales.

Henry Blackwood was born in 1770, the fourth son in a family of landowners in County Down, Ireland. He went to sea at the age of ten in the frigate *Artois* under the patronage of a fellow Ulsterman, Captain John Macbride of County Antrim, and within four months he was in action against the Dutch at Dogger Bank. He saw some service in peacetime, as signal midshipman to Admiral Lord Howe during the mobilization of 1790, and was promoted lieutenant later that year. In 1791–92 he went to France to learn the language as Nelson had done eight years earlier – though Blackwood was far more successful. The Revolution was in progress and he was drawn towards Paris. He was imprisoned for a time on suspicion of carrying political letters, but released. Later he attended meetings of Jacobin Clubs and was in the city when

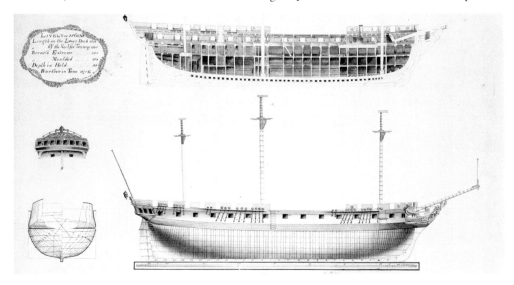

A plan and cross-section of the frigate Lively *showing some of the internal arrangements.*

the Royal Family was imprisoned and the Reign of Terror began. He was obliged to flee for his life, but he had learned far more about the French Revolution than most in the navy.

Blackwood became first lieutenant of the 74-gun *Invincible* under another Irishman and a friend of Macbride, Captain Thomas Pakenham, who regarded Blackwood 'as capable an officer as I have ever met with.' As such, he served in the first great fleet battle of the wars, the 'Glorious First of June', 1794, and was promoted to commander. He became a post-captain in June 1795. He commanded the *Brilliant* of 28 guns and off Tenerife in July 1798 he fought off two French 44-gun frigates, an action which earned him fame. In March 1799 he was given the *Penelope* of 36 guns and sent to the Mediterranean. As yet he had never met Nelson, but in March 1800 he led the chase of the last French survivor of the Nile, the mighty 80-gun *Guillaume Tell*, as she attempted to escape from Malta. The *Penelope* continually came up under the stern of the great ship and brought her guns to bear, while the Frenchman did not dare to turn to meet her for fear that the rest of the pursuing ships would catch up. Eventually the *Guillaume Tell*'s mainmast fell and she surrendered to a British squadron. Nelson would soon strike his flag. He wrote to Blackwood, '… I believe … I was your friend and acquaintance before I saw you. Your conduct and character, on the late glorious occasion, stamps your fame beyond the reach of envy.' He was put on half-pay at the end of the war in 1802.[2]

Blackwood was 'rather short, but of extraordinary strength and finely made, well set up, a fresh complexion, and small hands and feet. His dress was a gold-laced cocked hat, gold-laced coat and epaulettes, white pantaloons, and Hessian boots, a light crooked sabre, and a great shirt frill …'. In the days when orders had to be transmitted by voice he had the advantage of 'a wonderful organ' which 'might be heard a mile off.'[3] His first wife died in 1798 after three years of marriage; his second in 1801 after two years. His letters show he was very much in love with his third wife, Harriet Gore, whom he married in May 1803.

By this time Blackwood was seeking employment in the peacetime fleet. He wrote to the Admiralty on the first day of the year. 'I beg you will have the goodness to renew my application for employment, assuring your lordships of my constant readiness to serve.' He got no satisfaction and repeated the letter in May, after the declaration of war.[4] Eventually St Vincent gave him the command of the new *Euryalus*, still under construction. The frigate was launched on 6 June 1803 and towed round to Portsmouth to be rigged and fitted. Blackwood joined her there on the on 27 June. He had no crew, but forty convicts were employed in the heavy work of loading ballast and stowing the hold. A draft of twenty boys was sent on board from the Marine Society which specialized in recruiting waifs for the navy, and the ship's marines were able to do some of the work with the co-operation of dockyard artificers. The ship sailed out to anchor at Spithead and received its first draft of seventy-seven seamen, but still it was undermanned, because many seamen had gone to ground in the aftermath of the hot press that spring. The *Euryalus* went a few miles down the Solent to anchor off Lymington, where its press gangs picked up a few more men from passing merchant ships; but Blackwood remained unsatisfied with the quality and quantity of his men. The ship finally went to sea on 28 August 1803, nearly three months after her launch.[5]

Blackwood was not entirely sanguine with his new ship. She was of the same size as the *Penelope* and nominally had a similar armament. In fact her main guns, the 18-pounders on the lower deck, were longer than those of the previous ship and weighed more. He soon noticed that they were more difficult to handle; even in the *Penelope* with lighter guns, he had needed the whole crew to man them in action with none left over for a small-arms party. He wrote to the Admiralty of his present crew that 'four-fifths of that of the *Penelope* were more equal to manage her guns than all my present ship's company would have been, which now have metal from five to six hundred-weight more to handle, at least a man difference on each gun.' The Admiralty and the Board of Ordnance agreed in November 1804 that he needed lighter guns, but suitable carriages were not in stock. He was allowed ten extra men for his crew, but this order was lost and did not reach him for six months. In the meantime he had noticed that the extra weight of metal affected the ship's sailing qualities and in August 1805 he wrote, 'I have still on board the heavy long 18-pound guns, which from their overhanging the side much more than those of the proper establishment, I am

Captain Henry Blackwood, painted by John Hoppner and engraved by Charles Turner in 1833.

well convinced must weaken the ship, and in all weather act against her sailing.'[6]

Blackwood was first sent to join the Irish Squadron under Admiral Lord Gardner. He spent much of his time at anchor off either Cork or Dublin, and in September 1803 he complained to St Vincent. The First Lord offered no sympathy.

> The defence of the capital of Ireland appears to me the most honourable service (with the single exception of the defence of London) that an Officer can be employed upon, and when the Lord Lieutenant [of Ireland] has no further occasion for a force in Dublin Bay, Admiral Lord Gardner will find active service for the *Euryalus*.

Relations deteriorated further in December when St Vincent replied to another letter. He expressed his 'astonishment' at the 'most dangerous and mischievous tendency' expressed by Blackwood, and hoped that 'you will in future consider the obedience to the Orders you receive as the only principle of your duty.'[7] Nevertheless the *Euryalus* was transferred to the North Sea Fleet under Keith. Blackwood spent a productive year with the squadron off Boulogne, in the centre of the defences against invasion. In September 1804 he supervised an attack on the French using 'explosion vessels' and mines.[8] At the end of the year he went to the Channel Fleet.

Twice during the campaign of 1805, Blackwood's *Euryalus* played a decisive role in events. The first was purely by chance. In July 1805 he applied for leave of absence to see his wife who was in 'distress of a very serious nature.' Admiral Villeneuve's fleet was still at large and no-one could be spared; the Admiralty replied, 'the ship he commands being wanted for service, the leave of absence cannot be granted.'[9] He was sent back to the Irish station and on the way there he received news of Admiral Calder's action from a passing frigate. On 3 August 1805 the *Euryalus* arrived back in Cork Harbour and Blackwood went on board Admiral Thomas Drury's flagship with the news. Instead of being sent to patrol the north of Ireland as he had expected, Blackwood was instead ordered to go south to try to make contact with Nelson to convey the news. He was far too late for this, as Nelson had gone north; but in Lisbon he heard news that Villeneuve's fleet was on the move, and decided to look out for it.[10]

On Saturday, 17 August the *Euryalus* was in a heavy swell off the coast of Portugal with the frigates *Phoenix* and *Iris*, when they sighted three strange ships which were suspected of being the screen of the enemy fleet. Blackwood pursued one of them, but was delayed due to the loss of a studding sail boom; when he finally caught up, the stranger turned out to be an English ship from the South Seas. Two days later they stopped a Danish ship from the West Indies. Blackwood spoke to her captain, who quickly volunteered the information that he had sailed within 5 to 7 miles of a great fleet of thirty-five warships, twenty-seven of which he believed to be ships of the line, sailing south-south-east in a light easterly wind. The captain had made sure of his facts – he and his mate counted the ships more than twenty times. Blackwood was equally cautious about taking information on trust. He examined each of the Danish crew 'particularly and separately' but each came up with the same answer. It could only be the Combined French and Spanish Fleet, passing south towards the Mediterranean.

Blackwood immediately sent the *Iris* home with the news, and set all possible sail to the south to seek out the enemy and inform Admiral Collingwood, stationed with a weak force off Cadiz. He soon sighted 'a large fleet, the body of them bearing south-east and steering south-south-east', but he found it impossible to get round them to reach Collingwood. Therefore the Admiral was surprised and in some danger, until he withdrew. Next day, on the evening of 21 August, Blackwood at last joined Collingwood off Cadiz, and was sent home with the news the great Combined Fleet had taken refuge in the Spanish port, where it would join with more Spanish ships, to make a potentially huge force of ships of the line. Ten days later, 1.30 p.m. on 1 September, the *Euryalus* passed the Needles into the Solent, and anchored off Lymington where she had unsuccessfully tried to augment her crew by impressment two years before. Blackwood went ashore with his urgent dispatches.

On 14 September, after Blackwood had returned from Merton and London, the *Euryalus* finally got her new, lighter guns and carriages – just in time, because the next day she sailed with the *Victory* to join the fleet off Cadiz.

CHAPTER 11

Barham at the Admiralty

In the middle of Britain's greatest ever crisis, with invasion barges massed in Boulogne and a large enemy fleet lost to view and liable to appear anywhere without warning, the post of First Lord of the Admiralty was vacant in April 1805. It was, as the Home Secretary agreed, 'the Office next to that of Prime Minister of the most importance and of the Greatest Power and Responsibility.'[1] It could be offered to a senior politician, probably a member of the House of Lords, and in the last half century it had been filled for long periods by the Earls of Sandwich, Chatham and Spencer. But none of the available ministers seemed suitable. The post could equally well be held by a senior naval officer with political interests, and Pitt considered the admirals. St Vincent was out of the question in view of his support for the previous administration. Lord Gardner of the Channel Fleet was not considered suitable, while Lord Keith of the North Sea Fleet was a political maverick who had no experience at the Admiralty and was quite junior in the list of flag officers.

On the face of it, Pitt's choice of Sir Charles Middleton was a surprising one. The son of a customs officer in Leith, Middleton was a cousin of Lord Melville, which was not an asset in the circumstances. He was nearly seventy-nine years old. He was a full admiral but had never commanded a fleet. He was an experienced administrator, having served for twelve years as Controller of the Navy, and eighteen months on the Admiralty Board itself in the 1790s, leaving in a fury and throwing all his papers in a corner.[2] He had carried out many reforms, including the introduction of carronades and copper sheathing for ships' bottoms, but he was an awkward subordinate, always bombarding his superiors with unwanted advice, confident of his own importance and feeling slighted when he was ignored. Unlike Melville he had little political experience or interests. He had some enemies, including those of the St Vincent faction and other supporters of the former Addington government.

These were to prove advantages rather than defects. Middleton had been out of office for ten years, so was well rested. At the same time he was not completely out of touch with Admiralty affairs, for he had advised the Melville Board, particularly on emergency repairs to old ships so that they could augment the fleet in the crisis. His regular memos suggest that he had thought deeply about naval strategy and organization. Nor was political ability needed in the circumstances. Normally, one of the primary duties of a cabinet minister is to make sure that his department gets due funding and prominence in the cabinet, parliament and the country. This was not a problem in 1805, for no one doubted the need for a strong navy. The Navy Estimates had already been passed by Parliament. They provided for a fleet of 120,000 men, as strong as it had ever been. £3.5 million was allocated, the largest sum ever. Nor did Middleton have to fear political interference; at least one leading politician had turned down the office because of the grave responsibility involved. He was created Lord Barham and took office on 2 May 1805, three weeks after Melville lost the vote of censure.

Without Melville's heavy political baggage, Barham was able to focus his whole energy on the navy. The first place he looked was to the Admiralty Office itself. He knew from experience that the Board was an unstructured body, meeting every morning and considering everything that came before it, however trivial, in great detail. During his first month in

Sir Charles Middleton, Lord Barham, First Lord of the Admiralty in 1805.

The Admiralty Building in Whitehall, by Brown and Pettit.

The Admiralty Building in Whitehall, by Brown and Pettit.

office, Barham allocated specific duties to each of the members. As First Lord, he personally would 'take upon himself the general superintendence and arrangement of the whole.' The naval members of the Board were already known informally as the Sea Lords, but Barham was the first to give them specific duties. The senior one, by this date known as the First Sea Lord, was to deputise for the First Lord, and to supervise the business of the Admiralty itself, including the allocation of ships, officers and seamen, and the issuing of secret orders. He was also charged with ensuring that orders were carried out, particularly cruisers and convoy escorts acting away from the main fleets.

The Second Sea Lord was to deal with the business of the other Boards under the Admiralty – the Navy Board, Transport Board, Sick and Hurt Board, Victualling and Greenwich Hospital for retired seamen. The Third Sea Lord was to superintend the appointment of commissioned and warrant officers, quite a large task in a navy that included 4258 commissioned officers and masters. Barham did not think highly of the professional politicians on the Board, the Civil Lords. They were to 'keep the professional lords uninterrupted in the various important duties committed to their charge' by signing all the minor orders which passes through the office – 'protections, warrants and promiscuous papers.'[3]

Barham was backed by a strong Board of Admiralty, though it was almost as apolitical as himself. The most experienced member was Sir Philip Stephens, who had started work as an Admiralty Clerk fifty-four years before, and had worked up to become the First Secretary in 1783. He became a member of the Board in 1795, and survived the changes of government in 1801 and 1804. As late as 1806, although he was over eighty, it was remarked that Stephens 'repairs daily to town, and even at an advanced period in life still continues to busy himself about the affairs of ... the navy.'[4] The senior naval officer, the 'First Sea Lord' under the new rules, was Admiral James Gambier. Like Barham he was an Evangelical Christian, though unlike his lordship he did not know when to keep quiet about it. Barham wrote of his own service,

> I was sixteen years in the sea service before I became a captain, and never, during that time heard prayers or divine service performed aboard of any ship. ... As soon as I became a captain I began reading prayers myself to the ship's company of a Sunday, and also a sermon ... I did not indeed venture to further than Sundays ... and I should only have acquired the name of methodist or enthusiast if I attempted it.[5]

A meeting of the Board of Admiralty, by Rowlandson and Pugin. The figures are far too small for the background, but it shows the wind indicator above the globe, with rolled maps on the wall to the right.

Gambier, on the other hand, was not afraid to force his beliefs on other people. Swearing was punished by a wooden collar with two 32-pound shot attached to it. He became known throughout the fleet at 'dismal Jimmy' or 'preaching Jemmie'.

The Second Sea Lord was another Scot, Admiral Phillip Patton, born in Fife in 1739. Like Barham, he was the son of a customs officer. He had seen nearly fifty years of active service since he was a midshipman under Admiral Edward Boscawen in 1755. He was present at the taking of Louisbourg in Canada in 1758 and the battles of Lagos and Quiberon Bay in 'the year of victories' – 1759. He was involved in the taking of Havana in 1762. He served in frigates in the North Sea and Mediterranean during the peace of 1763–75. During the War of Independence he started in big ships, being flag captain to Admiral Digby during Admiral Rodney's action off Cape St Vincent in 1780. After that he served mainly in frigates in the North Sea and took part in a battle with the Dutch at Dogger Bank in 1781. In the next war, against the revolutionary French, he became a Commissioner of the Transport Board but there was a complicated dispute over his right to promotion to rear-admiral while serving in a civil post. He had won some respect by putting down a mutiny in the Prince George in 1779, and had helped deal with the mutinies of 1797. He was a thoughtful writer on naval affairs, particularly on the condition of the lower deck. In 1803, as a vice-admiral he was Keith's deputy in the North Sea Fleet charged with preventing invasion until he joined the Admiralty under his countryman Melville in 1804.

The Third Sea Lord was also a Scot, Captain George Stewart, Viscount Garlies. Despite the naval rank this was largely a political appointment. He was in poor health at the beginning of 1805 and needed a less active job than as captain of the *Ajax*. His father, the Earl of Galloway, had just given him control of his electoral interests in Scotland and Melville, always mindful of such matters, offered him a seat at the Admiralty, though he himself had gone before Garlies took office. It was agreed that Garlies worked hard in the post.[6]

Of the remaining Civil Lords, Sir Evan Nepean, like Phillip Stephens, had had considerable experience as an official, spending nine years as First Secretary of the Admiralty up to 1804. The Barham Board had only one member with neither naval nor administrative experience. William Dickinson, MP for Lostwithiel in Cornwall was the only purely political appointment. He was a close ally of Pitt and often made statements on behalf of the

Admiralty in the House of Commons. He did not impress the Opposition, who rated him 'one of the very worst politicians in the whole House.'[7]

Barham had to work hard in his new post, in view of his age.

> The charge I have taken upon me is, I own, a very heavy one, and the service so increased in every point of view as to bear no comparison with former times. I seldom have the pen out of my hand from 8 in the morning till 6 at night; and although I see no person but on public business, yet I don't find my own finished in that time; and if I did not make a point of doing so, the current business must overpower us.[8]

He did everything he could to delegate work and to efficiently organize his time. His memory, he admitted, was poor and he kept a day book in which he 'entered every thing of importance, … and scratched through the article when it was executed.' He tended to draft very rough short minutes, 'leaving them to be modified by the secretary or writing clerk'.[9] The office started late and Barham found that he could not get at essential papers 'from the non-attendance of the clerks'. He decreed that at least one from each department should be in the office by 10.00 a.m., and the rest should be at their desks by 10.30 a.m. Nevertheless he complained to a persistent correspondent that

> If you was acquainted with the number of letters which come daily into the hands of a first lord of the admiralty you would not wonder at his wish to divest himself of every one of a public nature by transferring it to the board. This is my own practice, and I could not undertake the department if it was otherwise.[10]

By these means Barham found some time to look at the most important matter of all – where was Villeneuve's fleet now, and where would it reappear in the world scene? Already by 1 July 1805 he knew for sure that it had been seen in the West Indies. Napoleon's ploy of luring forces there was completely transparent and Admiral Collingwood wrote, 'I think it not impossible I shall have these fellows coming from the West Indies again before the hurricane months, unless they sail from there directly for Ireland, which I have always had an idea was their plan; for this Bonaparte has as many tricks as a monkey.'[11] But there was

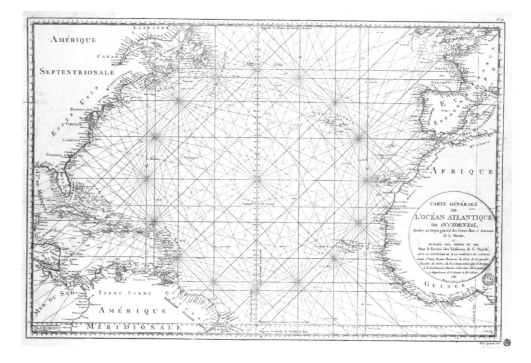

A French chart of the North Atlantic in 1791, produced by the Depot de la Marine.

no way of knowing where the French would turn up, perhaps to tip the scale in the region. Around 8 June Barham had made a list of the forces available to him in Western Europe. There were twenty-two ships of the line off the main French base at Brest, five off the smaller one at Rochefort and twelve off the north-west Spanish one of Ferrol, with two more which might be available, making forty-one. He planned to detach ten ships from Brest to reinforce the remnants of the Mediterranean Fleet, which he believed to be four ships under Admiral Bickerton off Cadiz, for it was quite likely that the French squadron would return there. This would be 'a strong force in the very spot where they may be expected.' He was inclined to believe that 'depredation and the destruction of our trade' was 'their grand object', rather than invasion, and planned to give priority to fast squadrons of two-deckers and large frigates to chase them.

Long-distance communication was the peculiar source of weakness in a world strategy. Warships and merchant ships from western Europe covered the seas at will, for their crews had learned to cope with the winds and use them to advantage. Colonies in India and the Caribbean were essential to the economic prospects of both Britain and France, and in that sense they lived in a global economy. Travel to and from these colonies was slow, but reasonably reliable. Despite the gradual advances in seamanship and shipbuilding over the preceding few centuries, virtually nothing had changed in long-distance communication. A message still could not travel any faster than the ship that carried it. True, there had been some changes in other forms of communication. On land, telegraph and semaphore stations could be set up and a message passed over a hundred miles in a few minutes, in good visibility. At sea, ships within sight could communicate with increasingly sophisticated signal codes. Beyond that, nothing had changed since the days of Vasco da Gama and Columbus. A message from India might take six months to reach home, one from the Caribbean would take two months, and in the meantime the government in London lacked information and control, and the officers on the spot had to make the best of the resources they had, and reach their own decisions. These facts were to dominate the naval campaigns of 1805.

Napoleon had many faults as a naval commander, which almost exactly balanced his enormous strengths in command of an army. In battle, his presence alone was said to be worth 40,000 men. But Napoleon knew comparatively little of the world he was sending his fleets into. Apart from the ill-fated expedition to Egypt, he had never left Europe or made

An Admiralty telegraph station on Southsea Common near Portsmouth.

a long sea voyage. He lacked the almost instinctive knowledge of winds and weather that came easily to Barham and Nelson, and even to far less successful commanders such as Calder and Gardner. Barham had not been to sea since 1778, but before that he had distinguished himself in the West Indies, so he knew these waters well. The Admiralty had no naval staff as such, so Barham relied on his own experiences, and those of his sea lords. Between them they had served in every important corner of the naval world, they knew the winds and currents at different times of year, the likelihood of storms or calms of each season. Anyone could of course look at a map to find out how far Martinique was from Cadiz, or the mouth of the English Channel from Brest, but that was meaningless. These seasoned officers knew what winds to seek out, what dangers to avoid. Unlike Napoleon, they knew the world outside Europe where a large part of the extensive naval campaign of 1805 would take place.

Their other great advantage was the ease with which they understood and delegated to the officers on the spot. Napoleon continually dictated to his admirals, because he did not trust their energy or courage. The British government could see the record of their own admirals over the last few decades, how they had crushed the French, Spanish and Dutch in battle after battle, how they had led successful expeditions against enemy colonies in the West Indies, South Africa, Ceylon and Egypt. Technically the cabinet was in charge of naval strategy and directed the movement of ships; in practice much of this power was delegated to Barham at the Admiralty. Between them, the sea lords were able to pick out the key points to defend, the probable lines of enemy movement, and the likely points of attack. There remained numerous imponderables.

Barham was in bed on the night of 8 July when important information arrived. Captain Bettesworth of the *Curieux* had left Nelson in the Atlantic 3 1/2 weeks earlier, and was carrying dispatches about the French movements. He reached Plymouth on 7 July, and made haste to London by road. When he got to the Admiralty in the middle of the night the servants were reluctant to wake Barham, until he woke naturally. He raged about the delay, but quickly took in the information Bettesworth was offering him.

It was not so much Nelson's dispatch that was interesting; Barham had already guessed that Villeneuve would return to Europe. More important, the *Curieux* had actually sighted the French after leaving Nelson, and followed them for several days as they continued to head north. It was clear that they were not going to the Mediterranean as both Barham and Nelson had thought, but further north. The enemy was evidently heading towards the English Channel and could be intercepted on the entry to European waters, either off Cape Finisterre in the north-west of Spain, or off Brest in north-west France. Barham's first thought was to take ships from Brest and send them to join Admiral Sir Robert Calder off Ferrol and Finisterre. He scrawled a minute for his clerks to draft an order, but then changed his mind. There was no point in weakening the Brest squadron, which might play a crucial role if the enemy got past Calder. Instead he decided to take the risk of withdrawing the squadron blockading the small naval port of Rochefort to reinforce Calder. They were to cruise 90 to 120 miles to the west of Finisterre for six or eight days looking for the enemy.[12]

Cornwallis, in charge of the Channel Fleet off Brest, knew about the French movements as soon as Barham did. Bettesworth of the *Curieux* had left a message with the port admiral at Plymouth as he passed through, and that was transmitted to Cornwallis by the 9 July. He sent it on to his subordinates, Stirling off Rochefort and Calder off Ferrol. Five days later Barham's dispositions were completed; Stirling joined Calder off Cape Finisterre, making a squadron of fifteen ships of the line.[13]

A week later, at noon on 23 July, Calder's lookouts sighted the Franco-Spanish force, 75 miles north-west of Finisterre. They assessed it as '20 sail of the line, also 3 large ships armed *en flute* [i.e. without their main guns] of about 50 guns each, with 5 frigates and 3 brigs'. Calder had several disadvantages. He was up against an enemy who, for once, had spent a considerable amount of time together and at sea, if not in battle. The weather was foggy (and night would fall towards the end of the battle). He was outnumbered by twenty ships of the line to fifteen. His main advantage, apart from the generally better quality and experience of British officers and crews, was that he was between the enemy and his bases and mission, so the French and Spanish would have to make some attempt to fight. In a confused action, two Spanish ships of the line were captured.

The Franco-Spanish squadron retreated into Ferrol and Napoleon's grand invasion plan, having ranged across both sides of the Atlantic, ground to a halt. Calder was pleased with himself, and hinted at a reward. He wrote to Barham,

> I have had the good fortune to have fallen in with the combined squadrons of Toulon and Cadiz upon their return from the West Indies. The action has been unique, having been fought in a fog at night. I hope your lordship and my royal master will think I have done all that it was possible to have been done. If so, and you should think me deserving of any mark of royal bounty, I beg leave to observe that I have no children, but I have a nephew, the son of an old faithful servant of the crown … to whom I hope His Majesty's royal bounty may extend, if my services may be though worthy of any mark by His Majesty.[14]

The immediate crisis was over by the time Nelson arrived home at Merton on 20 August. Barham knew little of the Admiral, for he had been out of office during his rise to fame since the Battle of Cape St Vincent in 1797. Even in 1798 he had no inkling of Nelson's great abilities, for he wrote in August that the force sent to the Mediterranean was not enough to attack Bonaparte 'with any hope of success.'[15] He was not to know that Nelson had already won the Battle of the Nile. By September 1805 Barham was calling him 'that distinguished officer' in a letter to the King.[16] Nelson, for his part, wrote to his old friend, Edward Berry, in August 1805, 'Lord Barham is an almost entire stranger to me.'[17]

This was the happiest period of Nelson's home life. Emma Hamilton soon arrived at Merton from Southend, and their daughter Horatia was already there. Nelson no longer had to share Emma's affections with Sir William (though oddly enough that arrangement does not seem to have caused Nelson any anguish). He had his own home, not his father's house where he had spent five years of intense boredom and rejection up to 1793. He had suffered no new wounds during the campaign, and his administration of the Mediterranean Fleet had been faultless, with no unfortunate political side effects. He was beginning to be accepted back in society and there was a steady stream of visitors from his past, including the Duke of Clarence, Lord Minto and Admiral Sir Peter Parker. According to the latter, 'I had a most hearty welcome. He looks remarkably well and full of spirits. His conversation is as cordial in these low times.'

Nelson was no longer on duty as commander-in-chief of the Mediterranean. As late as 29 August 1805, the connection between him and his flagship was not regarded as indissoluble. For the moment the Channel Fleet had the greater priority and the Secretary of the Admiralty wrote to Nelson that the *Victory* was to go to sea as soon as possible to join Cornwallis.[18] All the same, Nelson was in much demand as an adviser to the government,

Nelson's home at Merton in 1802, by Thomas Baxter.

and several times he made the 8-mile journey to London to meet the highest in the land. At first he had feared that he might have been censured for failing to find the enemy; but in the streets of London the people treated him as a hero, and Pitt took him into his confidence. On 23 August, Lord Castlereagh, the Foreign Secretary, had an extremely high opinion of him: 'I am now set up as a conjuror, and God knows they will very soon find out I am far from being one ...'.[19] On 1 September he was in Downing Street advising the Prime Minister that the Combined Fleet might well return to action and steps needed to be taken against this. He returned to Merton that night.

Nelson was already dressed at 5.00 the next morning when Captain Blackwood of the *Euryalus* arrived on the way from Portsmouth to London. He exclaimed, 'I am sure you bring me news of the French and Spanish Fleets, and I think I shall yet have to beat them.' Blackwood confirmed that he had the latest intelligence. The Combined Fleet of France and Spain had now sailed to Cadiz, where they joined yet more Spanish ships. From there they could threaten the Mediterranean and were watched only by Collingwood's small squadron. There are two contradictory accounts of Nelson's reaction. One claims that he immediately saw the opportunity, saying 'Depend on it, Blackwood, I shall yet give Mr. Villeneuve a drubbing.' Another has him much more nonchalant. 'All this was nothing to him. "Let the man trudge it who has lost his budget."' was his obscure comment. He knew that he would be recalled to duty, and travelled to London next morning.[20] Lady Hamilton wrote to Nelson's niece,

> I am again broken-hearted, as our dear Nelson is immediately going. It seems as though I have had a fortnight's dream, and am awoke to all the misery of this cruel separation. But what can I do? His powerful arm is of so much consequence to his Country.[21]

Thus on 2 September, exactly four months after Barham took office, London received the news from Blackwood. From this moment the southern Spanish port became the focus of British naval activity, and attention was transferred from the Brest Fleet, watched by Cornwallis. Barham drafted a new policy to send to the Prime Minister. Nelson's new Mediterranean command should extend as far outwards as Cape St Vincent, as he had wanted a year ago. He was to go out immediately in the *Victory* with such ships as were available, and reinforce and take charge of the blockade of Cadiz under Collingwood. But Barham still regarded the Cadiz blockade as the tail, rather than the dog, of the Mediterranean command. Having set up Collingwood's force to his satisfaction, Nelson was then to 'proceed himself to Gibraltar, and having settled everything there for the defence of the garrison and trade coming in and going out of the Mediterranean, to visit the other parts of his command and form such a squadron as will embrace every duty belonging to it ...'.[22]

Barham spared no effort to find ships for Nelson's fleet. According to an unauthenticated account, the First Lord gave Nelson a Navy List and told him to choose the officers he wanted to serve under him. Nelson replied 'Choose yourself, my Lord, the same spirit actuates the whole profession; you cannot choose wrong.' But according to the same account, Nelson did agree to choose the ships he most wanted and dictate their names to Barham's secretary; both admirals were aware of the unevenness of quality and condition of the ships of the line.[23]

Nelson returned to Merton for a last few days at home. According to Lady Hamilton, she was stoical about parting from her lover after such a short time. 'Even in this last fatal victory, it was I bid him go forth. Did he not pat me on the back, call me brave Emma, and said, "If there were more Emmas there would be more Nelson's."' On 13 September, according to Nelson's diary, 'Friday at $^{1}/_{2}$ past 10, drove from dear, dear Merton where I left all that I hold dear in this world to serve my King and Country.'[24]

CHAPTER 12

Cadiz

Admiral Villeneuve was a product of his times, just as much as his adversary Horatio Nelson. The British commander had grown up in an era when the British navy increasingly regarded itself as invincible, whereas Villeneuve had witnessed the other side of the same coin. Pierre Charles de Villeneuve had entered the Marine Royal as a cadet at the age of fifteen and was one of the few officers who did not go into exile as the Revolution became more extreme. He prospered in a navy that needed to maintain an active campaign with a large fleet, but was short of experienced officers. At the beginning of the wars in 1793 he was already a captain at the age of twenty-nine.

Admiral Pierre Villeneuve.

Villeneuve was a rear-admiral and third-in-command of Admiral Brueys' fleet in 1798, when it was attacked by Nelson at anchor in Aboukir Bay. He was in command of what Brueys intended to be the van of the fleet, until Nelson spoiled his plans by attacking at the wrong time, from the wrong end and on the wrong side. Villeneuve had no orders to move up in support of the rest of the fleet, and the wind was against him. Brueys' fleet was fatally damaged when his flagship blew up and most of the ships surrendered, before Villeneuve at the rear became engaged at all. He kept up a desultory fire for several hours during the night, until he finally made a decision to escape with the two remaining ships of the line and two frigates. At the time this was regarded as a success, saving something from a disaster, but the action was ambiguous to say the least, as were most of Villeneuve's efforts.

In strong contrast to Nelson, Villeneuve was by nature a pessimist, 'always ready to credit unfavourable news.'[1] His fleet was an enormous cuckoo in the nest. It was ever-growing, taking on more ships in the West Indies and at Ferrol and Cadiz. It was constantly hungry, especially after it had almost exhausted its own stores in the return crossing of the Atlantic. It quickly denuded the poor provinces of Spain where it anchored. Transport ships might have brought in supplies to the most unlikely places, but that was impossible with an enemy fleet off every port. Supplies by land were just as difficult in a mountainous country such as Spain. Nor was it possible to split the fleet between different ports. Movements by squadron would be highly dangerous in British-controlled seas, and it would be unwise to throw away the benefits of concentration, the only tactical advantage the allies had. The natural dynamic of the Combined Fleet was to move from place to place until it reached a port, perhaps Toulon, which could feed it.

Villeneuve had left Corunna on 10 August, hoping to head for Brest in support of the invasion plan. Fears (largely imaginary) of British ships in the Bay of Biscay caused him to turn south, which was perhaps fortunate for him, because the British were concentrating a large fleet under Cornwallis off Brest. Off Cadiz he brushed Collingwood's three ships aside without a fight, and anchored in the port on the evening of 20 August. There he found six more Spanish ships of the line to add to his fleet of eighteen French and nine Spanish, making a combined force of thirty-three.

The harbour of Cadiz was 'the finest in old Spain and the great emporium of the Spanish foreign trade' according to a British pilot book. The town itself was an ancient walled city at the end of a sandy peninsula running approximately north, 'on a very flat point, with

A view and chart of Cadiz in 1783.

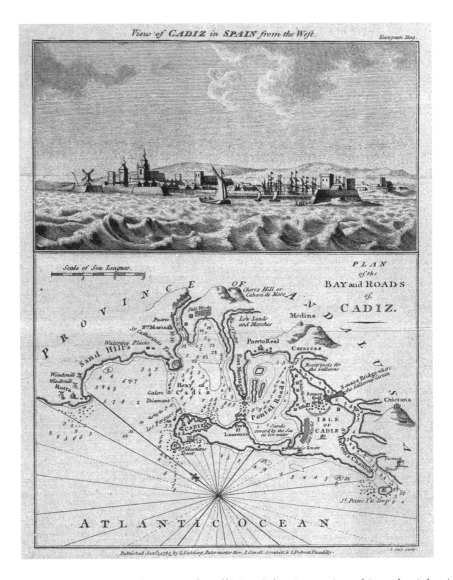

several steeples that are seen from very far off.' San Sebastian projected into the Atlantic to the west – 'it is all rocks above and under water that run a quarter of a league to sea.' To the east of the city, between it and the mainland, were several dangerous rocks – las Puercas, el Diamante marked by a buoy and la Galera off the point of Santa Catalina. To the north east of the city the bay of Cadiz cut into the mainland and seemed large enough; but its waters were too shallow for a fleet of ships of the line. The main channel, more than 4 fathoms deep, passed the city and gradually narrowed over 3 miles, to form what the French called the Grand Rade or Great Anchorage, rather open to north-westerly winds. After that the channel passed between the points of Matagorda and Puntal and curved round to the east, forming Puntal Road. This led in turn to the naval arsenal at Carraca, and to dry-docks yet further up the Sancti Petri river.[2]

On the face of it, Villeneuve had a strong fleet. It was generally believed that French ship design was better than British. Napoleon said, 'The French understand building better than their rivals, and French ships, the English themselves admit, are better than theirs. The guns are superior in calibre to those of the English by one fourth. These are two great advantages.' On the British side, Captain Edward Brenton claimed that 'the ships of France and Spain were generally superior to those of England, both in size, weight of metal and number of men, outsailing them both in fleets, and often in single ships, carrying their guns higher out of the water, and in all respects better found for the material of war.' But this was greatly exaggerated, and in any case sailing qualities depended as much on the crews as in any inherent qualities in the design of the ship. Nelson's chase across the Atlantic in July 1805, in which he gained a month on his opponents, should have been enough to dispel any myths about the sailing qualities of his ships. Numerous battles over the last fifty years had shown that the British ships could perform well in practice, including Quiberon Bay in 1759 when the French had been chased in a gale and heavily defeated.

French ship design had been highly innovative in the second quarter of the last century. With vulnerable land frontiers to defend, the army would always take priority and the French realized that they would never be able to outnumber the British in warships. Instead, they allowed a certain amount of initiative to their designers (at the same time when the British shipbuilders were rigidly controlled), they sent naval architects abroad to study design in Britain and the Netherlands, they founded schools of naval architecture and concentrated on the quality of individual ships rather than the navy as a whole. Instead of trying to control the sea for its own sake as the Royal Navy did, they would send out fleets of fast, well-equipped ships on specific missions – to support rebellions in Scotland, Ireland or America, to threaten an attack on Britain or her colonies in India or the Caribbean. In this period they evolved the two standard classes of the rest of the age of sail, the 74-gun ship of the line and the 'true' frigate.

The British had absorbed most of the lessons from the French by 1760, and by that time ship design had reached a plateau within the technology available. French ships were faster in light winds and good conditions, but British ships were far tougher, to withstand the pressures of constant blockade and patrol. British dockyards were far less enthusiastic about French design than sea officers, for they could see their faults when captured ships came back for repair after months at sea. This is not to say that French ships were inferior; they were nearly all well designed for the tasks they were intended to perform.

By the 1780s French design was no longer innovative and there was an increasing tendency to standardize plans down to the last detail. The chief naval architect of the time, Jacques-Noel Sane, produced standard plans for each type of ship. These continued in use through the Revolution and Empire and in 1813 it was noted on a draught of 1788 that it had 'been used without alteration between these two dates for every 80-gun ship built in all the ports of France from Vince to Anvers.' There was nothing inherently wrong with Sane's designs but the French navy did not leave the door open to further experimentation. The British had produced the carronade and had coppered their ships' bottoms, to be copied by the French. At Chatham, Robert Seppings would soon try new systems of construction and transform the whole field of ship design. Smaller navies such as the Danish and Swedish were fertile with ideas. But the French Revolution and the disruption in the navy seems to have reinforced

The plans of Villeneuve's flagship, the Bucentaure.

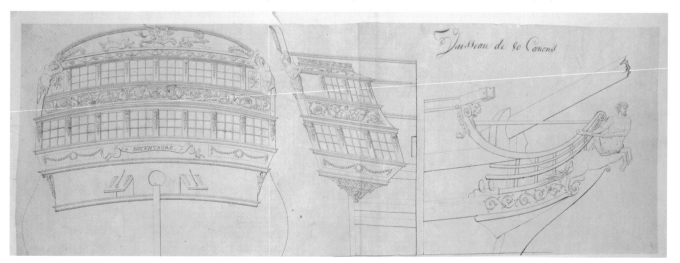

existing prejudices and there was no attempt at improvement by French ship designers.

The French had pioneered building large three-deckers of 110 and 120 guns, but none of these were with the Combined Fleet. All the French ships of the line in Cadiz were two deckers, therefore with better sailing qualities than the British 100s and 98s. Compared with the British fleet outside, which included five different types of ship of the line, the French had only two, 80s and 74s.

Villeneuve's flagship was one of four 80s, the *Bucentaure* of 1803. The type was a logical conclusion to the policy of building the largest possible ship for a given number of decks, for a Sane 80 was 8 feet longer than a 74 by the same designer. The six extra guns were significant, but even more important was the fact that an 80 had 24-pounders on her upper deck, while a 74 had 18-pounders. The broadside weight of a French 80, without carronades, was 1118 pounds in British measurement, compared with 943 for a British 98-gun ship. *Bucentaure* was the newest of the 80s, but none of the French ships were particularly old by British and Spanish standards. The oldest 80 was the *Indomptable*, launched in 1790. She was a private ship without an admiral on board, as was her sister, the *Neptune*; the *Formidable* of 1795 carried Rear-Admiral Dumanoir-le-Pelley, the second-in-command of the fleet.

The thirteen French 74s were as new as the 80s. Of the French-built ships, only the *Argonaute*, *Fougeaux*, *Mont-Blanc* and *Redoutable* were more than five years old. They were as large as any British 74, more than 180 feet long on the gundeck and of about 1800 tons. They had a slightly different armament, with two more guns on the upper deck and two less on the quarterdeck. The French fleet also included two British-built ships, the *Berwick* and *Swiftsure*, still bearing their old names to remind the British of their fallibility. The former, built in Portsmouth Dockyard in 1775, had been taken in 1795 by three French frigates. The *Swiftsure* had been built by Wells of Deptford in 1787 and was captured by a French squadron in 1801. The two ships were sisters to the *Defiance*, which was stationed outside Cadiz. To complete the irony, a new *Swiftsure* had been launched at Buckler's Hard in Hampshire in 1804 and had joined the blockading fleet.

The French ships of the line all had 36-pounder guns on their lower deck. With a different French system of weights, this made them equivalent to 39 pounds in British measure. The 39 pounds took them close to the British 42-pounder gun, already discarded because the ball was too heavy to handle effectively in action. This contributed to the slower rate of fire of the French ships.

Villeneuve's force included five frigates, all French, and all armed with 18-pounders. The French frigate was regarded as a triumph of design, combining medium gun power with excellent sailing qualities, but it shared some of the faults of their ships of the line. French frigates usually had a characteristic V-shaped midsection underwater, compared with the rounder section of British ships.

The poop, quarterdeck and forecastle of the Spanish 74-gun ship Montanes.

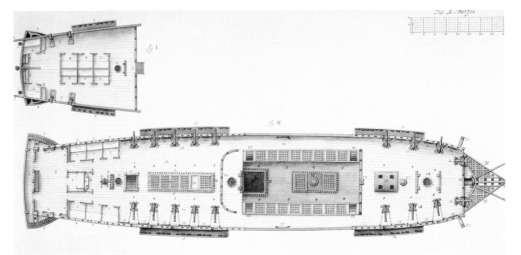

The Spanish ships at Cadiz were much less uniform than the French. There was a mixture of two- and three-deckers; ship design was a reflection of several different influences; obsolete types such as the 64 were still in service, as were several quite old vessels. In a sense they were more like the British than the French, which is not surprising, since Spain had an even larger and more far-flung empire to defend. In a similar style to the British, they went through phases of building cut-price ships to spread thinly round the world. And like the British, they were still able to learn from foreign practices, although by immigration rather than capture. They tended to produce sturdy ships rather than fast ones.

Spanish ship design was divided into three schools of thought, two of which were foreign. The Frenchman, Jean-Francois Gautier, lived in Spain from 1762 and was in charge of naval construction from the end of that decade. He built with light structure and high speed. Alongside this was the 'English' school, led by the Irishman, Matthew Mullan, who was joined by other Roman Catholic or Jacobite exiles, because they had difficulty in finding employment in England. Finally, there was the native Spanish school, headed by the naval architect, Romero y Landa.

The Spanish ships of the line at Cadiz ranged from 64 guns to 130, with three other types in between, including the universal 74 and 80-gun ships. The 130-gun, *Santisima Trinidad*, was an extraordinary ship by any standard. She had been built by Mullan in 1769 in Havana, where the Spanish had supplies of mahogany, which lasted well, and pine for the less essential parts. She was the largest ship in the world from the day of her launch as a 120-gun ship, but in 1795 she was reconstructed with an extra deck, making her the only four-decker ever built. Nelson had already encountered her at St Vincent in 1797, and only just failed to capture her then.

There were three other Spanish three-deckers present. The *Rayo* of 100 guns had been built at Havana in 1749 and was the oldest ship in any of the fleets. The *Principe de Asturias* of 118 guns had been built in the same place in 1793. The *Santa Ana* had been built at Ferrol in 1784. All were fine, powerful ships.

Villeneuve's fleet was not lacking in sea experience. Eight of his ships of the line, including all the 80s, had taken part in the chase across the Atlantic and in the inconclusive battle against Admiral Calder. But this had only reinforced his feeling of inferiority. He was 'not ... able to have any confidence in the state of the equipment of my ships, in their sailing powers, and in their concerted manoeuvres.'[3]

Despite its apparent strength, the Combined Fleet was not comfortable at Cadiz. The ships which had crossed the Atlantic had to repair a certain amount of damage caused by the weather or in Calder's action, such as the 'badly-wounded' foremast of the *Berwick*, the bowsprit of the *Mont-Blanc* and the cutwater in the bows of the *Scipion*. The *Swiftsure*, *Intrepide* and *Mont-Blanc* all had defects in their hulls which could only be remedied, if at all, by long repair in a dry-dock.[4]

On 16 September Villeneuve reviewed the state of the French ships under his command. Of eighteen ships of the line, ten were in good condition. His flagship, *Bucentaure*, was 'Suitable for any kind of employment; she sails well'. The *Algeciras* was 'a fine ship, sailing well', despite 'complaints of her being crazy.' The *Argonaute*, *Duguay-Trouin* and *Redoutable* were fine ships, 'fit for any employment.' *L'Aigle* was mediocre, 'In fairly good condition. An indifferent sailer, which is attributed to her old-fashioned stowage space and the age of her sheathing.' The *Formidable* was similar, for her poor coppering 'gathers barnacles and seaweed like a wooden sheathing.' The *Pluton* was even worse. 'This ship is crank, making much lee-way when close hauled, sailing passably before the wind.' Worst of all was the *Intrepide*. 'Sails very badly, the bottom is very bad.' In all, six of his ships of the line were less than satisfactory.

The crews were even more of a problem. That of the flagship, though it had been 'much weakened by the losses that have been sustained', was 'one of the best in the squadron.' That of *L'Aigle* was 'fairly good', the nucleus of the *Pluton*'s crew was 'very good', but most of the rest were 'weak in crew', largely because illness had reduced their numbers. The *Indomptable* had 'a very bad crew and very weak.'[5] There was no easy way to remedy this. The journey overland from France was long, and it could not be expected that seamen would travel such

A sailor and marine of the Spanish Navy.

a distance without large numbers of desertions, while the British blockade would ensure that no substantial reinforcements could arrive by sea.

The Spanish had begun the eighteenth century with a plan to man their ships with the minimum of compulsion. Fishermen and merchant seamen were to register with the government and be called up in turn, as with the French system, and in return they were given various privileges. This system had been under strain for the last twenty years. The number of seamen on the register remained static at about 65,000 from 1785 onwards and by 1805 it was declining, to reach 40,000 by 1808. Either the real number of seaman was declining, or many were evading naval service by becoming 'vagabond mariners' outside government control. The government attempted to fill out the crews with a levy of landsmen and Villeneuve complained, 'it is very distressing to see such fine ships manned with herdsmen and beggars and having such a small number of seamen.'[6]

After five months without major replenishment the Combined Fleet was already short of almost everything. It needed considerably more if the ships were to be restocked with three months' supplies so that they would be operationally useful. Villeneuve complained of 'the poverty of the port' and feared that the coming winter would reduce supplies even further. M. Le Roy, the French Agent-General in Cadiz, was an unfortunate choice – 'not gifted with a disposition that gains him the attachment of the men with whom he has to do business'. Moreover, French credit was very poor and there was no ready money available. Le Roy could only issue bills to be paid at an indefinite future date. If that was not enough, there was a financial crisis in Spain and the banks had suspended payments. Aid was on the way, in the form of hard cash from Madrid, but that only reached Cadiz on 24 September. Villeneuve's orders demanded that he completed his ships with six months of victuals, but that was impossible. Eventually he found enough for three months, except in ship's biscuit, of which he had only two and a half months supply.[7]

Villeneuve followed the state of the British forces off Cadiz, and studied reports from the lookout post high in the city. On 2 September there was reported to be a squadron of twenty-seven ships of the line and frigates to the south-south-west; the next day this was elaborated as seven three-decker and seventeen two-decker ships of the line, five frigates and two smaller vessels. On 4 September an inshore squadron of five ships of the line and a frigate was identified 'fairly close in' to Cadiz. On 28 September he was informed that the enemy fleet had been increased to thirty-one ships of the line with the arrival of a three-decker (the *Victory*) and two more ships of the line. By 8 October the fleet was aware that their opponents were led by the man they feared most – Admiral Nelson.[8]

A narrow harbour like Cadiz did not allow much chance for training in gunnery but Captain Lucas of the *Redoutable* modified his tactics to take account of this.

My ideas were always directed towards fighting by boarding. I so counted upon its success that every thing had been prepared to undertake it with advantage: I had had canvas pouches to hold two grenades made for all captains of guns, the cross belts of these pouches carried a tin tube containing a small match. In all our drills, I made them throw a great number of paste-board grenades and I often landed the grenadiers in order to have them explode iron grenades … I had 100 carbines fitted with long bayonets on board; the men to whom these were served out were so well accustomed to their use that they climbed halfway up the shrouds to open a musketry fire. All the men armed with swords were instructed in broadsword practice every day and pistol had become familiar arms to them. The grapnels were thrown aboard so skillfully that they succeeded in hooking a ship even though she was not exactly touching us.[9]

The French command structure for naval operations was seriously flawed. The Emperor, all-powerful and triumphant on land, had absolute power over the navy as well, but almost no understanding of how to use it. Napoleon is famously quoted as saying that an army marches on his stomach. More fundamentally, he knew that it moved and fought by the willpower of its leaders. Navies needed willpower, too, as Nelson well knew. But they also needed wind power, a factor which no admiral or emperor could control. A great seaman like Nelson might use the power of the wind to the full, but he would never make detailed plans that failed to take all the possibilities of wind and weather into account.

Under Napoleon was Decres, the Minister of Marine, who longed for something akin to the British set-up, which in fact would have made him less powerful, but less responsible, as an individual.

Napoleon Bonaparte as Emperor of France.

> Deign to form a council for the operations at sea; a board of admiralty, whatever may be agreeable to Your Majesty. But as for myself I feel that instead of being strengthened I am becoming more powerless daily. And to be candid, a Minister of Marine overawed by Your Majesty in those matters which concern the sea, is serving Your Majesty ill and is becoming a cipher as regards the glory of Your arms, if he is not becoming harmful to it.[10]

Decres longed for the situation of Barham, who was trusted implicitly by his political superiors to handle naval matters. But the same problem spread further down, as the Emperor no longer trusted admirals such as Villeneuve. Decres was on the defensive here, after recent failures.

> This business of Villeneuve is distracting me. I view it in the proper light. I can never believe it to be cowardice but rather that he has lost his head. Whichever of Your admirals these events had befallen I should be distressed about it; how much more so when it is to a man with whom I served my first campaign and with whom I have ties and friendship of 25 years standing.
>
> These events make me feel very wretched.[11]

On 2 October Villeneuve attempted to take his fleet out of Cadiz before the enemy fleet became too strong. He produced a rousing declaration for issue to his captains.

> The Fleet will see with satisfaction the opportunity that is offered to us to display that resolution and daring which will ensure its success, revenge the insults offered to its Flag, and lay low the tyrannical domination of the English upon the seas.
>
> Our Allies will fight by our side, under the walls of Cadiz and in the sight of their fellow citizens; the Emperor's gaze is fixed upon us. These motives of emulation are also the guarantees of a day honourable alike to the forces of our respective Sovereigns and to the glory of all the valiant men who will bear their part therein.[12]

The easterly wind turned to a westerly gale and the plan had to be abandoned.

Despite numerous setbacks, Napoleon resolutely clung to hopes of an invasion of Britain until late in August 1805. But relations with old adversaries, the Austrians, were deteriorating and he needed his army to fight them. On 24 August he ordered the camp at Boulogne to be disbanded and the Grand Army to move east.

Exasperated with Villeneuve's failure, Napoleon chose Vice-Admiral Francois Rosily to supersede him on 18 September. Decres wrote to Villeneuve,

> His Majesty the Emperor and King has just appointed Vice-Admiral Rosily to the command of the naval forces assembled at Cadiz and has given orders that you are to proceed to Paris in order to give an account of the campaign on which you have recently been employed.[13]

Communication by land was no faster than by sea, except when visual telegraphs were used. Rosily travelled south slowly from Paris, and by 18 October Villeneuve was aware that he had reached Madrid; 'the common report is that he is coming to take over the command of the Fleet.' Villeneuve was willing to serve as second-in-command under him, even though he must have feared that was not what Napoleon intended: '… it would be too terrible to me to lose all hope of having an opportunity of showing that I am worthy of a better fate.'

There were tactical factors that recommended an early exit from Cadiz. The enemy was clearly growing in strength; the Combined Fleet was not. Nelson was rumoured to be collecting bomb-vessels for an attack on the town and harbour, which might well succeed. Then, on 18 October, Villeneuve received intelligence, which gave him hope that he might succeed in his new mission, which was to support French armies in Italy. A convoy had been seen leaving Gibraltar with four ships of the line, presumably detached from Nelson's fleet, while another ship was under repair at Gibraltar and a sixth had been seen heading for the Rock. In fact they were Admiral Louis's squadron, which had left under protest a few days before. Villeneuve did not know that Nelson had in fact been joined by six more ships since that time, and assumed that his enemy was now down to about twenty-two ships. The wind was coming from the east, which was suitable for leaving Cadiz. It was 'a favourable opportunity to me to get under weigh.' At 8.00 a.m. on 20 October, as his ships headed slowly out of harbour, he wrote to his superiors, sharing the Emperor's fatalism about success in battle;

The whole Squadron is under sail except 3 line of battle ships, which I think are going to follow; …

In thus putting to sea, my Lord, I have only consulted my keen desire to comply with His Majesty's intention and to do my utmost to efface the dissatisfaction with which He has been filled by the events of the late cruise. If this one succeeds, I shall find it hard not to believe that everything was ordained thus, that everything has been combined for the greatest good of His Majesty's service.[14]

CHAPTER 13

The Revenge

The *Revenge* was one of the newest ships in the British fleet. She was launched at Deptford Dockyard in April 1805, to yet another design for a large class 74 by Sir John Henslow. Her construction was peculiarly slow, for she had been ordered nine years earlier and only begun in August 1800. Robert Moorsom was appointed her captain in April 1805, just as the ship was ready for launch. The need for ships was acute, and Moorsom had to get her ready as quickly as possible. On 12 April, the day before her launch, Moorsom commissioned the ship by reading out his orders from the Admiralty. It was not an impressive occasion, for Moorsom was the only commissioned officer who had arrived so far. The boatswain, carpenter, gunner, purser and cook were already on the ship's books, but apart from that there was no crew. The ceremony took place in the ghostly presence of six 'widows' men' – fictitious names entered in the muster books of every ship at the rate of one per hundred of the crew, whose wages would be paid into a fund for widows of men killed in action.

On 13 April the ship was launched into the River Thames and hauled alongside the hulk *Batavia*, a captured Dutchman. Despite his almost complete lack of human resources, Moorsom was now responsible for fitting the ship out and manning her. His first instinct was to turn to his old ship, the *Majestic*, now in dry-dock. He asked the Admiralty if her crew, already well known to him, could be transferred to the *Revenge*. The Admiralty had its own plans and replied that 'measures will be taken' to man the *Revenge*. Meanwhile, large teams of dockyard workers and men from ships under refit were sent out to get the masts, yards, rigging and sails of the new ship. On 4 May there were only thirty-three men borne in the

The Revenge *in later life, drawn by T. Robinson of Gosport.*

ship's company, including about twenty officers and Moorsom's three servants, transferred from the *Majestic*. There were also seven boys and forty-four marines, plus 126 'supernumeraries', the men from the dockyards and the other ships.

The dockyard riggers did their work and a month after her launch the ship was ready to sail 15 miles down the Thames to Long Reach near Dartford, where the even heavier task of fitting her guns would be carried out. These were brought out by tender from the Ordnance Depot at Woolwich. The barrels of the heaviest guns, the 32-pounders of the lower deck, weighed 2½ tons each. They were hoisted in one by one using tackles rigged from the yardarms and then hauled in through the gunports and lowered on to the wooden carriages. There was little relief when the lower deck was finished on 24 May, for the 24-pounders of *Revenge*'s upper deck weighed 2¾ tons each. There was a problem with the lighter guns of the forecastle. Moorsom had prepared the ship for 12-pounders but the Ordnance Depot sent 9-pounders. The Admiralty, perhaps feeling it had been bothered by too many letters from Moorsom, told him that 9-pounders were what the establishment said and he would have to make do with them.

The actual crew of the *Revenge* remained very small – just forty-four men on 31 May, plus twenty-nine boys and 110 marines. Moorsom was concerned about his lack of officers. Lieutenants Hole, Pickernell and Harford had not yet joined, though their Admiralty orders had instructed them to 'make all possible haste' in getting to their ship. Moorsom asked the Admiralty to order them to their duty. Their lordships did not want a new and powerful ship of the line left inactive during a developing naval crisis, so they went one step further. They took three lieutenants out of ships in the area without waiting for them to be superseded by others, and sent them to the *Revenge*. Thus John Holcombe left the sloop, *L'Utile*, while John Berry was taken out of the storeship *Serapis*. On 5 June, as the *Revenge* was ready to put to sea, the ship was still short and Moorsom wanted to give a temporary commission to John Campbell, a master's mate, but Lieutenants Hole and Pickernell turned up soon afterwards and the ship finally had its complement of six lieutenants.

In the first week of June the ship sailed 20 miles further down river to the great naval anchorage at the Nore, and large drafts of men were sent from the receiving ship *Zealand*, which was almost permanently anchored there to hold seamen pressed from merchant ships entering the Thames. By 8 June the *Revenge* had a total of 618 in her crew, including 480 officers, seamen, landsmen, servants and artificers, twenty-eight boys and 110 marines. By 17 June she had 629 on her muster book, little short of the complement of 640.

The drafts from the *Zealand* included two young men with their own stories to tell. John Martingale Powell wrote regularly to his mother, 'Next door to the Assembly House, Battle Bridge, Pentonville, near Bagnigge Wells, London.' He was twenty-one years old and had served in East India Company ships. He had already spent several weeks in the *Zealand* but was not discontented, although, as he told his mother, 'blasphemy reigns' and he was unable to read his Bible as recommended.

I once attempted to pass part of the day in such manner as I ought well convinced that nothing will prosper without it but I was interrupted so many times that I thought it better to do no good myself rather than make others do worse so I imploy this time in writing to you.

When a draft of men was sent on board the 64-gun ship *Stately*, Powell was pleased not to be with them as the officers of the ship had 'a very bad character'. Instead he was sent to the *Revenge* on 5 June.

Powell was pleased that he was a volunteer for the navy. As such he was treated better than the pressed men who arrived in tenders when he was in the *Zealand*. He heard a rumour that a large East India Fleet had been captured in June 1805. It was untrue, as was the report that Nelson had taken ten ships of the line with very little loss, but Powell was grateful not to be in a relatively defenceless merchant ship. Furthermore, the naval ships were better manned. While the *Revenge* was at anchor in the Downs he wrote,

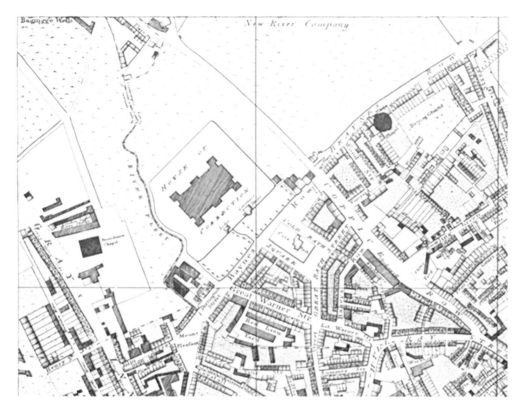

A detail from William Faden's map of London, 1813, showing the area where Powell lived.

We keep watch the same here as at sea, ie four hours up and the same down. I am in the starboard watch so that when the larboard watch is on in a morning we can sleep till 7 or 8 o'clock and sometimes longer, which I could not do in an Indiaman. We have very little work to do and plenty of men to assist when any work is to be done. Some days we have but little to do but on others nobody would believe that is unused to the sea what a hurry we are all in. As a proof of it, last Monday I ate one part of my breakfast upon deck, another in the mizzen top and finished it on the mizzen topsail yard.

One might suspect that Powell presented an optimistic picture to reassure his mother, but other phrases must have caused her heart to sink. Powell acknowledged that she was 'so much concerned for my safety', but he also wrote that 'a man of war is much better in war time than an Indiaman for we laugh at and seek the danger they have so much reason to dread and avoid.' Later he was anxious to get to sea again, for 'French hunting … is a glorious sport.'

Powell was a mizzen topman, with the right combination of age and experience to work aloft, albeit on the smallest of the ship's three masts. In action he was stationed at one of the 32-pounder guns on the lower deck, and was proud of the heavy armament, that his ship was 'of great force'. He had 'the most agreeable shipmates that can be.' He had no enemies on board, 'they either love me or fear me.' As a literate seaman he was able to write letters for his messmates, which increased his popularity, but gave him a dilemma.

I have been requested by one of the women on board to write out a certificate of marriage between her and one of the men, she telling me she had forgot to bring the right one with her on board and that she might perhaps have occasion for it she should be glad if I would make one out and she would direct me how to draw it up but this I absolutely refused to do well knowing the consequence of forgery.

This is a rare reference to women serving on board ship at this time. It was quite common for them to come on board while a ship was in port, and indeed the Admiralty orders expressly allowed seamen's wives to visit them. This was generally interpreted rather liberally, except by Lord Gambier, before he joined the Board of Admiralty. While a captain he had enforced the rule that 'none but married women' were allowed to visit the men on board ship. In almost all other ships, local prostitutes made a habit of visiting, and the scene was described by Powell's shipmate, William Robinson.

> On the arrival of any man of war in port, these girls flock down to the shore, where boats are always ready; and here may be witnessed a scene, somewhat similar to the trafficking for slaves in the West Indies. As they approached a boat, old Charon … surveys them from stem to stern, with the eyes of a bargaining jew; and carefully culls out the best looking, and the most dashingly dressed. …

> After having moored out ship, swarms of boats came round us; … a great many were freighted with cargoes of ladies, a sight that was most gratifying, and a great treat. … So soon as these boats were allowed to come alongside, the seamen flocked down pretty quick, one after the other, and brought their choice up, so that in the course of the afternoon, we had four hundred and fifty on board.[1]

Although this was common enough at Spithead, the Downs or Torbay, it was not a privilege that the men of the Mediterranean Fleet enjoyed. The lands around the Maddelena Islands were sparsely populated and difficult of access, and Nelson had no intention of drawing too much attention to his presence. It is unlikely that the men of the *Victory* enjoyed feminine company of any kind during their two years with the fleet.

During Nelson's Nile campaign of 1798, it had clearly been quite common for women to go to sea as wives of crew members, though the regulations decreed that ships were 'not to carry any woman to sea … without orders from the Admiralty.' Seaman John Nicol of the *Goliath* noted that in battle 'the women behaved as well as the men', and his captain, Thomas Foley, risked the wrath of the Admiralty's accountants by putting four of them on the muster roll for victuals after the battle. Many years later a few women applied for medals for the Battle of the Nile and were refused on the grounds that it would open the way to innumerable applications.

But there are almost no references to women at sea during the Trafalgar period, except

An unflattering view of women coming on board a ship.

for the one by Powell. Robinson makes it clear that women were not to be found in the *Revenge* later on, when he wrote, '… our crew, consisting of six hundred and upwards, nearly all young men, had seen one woman on board for eighteen months, and that was the daughter of one of the Spanish chiefs, who made no stay on board …'[2] On board the Britannia, Lieutenant Halloran wrote a poem highlighting the irony of the situation and read it to an audience which included Rear-Admiral the Earl of Northesk.

> My Lord and Gentlemen – alas! off Cadiz,
> How hard it is we can't address the Ladies!
> For 'if the brave alone deserve the fair,'
> BRITANNIA'S Sons should surely have their share![3]

Clearly there had been some significant cultural shift in the seven years since the Nile. Certainly Barham and Gambier at the Admiralty would have enforced this if they had the power, but there is no sign of any stream of orders from the Admiralty. In any case it was mainly a matter for individual captains. Those of Nelson's 1805 fleet were evidently of a different generation, looking forward to Victorian primness rather than backward to Georgian licentiousness.

Powell continued to take an interest in the opposite sex ashore, unlike his colleague, Robinson, whose nickname of 'Jack Nastyface' hinted at a lack of personal charm. Powell was surprised and pleased to hear that Miss E. Page was married, as it would be 'the means of preventing her pursuing the road to ruin.' Mrs Powell was keen that her son keep up his hopes with 'Miss Y', but he replied,

> I have long since renounced them in favour of a gentleman 'worth thousands', never-theless it would be some consolation to a (real) lover to hear that his mistress was not engaged for life to such an old and superannuated figure as he is I am much incensed against him but I will not say any more on the subject lest if I do you should suspect me of being more enraged than I really am.

Powell also declared his love for Miss Springwell, but rebuked his mother.

> I must stop to reproach you for writing her name so obscurely, which I dare say you did intentionally for it was almost half an hour before I could find it out, which greatly perplexed me. I mounted my stilts and did not get down for a good while. Present my love to her and tell her I sincerely hope she and her father are well but as for her mother it is vain to hope she has not got some indisposition.

Robinson, aged twenty from Farnham in Surrey, was also a seaman of moderate experience when he arrived on board the *Revenge*. He had volunteered in London in May 1805, but repented when he was sent down to the hold of the receiving ship off the Tower of London to spend the night 'with my companions in wretchedness, and the rats running over us in numbers.' Things did not improve next morning when he and nearly 200 companions were put into a tender to take them down river to the fleet.

> Upon getting on board this vessel, we were ordered down in the hold, and the gratings put over us; as well as a guard of marines placed round the hatchway, with their muskets loaded and fixed bayonets, as though we had been culprits of the first degree, or capital convicts. In this place we spent the day and the following night huddled together, for there was not room to sit or stand separate; indeed, we were in a pitiable plight, for numbers of them were sea-sick, some retching, others were smoking, whilst many were so overcome by the stench, that they fainted for want of air.

The tender finally arrived at the Nore, where two men tried to desert by swimming ashore

An engraving by I. C. Schetky showing a woman looking at casualties on board a warship.

with their clothes tied round their necks. One got away, the other stuck in the mud and had to be rescued by a boat. The rest, including Robinson, were drafted on board the *Zealand* at anchor there, and he went with a draft to the *Revenge* on 5 June, the same day as Powell.

More than thirty years later, Robinson published a rather scurrilous, but not inaccurate book under the name of Jack Nastyface, about his time in the *Revenge*. Yet most of his complaints were directed at Captain Charles Elphinstone Fleming, who succeeded Moorsom early in 1806. His only real complaint during the Moorsom period was about the tyranny of a young midshipman.

> He was a youth of not more than twelve or thirteen years of age: but I have often seen him get on the carriage of a gun, call a man to him, and kick him about the thighs and body, and with his fist would beat him about the head; and these, though prime seamen, at the same time dared not murmur.

This was Edward F. Brook, registered in the muster book as thirteen years old. He was probably a protégé of the Captain, for he was a fellow Yorkshireman. Robinson's account has been cited as an example of persistent naval tyranny, for example in John Masefield's *Sea Life in Nelson's Time* of 1905, but there is no indication of how often this happened during the four and a half months in which Brooks and Robinson were together in the *Revenge*. During a rapid expansion of the navy, which brought it from 50,000 men in 1803 to 120,000 in 1805, there must have been many appointments of unsuitable officers.

Moorsom was one of the least famous of Nelson's captains. The son of a magistrate in Whitby, Yorkshire, he had enjoyed the support of Constantine Phipps, later Lord Mulgrave, who had also been Nelson's superior during an Arctic exploration voyage in the 1770s. He had seen much service as a midshipman in the War of Independence and had served in peacetime in the West Indies as captain of the Astrea frigate. He had commanded the *Hindustan* of 54 guns during the last war, but had seen little action. Moorsom's presence at Trafalgar would earn him a place in James Ralfe's four-volume collection of biographies of distinguished naval officers, but even that eulogist could find little to say about him, devoting half the entry to a general dissertation about the virtues of naval officers.

Moorsom took a good deal of kindly interest in the men under him, and was prepared to risk rebuff by the Lords of the Admiralty in pressing their cases. As he parted with his old crew of the *Majestic* in April 1805, he wrote several letters to the Admiralty about their welfare. James Ford of Penzance was an unusually rich seaman who had come into £550 on his twenty-first birthday, but there was no sign of the money from his father's executors. The Admiralty replied that it was nothing to do with them. Seaman James Dickinson was even wealthier and Moorsom asked the Admiralty to give him leave of absence to try to sell his property at Blackwall near London, which had been valued at £700 before he was impressed into the navy. William Gally had served eleven years and was well qualified for a gunner's warrant. Moorsom arranged permission for him to go to London for the examination, but his certificate of service had gone astray during frequent moves and Moorsom advocated his case.

As he moved into the *Revenge*, Moorsom found himself dealing with various pressed men. Henry Wigmore was a native of Hanover so not liable for service, but he had accepted the King's bounty, so the Admiralty ruled that he had to stay. Samuel Worthington Bradbury was an apprentice from Putney who had enlisted under the false name of Taylor, but he, too, had taken the bounty and had to stay. Robert Telford, chief mate of the collier *Friends of Sunderland*, had been taken against the law and was to be released. Daniel McKerley had once worked as an usher in Burney's Naval Academy in Gosport and Moorsom wanted him appointed as schoolmaster of the *Revenge*; but the Admiralty ruled this out, as he had not passed the examination at Trinity House. Seaman Michael Moore had allotted some of his wages to his family but part of the money seemed to have gone astray. Again the Admiralty, becoming more impatient with Moorsom's letters, wrote back that it was nothing to do with them. It is not surprising that John Powell regarded his captain as having a 'very admirable disposition.'

On 8 June 1805 the *Revenge* raised her anchor and sailed from the Nore. She anchored for a week at the Downs to await a favourable wind to take her down the English Channel. Local traders were allowed to come on board by boat and Powell found much dishonesty around him.

> ... Any inexperienced person may be taken in by a set of abominable wretches like them when the men received their money they were ready to tear themselves to pieces to buy them new things. One man belonging to another ship had received one hundred pounds and getting drunk the next morning he lost it all every farthing. On the day appointed for payment about two hundred jews came on board bringing with them all sorts of slop, watches, hats, rings, lockets, telescopes etc. It was exactly like a fair. There was also provisions of all sorts to be sold together with gingerbread and cakes which many of the men were fools enough to buy. One man gave eight guineas for a watch and the next morning he found it was good for nothing. Another gave thirty shillings for a hat that was not worth 12, so that's the way that they are always so poor or they usually are. One man got his pocket picked out of twenty six pounds and marine got a flogging for robbing his messmate of six and twenty shilling, but that is only a specimen of their tricks. As for me, as soon as I got mine I locked it up.

But he did indulge himself in buying a cake and some soap for 4 shillings. 'I have got the character of a miser and credit of having plenty of money for they are all very sure I did not spend it and must have it.'

At Spithead the *Revenge* took on more stores, and by the time she sailed on 16 July, she had 224 tons of water in 478 casks at the bottom of the hold, along with 14 tons of beer in thirty-two casks, 4 tons of wine and 16 of spirits. On top of the water in the hold she had 3832 pieces of beef weighing 13 tons, 7558 pieces of pork at about the same weight, as well as casks of peas, suet, oatmeal, flour and raisins. The butts, puncheons, hogsheads, barrels and firkins themselves weighed a total of 63 tons, rather more than the crew of 640 men and their belongings at 47 tons. Bread (45 tons) and cheese were stored in bags rather than casks. There was nearly a ton of candles, 45 tons of wood and 50 of coal for the galley stove, and $2^{1/4}$ tons of slop clothing for the crew. Fully fitted and stored for foreign service, the *Revenge* drew 24 feet 6 inches of water at her stern, and the lowest point of her gunports was 5 feet 3 inches out of the water.[4]

The *Revenge* had a new and inexperienced crew, men who had never served together before, and many who had never served in the navy. It was the reverse of hand-picked, for the Captain had had to accept the drafts sent to him by the *Zealand* and other ships.

Moorsom was doing his best to pull them into shape, but his log suggests that it was not going well. His first flogging in the *Revenge* was on 24 May at Long Reach, when the ship was still manned almost entirely by supernumeraries. John Conly was punished for 'breaking into the hold and broaching beer', a fairly serious offence in any captain's book. On 27 June, after the regular crew had taken over, two men were punished for insolence and contempt, and after that floggings at the gangway took place once or twice a week. William Robinson was careful in his description of such occasions.

> About eleven o'clock, or six bells, when any of the men are in irons, or on the black list, the boatswain or mate are ordered to call all hands; the culprits are then brought forward by the master at arms .... All hands now being mustered, the captain orders the man to strip; he is then seized to a grating by the wrists and knees; his crime is then mentioned, and the prisoner may plead, but, in nineteen cases out of twenty, he is flogged for the most trifling offence or neglect.

Captain Capel of the *Phoebe* describes the procedure on board his ship in more detail. A few years after the great mutinies, he was taking no chances of sparking a revolt.

> In time of punishment the Marine Guard to be under arms on the quarterdeck, the marines paraded on the gangways, the officers to be in uniform, the mates and warrant officers in the waist to mix with the people and a lieutenant to attend in the outer rank to see no irregularity committed and every person … attentive during punishment and any irregular behaviour among the people to be immediately reported.[5]

Moorsom was usually quite moderate in the amount of lashes he awarded, often giving six rather than the more common twelve; but on 25 July he gave one seaman twenty-four lashes for drunkenness. In the middle of August one man was forced to run the gauntlet for theft, a punishment described by Robinson.

> The criminal is placed with his naked back in a large tub, wherein a seat has been fixed, and his hands lashed down his sides: this tub is secured on a grating, and is drawn

The plans of a pressing tender, c. 1800, showing the stoutly-constructed 'Room for Imprest Men' below decks.

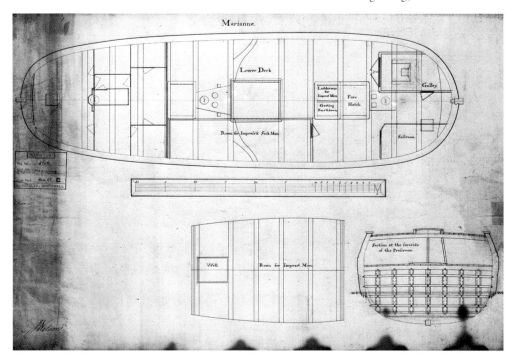

The Point of Honor.

Gᵉᵒ Cruikshank feᶜᵗ

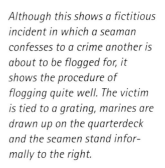

Although this shows a fictitious incident in which a seaman confesses to a crime another is about to be flogged for, it shows the procedure of flogging quite well. The victim is tied to a grating, marines are drawn up on the quarterdeck and the seamen stand informally to the right.

round the decks by the boys, the master-at-arms with his drawn sword pointing to the prisoner's breast. The cavalcade starts from the break of the quarter-deck, after the boatswain has given the prisoner a dozen lashes, and the ship's crew are ranged round the decks in two rows, so that the prisoner passes between them, and each man is provided with a three yarn knettle; that is, three rope yarns tightly laid together and knotted. With this, each man must cut him, or be thought implicated in the theft.

The *Revenge* was a fine ship. Even Captain Codrington, despite natural pride in his own ship, had to admit that. '"Orion" sailed yesterday I think better than anything excepting "Revenge", whose superiority is very conspicuous.'[6] But her discipline had not improved by the time she arrived off Cadiz on 30 August, to join Admiral Collingwood. Just three days later one marine was given six lashes for gambling, and four seamen and five marines were given a dozen each for drunkenness.

CHAPTER 14

Officers

In contrast to the seamen, the Royal Navy never had any difficulty in recruiting officers. While the seamen hid from the press gang in every nook and cranny, the waiting room of the Admiralty was a hive of activity with officers soliciting appointments. Captain Edward Rotherham complained of 'Being obliged after having attended daily at the Admiralty for three years soliciting a ship to repair at a moment's notice with an acting order for one, ready for sea at Plymouth …'.[1]

Several conditions were needed to make a career in the naval profession possible. A candidate needed enthusiasm and ability, as well as good naval connections. Love of the sea was clearly an important draw and was sometimes found in a boy from a non-naval family. John Franklin was brought up in Spilsby, Lincolnshire, 11 miles from the sea. A holiday visit to Saltfleet at the age of twelve fascinated him and attracted him to a sailor's life. His father resisted – 'he would rather follow his son to the grave than to sea' – but after two years he was persuaded to let him go on a merchant voyage from Hull to Lisbon. This only reinforced the boy's wishes. His father gave way and entered him as a Volunteer First Class in the 64-gun *Polyphemus*.[2]

The waiting room at the Admiralty in peacetime, with officers soliciting appointments, by Marryat and Cruikshank.

A commission in the navy offered a unique way to serve king and country with the highest honour, while still providing the chance to make large sums of money. It was particularly attractive to members of the aristocracy, especially younger sons who had to make their own way in the world, or those from impoverished branches of the nobility, especially in Scotland, who hoped to restore family fortunes without descending into commerce. It was equally attractive to rising commercial and professional families from the middle class, who could gain honour by service to the King, without losing sight of the need to make money. Jane Austen's Sir Walter Elliot objected to the navy 'as being the means of bringing persons of obscure birth into undue distinction, and raising men to honours which their fathers and grandfathers never dreamt of.'[3]

It was not the salary alone that attracted young men. Officers often had to pay their own expenses, including uniforms, travel to and from their ships, and food consumed in excess of the normal ships' provisions as issued to the seamen. Edward Rotherham, as a lieutenant in the 1790s, complained about the cost of this. He spent nearly £20 travelling from his home in the north of England to Plymouth, and £2 more for lodgings while his ship was got ready. He had to pay a guinea (£1.05) for his commission, and then £7.15.0 (£7.75) for his uniform plus a greatcoat, fourteen shirts, a gold-laced hat, twelve pairs of stockings, six pairs of shoes and one of boots. If he was going to the West Indies he would need three waistcoats and breeches to suit the climate, plus two pairs of 'Muskito trousers'. He needed a telescope, a sword and belt, a speaking trumpet, and 6 pounds of hair powder (although that was probably out of fashion by 1805). He might pay £6.18.0 (£6.90) towards wardroom furniture, and £10 as his first contribution to the provisions and stores for the officers. He took 5 guineas (£5.25) for pocket money, making a total cost of over £90. Rotherham complained that this was more than a year's pay of £72. 'This good officer hath served one whole year in defence of his King and country, his clothes worn out and stock exhausted, finds himself in debt £18/17/101/2'.

It was the chance of prize money that made the economic position of officers acceptable. Frederick Hoffman's mother was persuaded to let her son go to the navy after consulting a naval friend.

'Do you really think, Captain Elphinstone,' said my mother, with a half-sorrowful countenance, 'that it would be to his advantage?' 'Most assuredly,' replied he, 'as I think it very likely war will soon be declared against that unhappy and distracted France, and he will have a very fair chance of making prize money, and in time will gain his promotion.'

'Quit the room for a short time, my love,' said my mother to me. In about a quarter of an hour, which I thought an hour, I was sent for. Captain Elphinstone had taken his leave. I found my mother still very pale. 'I am afraid, dear boy,' she began, 'that Captain Elphinstone has almost persuaded me against my will. He has spoken of the prospects of the Naval Service in so favorable a manner that I am nearly tempted to let you enter it, and should war unhappily be declared against our unfortunate neighbours, the French, and my friend Captain Markham be appointed to a ship, I believe I must make up my mind to be persuaded and let you have your wish.'

A parent did not have to pay directly for a boy's entry to the navy, but he would have to find money for his uniform, instruments, books and travel. In May 1804 Nelson estimated this at £70 to £100, 'besides his yearly stipend.' John Franklin's elder brother resented the time he spent 'continually running after this nasty cloaths-buying business' but was proud of John's final appearance; 'the dirk and cocked hat, which are certainly very formidable, are among the most attractive parts of the dress.'[4]

At the end of 1803 Captain Hardy of the *Victory* agreed to find a place for John Mansfield, son of his friend the Mayor of Dorchester.

If your son John is determined to go to Sea the sooner the better I think. It will be necessary for you to point out to him all the inconveniencies attending to our profession, & that he must make up his mind to encounter numberless hardships; with that & a good constitution I have no doubt but he will do very well.

Hardy found him a berth in the *Defiance* under Captain Phillip Durham, who 'pays particular attention to the education of his youngsters & himself is very clever in his profession.' The boy arrived in the Mediterranean a few months later and made a promising start. As Hardy comments in a letter to his father,

John appears quite satisfied with his situation & has got the better of Sea Sickness. He Dined yesterday with Lord Nelson … you may depend on my taking every care of him, & you may make yourself quite easy about his money concerns, all that I will strictly attend to. Captain [Durham] speaks very highly of his Disposition and I have no doubt he will do very well.[5]

As well as financial and naval support from his own family, an ambitious officer needed to develop his relationships within the navy, which was, in effect, a series of overlapping groups of interests. There was no formal training scheme. Each captain had his own way of training his officers – though some had no system at all. Captain Capel of the *Phoebe* was one of the longest-established members of the Band of Brothers, but Nelson had doubts about his style of leadership. 'Capel, although, I am sure, very kind to younkers, I do not think, has the knack of keeping them in high discipline; he lets them be their own masters too much.' Hardy lamented that his nephew had been 'so much neglected' in the frigate *Ambuscade* under Captain –, though he 'appeared quite clean' when he came on board the *Victory*.[6]

On the other hand, Captain Codrington of the 74-gun *Orion* allowed the youngsters

A young man, on the ladder to the right, is shocked on his first introduction to the midshipmen's berth.

… to take charge of the deck in the day time, taking care of course, that he or the Commander or First Lieutenant or Master were in sight, in case of anything going wrong. Nothing so habituates a young boy to consider the nature and casualties of his profession or his practice. A squall to windward, what shall I do? Are the men at their stations to shorten sail? A vessel is crossing us will she weather? Are we on tack to bear up or hold the wind? Are the yards properly braced up, and the bowlines hauled? Are the topgallant sheets home and the jib taut up? What shall I do if the captain tells me to shorten, or make sail? And a thousand such like cogitations exercise a boy's mind in a way which walking to leeward and repeating orders could never affect.[7]

Apart from the quality of his training, the very speed of a young man's introduction to the navy might be bewildering. Frederick Hoffman had never seen a ship of the line before October 1793, when he saw a squadron of twelve anchored at Spithead as he was rowed out to join the frigate *Blonde*. His ship sailed within days and was soon in action with a French frigate. A few weeks later he was in the West Indies, having crammed more experience into his first two months than a shore-based brother would see in a lifetime.[8] Archibald Nagle joined the *Royal Sovereign* as a Volunteer First Class on 2 September 1805, and was in a great fleet battle seven weeks later.[9]

Not all young men found a seagoing career to their taste. Most ships had about eight midshipmen and captain's servants for every commissioned officer, so it was clear that not all of them would make the grade. Many, in fact would drop out after a voyage or two. Early in 1805 Hardy wrote of a protégé, 'I think my nephew John has acted a very wise part in quitting the Navy, for I fear his delicate constitution would not have agreed with our very rough and uncertain service.'[10] Another unsuitable young man was found in the *Bellerophon* in the same year, and his officer wrote of him,

> Young Markland does not appear to be near so well calculated for a sea life and as he wishes to follow some profession in preference, I am of opinion his friends would do well to allow him to do so, as he is quite young and this is his first trip to sea. He is a very fine boy but too mild and delicate to encounter the variety of unpleasant occurrences to which a sailor is exposed.[11]

As he neared the end of the six years' service, a midshipman might be promoted to master's mate with an increase in pay, though it did nothing to increase the formal chances of promotion. In the *Defiance*, Master's Mate James Spratt had a reputation as a dashing young man. He was known for rescuing men from the sea; for the great majority of seamen could not swim and the officers, fearing desertion, did not encourage them to learn. In one case he saved a swimmer from two sharks by distracting them with food dropped elsewhere. When Seaman Owen Davies, 'a huge fellow and Welshman' fell asleep on the cathead in a flat calm and dropped into the water, Spratt was soon in beside him. 'I soon had him under the fore chains and got him on board, wide awake and not much the worse of his dip.'

Spratt, an Irishman from near Dublin, was immensely proud of his skill as a swordsman and in less formal means of fighting and was encouraged by Captain Durham. A party of seamen was trained to be useful in the event of boarding an enemy ship, when hand-to-hand fighting would be needed. Spratt taught them French and English styles of swordplay with the cutlass, 'which I was pretty expert at, and which the seamen were very deficient in those days.' He mixed in some instruction in his own country's weapon, the 'shilela' as he spelled it. He worked long hours with them, 'in my watch or not' and boasted that they could 'pick any tooth out of an enemy's jaw without disturbing the one next to it.' Durham was pleased and told Spratt that 'if we came into action he intended giving me an opportunity of signalizing myself.'

William Badcock was appointed to the 98-gun *Neptune* in May 1805 and Captain Thomas Fremantle decided to give him a chance at the lieutenant's examination. He was sent to Somerset House in London, the main office for several departments of the navy, and found himself before three captains, including Sir Andrew Snape Hammond, 'whose character for turning mids back frightened me not a little.' He encountered a failed midshipman on his way out, and entered in a state of great nervousness. The captains were civil and allowed him to sit for a few minutes to regain his composure. The questioning began.

> I was desired to stand up, and consider myself on the quarter-deck of a man-of-war at

A deck scene with the rain coming down and the young midshipman in the foreground regretting his lack of warm clothes.

Spithead – 'unmoor' – 'get underway' – 'stand out to sea' – 'make and shorten sail' – 'reef' – 'return into port' – 'unrig the foremast and bowsprit, and rig them again.' I got into a scrape after reefing for not overhauling the reef tackles when hoisting the sails. However, they passed me, and desired me to come again the next day to receive my passing certificate. I made the captains the best bow I could, and, without staying to look behind me, bolted out of the room, and was surrounded in a moment by the other poor fellows, who were anxiously waiting their turn to be called in for examination, who asked what questions had been put to me, and the answers I made, &c.

But for the moment there was no vacancy for a lieutenant and Badcock remained in the *Neptune* as a 'passed midshipman'.

Lieutenants could come from a broad social range. Some men were commissioned from the lower deck; others came from lower middle-class backgrounds. Richard Spear, lieutenant of the *Conqueror* in 1805, was a bank clerk in Dublin before he entered the navy 'under the auspices of the first Lord Gardner, and was subsequently patronized by the Marquis of Hastings.' A single wardroom could include men from many backgrounds. In October 1805 the *Spartiate* had two lieutenants from the highest ranks of society. Frederick Thomas, acting lieutenant, was the son of a baronet of Glamorgan and Hon. Michael de Courcy, a supernumerary lieutenant travelling as a passenger, was the third son of the Irish peer Lord Kinsale. James Clephan, the second lieutenant, came from a very different background. A Scot from Fife, he had served his apprenticeship in merchantmen and was employed as a mate in 1794 when he was pressed into the navy as an able seaman. After fifteen months he reached the quarterdeck as a master's mate and he was promoted lieutenant in 1801 after conspicuous gallantry in 'cutting out' a French corvette near Brest. His immediate superior, John McKerlie, the first lieutenant, was another Scot who claimed descent from a medieval warrior. Of the warrant officers the purser, Digory Forrest, was the son of an official of the naval Victualling Office and was later knighted.

Officers, as beneficiaries of the British class system, were usually keen to keep it intact when possible. When it was found that a young man 'of genteel family, with good expectations' had enlisted as a marine, Nelson ordered his discharge from one of the ships under his command.

The most vital and demanding duty of a lieutenant, apart from the first lieutenant, was to serve as officer of the watch, taking charge of the ship for a four-hour spell. His most important task was the efficient sailing of the ship. According to Captain Capel's orders for the *Phoebe*, 'The officers of the watch are to pay the strictest attention that the sails are well set, topsail sheets close home, jib and staysails taut up, and whenever a jib or staysail is hauled down, it is to be immediately neatly stowed.' He was to muster the men twice during each watch and to keep them on deck, except in bad weather when they were allowed to shelter under the half-deck.[12]

Outside watchkeeping hours, a lieutenant was in charge of a division of the ship's company, of perhaps a hundred men. Divisions were assembled at least once a week on most ships, and the officers inspected the clothing and the cleanliness of the men.

Nelson had two admirals under him in October 1805, plus twenty-five captains of ships of the line, four frigate captains, two lieutenants in acting command of ships of the line and two lieutenants in command of smaller vessels. Captains tended to be slightly higher in the social scale than the lieutenants, for naval and political patronage counted for a good deal. But of the twenty-eight admirals and captains in the fleet, only three came from the highest ranks in society. Admiral Northesk was an earl himself, and Thomas Bladen Capel of the *Phoebe* was the son of an earl. George Johnstone Hope of the *Defence* was a grandson of the Earl of Hopetoun. About a dozen of the others were the sons of landowners, including Eliab Harvey of the *Temeraire*, whose father was also an MP, and Henry Blackwood of the *Euryalus*, whose father was a baronet. Like Nelson, Henry Digby of the *Africa* was the son of a clergyman, but not just a country parson – he was the Dean of Durham and a Chaplain to the King. Edward Rotherham of the *Royal Sovereign* was the son of a doctor, and Edward Berry of the *Agamemnon* and Cuthbert Collingwood were sons of merchants. Henry William Bayntum of the *Leviatha*n was the son of a diplomat, the British consul-general in Algiers.

A large proportion had naval ancestry of one kind or another, which was always useful in a career at sea. Francis Laforey of the *Spartiate* was the son of an admiral, as was Richard King of the *Achille*. James Nicoll Morris of the *Colossus* was the son of a naval captain, and the father of the *Conqueror*'s Israel Pellew was rather lower in the scale as the captain of a Dover packet boat. The father of John Cooke of the *Bellerophon* had been a cashier in the Admiralty. Only William Prowse of the *Sirius* had come up the hard way. He had joined the navy as an able seaman in 1771 and did not become a midshipman for seven years.

Most of the captains of the ships of the line were in their forties and had served nine to fifteen years in the rank; though the flag captains – Thomas Hardy of the *Victory*, Edward Rotherham and Charles Bullen of the *Britannia* – had only seven, five and three years seniority. Some with rather poor connections or undistinguished abilities – William Prowse, Richard Grindall of the *Prince* and Edward Rotherham – were in their fifties as they had not reached the rank of captain until quite late in life. Conversely, the younger captains were usually well connected. Laforey and King, the admirals' sons, were thirty-eight and thirty-one. Hope and Blackwood, from titled families, were thirty-eight and thirty-five, while Digby, with connections in the church and at court, was thirty-five.

The four frigate captains had less seniority in the rank than those in command of ships of the line, as might be expected. Blackwood was the most senior, with ten years in the rank, and from that point of view he was well qualified to command a ship of the line. Capel and Thomas Dundas of the *Naiad* had seven years, while Prowse, a lower deck entry, had eight years.[13]

Every one of the captains had been in action several times and some, like Hardy, had fought in many of the most famous actions of the last twelve years. Three quarters of them had already been in at least one fleet battle during the previous two wars.

In contrast to the military side of naval life, every officer had a great deal of paperwork to do. In order to claim his pay, a captain had to present a large number of forms and books. In July 1804 Captain Bayntum sent in his books and papers for the last year in command of the *Leviathan* – twenty-eight documents, including ship's logs, lists of the ship's company and their financial affairs in different forms – '1 ship's book, complete, 1 alphabetical list, 1 complete book' – the expense books and the 'supplies and returns' of the warrant officers such as the boatswain, carpenter, gunner and purser, reports on the remaining stores of warrant officers who had been relieved, and some which invited a nil return, such as '1 certificate of no new observations'.[14]

If there were irregularities in the accounts, an officer might have the missing money deducted from his own pay. In August 1804 the *Leviathan* was loading bags of bread from the transport *Amity* when one fell overboard. Nelson ordered the masters of three other ships to go on board and,

> strictly and carefully survey the bag of bread complained of as above, taking care to see every particle of it particularly picked, and the dust wiped off, in order that as much as possible of it may be saved for further use. ... You are further hereby directed strictly to inquire whether to blame is to be attached to any individual for the said loss, in order that it may be charged against his growing wages.

The great cabin of a ship of the line, with doors leading to the quarter gallery.

In May 1805 it was found that four seamen of the *Leviathan* had allotted sums to their families from their pay, but these were not paid. When the Navy Board wanted to deduct the money from Bayntum's pay, he was incensed. He cancelled the first draft of his letter, but the second was scarcely conciliatory.

> I can only say it would have been odd if any notice had been taken of the allotments; your letter was the first information on the subject; therefore I must express my surprise that those persons who have little other employment than to examine ships' books have been so negligent as not to have found it before. ... Having shown that blame does not attach to me, it is with regret that I am obliged to complain of the rudeness of your letter. ... The constant threat of stopping pay seems to be dealt out indiscriminately.

Besides the 'sea officers' who were eligible to become captains and admirals, there were several specialists in every wardroom and gunroom. The marine officers were the only ones who were actually commissioned – the rest were warrant officers.

In the past the navy had used soldiers when there were not enough marines available, but St Vincent was strongly against this, for it was difficult to enforce naval discipline on army officers. He strongly favoured the marines, and in 1802 he ensured that they took on the title 'Royal' for the first time. Officers were appointed by recommendation to the Board of Admiralty, so no particular experience or qualifications were needed, except the status of a gentleman. Commissions were not purchased, as in the army, so the career was open to those whose families had status but little money, and to young men who were too old to start the long training process for a naval officer. It was also a family career, and Second Lieutenant Samuel Ellis of the *Ajax* had three brothers in the navy and the marines.[15] Their training at the marine barracks was short and tended to concentrate on drilling the men with their arms. Promotion was by seniority and tended to be very slow, despite the expansion of the corps under St Vincent. Captain Thomas Timins of the *Dreadnought* had already served twenty-seven years, Captain Palmes Westropp of the *Achille* had served twenty-five.[16]

A 74-gun ship usually had a captain in command of the marine detachment, with two lieutenants, all of who lived in the wardroom. Many of the marines were dispersed round the ship in the more basic seaman's duties, while the others acted as sentries, so the marine officers tended to have too little to do, except to drill the men on occasion. Ten years after Trafalgar, Captain Robert Clarke wrote of the 'weary tedium' of his life on voyage to the West Indies.[17]

Masters were essential in the running of the ship. Some, such as William Wilkinson of the frigate *Sirius*, had once been midshipmen and therefore potential commissioned officers; most had been mates in the merchant service where they had learned seamanship, ship-handling and navigation to a high degree.

Luke Brokensha of the *Revenge* was thirty-eight in 1805. He had served as a master's mate in the sloop *Fortune* at the end of the last war, and master of the 44-gun *Severn* in 1803. That ship was lost in the Channel Islands in August but Brockensha came out of the affair with credit. Captain D'Auvergne wrote to the Navy Board that he was 'a young man of distinguished merit … to the most indefatigable application he joins commendable zeal and desire of improvement.' He recommended an appointment to a good frigate, which was agreed by the Navy Board until they went even further and sent him to the 74-gun *Revenge*. Captain Moorsom was pleased with him. 'He is a good seaman, and conversant in the present practice of observation of the sun, moon, and stars as far as may be necessary for the purposes of navigation.'[18]

Richard Turner of the *Defence* was from Exmouth in Devon. He had served in the merchant marine, like most masters, and passed as master of a sloop in 1797, being qualified in the standard phrase, 'from the Downs thro' the Channel to the Westward and pilot in and out of Spithead, the Needles and Plymouth Sound.' He served under Captain Popham in the *Romney* and was 'strongly recommended' to Captain Hope, who took him into the *Defence*.[19]

William Wilkinson first appeared in the Royal Navy as a midshipman on board the Dutch prize *Texel* in March 1801, blockading the North Sea ports. He was twenty-two by this time, and in view of his age and quick promotion it seems likely that he had spent some years in the merchant service, and was possibly a mate pressed into the navy. He first passed as a master in August 1801. He would not have been eligible for a commission as a lieutenant after only five months in the navy, so he presumably chose the quickest route to the quarterdeck in what was still expected to be a long war. The Navy Board noted that 'The *Rambler* at Portsmouth is very much in want of a master and may if apprised have this man.' He joined the ship and spent some months patrolling the French coast in the difficult waters between La Hogue and St Malo. He went to the *Sirius* in March 1803, but his health was poor and he spent two months in hospital at Plymouth early in 1804 before returning to his ship. He fought in Calder's action in the summer of 1805.[20]

Frederick Ruckert of the *Euryalus* had been born in Prussia but he joined the navy in the sloop *Speedy* at Gibraltar in 1793. He soon attracted notice and was transferred to the gun-brig *Vanneau*, in which he served for three years before becoming a midshipman in Nelson's *Captain* in 1796. It was difficult for a man of foreign birth to get a commission in the Royal Navy, which is perhaps why he became second master of the *Ville de Paris*, Sir John Jervis's flagship. In 1797 he became master of the brig *Mutine* under Captains Hardy, Capel and Hoste, all well-established as members of Nelson's Band of Brothers. He fought at the Battle of the Nile and helped to deliver Nelson's dispatches to Naples. In February 1804 he was officer of the watch of the 24-gun *Champion* when she collided with the sloop *Lynx*. He and the first lieutenant of the *Lynx* were found jointly responsible, but let off with reprimands 'in consideration of the good characters given to them by their respective commanders', and recommended 'to be more careful in future.' His references were 'very strong' and he was appointed to the *Euryalus* later that year.[21]

Naval surgeons often found their position ambiguous on board ship. They had only recently ended the link with barbers, and still most of them learned the trade by apprenticeship rather than university. They were sensitive about the 'strict and distant behaviour' of commissioned officers towards them. They regarded themselves as 'men of liberal education and sentiments', but there were some who did not live up to the ideal. As recently as 1800 Surgeon Whyte of HMS *Atlas* complained of surgeon's mates who could not read Latin or spell common English words, or who 'could neither perform a simple operation of vensection, nor make up the most common medical preparations.' After numerous petitions, including one to Nelson in 1803, the status of surgeons was eventually improved in January 1805. They were to be eligible for half pay when not employed and were given a uniform and a substantial pay rise. The surgeon lived in the wardroom. In a 74-gun ship he had two assistants, who lived in the cockpit with the midshipmen.[22]

The surgeon had to co-operate with the captain and the purser to maintain the health of the ship, but he had a good deal of latitude.

> A naval surgeon of abilities and circumspection is generally the most independent officer in the ship, as his line of duty is unconnected with the others. He has the entire charge and management of the sick and hurt seamen on board his ship; he is to perform surgical operations on the wounded as he may deem necessary to the safety of their lives; and to see that the medicines and necessaries are good in kind, and administered faithfully to the sick patients under his care.[23]

It was common for each surgeon to devise his own strategy, and he was faced with peculiar problems according to the nature of the service. Movements around the world were very slow by modern standards, but were faster than the medical and logistic systems of the age could cope with. When the *Leviathan* returned from the West Indies in 1803, the 300 remaining members of her crew were employed in rigging ships in Portsmouth Dockyard during the great mobilization. This caused serious health problems, according to her new surgeon, William Shoveller, 'the consequence of their being thus exposed was febrile diseases, catarrhs, rheumatism and cough with dyspnoea.' In February 1804 the crew was completed by newly pressed men, some of whom were poorly clothed but had already used up their advances of wages. There was no mechanism to supply them with clothes and Shoveller noted,

> … these people have been principally the subject of fever – the typhus kind. Every possible care and attention was paid to them, and though rather destitute of clothing, they were at least obliged to keep their fresh clean, the people regularly mustered every Sunday and Thursday by the Captain, who with my assistance inspects them minutely and individually.

Shoveller insisted that the deck be cleaned without using water, in order to prevent further rheumatism.[24]

A surgeon's medicine and tool chest.

Surgeon James Fullarton of the *Prince* was also worried about rheumatism, and recorded some of his cases in detail during the spring and summer of 1805 when the ship was engaged in the blockade of Brest. When a nineteen-year-old marine was sent over from another ship, Fullarton found

> … his leg contracted as to be almost parallel with the thigh, the consequence it appears of a rheumatic --- of the joint. By being placed in a frame and gradually extended in a few weeks, it relaxed so far as to form a right angle with the thigh, but its further extension excited so much pain and occasioned such inflammation as obliged me to desist from the attempt.

The young man was sent ashore to the hospital at Gibraltar.

There were accidents caused by the usual hazards of the seaman's life. William Bryon, a twenty-one-year-old seaman,

> … when employed aloft … by accident fell from the top and was taken to the sick berth in a state of insensibility from which however he soon recovered. On examining him the principal injury appears to have fallen on his [head], a large portion of the scalp being contused and detached. … He also complained of severe pain in his back on which there is no appearance of any external injury.[25]

The purser was as much a businessman as a naval officer. He had to produce a bond of up to £1200 as security. He was paid rather less than other officers, and in return he expected to make a profit on saving certain provisions. Despite his lack of military status, William Murray of the *Orion* had once taken command of the frigate *Ambuscade* in the most unfortunate circumstances. The ship was attacked by the French *Bayonaise* off the French coast, but her captain was incompetent and the crew was ill disciplined. Five officers were killed in quick succession and the captain was wounded. Murray took charge but an explosion of cartridges blew out most of the stern and the crew panicked. Murray had to surrender the

A purser, drawn by Thomas Rowlandson.

ship, a rare example of a British vessel of the age being beaten by one of inferior force.[26]

Naval chaplains did not get a pay rise with the other officers in the early 1800s, and their status remained indistinct, for they were not fully recognized as members of the wardroom. Nevertheless, about half of the ships of Nelson's fleet carried a chaplain in October 1805, perhaps reflecting a slight rise in religious devotion, and the desire of many clergymen to serve their country. They were mostly to be found in the bigger ships where their flocks were larger, and there were none in the frigates. They were not all men of ill repute as legend sometimes suggests; after leaving the navy, most settled down to very respectable livings as country parsons. John Greenly of the *Revenge* became a minor canon of Salisbury Cathedral, perpetual curate of St Thomas and Rector of Sharncote in Wiltshire.[27]

None of the warrant officers would expect to share in the glory of the commissioned officers, and their promotion prospects were poor. They made their reputations, not in a few hours in the heat of battle, but over many months of administrative, medical and disciplinary work.

CHAPTER 15

Collingwood and the Stick

Cuthbert Collingwood as an admiral, painted by Henry Howard.

In the whole of the Royal Navy there was no officer who knew Nelson better than Cuthbert Collingwood. He had been born eight years before Nelson, but had followed a more normal career path and did not reach the crucial rank of captain until a few months after Nelson and, as such, he was always behind him in rank and seniority. They first met in 1773 when Nelson was fifteen, and five years later they served together in the frigate *Lowestoffe* during the War of Independence. They soon developed what Collingwood described as 'habits of great friendship.' In the mid 1780s Collingwood commanded a ship in the West Indies alongside his brother Wilfred, at a time when Captain Nelson was the senior officer on the station. The Collingwoods followed Nelson in enforcing the Navigation Acts by seizing American vessels, despite great local unpopularity. Cuthbert's and Nelson's shared experience brought them together and in 1785 they produced drawings of each other in Commissioner Moutray's house at Antigua. At one stage both were in love with Mrs Moutray, and the evidence suggests that the lady preferred Cuthbert. He went home in 1786, his brother died at sea a year later.

Collingwood fought at the Glorious First of June in 1794, when he was flag captain of the *Barfleur* under Rear-Admiral Bowyer. He commanded the *Excellent* at St Vincent in 1797; his ship was towards the rear of the British line. After Nelson, in the *Captain*, broke away to attack several large ships, Collingwood was the only captain to follow him, and earned Nelson's eternal gratitude by relieving him at a tight moment.

> My dearest friend, 'A friend in need is a friend indeed' was never more truly verified than by your most noble and gallant conduct yesterday in sparing the Captain from further loss; and I beg, both as a public officer and a friend, you will accept my most sincere thanks.

Like Nelson, Collingwood had a great talent for training young men into officers. Jeffrey de Raigersfield joined the *Mediator* as a captain's servant in 1785 at the age of twelve, and soon felt his influence.

> ... After prayers (which the Captain used to read himself to the ship's company upon the quarter deck) on a Sunday, the midshipmen were sent for into his cabin, and there he would question each according to their capacity as to the knowledge they had gained during the week ... .' He was a reserved man, a good seaman and navigator, and well read in the English classics; and most heartily do I thank him for the care and pains he took to make me a seaman...[1]

Collingwood was a Newcastle man and remained in close contact with his native Northumberland all his life. He took a personal interest in young officers from that area, and even in men on the lower deck. While serving in the *Venerable* in 1803 he took on a draft of 200 Newcastle volunteers and reported that they were 'a set of stout young men and a great addition to my strength …'. But if they expected to serve continually under Collingwood they would have been disappointed, for he had an unfortunate habit of being moved from ship to ship, and was only able to take a few men with him. Collingwood had more than his share of moves, because of the exigencies of war and partly because Nelson believed he was favouring one of his oldest friends.

Collingwood began the war in 1803 in the aptly named *Venerable*, a 74 that had been built in 1784 and had served as Duncan's flagship at Camperdown in 1797. She came into Cawsand Bay to replenish in December 1803 and was soon found wanting.

> We began by discovering slight defects ... And the further went in the examination, the more important they appeared, until at last she was discovered to be so completely rotten as to be unfit for sea. We have been sailing for the last six months with only a sheet of copper between us and eternity.[2]

The *Venerable* was sent to Plymouth for repair and Collingwood shifted his flag to another 74, the *Culloden*. She was a year older than the *Venerable*, but had just spent twenty-one months in dock at Plymouth for a 'large repair'.

During his service in the *Culloden*, Collingwood had a young seaman, Robert Hay, under his command, and he provided a detailed pen-portrait of the mature Collingwood and his way of running a ship.

> Collingwood, in short, take him all in all, will perhaps stand second to none that ever hoisted a flag. He was as careful of the ship and her stores as if he had been sole owner. Scarcely could she be put about at any hour of the night but he would be on deck. There, accompanied by his favourite dog, Bounce, he would stand on the weather gangway snuffing up the midnight air, with his eye either glancing through his long night glass all round the horizon, or fixed on the light carried by Cornwallis in the *Ville de Paris*, the van ship of the weather line. When the ship was round and the bowlings hauled, he would exchange a few kindly words with the lieutenant of the watch, and then retire to his cot. Duties of every kind were carried on with that calmness and order and regularity and promptness, which afford a strong evidence of the directing hand of a master spirit. No swearing, no threatening or bullying, no startings were to be seen or heard. Boatswain's mates, or ship's corporals, dared not to be seen with a rattan, or rope's end in hand; nor do I recollect a single instance of a man being flogged while he remained aboard. Was discipline neglected then? By no means. There was not a better disciplined crew in the fleet.[3]

But the log of the *Culloden* suggests that Hay's memory was at fault in at least one respect. There were fewer floggings than in many ships, but they were not unknown. At least thirteen men were punished during the period Collingwood was on board, including one man who got twenty-four lashes for drunkenness in March.[4]

One officer in the Culloden had a habit of referring to individual men as 'You, Sir.' Collingwood answered this by example.

> Going aft when he found the Lieutenant near the break of the poop, he addressed himself to the steersman, but loud enough to be heard by the Lieutenant.

> 'Jenkins, what is that man's name in the weather-rigging?'
> 'Dan Swain, your honour.'

> Forward the Admiral goes, and putting his hand instead of a speaking trumpet to his lips looked up and called out,
> 'Dan Swain.'
> 'Sir.'
> 'The after end of that ratling is too high; let it down a handbreadth.'

'Aye, aye, Sir.'

The Lieutenant knew right well for whom this hint was intended and forthwith expunged You-Sir from his vocabulary.[5]

Captain Edward Rotherham, engraved by Robert Pollard in 1806.

Hay summarized Collingwood by writing, 'A better seaman – a better friend to seamen – a greater lover and more zealous defender of his country's rights and honour, never trod a quarterdeck.'[6]

In May 1804 Collingwood shifted his flag to the three-decker *Prince*, 12 miles off Ushant. She was a notoriously slow ship but as a three-decker she had extra accommodation. The boats of the Culloden were employed for four hours in the afternoon of 7 May, carrying the Admiral's furniture, clothing, papers and personal belongings. They stopped at 8.00 p.m. but resumed the next morning. 'AM at 4 hove to and sent the remainder of the admiral's things on board the *Prince*. At 6 the admiral joined the *Prince* and left the ship, hoisted in boats.'[7] In June, as the ministry changed in London, Collingwood complained, 'The latter Admiralty shifted me about from ship to ship, but I hope now I shall get settled in one.'[8] He could not have been happy a few weeks later when he moved again, to a newer three-decker, the *Dreadnought* of 1801, although this time the transfer was effected in the relative shelter of Cawsand Bay near Plymouth. The move did allow him to bring across his former officers from the *Culloden*, who had been displaced from that ship when Sir Edward Pellew took her over as his flagship.[9]

Collingwood was not impressed by the captain of the *Dreadnought*, Edward Rotherham, who had neither ability nor manners. He was

… such a stick, I wonder how such people get forward. He should (I firmly believe) with his nautical ability and knowledge and exertion, have been a bad Lieutenant to this day. Was he brought up in the Navy? For he has very much of the stile of the Coal trade about him, except they are good seamen.

Even a young midshipman was fully aware of the Admiral's feelings, and Hercules Robinson wrote many years later.

Collingwood's dry, caustic wit lives before me in the recollection of his calling across the deck his fat, stupid captain – long since dead – when he had seen him commit some monstrous blunder, and after the usual bowing and formality – which the excellent old chief never omitted – he said: 'Captain, I have been thinking, whilst I looked at you, how strange it is that a man should grow so big and know so little. That's all sir; that's all.' Hats off; low bows.[10]

Despite appearances, Rotherham came from a very intellectual family. He was from Hexham, less than 20 miles west of Collingwood's birthplace of Newcastle. His father was a local doctor, and senior physician at the local infirmary as well as 'a person of general science'. His brother had studied under the celebrated Linnaeus in Sweden and became Professor of Natural Philosophy at St Andrews University in 1795. Edward himself had been educated in mathematics by his father and by Dr Charles Hutton, who ran a mathematical school in Newcastle before moving on to higher things in London. But little of this seems to have rubbed off on young Edward, who was apprenticed, as Collingwood suspected, in the coal trade. Perhaps he did not serve long enough in colliers to learn the seamanship which had given Captain James Cook a good start in life, for he entered the Royal Navy during the War of Independence and was commissioned as a lieutenant at the very end of that conflict, in April 1783. By 1794 he had built up enough seniority to serve as first lieutenant of the *Culloden* during the 'Glorious First of June'. He was promoted to commander and took charge of a storeship on the Mediterranean station. Finally, after service in command of the small frigate *Lapwing* in the West Indies, he was promoted captain in August 1800, at the age of about forty-seven.

But Rotherham was a more complex character than Collingwood gave him credit for. His large and beautifully written 'Commonplace Book'[11] suggests that he had acquired a little of his father's interest in figures, though he tended towards arithmetic and statistics rather than pure mathematics. He made a meticulous list of the ships of the Royal Navy, perhaps in 1788 when he was on shore. There were detailed accounts of the ropes used for rigging different classes of ship, providing information that has not survived for the historian in any other form. He collected and personally transcribed sailing directions for most of the major ports of the Mediterranean. He had tables for dividing up the crew of every class of ship for keeping watch, mooring, reefing and furling sails and in fighting, suggesting that his interest in seamanship was theoretical rather than practical. He shows strong signs of disillusionment with the naval service. His 'Growls of a Naval Life' include the following:

Being engaged to one of the most engaging parties that was ever formed for your amusement, or to an assignation to one of the most desirable who ever ventured to be alone with man, and an order is issued on the alarm of invasion, that every officer and man must sleep on board till further order.

Endeavouring to repose after the fatigue of being up all night in a gale of wind and not having room in your cabin for a cot to swing without striking a gun, the ship's side or bulkhead, with a leak dripping in your bed...

All of these, however, seem quite tame compared with his 49th article.

After being maimed in battle to be obliged to suffer the slow and erroneous amputation of a doubting unskillful surgeon by the light of a purser's short dip.

He makes no mention of other obvious fears, such as death by drowning or in battle.

It is not clear how far this relates to Rotherham's personal experience, for it was in the nature of a commonplace book to copy out pearls of wisdom from many sources. Yet it was clearly written by a captain of a ship of the line who had seen considerable service. Nelson and Collingwood both had their moments of despair, but it is difficult to believe they would have become so disillusioned.

All this nautical lore was mixed indiscriminately in Rotherham's 'Commonplace Book' with pages on religion, law, politics and columns of statistics on the population of England and births and deaths in Devonshire, where he settled with his family. These high-minded texts are not separated from a kind of humour that would have been more appropriate in the midshipmen's berth than the great cabin. One poem, apparently copied in the 1800s when Rotherham was already a captain, hinges on a retired, or 'yellow' admiral sitting on some faeces while courting his 'Buxom chamber maid' on Portsmouth beach and ends in the liberal sentiment,

Now God preserve our jolly tars
Captains and Admirals too
And let them each enjoy their lass
At home like me and you

His 'Naval Growls' includes one which admits to sexual desires among senior officers.

Being disturbed from a dream in which a lovely female is the object, and rapture approaching, by a most sudden and violent squall ...

There is no sign that the *Dreadnought* was a happy ship under the rule of Collingwood and Rotherham. Despite the Admiral's benign reputation, floggings were numerous and savage. On 15 April 1805, for example, eight men were flogged with up to thirty-six lashes, and ten were punished on 8 August.[12] All the same Collingwood considered, by October, that the ship was well manned. He trained his men hard in gunnery and soon achieved a target of three rounds in five minutes. His supporters even claimed that the crew of the *Dreadnought* could load and fire three rounds in three and a half minutes, a remarkable achievement if true.[13]

Lieutenant James Clavell was very different from Rotherham in Collingwood's estimation – 'the spirit of the ship.' He was twenty-six years old, the son of a vicar from the Isle of Wight who clearly had good naval connections, for his son was borne on the books of warships from the age of one. He actually joined in 1792 at the age of thirteen and served in the *Victory* from 1793 to 1797 under several successive admirals, including St Vincent. He was ashore with Nelson in 1795 at the sieges of Bastia and Calvi. He first served directly under Collingwood in April 1797 when he transferred to the *Excellent* with an acting commission, and he was confirmed as a lieutenant eighteen months later at the age of nineteen. He rejoined Collingwood when he commissioned the *Venerable* in May 1803 and followed him from ship to ship, always as his first lieutenant, although this required some manipulation of postings, since Clavell was relatively junior in the rank.

Collingwood was senior officer in the key station off Cadiz from his arrival there on 8 June 1805, with a small and largely decreasing force of ships. On 20 August he had a brush with Villeneuve's fleet as it sailed into the port. As he wrote to his wife,

> I have very little time to write to you, but I must tell you what a squeeze we had like to have got yesterday. While we were cruising off the town, down came the combined fleet of thirty-six men of war; we were only three poor little things, with a frigate and a bomb, and we drew off towards the Straits [of Gibraltar], not very ambitious, as you may suppose, to try our strength against such odds. They followed us as we retired, with sixteen large ships; but on our approaching the Straits they left us, and joined their friends in Cadiz, where they are fitting and replenishing their provisions. We, in our turn, followed them back, and to-day have been looking into Cadiz, where their fleet is now as thick as a wood.[14]

Following this incident the fleet off Cadiz was built up as quickly as possible. Not everyone welcomed Collingwood's leadership. Captain Codrington of the *Orion* had been there since mid-August, and much preferred the easy-going, sociable rule of Sir Robert Calder, who had 'the most laudable inclination to promote society, and that harmony so essential to a fleet destined to act well together …' Collingwood, in contrast, was 'another stay-on-board Admiral, who never communicates with anybody but upon service … we stand a very good chance of forgetting that anything like society is known among men.' Codrington longed for a change in command, and wrote on 4 September,

> Is Lord Nelson coming out to us again? I anxiously hope that he may be; that I may once in my life see a commander-in-chief endeavouring to make a hard and disagreeable service as palatable to those serving under him as circumstances will admit of, and keeping up by his example that animation so necessary for such an occasion.

The next day Codrington was summoned on board Collingwood's flagship after the Admiral considered him inattentive to some of his orders. He was pleasantly surprised when the Admiral listened to his problems, and found him 'good-humoured, chatty and communicative.' In September there was a court martial on board Calder's *Prince of Wales*, and the rules of the service demanded that the second-in-command of the fleet should preside and at least five captains should be present. This grim occasion provided an opportunity for socialization. According to Codrington, the trial was followed by

> as social a dinner as I was ever at; and the beautiful music his band gave us to make our wine relish, made us all regret the more the difficulty of repeating our visit. It was … a most animating sight; an admiral surrounded by twenty of his captains in social inter-

course, showing a strong desire to support each other cordially and manfully in the event of a battle taking place.

Calder was far inferior to Nelson as a leader, though he shared at least some of his techniques. But Codrington still longed for the real thing. 'For charity's sake send us Lord Nelson, oh ye men of power!'[15]

Codrington dreaded the prospect of a long blockade more than anything else and wrote to his wife,

> The truth is that our heads are so perpetually crammed with ship matters, which we are of necessity obliged to give our whole attention to, that we cannot receive affairs of less immediate moment, although alone interesting to those anxious about us. It would be little to tell you that yesterday we wore ship, and the day before we tacked ship; although any difficulties attending these simple acts on account of weather or situation might, attract all our interest and require all our skill and exertion; and to us even, the interest ceases when the act terminates.[16]

When Nelson was given overall command of the fleet, Collingwood showed no resentment. He was forewarned by a brief message sent ahead by new ships joining, although the second part of the message was probably not welcome.

> My dear Coll.,
> I shall be with you in a few days, and I hope you will remain Second in Command. You will change the *Dreadnought* for the *Royal Sovereign*, which I hope you will like. Ever, my dear Collingwood, most faithfully yours,
> Nelson and Bronte[17]

The stern of the Royal Sovereign.

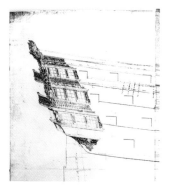

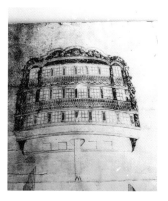

If Collingwood had his doubts about the change of ship, he can be forgiven. It was only seven months since Nelson had complained about the *Royal Sovereign* in that 'she has very much retarded the Squadron in its pursuit of the Enemy to Alexandria.' Nelson was aware that this was not due to any defect in the design of the ship; it was just that she had not been coppered for six years. The copper had worn off in many places, making the ship foul. At Nelson's request the ship had been sent home to Portsmouth to be re-coppered and repaired.

The *Royal Sovereign* had been ordered in 1772, before the *Victory* had ever seen active service. She was designed by Sir John Williams, who succeeded Sire Thomas Slade as Surveyor of the Navy and remained in his shadow even before he declined in his old age. The new ship was slightly shorter than the *Victory* on the gundeck though a little broader and deeper, so her tonnage was registered at 2175 compared with the *Victory*'s 2142. With the usual low priority of large ships in peacetime, she was not started until 1774, and she got no more attention in wartime, for precedence was given to other ships which could be completed sooner. She was finally completed in 1786, having spent the whole of the American War on the stocks. She was sent to sea briefly in the following year during a mobilization caused by the threat of war, but went back into ordinary after two months. The same thing happened during the 'Spanish Armament' of 1790 and it was 1793, more than twenty years after her first order, that she finally went on active service, as the flagship of Vice-Admiral Thomas Graves as part of Admiral Howe's fleet in the Channel. She took part in the 'Glorious First of June' in 1794, but her finest hour came in the following year. Flying the flag of Admiral Cornwallis, she was leading four 74s and two frigates along the French coast when they were chased by a much stronger French force. Though two of the 74s were in poor sailing condition, the Admiral managed to defend all of them in a masterly action known as Cornwallis's retreat.

The *Royal Sovereign* sailed from Plymouth on 10 September 1805 after a minor refit and re-coppering in a dry-dock there. She arrived off Cadiz on 8 October, but there was some delay before Collingwood transferred to her. Nelson was encouraging and told

Collingwood, 'I am sure you will admire her as a far better ship than the *Victory*.' He was disparaging about the qualities of the Collingwood's present ship and wrote to him on the 12th, 'I am sure you felt for poor *Dreadnought*'s movements yesterday.' But Collingwood was defensive and wrote back, 'The *Dreadnought* certainly sails very ill, but it is her only fault; for no ship is better manned, and in every respect better conditioned.'

It would not have been practical to move *Dreadnought*'s crew into the *Royal Sovereign*, but Collingwood was keen to take some of his officers with him. For some reason he decided to take Edward Rotherham – perhaps he had discovered some qualities in him in the six weeks since he called him 'such a stick'. He also took James Clavell, still as his first lieutenant.

The *Royal Sovereign* had already gone through enough instability of her own. She had had no less than five captains since 1800 by the time Mark Robinson was superseded by John Conn on 13 September 1805. But that command lasted only a month until the boats were hoisted out again and Collingwood and Rotherham came on board. Such inconstancy did much to disrupt a crew, as each captain might well bring his own ideas, discipline and organization with him. As Commander G. P. Monke wrote in 1806, much of the mutiny and disaffection of the navy was caused by the 'mutability of the system of discipline too often introduced by different commanders in different ships, and even by the same commander in the same ship'. Regulations were 'introduced and abolished according to [the captain's] sole will and caprice, it may be conceived what inconsistency and confusion must, in the progress of time, have arisen from such a contrariety of opinion on certain points of discipline and duty.'[18] Crews were likely to be disrupted every time the captain changed.

With an incompetent captain and a disrupted crew the *Royal Sovereign* might have failed the ultimate test of battle which was about to present itself; or would a highly competent admiral and first lieutenant be enough to make up for that? Anticipating battle, Collingwood took good care to drill his men in gunnery, but there was not much time.

CHAPTER 16

The Fleet

Nelson, painted by Sir William Beechey.

At 6.00 a.m. on 14 September 1805 Nelson arrived back at Portsmouth from Merton, after a coach journey of seven and a half hours. He breakfasted at the George Hotel then called on Sir Charles Saxton, the Commissioner of the Dockyard. He returned to the George and was joined by two government ministers, George Rose and George Canning. He had intended to walk to the sally port a few hundred yards away at the end of the High Street to be rowed out to his flagship, but a large crowd had gathered, making passage impossible. He slipped out of the back door and headed towards the beach at Southsea where the 'bathing machines' were situated. He passed down a tunnel through the fortifications to meet a waiting boat, but he had not managed to evade the crowds. According to an American visitor,

> By the time he had arrived on the beach some hundreds of people had collected in his train, pressing all around and pushing to get a little before him to obtain a sight of his face. I stood on one of the batteries near where he passed and had a full view of his person. As the barge in which he embarked pushed away from the shore, the people gave three cheers, which his lordship returned by waving his hat.

Nelson turned to Hardy and remarked, 'I had their huzzas before – I have their hearts now.'[1]

Nelson was rowed out to the *Victory* with the two politicians. It was 5 miles to the anchorage at St Helens off the Isle of Wight, and he arrived on board at 11.30 a.m., when the flag of a vice-admiral was hoisted at the head of *Victory*'s foremast. There was time to dine with his friends in the great cabin, before they were rowed ashore. At 8.00 a.m. on Sunday the 15th, the *Victory*'s anchor was raised and she sailed out of the Solent. Three other ships of the line were at Portsmouth bound for the Cadiz fleet, but none was ready; Nelson sailed in company with Blackwood's *Euryalus*. There were a few changes in the *Victory*'s officers. Dr Gillespie had left and there was now no Physician of the Fleet. The new surgeon of the *Victory* was William Beatty, a man of undistinguished history and accomplishments. Among the new midshipmen was Francis Edward Collingwood of Milford Haven in Wales, the nephew of an admiral and son and grandson of naval officers but now orphaned, a protégé of Nelson's friend Lord Grenville. He was twenty years old, 5 feet 11 inches tall, of 'good character' and had passed for lieutenant.[2]

The winds in the English Channel were foul, there was a 'nasty, blowing night' on the 16/17 September, and progress was slow. Off Plymouth on the 17th Nelson signalled for any ships earmarked for his fleet to come out and join him. Two did, the 74s *Thunderer* and *Ajax*. Next day he was off the Lizard, and therefore almost out of the channel. Two days later he exchanged salutes with Rear-Admiral Stirling's squadron blockading the Spanish in Ferrol, and on the 25th he was in sight of the Rock of Lisbon, marking one of the few friendly harbours in the area. He sent the *Euryalus* on ahead with a message to Collingwood, ordering him that no gun salutes were to take place when he joined, and there was to be no hoisting of colours – 'it is well not to proclaim to the Enemy every ship which may join the

Fleet.' Three days later, at 6.00 p.m. on 28 September, he found the fleet 15 miles east of St Sebastian's Lighthouse and took command of a force of twenty-nine ships of the line. He wrote to his friend, Sir John Acton, 'After being only twenty-five days in England, I find myself again in command of the Mediterranean Fleet. I only hope that I may be able, in a small degree, to fulfil the expectations of my country.'[3]

Captain Codrington of the *Orion*, who had longed for Nelson's return, wrote immediately, 'Lord Nelson is arrived! A sort of general joy has been the consequence, and many good effects will shortly arise from our change of system.'[4] Nelson immediately began to get to know the ships of his fleet and, even more important, his captains.

Fundamentally, Nelson's new fleet had much in common with the French and the Spanish. In past ages, when the English fought the Spanish Armada in 1588, or the Dutch between 1652 and 1674, there had been significant differences between the aims and practices of the rivals. By 1805, there had been constant antagonism or warfare between the great western European powers for more than a century, but comparatively little had changed in the basic technology of the sailing ship. There had been much convergence, for ideas were exchanged by means of espionage, learned books and articles, emigration of shipwrights and the study of captured warships.

Besides augmenting the size of the fleet, the capture of enemy warships gave the British Navy one of its prime sources of ideas. The French *Invincible*, captured in 1747, was one of the first to be copied, and a ship based on her design was now with Nelson. The *Courageaux*, captured in 1761, was even more influential and eventually forty-six British warships were to be based on her design. Of twenty-seven British ships of the line with Nelson in October 1805, three – *Belleisle*, *Canopus* and *Tonnant* – had been captured from the French, and four more were copied from French designs. The French navy had captured fewer ships than their enemy, but it made full use of its prizes, partly for prestige reasons. With the Combined Fleet at Cadiz were the *Berwick* and the *Swiftsure*, both prizes. But neither the French nor the Spanish ever made direct copies of captured ships.

A single ship of the line had fire power equal to that of an army. It had more guns than any but the largest fortresses on land, but it had several grave weaknesses. Obviously it depended on the wind for its movement. It was made of wood, so it was relatively weak and highly inflammable. As such, it was reluctant to fight directly with land forces, which had an indestructible base and might use explosive or heated shot against ships.

Furthermore, the sailing warship was immensely powerful on its sides but very weak on its bow and stern. The average ship of the line had about 40 guns firing on each side, with perhaps 2 firing forward and 4 aft. The sides of the ship were built with very strong timbers but the stern, in particular, was fragile, with a flimsy structure round the large windows of the officers' cabins.

The fundamental reason for this was that a ship of the line was long and narrow and so could carry more guns on her sides. However, some types of ship, such as the rowing galley and later, the submarine, were actually much longer than a ship of the line in proportion to their length, but carried mainly forward-firing armament. A ship of the line, unlike a galley, was designed to cram the maximum amount of fire power into a small space. Large warships of the twentieth century relied on a small number of large guns, but that option was not open to the warship designers of the eighteenth and early nineteenth centuries. The size of each individual gun was limited by the weight of shot that a single man could lift efficiently in battle. The largest in common use had 42-pound shot but these were already out of favour, because in battle it was found the weight slowed down the rate of fire. In 1777 Admiral Keppel asked for the *Victory's* 42-pounders to be exchanged for 32-pounders, on the grounds that 'it may, on board ship, be fired much oftener than a larger gun' and that 'the lesser guns may be used in service at particular times, when guns of 42 pound ball cannot be managed at all.' The 32-pounder remained the standard size of gun for the lower decks of British ships of the line. The only way a ship could carry a large gun power was to fit the sides with as many guns as she could carry, until excessive weight began to affect her sailing qualities.

This way of arming ships evolved in the first half of the seventeenth century, and it soon led to the obvious conclusion that the fleet had to fight in a single line to make the maximum use of its fire power without one ship getting in the way of another. For the next century there was a tendency for admirals to impose more and more discipline on their fleets and to make the line of battle ever more rigid. This had an effect on ship design, for no serious attempt was made to arm the bow and stern, or to protect them from enemy fire, as every ship was expected to be covered by the next in line. For the half century up to 1805, tactics tended to become more daring, culminating in Nelson's own battles. Ship design had not entirely caught up with these developments, in Britain, France or Spain.

One consequence of the line of battle was that a ship had to be strong enough to stand in it. In the old type of melée battle, as fought before the 1650s, a small ship could seek out an opponent of her own size, or combine with others to attack a larger one. With the line of battle each ship had to stand and fight with the opposite ship in the enemy line, however large she might be. Since the late seventeenth-century, warships had been divided into two types: the 'ships of the line', which were large and powerful enough to stand in the line of battle, and those that could not. The latter group included, in descending order of size, frigates, sloops, corvettes, brigs, schooners and cutters, as well as many small types used for patrol, escort, scouting, dispatch-carrying and numerous other duties. They could be very important in a war against commerce, but in a fleet battle the ship of the line was paramount. A few frigates were needed for scouting and a few smaller vessels for carrying dispatches, but each fleet measured its strength in 'sail of the line'.

To carry enough guns to fight in line, a ship needed at least two complete gundecks. Such a ship could carry up to 84 guns, though most had 74. Three-deckers usually had about 100 guns, although the Spanish had some of 110 to 112 guns. Some ships were being built with 120 guns, but none of these were at Cadiz or in Nelson's fleet. The largest Spanish ship, the *Santisima Trinidad*, was virtually a four-decker with about 130 guns.

Lord Barham had done his best to hand pick the best ships for Nelson's fleet, but he was very much hampered by the need for haste. Due to the failure of St Vincent's reforms, the fleet was in relatively poor physical condition. In practice he had to send those ships that were available, and in good enough condition to stand a winter in the Atlantic Ocean off Cadiz. The haste accounts for the varied sailing qualities of the different ships; but as a general rule, the larger ships with a given number of decks were the best. Three-decker, 100-gun ships sailed better than 98s, which were, in fact, much more different than the mere

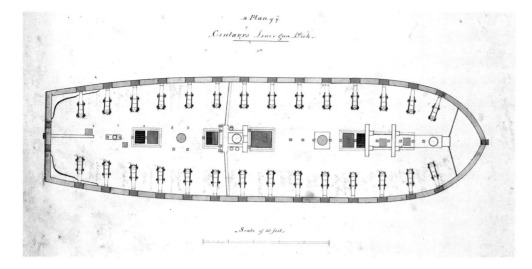

The gundeck of the 74-gun Centaur.

absence of two guns suggested. Two-decker 80s or 74s sailed better than 64s. The *Victory* had always been regarded as a good sailer for a three-decker. The 100-gun *Royal Sovereign*, now the second flagship under Collingwood, had a history of bad sailing but had benefited from a period in dry-dock where her copper was repaired.

The four 98-gun ships were perhaps the worst in the fleet, The *Neptune* was 'never a good sailer', the *Dreadnought*, 'from her present heavy sailing, could never keep up with the fleet in a chase' while the *Prince*, like the 100-gun *Britannia*, sailed 'most wretchedly'. Only the *Temeraire* escaped criticism.[5] However, three-deckers were well regarded as fighting ships at this time. Many considered each the equal of two two-deckers, particularly in a close-range action. According to one French tactician,

> When it comes to boarding they dominate vessels of lower rate. The small-arms fire of large ships commands that of small ones; all the shot plunge and get home over the bulwarks. … the crew can get down to board a small ship more easily than they can climb onto a big one. In heavy seas big vessels can use their lower batteries more easily … Large ships, too, have greater solidity and better resistance to attack.

But Nelson's own view on the relative values is unknown; all he said was that two-deckers alongside an enemy were 'better then three-deckers a great distance off'[6]

In general the two-deckers, with much less area of hull to catch the wind, were far better sailers. The sole 80-gun ship in the fleet, the ex-French *Tonnant* (the *Spartiate* had been reduced to 74 by the time of Trafalgar), was highly regarded. According to Frederick Hoffman, who served as a lieutenant in her during the battle, she was 'a glorious ship of ships ... an equal match for any ship afloat.'[7] The 74-gun *Defence* of 1763 was one of the oldest ships in the fleet, but her design perhaps reflected the genius of Sir Thomas Slade,

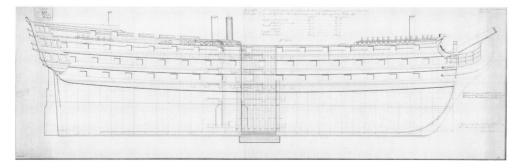

The plans of the Prince, showing how the ship was lengthened in 1796. She remained one of the slowest sailers in the fleet.

who had also produced the *Victory*. Midshipman Thomas Huskisson wrote, 'Neither up to that time nor subsequently did we ever meet with a ship of any class that sailed as well as the *Defence*, and I have no doubt that she was one of the fastest ships in the service on all points of sailing.'[8] Captain Duff wrote of the *Mars*, 'I think she sails much better than the generality of ships, answers her helm well, is easy in a sea, very weatherly and in every respect a good ship, and could I bring her more on an even keel I am convinced she would answer even better.'[9] The *Defiance*, Captain Durham believed was 'the fastest sailing ship of her rate in the British navy.'[10]

The smallest two-deckers still in general service, the 64s, were generally recognized as obsolete. They had only 24-pounder guns as their main armament instead of 32-pounders. The French had stopped building them two decades ago and in battle each was likely to find itself against an enemy ship of much superior force. It was reported in 1795, 'there is no difference of opinion respecting 64-gun ships being struck out of the rates. It is a fact that our naval officers either pray or swear against being appointed to serve on board them.' Barham himself tended to agree with this and he preferred them to serve in the minor foreign stations where they were less likely to encounter strong opposition.[11] Yet this was only half the story. Nelson had been appointed to the 64-gun *Agamemnon* in 1793, after several years on the beach. He considered her a glorious ship, no doubt influenced by a return to command after such a long period of rural boredom. The same ship joined the fleet off Cadiz on 13 October under Nelson's old friend and flag-captain, Sir Edward Berry. According to the editor of Nelson's letters he rubbed his hands with glee, which was impossible in the circumstances; more credibly, he exclaimed, 'Here comes Berry; now we shall have a Battle.'[12] There were two other 64s in the fleet, the *Polyphemus* under Robert Redmill and the *Africa* commanded by Henry Digby.

The frigate was next in the naval pecking order, with a distinct gap between it and the ship of the line. Like the 74, the type had evolved in France in the second quarter of the eighteenth century, after several failed attempts to find a compromise between speed and gunpower. The main characteristic was that the lower deck was unarmed, and needed no gunports. The ports of the upper deck were higher out of the water, which meant that the ship could heel more in the wind, and therefore carry more sail. The guns were lighter than on a ship of the line – 12-pounders on the older ships, 18-pounders on more recent ones, compared with 32-pounders on a standard ship of the line. The hull did not have to bear such a heavy weight, so its underwater lines could be finer. Frigates were usually smaller than ships of the line – a 36-gun frigate with 18-pounder guns was 140–150 feet long on the gundeck compared with 180 feet for a large 74. A 36-gun frigate was measured at 900–1000 tons, just over half that of a 74-gun ship. A 36 carried a crew of 264 men, compared with 590 for a standard 74. Frigates were glamorous ships compared with the rather staid ships of the line and were usually commanded by younger captains.[13]

On 7 October Nelson reviewed his strength in frigates. There were seventeen under his command at that moment, but three of these were in poor condition and would be sent home at the first opportunity. In addition seven ships were at home and would be sent out as soon as they were ready, so potentially he had twenty-one frigates under his command. Nelson estimated that he needed a dozen for duties away from the main fleet, supporting Gibraltar, Malta and Sir James Craig's expedition to Italy, or patrolling off vital headlands. For the main fleet itself he needed eight frigates and two smaller vessels.

> To be constantly with the Fleet off Cadiz, 8 Frigates and 2 Sloops. 2 Frigates and 2 Sloops to go to and from Gibraltar with Convoys, and to relieve the others to refit; and the 2 Sloops to go occasionally to Lisbon with dispatches, and for Purser's necessaries.

Nelson would be only one frigate short when the new ships arrived, but in the meantime he lamented the position. 'How I long for frigates!' he wrote to Collingwood on 6 October.

Frigates were in demand simply because they had so many uses. A modern historian lists eight with the main fleet – strategic reconnaissance, tactical reconnaissance, support in fleet engagements, squadron action, blockade duty, in coastal operations, amphibious warfare and miscellaneous duties. Independent of the battle fleet, they could escort convoys, cruise against enemy trade and 'annoy' the enemy in various ways.[14]

Despite a few weaknesses, Nelson was not dissatisfied with what he saw. As he told the Secretary to the Admiralty on his arrival, 'the Fleet is in very fair condition and good humour, and their Lordships may be assured that every exertion of mine shall be used to keep it so, and in a state to meet the Combined Fleet whenever they come out.'[15]

Nelson had refined his tactical ideas since the voyage from the West Indies. During his stay at Merton he was visited by Captain Richard Keats, who had commanded the *Superb* during the chase. As they walked in the garden one morning, Nelson explained his latest plan, which involved putting the fleet into three divisions. One, led by Nelson himself, would cut the enemy line of battle 'about one-third of their Line from their leading ship.' The other division, under the second-in-command, would attack the portion which had been cut off and create 'a pell-mell battle' in which the British advantage in gunnery would be used to the full. The smallest division, which would include the fastest sailing ships, would be stationed 'in a situation of advantage', under an officer of initiative and would attack where it seemed most useful.

Now it was time to explain these ideas to the captains of the fleet. He arrived off Cadiz too late in the evening of 28 September, but next day he called half the captains on board the *Victory* to explain his plans, and the rest the following day.[16] Nelson was ecstatic with the reception.

> … when I came to explain to them the 'Nelson touch', it was like an electric shock. Some shed tears, all approved – 'it was new – it was singular – it was simple!'; and from the Admirals downwards, it was repeated – 'It must succeed, if they will allow us to get at them! You are, my Lord, surrounded by friends whom you inspire with confidence.' Some may be Judas's; but the majority are certainly much pleased with my commanding them.[17]

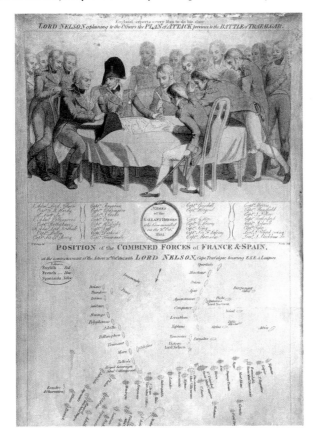

Nelson outlines his plans to his captains – although the actual battle, as shown below, was rather different from the plan.

Nelson's tactical plans, as outlined before Trafalgar.

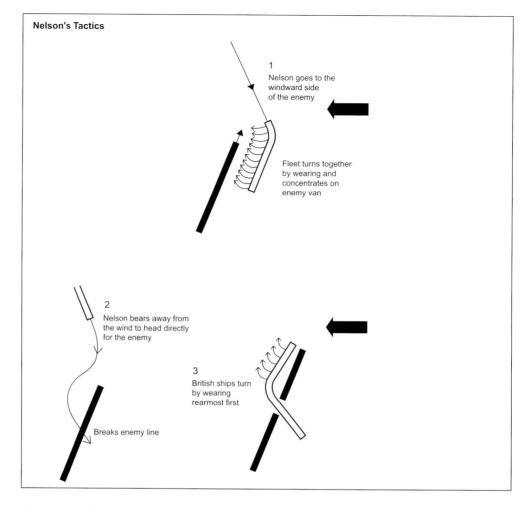

Nelson's Tactics

1
Nelson goes to the windward side of the enemy

Fleet turns together by wearing and concentrates on enemy van

2
Nelson bears away from the wind to head directly for the enemy

Breaks enemy line

3
British ships turn by wearing rearmost first

Nelson put his ideas on paper. They were edited by John Scott the secretary, and copied for distribution to the fleet on 9 October, eleven days after Nelson's arrival. He expected to have forty ships under his command against forty-six of the enemy, and he believed that it would be impossible to form up such a fleet and bring it into battle 'in variable winds thick weather, and other circumstances which must occur.' Therefore the fleet was to be divided into two squadrons of sixteen ships each, under himself and Collingwood. The advanced squadron, of eight 'of the fastest sailing Two-decked ships' would join with whichever line needed it most to make up a squadron of twenty-four ships. Collingwood, in charge of one of the squadrons of sixteen, would have 'the entire direction of the Line to make the attack upon the Enemy' after Nelson's intentions were made known.

Nelson was aware that things did not always go according to plan.

Something must be left to chance; nothing is sure in a Sea Fight beyond all others. Shot will carry away the masts and yards of friends as well as foes; but I look with confidence to a Victory before the Van of the Enemy could succour their Rear, and then that the British Fleet would most of them be ready to receive their twenty Sail of the Line, or pursue them, should they endeavour to make off.

If the enemy had the wind behind him, Nelson would lead his own squadron into battle by cutting the enemy line a few ships ahead of its flagship, which could be assumed to be in the centre. The advanced squadron would attack just aft of the center, to make sure that the commander-in-chief was taken. The second-in-command would attack about twelve ships from the enemy rear, and that part of his fleet would be overwhelmed. If the British had the wind behind them, the three squadrons would form an echelon parallel to the enemy, as close as possible to his centre. The second-in-command's squadron of sixteen ships would then alter course together towards him, setting as much sail as possible and concentrating on the twelve rearmost of the centre of the enemy line. Nelson's squadron would then cover the rest of the fleet, 'taking care that the movements of the Second in Command are as little interrupted as is possible.'

In a key passage, Nelson acknowledged that no amount of planning and control could ensure victory:'… in case Signals can neither be seen or perfectly understood, no Captain can do very wrong if he places his ship alongside that of an enemy'.[18]

On the same day Captain Moorsom of the *Revenge* began a policy that would eventually prove very popular with the crew. Planks were hung over the side and men began to paint the sides of the ship in the famous 'Nelson chequer'. Captain Codrington of the *Orion* had first noticed the new style in August on the eight seasoned ships which had been with Nelson in the chase across the Atlantic. 'Although their ships do not look so handsome as objects, they look so very warlike, and show such high condition, that when once I think 'Orion' fit to manouevre with them, I shall probably paint her in the same manner.' But at the end of September he was more skeptical.

> I shall endeavour to preserve my yellow band, although I intend following the admiral's whim as to the two streaks; but, as all small ships are much disfigured by this attempt to look large, like the frog in the fable, I shall divide betwixt the line of the ports and the sheer of the ship…[19]

Officers and men began to adjust to the boredom of blockade service. William Ram, the gloomy midshipman who had joined the *Victory* that spring, was delighted to be asked to dine with the Admiral soon after the arrival off Cadiz, and was even more pleased when Nelson arranged his promotion to lieutenant, at the age of twenty-one. But an ambitious young officer was never satisfied, and he wrote to his sister, 'now I'll wait for a Captain Commission, you see we are never content, no sooner we get one piece of good fortune than we are distracted to get more.' By 13 October he was already impatient.

> I begin already to be tired of this Station, the sameness that runs through the Navy (I mean principally the Line of Battleships) is intolerable, and tho' in daily hopes of the Enemy giving us an opportunity of signalising ourselves, yet alas, day follows day no enemy comes and the same anxiety is printed on my brow.[20]

Since the fleet was static rather than in a chase, and plenty of warning might be expected of an enemy movement, it was possible for captains to socialize together. As well as dinners on board the *Victory* with the Admiral, Codrington dined in Captain Hope's *Defence* with Brown of the *Ajax* on 3 October, but four days later he was unable to return their hospitality because they were too far to windward. Nevertheless he had 'a very passable day with two other brother captains.'[21]

Cadiz was nearly a thousand miles closer to the English Channel than Toulon and contained a much more powerful fleet, so Nelson could not risk taking his whole force away at any one time to take on provisions and to tempt the enemy out. It was not customary to send storeships out to the fleet, partly because of fear of enemy attack on the convoy, partly because of the difficulty of finding the fleet, and largely because it would be very hard to transfer stores in a rough sea. Therefore Nelson had to send ships in squadron by squadron rather than singly, in case the detached force should meet the enemy. Thus on 3 October he called Rear-Admiral Thomas Louis of *Canopus* on board the *Victory*. He came with his flag captain, Francis Austen, who had been promised a battle 'alongside a French 80 gun ship.' He was told that Nelson had decided to send his squadron to Gibraltar and Tetuan for stores. As they parted Louis protested. 'You are sending us away my Lord – the enemy will come out, and we shall have no share in the battle.' Nelson replied,

> My dear Louis, I have no other means of keeping my Fleet complete in provisions and water, but by sending them in detachments to Gibraltar. The enemy will come out, and we shall fight them; but there will be time for you to get back first. I look on *Canopus* as my right hand and I send you first to insure your being here to help beat them.

Louis sailed at 6.00 p.m. that day, in the *Canopus* with the *Queen*, *Spencer*, *Zealous*, *Tigre* and frigate *Endymion*. But the squadron was to play a decisive role in history without firing a shot. When observers in *Algeciras* informed Villeneuve that the ships were off Gibraltar, the news persuaded him that Nelson's fleet was weak enough for him to come out.

The repercussions of Sir Robert Calder's action on 23 July still reverberated throughout the fleet, although only four of the ships in Nelson's fleet had taken part in it. Calder was with the fleet when Nelson arrived. He was deeply disappointed with the public reaction to his failure to pursue the enemy. He read in the newspapers that

> John Bull thought I might have done more; but I never dreamt that any prejudices could have gone forth so as to have in any manner affected my character as an officer for as a man, in not having brought the enemy to action on the succeeding day, after the victory I had obtained over them.

He demanded a court martial as a 'necessary evil' to clear his name. It would be a very cumbersome procedure, which needed at least five captains to sit on the court for many days, so it could only be held in one of the home ports without disrupting the service. Furthermore, Calder felt 'compelled to call upon most of the captains who were with me in the action, in order to refute the malicious reports and to clear all my character from suspicion.'[22]

There was much sympathy for Calder in the fleet. Nelson wrote,

> Who can, my dear Fremantle, command all the success which our Country may wish? … I have had the best disposed Fleet of friends, but who can say what will be the event of a battle? and it most sincerely grieves me, that in any of the papers it should be insinuated, that Lord Nelson could have done better. I should have fought the enemy, and so did my friend Calder; but who can say that he will be more successful than another?[23]

Captain Codrington was a fierce supporter of Calder, though he had not been present at the action.

> I maintain that the utmost that can be brought against Sir Robert Calder, then, is a small error in judgment; but I by no means admit that such charge can be made good. … And I trust … the public will yet see the cruelty and injustice of thus persecuting a man who has served his country faithfully, and with the credit of a good and brave officer, for more than five and forty years … And are we, with such a prospect before us, to eat salt beef and get the scurvy in a prison for eight or nine months, &c. &c. &c., for thirteen shillings a day?[24]

Witnesses were needed for the trial, which meant that Captain William Brown of the *Ajax* and Captain William Lechmere of the *Thunderer* had to be sent home, leaving their first lieutenants in command. Calder had asked Captain Phillip Durham of the *Defiance* to attend, and at first he agreed, but by 7 October he was having second thoughts and wrote to Nelson, '… the enemy in great force are on the eve of sailing, I cannot volunteer quitting the command of a line of battle ship entrusted to me at so critical a moment.' He wrote to Calder at the same time. 'However painful it may be for me to see the necessity of avoiding such a risk at such a crisis, yet I must feel on the occasion that the dictates of private friendship must yield to those of public duty.' Calder was mortified and wanted Durham ordered to attend, but Nelson did not comply.[25]

There was another shock for Calder in Nelson's orders from Barham. Since Calder's flagship, the *Prince of Wales*, was a powerful three-decker, he was to go home in a frigate. As reinforcements continued to join the fleet – the 100-gun *Royal Sovereign* on 8 October, the 74-gun *Belleisle* on the 10th – by the 13th Nelson felt strong enough, both morally and materially, to defy Barham's orders. He found Calder in 'a very distressed state' about the potential loss of his flagship and decided to allow him to go home in the *Prince of Wales* after all, making the rather specious excuse that 'she wants several little things done to her, perhaps instead of Gibraltar Mole it will be nearly as quickly done by her going direct to Spithead.'[26]

As it turned out, Nelson had twenty-seven ships of the line, four frigates and two smaller vessels under his direct command on 19 October. If they were fully manned they would have 19,081 men on board, out of 28,860 for the whole of Nelson's command, or about two-thirds of his strength. In total they made up about 15 per cent of the men in the Royal Navy at that moment.

After Admiral Louis had sailed with his squadron on 4 October, to take on stores, Nelson ordered Captain Duff of the *Mars* to take the post of honour in charge of the Inshore Squadron.

> As the Enemy's Fleets may be hourly expected to put to sea from Cadiz, I have to desire you that you will keep, with the *Mars*, *Defence*, and *Colossus*, from three to four leagues between the Fleet and Cadiz, in order that I may get the information from the Frigates stationed off that Port, as expeditiously as possible. Distant Signals to be used, when Flags, from the state of the weather, may not readily be distinguished in their colours. If the Enemy be out, or coming out, fire guns by day and night, in order to draw my attention. In thick weather, the Ships are to close within signal of the *Victory*: one of the Ships to be placed to windward, or rather to the Eastward of the other two, to extend the distance of seeing; and I have desired captain Blackwood [in command of the frigates which were still closer to the port] to throw a frigate to the Westward of Cadiz, for the purpose of an early and easy communication.

Codrington of the *Orion* had his doubts and wrote to his wife, 'So distant Lord Nelson keeps us from Cadiz, I think it very possible they may contrive to give us a good run for it.'[27]

This time no-one expected a long wait like the one off Toulon earlier in the year and as early as 9 October there were signs that something was happening with the Combined Fleet. According to Nelson's diary, 'Fresh breezes E. received an account from Captain Blackwood that the French ships had all bent their topgallant sails. Sent the Pickle with him with orders to have a good look.' The next day it was reported that the enemy was 'ready for sea and at the very harbour's mouth.'[28]

They were still there on 14 October, when Nelson ordered new dispositions for the fleet.

> Placed *Defence* and *Agamemnon* from seven to ten leagues West of Cadiz and *Mars* & *Colossus* five leagues East from the Fleet, whose station will be from 15 lgs. to twenty West of Cadiz, and by this chain I hope to have a constant communication with the frigates off Cadiz.[29]

Captain Duff was a very late recruit to the 'Band of Brothers'. He knew comparatively little of Nelson when the *Victory* arrived on station on 28 September, for their services had never brought them together. Duff went on board the flagship on 13 October for 'a very merry dinner.' Nelson was 'certainly the pleasantest Admiral I ever served under.' On 18 October, in one of his last letters, he wrote to Sophie, 'You ask me about Lord Nelson, and how I like him. I have already answered that question, as every person must do that ever served under him.' He was already falling under the spell of the great admiral and his men, like those of several other ships, were painting the sides of the ship in the 'Nelson chequer'.

Meanwhile the routine work of the ship continued. The carpenters of the *Mars* spent the early weeks of October repairing bulkheads which had been broken when the ship had been cleared for action during a false alarm, making a new pump to replace the old decayed one, making canvas pipes to carry the human waste out of the ship's heads, and in menial work such as new broom handles.[30]

On the evening of 19 October the *Euryalus* was 4 miles off Cadiz in 'Light Vearrable Airs and Clear,' according to the erratic spelling of her Prussian master, Frederick Ruckert. As night fell the officers began to notice 'Enemy making Signals between Rota and Cadiz & about the coast.' Between 3.30 and 4.00 a.m. the ship was tacked and more sail was set as the watches changed over. As the sun rose they saw 'the Enemys Ships in Cadiz having thir top Gallt Yards a Cross & Eight Ships ther Top-Sail Yards hoistd at the Mastheads' – they were getting ready to sail. By 7.00 a.m. it was clear that the leading ships had raised their anchors and were heading out of the harbour. Captain Blackwood sent the frigate *Sirius* to repeat signals to the lookout ships and then to the flagship.[31]

The *Mars* was on station in sight of Cadiz when the *Euryalus* made the signal 'that the Enemy was coming out of Port'. The *Mars* repeated the signal, giving Nelson warning to prepare for the great battle. Then the crew of the *Mars* were 'employed making the ship perfectly clear for action.'

William Pryce Cumby, first lieutenant of the *Bellerophon*, was the first in the main body of the fleet to spot the *Mars*'s signal. Cumby called the captain and asked permission to repeat it to the rest of the fleet, but Cooke was sceptical – he would not repeat a signal of such importance unless he could read it with his own eyes. Cumby took the opposite view – 'The very circumstance of the importance of the Signal added to my own perfect conviction of the correctness of my statement founded on long & frequent experience of the strength of my own sight, induced me again to urge Captain Cooke to repeat it ...'.

Cooke relented a little, saying that if anyone else could recognize the signal, he would indeed repeat it, but according to Cumby,

> None of the Officers and Signalmen however were bold enough to assert positively as I did that the flags were No 370 & I had the mortification to be disappointed in my anxious wish that the *Bellerophon* should be the first to repeat such delightful intelligence to the Admiral.

Before long, the *Mars* hauled down this signal and now made the distant signal No. 370, which used balls and shapes in different parts of the rigging and was easier to read from a distance. Cumby was confirmed in his belief, but before the *Bellerophon* could repeat it, the *Victory* herself acknowledged the *Mars*'s signal. Nelson noted in his diary, 'Fine weather. Wind Easterly. At 1/2 past 9 the Mars being one of the Look Out ships made the signal that the Enemy were coming out of Port. Made the signal for a general chase SE.'[32] Cooke had been invited to dinner with the Admiral that day, but this was immediately cancelled.[33]

Blackwood sent the sloop *Weazle* to Gibraltar to inform the British forces there, while the schooner *Pickle* went north to tell any ships that might stray into the area. Blackwood found a few minutes to write to his wife.

> What do you think, my own dearest love? At this moment the Enemy are coming out, and as if determined to have a fair fight; all night they have been making signals, and the morning showed them to us getting under sail. They have thirty-four sail of the line, and five Frigates. ... At this moment we are within four miles of the enemy, and talking to Lord Nelson by means of Sir H. Popham's signals, though so distant, but repeated along by the rest of the Frigates of this squadron. You see also, my Harriet, I have time to write to you, and to assure you that to the last moment of my breath I shall be as much attached to you as man can be, which I am sure you will credit. It is very odd how I have been dreaming all night of my carrying home dispatches. God send so much good luck! The day is fine; the sight, of course, beautiful. I expect, before this hour tomorrow, to have carried General Decres on board the Victory in my barge,

which I have just been painting. God bless you. No more at present.[34]

Nelson's first decision was to order the fleet into a 'general chase' to the south-east, in which each ship would make its best way to the enemy, in no order of battle. He apparently planned to intercept the enemy as he entered the Mediterranean. He soon revised this and ordered his ships to take up a pre-arranged order of sailing, though his slowest three-deckers, the *Britannia*, *Prince* and *Dreadnought*, were to take station as most convenient; in practice the 'general chase' signal seems to have been observed. According to Codrington,

> It was nearly calm, and has continued so ever since, till towards evening, but we have now a nice air, which fills our flying kites and drives us along at four knots an hour. 'Orion', true to the affection we bear for her, has now got a-head of all but the 'Belleisle', although she started in the very middle of the fleet, half of which were to windward and half to leeward.[35]

Nelson hoped that the easterly wind would bring Admiral Louis with his squadron out of Gibraltar, and by 1.00 a.m. he was in sight of the Rock, with his ships hove to, or stopped in the water, to await both friend and enemy.[36] At 8.00 a.m. on 20 October Nelson called Collingwood on board the *Victory*. Collingwood suggested an immediate attack, but Nelson was cautious – perhaps he feared the engagement would take place too late in the day and go off at half-cock.[37]

Blackwood spent the morning of the 20th watching as the enemy came slowly out of Cadiz harbour. Twenty-nine of them were out by 8.20 a.m. when a ship came into sight, towing another and steering straight for the enemy. She was soon recognized as the *Agamemnon* towing a prize, but it took some time to attract her attention by gunfire and signals. Thirty-four of the enemy were out by 8.50, and an hour later there were 'Strong Breezes and thick with Rain', and the enemy was lost sight of for a time. Further out with the fleet there was despondency, for the captains thought that the enemy fleet was further ahead than it actually was, and were expecting to sight them any minute. Codrington wrote to his wife in despair,

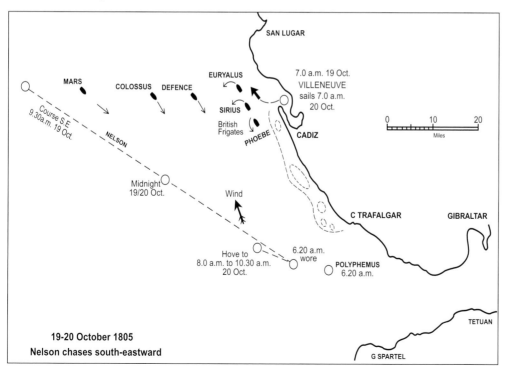

The situation on the eve of battle, showing the position of Nelson's fleet and the line of frigates and ships of the line to send messages to him.

All our gay hopes are fled; and instead of being under all possible sail in a very light breeze and fine weather, expecting to bring the enemy to battle, we are now under close-reefed topsails, in a very strong wind with thick rainy weather, and the dastardly French returned to Cadiz. Had they persevered we should certainly have come up with them, from the decisive dash we made for the Gut of Gibraltar.[38]

At 12.30 the weather cleared a little and the officers of the *Euryalus* were relieved that the enemy was still in sight, and still holding his course. Blackwood sailed out to look for Nelson's fleet and at 2.00 p.m. he saw it to the south-south-west. Ten minutes later he told the *Sirius* that he was going to join the Admiral, and at 3.00 he was exchanging signal numbers with the rest of the fleet. At 3.20 p.m. he signalled Nelson with the news he wanted to hear – 'Enemy appears determined to push to the westward.'[39] From past experience off Toulon and in the Atlantic campaign, Nelson knew just how easy it was to lose an enemy fleet. When he signalled to Blackwood, 'I rely on you that I do not miss the enemy', all the frustrations of the last two years were in the flags which fluttered from the *Victory*'s masts.[40]

Blackwood stayed within 2 or 3 miles of the enemy fleet during the hours of darkness, shifting sails and manoeuvring to keep a suitable distance and signalling regularly to Nelson. The anxiety and hard work of the night are scarcely recorded in the ship's log, but there must have been relief as the next day dawned; 'at Day light the Body of the Enemy's Fleet ESE 5 or 6 miles English Fleet WSW'. Now there was little that could prevent a battle taking place that day.

CHAPTER 17

Into Battle

Nelson rose soon after dawn on the morning of 21 October. According to Surgeon Beatty, he came on deck

> … dressed as usual in his Admiral's frock-coat, bearing on the left breast four stars of the different orders which he always wore with his common apparel. He did not wear his sword … It had been taken from the place where it hung up in his cabin, and was ready on his table; but it is supposed he forgot to call for it.[1]

He was in good spirits and spoke with the officers already on deck about the prospects for a great victory, saying to Hardy that he would not be satisfied with capturing less than twenty sail of the line. At 6.40 a.m. he ordered the hoisting of the signal 'prepare for battle', which was 'Answered by the Fleet immediately, which was complied with.'

Collingwood, too, was an early riser. Smith, his servant, went into his cabin at 6.00 a.m. and found him up and dressing. They looked out of the window to see the enemy fleet, Collingwood remarking that 'in a very short time, we should see a great deal more of them.' He shaved with great composure and went on deck where he met Lieutenant Clavell, who had put on boots for the occasion. The Admiral advised him. 'You had better put on silk stockings, as I have done: for if one should get shot in the leg, they would be so much more manageable for the surgeon.' Collingwood then went below decks, offering words of encouragement to the men. 'Now, gentlemen, let us do something today which the world may talk of hereafter.'[2]

Captain Codrington of the *Orion* had slept well in his cot, 'although the enemy were ranged under our lee, knowing that it was not Lord Nelson's intention to give them battle till the morning.'[3] Lieutenant Cumby of the *Bellerophon* was wakened at 6.00 a.m. by his friend and messmate, Edward Overton, the master of the ship. 'Cumby my boy turn out, here they are all ready for you, thrice and thirty sail of the line close under our lee & evidently disposed to await our attack.' Cumby leapt out of bed and dressed himself, then said a short prayer 'for a glorious victory to the arms of my country.' He was soon on deck where he saw the enemy fleet 'to leeward standing to the southward under easy sail, and forming line on the starboard tack.'[4]

Lieutenant Paul Nicolas, the junior marine officer of the *Belleisle*, noted the men's enthusiasm.

> I was awakened by the cheers of the crew and by their rushing up the hatchways to get a glimpse of the hostile fleet. The delight manifested exceeded anything I ever witnessed, surpassing even those gratulations when our native cliffs are descried after a long period of distant service.[5]

The men of the *Belleisle* had breakfast not long after 9.00, when the officers met together. In the view of Nicolas, 'though each seemed to exult in the hope of a glorious termination to the contest so near at hand, a fearful presage was experienced that not all would unite again at that festive board.'[6]

Around 10.00 a.m. each of the ships got ready for battle, using a routine they had practiced many times. The galley fire was extinguished, for if it was hit the flames might cause the whole ship to catch fire. There would be no more hot meals until after the battle. Chains were fitted to the lower yards so that they would not be shot away in action, immobilizing the ship and crashing down on to the heads of the crew below. Partitions of all the cabins from the lower deck upwards were dismantled. Non-essential stores were jettisoned as the ships approached the enemy. Most crews threw wooden chicken coops overboard – the unfortunate occupants, who had kept the men supplied with fresh eggs over the last few months, seem to have gone with them. Some ships had pigsties or sheep pens with fresh food for the officers, but these went, too – though this did not include a sheep that Nelson had sent on board the *Leviathan* in the West Indies, which survived the battle to become a valued possession of Captain Bayntum's family.[7] The *Thunderer* ditched an arms chest, a 'moveing pantry', a wood screw bolt, five small deal tables, a larger elm one and fourteen officers' canvas beds. The *Leviathan* went even further in getting rid of the officers' comforts: the bulkheads of the wardroom, the partitions of the officers' cabins, three wainscot tables, a small writing desk and eight small deal tables, along with the tables and stools used for seating the ship's company, and washboards which fitted at the bottoms of the gunports to help keep out spray. One wonders how much enthusiasm the crews showed in disposing of the comforts of their betters. One also wonders how many warrant officers used it as a chance to account for stores that had been damaged or embezzled over the months.[8]

On the poops and quarterdecks of each ship, captains and admirals took their places. Collingwood, as seen from the *Euryalus* close by, was 'walking the break of the poop with his little triangular gold-laced cocked hat, tights, silk stockings, and buckles, musing over the progress of the fight, and munching an apple.'[9] The first lieutenant of each ship stayed with the captain, ready to advise and take over command if needed. The master was there, too, as an expert adviser on navigation and seamanship. In the *Bellerophon*, Captain Cooke was aware of the possibility of his being 'bowl'ed out' by enemy shot and he decided to take his first lieutenant, William Pryce Cumby, into his confidence. Cumby pointed out that the same shot might kill him also, and suggested that Edward Overton, the master, should also be involved. Cooke agreed and each read a copy of Nelson's memorandum and Cooke asked

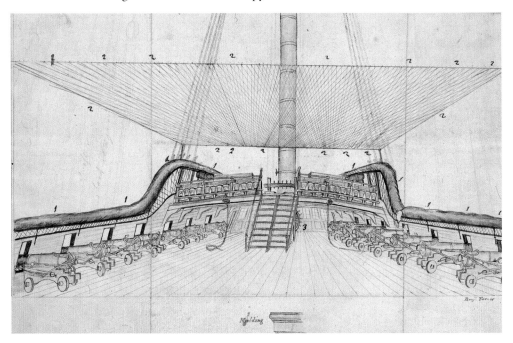

The quarterdeck of the Venerable *before the Battle of Camperdown in 1797. The partitions of the captain's cabin have been struck down, and a net stretched overhead to protect the men from falling debris from masts and rigging.*

whether they understood it. Cumby replied that the instructions were 'so distinct & explicit, that it was quite impossible they could be misunderstood.'[10]

Captain Rotherham, if his 'Commonplace Book' is to be believed, was accompanied by two midshipmen as aides de camp 'to pass the word', by taking messages to the other parts of the ship. Each ship had a signal officer, usually a lieutenant in a flagship and a midshipman in a private ship – Midshipman Thomas Huskisson did the duty in the *Defence*, under acting-Lieutenant James Plumridge. Two or three seamen stood by to hoist signals when required, while the officers kept their telescopes trained on the flagship and on the frigates which might repeat important messages when the principals were out of sight. In the *Defiance*, Captain Durham assembled James Spratt's boarding party on the quarterdeck and 'told them should we be boarded or have occasion to board he had no doubt that Mr Spratt would lead them to glory.' Spratt was flattered and made a low bow to the Captain. The men gave three cheers and went back to their stations at the guns.[11]

Lieutenant Cumby had chosen petty officers to steer the *Bellerophon* in battle. In charge was William Hayter of Gosport who had served in merchant ships for thirteen of his forty-six years, and in the navy for seventeen more. He was grey haired and hard of hearing, which must have been a disadvantage in the circumstances. William Ferguson from North Shields was thirty-nine and was 'a trusty fellow' who had served thirteen years continuously in the Royal Navy. John Stewart had sailed for eleven years in the coal trade from Berwick, and an equal time in the King's service. In 1792 he had married Helen Hunter of Plymouth and two of their children were alive; his family history was recorded in a tattoo on his right arm. William Yell, only 5 feet 1½ inches tall, had sailed in coasters from Harwich for twelve years, followed by thirteen in the Royal Navy.[12]

In action, the most basic unit was the single gun. The barrel was a long tube, cast in iron. Over the last twenty years Thomas Blomefield of the Board of Ordnance had worked with iron founders in Scotland and the north of England to improve the quality of metal, so that guns could withstand a greater rate of fire. The form of the barrel had been simplified and it now had a round breech and a ring to hold the rope that secured it. It tapered towards the muzzle. At the top of the breech was the touch hole, used to light the powder, by means of either a match or a flintlock. Just behind the centre of the barrel were the trunnions, which allowed it to pivot for elevation.

The wooden carriage was supported by four wheels known as trucks. A thick rope, the breeching rope, secured the gun to rings on the side of the ship, with room for it to recoil. A pair of thinner ropes, the gun tackles, passed through blocks and tackles and were used to haul the gun out to the gunports for firing – this process, 'running out' the gun, was the most labour-intensive activity in a battle. A third kind of rope, the train tackle, was used to hold the rear of the carriage to rings near the centre of the ship, so that it would not run out by accident while the ship was heeling. Wedges were driven under the breech to elevate the gun. Training from side to side was more difficult. It could be done by hauling unequally on the gun tackles on each side, with fine adjustments by leverage by means of a lever called a handspike.

The crews laid out their equipment beside their guns. The wooden rammer would be used to push cartridge and ball in against considerable air pressure. The 'flexible rammer' was made of stiffened rope and could be used for the same function when the gun was close to a gunport. The sponge was used to wet the inside between shots, so that the next cartridge would not be set off by a burning fragment as it was loaded. An iron 'worm' at the end of a wooden pole would be used to take spent cartridges out of the gun. Cartridges of powder were brought up from the magazine in limited numbers and laid out behind the gun. Cannonballs were already there, placed in holes drilled round the wooden coamings of hatches.

The heaviest guns were the 32-pounders on the lower decks of the ships of the line. If fully manned there were fourteen men for each pair of guns, one on each side of the ship. In conventional battles where the ships fought in line some distance apart, it was unlikely that guns would be needed on both sides at once, and the two crews could combine. In the new Nelsonic style of battle, it was quite likely that ships would be engaged on both sides as they crashed through the enemy line. In some ships it was ordered that each group of

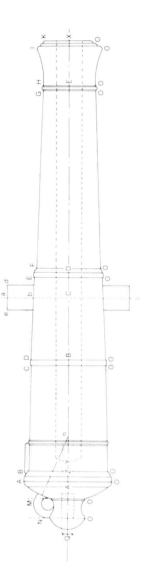

The details of the construction of a Blomefield pattern gun, as used at Trafalgar.

fourteen should operate two guns side by side on the same side of the ship, as there was less distance for the men to travel. The more skilled men, the loaders and aimers, would stay with the same gun while a party would move from one to the other to do the heavy work of hauling the gun out through its port.

The men were dressed for battle. In the *Belleisle*, 'Some were stripped to the waist; some had bared their necks and arms; others had tied a handkerchief round their heads; all seemed eagerly to await the order to engage.'[13]

Midshipman William Badcock was in charge of the five midship guns on each side of the *Neptune*'s main (lower) deck.[14] Midshipman Robert Patton, of the *Bellerophon*, was 'stationed at two guns and opposites on the lower deck, a little abaft the mainmast and not far from the after hatchway ladder.'[15] As such they had two roles. One was to pass orders from the captain, to use a particular type of charge or shot or to concentrate on one part of the enemy. The other, requiring more initiative, was to reorganize the men of the gun crews, as required, to cope with casualties.

Seamen had almost a free hand in choosing their messmates, and often men from the same town or district would congregate together. West country accents might predominate at one table, Scottish at the next and the almost illicit Irish Gaelic at another. However, it might have been different in gun crews, because the men were chosen by their officers to give the right balance of experience for the job in hand. But there seems to have been congregations of particular nationalities in certain guns, which might suggest the officers and men reached some kind of understanding.

The crews on the upper deck doubled as sail trimmers when required, so they included some of the most experienced men. The party on the first gun on the *Bellerophon*'s forecastle were seasoned enough to know how exposed their position was and some of them bore scars of previous battles and accidents. Thomas Jones, a thirty-four-year-old Welshman, had broken his nose in a fall. Owen Roberts, another Welshman, had lost the third finger on his left hand. Samuel King, a forty-year-old American from Philadelphia with fourteen years' naval service, had a scar on his upper lip. Joseph McCrea from Aberdeen had been at sea since he was fourteen and had sailed in the Baltic trade for eight years before entering the Royal Navy. He was 'much scarred in the throat from scrofula.' He served with three other Scots, two of whom were experienced merchant seamen. Peter McFarlane, a very stout, muscular man from Kirkcaldy, had spent five years in the Baltic trade and nine in the Royal Navy. William Taylor had spent less than three years in the King's service but almost two decades in the West India trade. He came from Banff in the north of Scotland but had a wife in Plymouth. Robert Dowey, a twenty-eight-year-old former weaver from Newburgh in Fife, was 'well made' and 'good looking' according to his officers. Peter Johnson was a

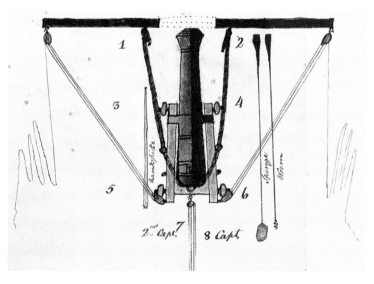

The position of the men round a 9-pounder gun on the frigate Amazon, 1799. Each man is denoted by a number.

Swede from Karlscrona, thirty-nine years old with fifteen of these at sea. He was tattooed with a flowerpot on his right arm. Richard Schofield of Yorkshire had spent five years in the Jamaica trade and twelve in the Royal Navy. He was tattooed with signal flags on his right arm and a pierced heart on his left. John White from London was the tallest man in the crew at 5 feet 10 inches, as well as the oldest at forty-one. He was also tattooed, with the letters SBMM on the back of his left hand.

Two decks below, the men on the seventh 32-pounder on the lower deck were slightly less experienced. James Marshall, the gun captain, was the oldest man in the ship at fifty-six, having served seventeen years in the Newfoundland trade and thirteen in the Royal Navy. He was quite tall at 5 feet 9 inches, and had lost his left eye. He came from Waterford, although he had lost his Irish accent. He had only one countryman in the gun crew. Thomas McNally was a former butcher from Kildare with a wild look in his face. Far more exotic was John Hachett, a tall American Negro from Maryland. He had spent at least eight years at sea since the age of fourteen, and had not been in his native land for ten years; possibly he was a runaway slave. John Signieur was a Frenchman from Bordeaux, perhaps a French royalist, who had been pressed out of a British merchant ship in 1794 after seven years' service at sea. William Gardner, a brazier of Bristol, had spent five of his twenty-six years in the navy, while Cicero Adams, a shoemaker from Cambridgeshire, had only started his sea career at forty-two and had served for six years. Henry Park from Scarborough had spent twenty years at sea, two thirds of them with the Royal Navy.[16]

In most ships it was normal for boys to carry powder from the magazines to the guns, inside round wooden cases to protect them from accidental sparks. In the *Mars* Captain Duff forbade this and ordered that 'proper men', that is, responsible members of the crew, be allocated to handle the powder, while the boys would swab the decks to remove any loose powder.[17] Usually the guns were kept loaded in wartime, with a lead apron over the touch hole to prevent accidents. In the *Mars* Duff planned to load each of his lower deck guns with two round shots for the first and second broadside, doing the maximum physical damage to the enemy hull. The guns of the upper deck would have one round shot and one load of grape shot, to inflict injuries on the enemy crew.[18]

In the magazines in the bowels of the ship, cartridges had already been made up by enclosing powder in linen or paper. In the grand magazine in the bows of the *Victory* Gunner Rivers took charge. One seaman took the cartridges out of their bins and gave them to another who put them in round wooden cases for safety as they were carried around the decks. A man stood on the magazine ladder to hand them up, while another passed empty cases down to be refilled. For reasons of space and safety only a proportion of the powder was made up into cartridges before the battle, so a seaman opened up the paper of new cartridges for another to fill them. Other men did the same job with 18- and 12-pounder cartridges, while the cooper and his assistant opened new barrels as required. One man tended the lamp in the light room, which was kept entirely separate from the magazine itself for safety reasons – the light shone through glass panels to the magazine. The middle magazine in the centre of the ship handled cartridges for the 18-pounders on the middle deck and was manned by seven men. The after magazine had the ammunition for the 12-pounders on the upper deck, quarterdeck and forecastle, and had a similar number of men.[19]

Around 10.00 a.m., Captain Blackwood of the *Euryalus* noticed that the enemy ships were 'wearing' – turning round by presenting their sterns to the wind, and heading in the opposite direction, back towards Cadiz. The British officers naturally assumed that they had had second thoughts in view of the strength of the opposition, and were trying to escape a battle. In fact Villeneuve had interpreted Nelson's movements as an attack on the rear of his line (now its head) and was manoeuvering to protect it.[20]

More than half a century after the event, the reminiscences of Midshipman Hercules Robinson of the *Euryalus* took on a glow of nostalgia.

There is now before me the beautiful misty sun-shiny morning of the 21st October. The delight of us all at the idea of a wearisome blockade, about to terminate with a fair stand-up fight, of which we knew the result. The noble fleet, with royals and studding sails on both sides, bands playing, officers in full dress, and the ships covered with ensigns, hanging in various places where they could never be struck.[21]

Lieutenant Hoffman, who had transferred to the *Tonnant* early in 1805, noticed the same enthusiasm. 'We answered with alacrity the signal to make all sail for the enemy. The sails appeared to know their places and were spread like magic.'[22]

Several ships had their own bands, unrecognized by any Admiralty regulation. William Robinson was shocked earlier in the year when the captain of the *Revenge* had pressed some men from an East Indiaman he had been escorting. Having listened to the Indiaman's band for several days, he made a point of taking the two best musicians to increase the *Revenge's* own band. According to Robinson, this was 'for the captain's amusement, and not to strengthen our force to engage an enemy.[23] The band in Hoffman's previous ship, the *Minotaur*, was formed by more legitimate if less successful means. According to Hoffman,

> Our gallant and would-be musical captain consulted us all respecting harmonious sounds, but alas! we were weighed in the musical balance and found wanting. This, however, did not discourage him. … it was determined nem. con. that a pease-barrel should be manufactured into a big drum, that two ramrods should be metamorphosed into triangles, that the two bassoons and the hautboy taken in the French frigate should be brought into action without loss of time, that the marine and ship's fifer, with the marine drummer, should be drilled with the others, under the direction of the sergeant, and a horrible confusion of unmusical sounds they made for more than six weeks.[24]

Competent or not, the bands assembled on the quarterdecks of the ships. Some played *Rule Britannia*, some *Downfall of Paris* and the *Minotaur's* played *Britons Strike Home*.[25] In light winds the sounds carried far over the water, and the cacophony was amazing to friend and foe alike.

Apart from the noise of the bands and the orders of the officers, the crews were supposed to be quiet. Captain Duff ordered 'The strictest silence to be observed by the Men at their Guns, and the Officers are directed to prevent any unnecessary noise and confusion.'[26] But there were whispered conversations, at the very least, as the ships were got ready.

> In such a bustling, and it may be said, trying as well as serious time, it is curious to notice the different dispositions of the British sailor. Some would be offering a guinea for a glass of grog, whilst others were making a sort of mutual verbal will, such as, if one of Johnny Crapeau's shots (a term given to the French) knocks my head off, you will take all my effects; and if you are killed, and I am not, why, I will have yours, and this is generally agreed to.[27]

Officers did a final tour of the gundecks to make sure that all was in order. In the *Bellerophon*, Lieutenant Cumby noticed how some of the crews had chalked 'Victory or Death' in very large letters on the barrels of their weapons, and thought this 'a very gratifying mark of the spirit in which they were going to their work.' It was now 11.00 a.m., but the ship was not likely to be in action for at least an hour. The Captain ordered the hands be piped to dinner, so that they could go into battle with a full stomach. Since all the tables and bulkheads had been taken down, the officers ate cold meat on the fixed structure round the rudderhead.[28] The *Victory's* men were issued with 'Dinner and grog' at 11.00 a.m., and at the same hour Codrington of the *Orion* 'gave the ship's company their dinner, and ate the leg of turkey myself, which was prepared beforehand, so that … we were all strong, fresh, hearty and in high spirits.'[29]

Not all the captains were so far-sighted. In the *Tonnant* the men were only issued with a small amount of cheese and half an allowance of grog as they entered the battle, at about their normal dinner-time of 12 noon. As a result they would fight 'on nearly empty stomachs.'[30]

Some men acknowledged the possibility of death and had already written letters to be sent on in that event. Thomas Aikenhead, a young midshipman in the *Royal Sovereign*, wrote to his father,

> We have just piped to breakfast – thirty-five sail, beside smaller vessels, are now on our beam, about three miles off. Should I, my dear parents, fall in defence of my king, let that thought console you. I feel not the least dread on my spirits. Oh! my parents, sisters, brothers, dear grandfather, grandmother, and aunt, believe me, ever yours.

And to his sister,

> Accept perhaps for the last time your brother's love; be assured, I feel for my friends, should I die in this glorious action – glorious, no doubt, it will be. Every British heart pants for glory. Our old Admiral (Vice Admiral Collingwood) is quite young with the thoughts of it. If I survive, nothing will give me greater pleasure than embracing my dearest relations. Do not, in case I fall, grieve – it will be to no purpose. Many brave fellows will, no doubt, fall with me, on both sides. Oh! Betsey, with what ardour I shall, if permitted by God's providence, come to England to embrace you all.[31]

Midshipman Robert Smith of the *Victory* tried to put a brave face on it.

> Most dear and honor'd parents,
> As I expect to be in action tomorrow morning with the Enemy of our Country, the idea of which I assure you gives me great pleasure, in case I shall fall in the noble cause I have wrote these last few lines to assure you that I shall die with a clear conscience, pure heart and in peace with all men.

He had two final requests – that his parents would pay his respects to all his friends, and that 'you my dearest of Mothers will not give way to those low spirits which you are subject …'[32]

Captain Blackwood of the Euryalus had similar feelings. Following his letter of the evening of the 19th, he wrote at 8.00 a.m. on the 21st,

> The last 24 hours has been most anxious work for me; but we have kept sight of them, and at this moment bearing up to come into action. Lord N 27 sail of the line. French 33 or 34. I wish the six we have at Gibraltar were here. … My dearest dear Harriet, your husband will not disgrace your love or name: if he dies, his last breath will be devoted to the dearest best of wives. Take care of my boy; make him a better man than his father.

At this point Nelson signalled Blackwood to come on board the flagship, along with the three other frigate captains. He was rowed over, expecting to be transferred to one of the ships of the line whose captains had gone to the Calder court martial. But Nelson had no intention of losing his best frigate captain. The visit, as Blackwood wrote later,

> … was only to talk and explain to me what he expected from the frigates in and after the action; to thank me, which he did but too lavishly, for the service I had afforded him, the intelligence and look-out we had kept; and to tell me, if he lived, he should send me home with dispatches …

This would have been a great honour, which would almost certainly have led to a knighthood. Nelson decided to keep Blackwood on board until the last moment, in case any further instructions were needed.[33]

Blackwood was concerned about the position of the *Victory* at the head of the line, where she would attract most of the enemy's fire during the approach. He discussed it with Hardy,

Nelson's coat as worn at Trafalgar, with the stars of his four orders.

and when Nelson remarked in characteristic vein 'I'll give them such a dressing as they never had before,' Blackwood boldly suggested that he might transfer his flag to the *Euryalus* where he would be in less danger. Nelson would not hear of it, so Blackwood tried to persuade him to allow one of the other large ships, the *Temeraire*, *Neptune* or *Leviathan*, to take the lead. Nelson agreed and he hailed the *Temeraire*, which was sailing abreast of the *Victory*. Since he could not be heard, Blackwood was sent over with the message but meanwhile, according to one report, Lieutenant John Yule, in command of *Victory*'s forecastle, found that one of the studding sails was badly set and took it in to reset it. Nelson spotted this and thought Yule was reducing sail without orders. He rushed forward to upbraid him. The sail was replaced and the *Victory* drew ahead of the *Temeraire*. Blackwood returned to find that Nelson was increasing sail and the *Temeraire* could not overtake. Later, on the final approach to battle, Nelson signalled her again with an order to stay astern of him.[34]

The Admiral began to make his personal preparations. He wrote a codicil to his will that morning, witnessed by Hardy and Blackwood. Lady Hamilton's services to the nation were recommended for attention, and he left her 'a Legacy to my King and Country, that they will give her an ample provision to maintain her rank in life.' He referred to Horatia Nelson Thompson as his 'adopted' daughter and demanded that she use the name of Nelson only. He began to write in his private diary,

May the Great God, whom I worship, grant to my Country, and for the benefit of Europe in general, a great and glorious Victory; and may no misconduct any one tarnish it; and may humanity after Victory be the predominant feature in the British Fleet. For myself, individually, I commit my life to Him who made me, and may his blessing light upon my endeavours for serving my Country faithfully. To Him I resign myself and the just cause which is entrusted to me to defend. Amen, Amen, Amen.

Lieutenant John Pasco was also concerned with his private position. He was senior to Lieutenant John Quillam, first lieutenant of the *Victory*, by more than three years but Nelson had made Pasco his flag lieutenant. This was certainly a post of some honour, a close aide to the Admiral and his voice in making signals to the other ships, but the first lieutenant was guaranteed promotion in the event of a victory, the flag lieutenant was not. He resolved to speak with Nelson about it. At about 11.00 a.m., 'on entering the cabin, I discovered his Lordship on his knees writing [the furniture had been cleared away for battle]. He was then penning that beautiful Prayer. I waited until he rose and communicated what I had to report, but could not at such a moment, disturb his mind with any grievances of mine.'[35] Pasco remained as flag lieutenant destined to play a vital part in the symbolism of the action.

There was much concern about Nelson's safety. His uniform, though not the full dress of an admiral, might attract the attention of enemy marksmen by its epaulettes and stars. Beatty the surgeon suggested to Scott the chaplain that he might be persuaded to cover them with a handkerchief. Scott the Secretary intervened: 'Take care, Doctor, what you are about: I would not be the man to mention such a matter to him.' Beatty lingered on deck, but had still not spoken when Nelson ordered everyone to their stations for battle. He went down to the cockpit, where he would see Nelson later in the day in different circumstances.

Blackwood was still on board the *Victory* awaiting further instructions and occasionally conversing with Nelson when, about 11.30 a.m., the Admiral decided to send a signal as a 'fillip' to the fleet. He considered for some time then went to the signal lieutenant on the poop. 'Mr. Pasco, I wish to say to the fleet, "England confides [i.e. is confident that] that every man will do his duty."' Pasco pointed out that in the new signal code devised by Sir Home Popham all the words could be made by three-flag combinations, except 'confides' and 'duty', which would have to be spelled letter by letter. He suggested 'expects' instead of 'confides' and Nelson replied, 'that will do, Pasco, make it directly.'[36] At the time Blackwood slightly misinterpreted the signal as 'England expects every officer, and man will do their utmost duty.'[37]

Victory and Euryalus *enter the battle. Engraved by R.H. Nimmo.*

In the *Royal Sovereign*, Collingwood's first reaction to the flurry of flags was to say 'that he wished Nelson would make no more signals, for they all understood what they were to do.' He changed his mind when he saw the message in the signal, and 'expressed great delight and admiration.'[38] In the *Defence*, Captain Hope chose not to broadcast the signal throughout the ship.[39] Did he feel it was unnecessary with so many other things to do, or was his Scottish pride offended by the use of England? In any case the men of the *Defence* knew something was happening from the reaction of the other ships. According to Lieutenant Hoffman, 'It was answered with three hearty cheers from each ship, which must have shaken the nerve of the enemy.'[40] Lieutenant Cumby of the *Bellerophon* agreed that it 'produced the most animating and inspiriting effect on the whole fleet.'[41] Even Seaman William Robinson of the *Revenge* abandoned his cynicism.

> … could England have seen her sons about to attack the enemy on his own coast, within sight of the inhabitants of Spain, with an inferior force, our number of men being not quite twenty thousand, whilst theirs was upwards of thirty thousand; from the zeal which animated every man in the fleet, the bosom of every inhabitant of England would have glowed with indescribable patriotic pride; for such a number of line-of-battle ships have never met together and engaged, either before or since.[42]

In some ships, such as the *Royal Sovereign*, *Belleisle* and *Neptune*, the men were ordered to lie flat on the decks, although the officers stayed upright to observe the action and set an example of coolness.[43] In the *Victory* Lieutenant Louis Roteley of the marines remembered his father's advice. 'Louis, you will soon be in battle … whatever you do, be sure to keep your head erect in battle, never bow to a Frenchman's shot, it is folly, for when you hear the ball's whistle you are safe, the ball has passed harmless before you can hear it.'[44]

As the ships approached the enemy at speeds of 2 or 3 knots, Nelson had to decide exactly where his line should attack. One possibility, allowed for in the original plan, was to cut it at about a third of the way from the head, sealing off a section to be eliminated by him and Collingwood. Another, more traditional for an admiral and appealing more directly to Nelson's well-developed sense of honour, was to head for the enemy flagship, probably in the centre of the line. But there was a difficulty here, for the allied fleet had still not hoisted its flags. Was Villeneuve still in command, in his old flagship, the *Bucentaure*? Or did the new tactics signal that Vice-Admiral Rosily had taken over, perhaps with his flag in the largest ship in the fleet, the unmistakable *Santisima Trinidad*? There was a much more fundamental question – what would the enemy do? Clearly he was retreating towards Cadiz, but would he continue to do so when that seemed increasingly unlikely to succeed? Nelson's greatest fear was that a large part of the fleet would escape, so he sailed to intercept with the head of the Franco-Spanish line, apparently abandoning the idea of containment.

As his ship approached the enemy, Collingwood began to consider another tactic, mentioned in the original plan but apparently unauthorized by Nelson except in his general instruction that the second-in-command should have complete control of his division 'after the intent of the commander-in-chief had been signified.' Before 9.00 a.m. Collingwood attempted to put his division into a 'line of bearing', instead of a 'line astern' of the Admiral. This meant that he wanted the other ships to come abreast of him on a particular bearing, so that they would all come into action at once. Clearly this could have a great tactical advantage, but it would slow the general progress while the other ships caught up with the flagship, which was not Nelson's intention. It was a difficult manoeuvre to execute in any case, and for that reason it had largely fallen into disuse. Collingwood was half-hearted about the orders, and he soon came to see that Nelson had no intention of shortening sail himself. Though he ordered individual ships to 'make all possible sail with safety to the masts', Collingwood did not slow down his own flagship to give them any chance to catch up.[45]

In the *Royal Sovereign* as in the *Victory*, the stunsails forced officers into decisions in the final

The position at the start of the battle, from Corbett's Campaign of Trafalgar.

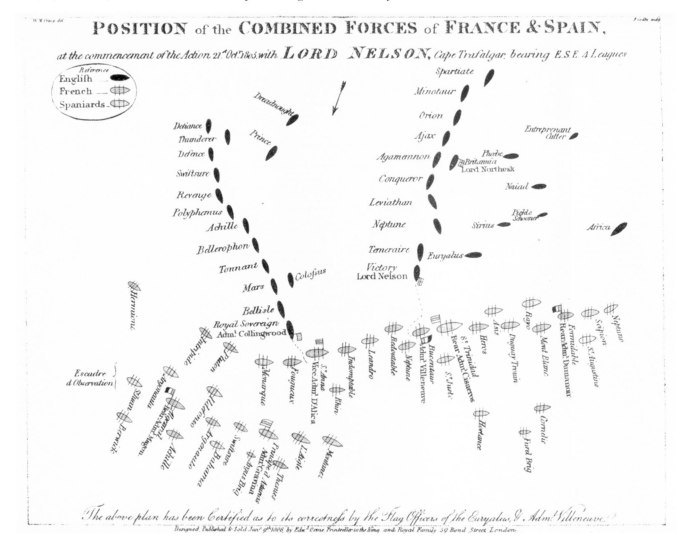

stages of the approach. Clavell, the first lieutenant on the *Royal Sovereign*, was keen to set them to speed the advance, but Collingwood was hesitant, since the ship was already some way ahead of the others. 'The ships of our line are not yet sufficiently up for us to do so now; but you may be getting ready.' Ten minutes later the sails were ready to hoist and Clavell looked expectantly at his admiral, who nodded. Clavell went to Captain Rotherham, his nominal superior and told him that the Admiral wanted him to make all sail. Thus decisions were made in the *Royal Sovereign*. The stunsails were hoisted and the ship began to move slightly faster through the water. Soon she was about a mile ahead of the nearest friendly ship.[46]

At midday Nelson displayed his foresight by ordering another signal, 'prepare to anchor'.[47] He had perhaps noticed the strong swell that was coming in from the ocean, despite the light winds. He knew this meant a storm somewhere out in the Atlantic and that his potentially battle-damaged ships would be vulnerable. Anchors were to be attached to their cables and made ready to drop with the minimum of effort.

About the same time the first shot rang out, the enemy hoisted their flags and the battle began. One French captain wrote,

> … the Combined Fleet ran up their colours; this was done in imposing style in the *Redoutable*; the drums were beating and the musketry presented arms to the standard, it was saluted by the executive and crew with seven cheers 'Vive l'Empereur!'[48]

CHAPTER 18

The First Round

At about midday on Monday, 21 October, the *Royal Sovereign* was the first British ship to engage in what became known as the Battle of Trafalgar. Collingwood was eight years older than Nelson, but he had always been just behind him. As Midshipman William Rivers of the *Victory* put it, 'It is a strange coincidence that Collingwood should have succeeded Nelson five times, first in the *Lowestoffe*, the *Bristol*, the *Badger*, the *Hinchinbrooke* …' – his most celebrated succession of all would take place later in the day.[1] Collingwood was just ahead of Nelson for once. There is a suspicion that in his haste he neglected some rules of tactics. Because of confusion over his orders for a line of bearing, because of the poor sailing of some of his ships and his impatience to get into the fight ahead of his chief, the division was far more strung out that it need have been. In his rush to battle Collingwood had got some way ahead of his second ship, *Belleisle*, far further than the *Victory* was ahead of the *Temeraire* in the other line.

As the *Royal Sovereign* came close to the enemy line, several ships opened fire. Immediately the British ships broke out their white ensigns on their sterns, supplemented union flags hung from the stays of the main topmasts and fore topgallants, for Nelson was determined to do everything he could to allow his ships to identify themselves in the fog of war. Noting that he was about to engage before the *Victory*, Collingwood remarked to Captain Rotherham, 'What would Nelson give to be here!' He intended to rake the Spanish 112–gun ship *Santa Ana*, now conspicuously flying the flag of Rear-Admiral Alva. As the leading ships moved closer to the enemy line, they reached the first moment of real danger but, as Midshipman Hercules Robinson of the *Euryalus* put it, 'the fire would scarcely be opened till the approaching ship was within four hundred yards, and as this ground would be over in five or six minutes, she would not have to encounter more than a couple of broadsides into her bows, and then would have ample revenge in a double-shotted broadside into her opponent's stern.'[2]

Collingwood passed under the stern of the *Santa Ana* and fired a broadside along her decks. This, the first British fire in the action, was devastating. Fourteen guns were put out of action, and up to 400 men were killed or wounded. The French 74 *Fougeaux*, just astern of the *Santa Ana*, was fired on by the *Royal Sovereign*'s starboard broadside, but to much less effect; *Fougeaux* was presenting her bow rather than the highly vulnerable stern, and the fire was at much longer range.

Collingwood now took the *Royal Sovereign* alongside the *Santa Ana*, so close that their yards were locked together. But the Spaniards had anticipated such a move, and the starboard guns were ready. A first broadside struck the British hull, and the impact caused it to heel so much that two strakes of plank were momentarily lifted out of the water. The *Royal Sovereign*'s studding sails, the most delicate of canvas, were shot away, and one fell on to the hammock rails on the gangway. Collingwood, combining coolness with economy, called Lieutenant Clavell and the two officers stowed it in one of the ship's boats. The British return fire was severe. Midshipman George Castle, in charge of some of the 32-pounders on the lower deck, later wrote to his sister, 'I can assure you it was glorious work. I think you would have liked to have seen me thump into her quarter.'[3] Captain Rotherham was also behaving well in action. He wore a large cocked hat, 'rather a remarkable one', and was asked why he exposed himself so much to sharpshooters. 'I have always fought in a cocked hat, and I always will.'[4] At this point he felt the enemy ship was already beaten and congratulated the Admiral. 'She is slackening her fire and must soon strike.'

The *Royal Sovereign* was still the only British ship in action, and the enemy was not inactive. The French *Fougeaux* copied the *Royal Sovereign*'s own manoeuvre and raked Collingwood's ship from astern, though at comparatively long range. The powerful French 80-gun ship, *Indomptable*, engaged her on the quarter while the Spanish two-deckers *San Justo* and *San Leandro*, ahead of the *Santa Ana* in the original line, were firing from ahead. The *Royal Sovereign* paid the penalty for being so far ahead of the rest of the squadron. Collingwood ordered his marines off the exposed poop deck, although he stayed there himself for a little longer. The *Fougeaux* came in closer, but was driven off by the *Royal Sovereign*'s quarterdeck carronades. Relief came after fifteen or twenty minutes of this close action when Captain Hargood's *Belleisle* sailed into the gap between the *Royal Sovereign* and *Santa Ana* on one side, and the *Fougeaux* and *Indomptable* on the other. This part of the action would eventually be reduced to a single-ship duel between the two three-deckers.[5]

The *Belleisle* had overtaken the slower *Tonnant* earlier in the day. As she approached about fifteen minutes behind the flagship, the band had ceased to play and 'an awful silence prevailed in the ship,' interrupted by Captain Hargood's cries to the helmsman – 'Steady! Starboard a little! Steady so!' The first enemy shot took the head off a young marine, and soon Hargood was hit and bruised from the throat to the waist, but he stayed on deck. The crew continued to lie on the deck and some were tempted to rise, to be restrained by cries of 'Lie down there, you, sir!' Paul Nicolas, the sixteen-year-old marine lieutenant with less than three weeks' experience, felt an urge to join them until his superior, Lieutenant John Owen, whispered, 'Stand up and do not shrink from your duty!' Ebenezer Geale, the first lieutenant, suggested turning the ship briefly to fire a broadside but the Captain snapped, 'No, we are ordered to go through the line, and go through we shall, by —.' Geale was killed soon afterwards, by which time there were about sixty casualties. At last Hargood gave the order 'Stand to your guns!' The ship passed through the enemy line between the *Fougeaux* and the Spanish *Santa Ana*, firing broadsides at each as she went. It was observed by Midshipman George Westphal of the *Victory*, who had left the gundeck to make a report to his first lieutenant. Everyone had expected her to fire sooner,

> … the enemy having been firing at her and, indeed, having *visibly* damaged her spars some time previously: but the *Belleisle* still reserved her fire until she had brought both broadsides, as appeared to us in the *Victory*, to bear upon ships on each side of her, and was within pistol shot, when her two broadsides were discharged spontaneously [sic], and with the precision of a volley of musketry; upon seeing which Lord Nelson exclaimed, 'Nobly done Hargood.'[6]

The *Belleisle* paid a high price for her Captain's daring and restraint. She was soon surrounded by several of the enemy and pounded on all sides. The *Fougeaux* rammed her amidships and then shot her mizzenmast away. The French *Achille* came up against her quarter but the *Belleisle* was unable to respond because the wreck of the mizzen and its sails masked her guns; at 2.00 p.m. young Lieutenant Nicolas was standing under the break of the poop helping the seamen run out a carronade, when he heard the cry 'Stand clear there! Here it comes!' He looked up to see the mainmast falling over the side just above him. Then the French *Neptune* joined in the fracas and completed the destruction of the British ship's rigging. 'In this unmanageable state we were but seldom capable of annoying our antagonists, while they had the power of choosing their distance, and every shot from them did considerable execution.'[7] The *Belleisle* had 'scarcely seen the British colours since one o'clock'. She suffered severe damage. She lost all her masts, boats and anchors, and on her hull 'Ports, port-timbers, channels, chain-plates, all exhibited unequivocal marks of the terrible mauling she had received.'[8] Lieutenant Nicolas visited the cockpit and found a scene beyond his comprehension.

> My nerves were but little accustomed to such trials, but even the dangers of the battle did not seem more terrific than the spectacle before me. On a long table lay several anxiously looking for their turn to receive the surgeon's care, yet dreading the fate which he might pronounce. One subject was undergoing amputation, and every part was heaped with sufferers: their piercing shrieks and expiring groans were echoed through this vault of misery; … what a contrast to the hilarity and enthusiastic mirth which reigned in this spot the preceding evening![9]

The *Belleisle* had 126 killed and wounded, nearly a quarter of her crew. She was the only British ship to lose all her masts.

Captain Duff's *Mars* was the third British ship in action, after the *Royal Sovereign* and *Belleisle*. By noon she was already beginning to feel the effect of the enemy's long-range shot from the *San Juan Nepomuceno*, *Pluton*, *Monarca* and *Algeciras*. Duff was on the quarterdeck as his duty demanded, while his son, Norwich, had been found slightly safer duties below deck. Duff intended to cut between the Spanish 74-gun *San Juan Nepomuceno* and the French 74 *Pluton*, but the French ship pulled ahead to overlap with the *San Juan*, closing the gap. Seeing the danger of being raked by the *Pluton*, Duff tried to get ahead of her and towards the Spaniard, but his rigging was already damaged and more ropes and sails were cut by the fire of the French ship as she approached. The *Mars* was now in danger of running her bows into the port side of the *Santa Ana*, whose other side was engaged with the *Royal Sovereign*. To avoid this Duff could only order the ship to turn head to wind, exposing her stern to the French *Algeciras* and the Spanish *Monarca*.

The *Leviathan*, under Captain Bayntum, arrived in time to prevent disaster, but now the *Mars* was under fire from the *Pluton* and the *Fougeaux* (still engaged with the *Belleisle* on her other side). The *Fougeaux* was beaten off and it was thought that she had surrendered, but in fact her colours had been shot away, and she continued to fire. On the poop of the *Mars*, Thomas Norman, the captain of marines, noticed *Fougeaux* dropping astern, and feared that she was getting into a position to rake the *Mars*. He ran down to the quarterdeck to inform the Captain, but the wind had dropped and it was impossible to manoeuvre. Duff asked, 'Do you think our guns would bear on her?' and the Marine Captain replied, 'I think not, but I cannot see for smoke.' Duff decided to let the guns fire on the ships they could see and went to the end of the quarterdeck to look over the side. He ordered his aide-de-camp, Midshipman Alexander Arbuthnott, to go below and order the gun crews to be pointed aft, towards the *Fougeaux*.[10] At that moment a broadside was fired, by either the *Fougeaux* or *Pluton*. The situation is described by Midshipman James Robinson from Banff:

> It was then the gallant Captain fell. I saw him fall. His head and neck were taken entirely off his body, when the men heard it, they held his body up and gave three cheers to show they were not discouraged by it, and they returned to their guns.

According to the ship's log, the poop and quarterdeck were 'nearly cleared' of men. The braces and much of the running rigging was shot away, leaving the ship 'entirely unmanageable'. Lieutenant William Hennah took command. The *Fougeaux* and *Pluton* turned their attention to other tasks, giving some relief. The *Mars* drifted for the next two hours, occasionally coming under fire from passing ships.

The *Tonnant* was a powerful 80-gun ship, the only one in Nelson's fleet that day. Captain Charles Tyler headed her between the French *Algeciras* and Spanish *Monarca*. The latter ship, badly handled by her captain, allowed the *Tonnant* to get close by her stern and fire a devastating raking broadside which swept the Spanish decks. The *Tonnant* came alongside her, but the Spanish flag was hauled down after a few shots and it was believed she had surrendered. The ships separated and the *Algeciras* came up from behind and tried to cross the *Tonnant*'s stern. Captain Tyler managed to evade this and the two ships became entangled, side by side. Though the position was to *Tonnant*'s advantage, Tyler was wounded and the crew had to fight off an attempted boarding by the men of the *Algeciras*. Eventually the power of the heavy guns prevailed and the French surrendered. The *Tonnant* suffered twenty-six killed and fifty wounded, less than any other ship of the first wave, and could claim to have forced the surrender of two ships single handed – though the *Monarca* later reneged and re-hoisted her flag while the fight with the *Algeciras* was raging.

As the *Bellerophon* came into action fifteen minutes behind the *Tonnant*, Captain Cooke resolved to hold his fire until he was passing through the enemy line. But in the last few hundred yards of the approach, the ship began to suffer casualties and damage. The men's spirits fell due to the failure to reply, and the knowledge that enemy gunfire would create a kind of smokescreen. At 12.20 Cooke gave the order to open fire, ten minutes before the ship broke through the enemy line, passing astern of the French *Montanes* and the Spanish *Monarca*, as she dropped out of her battle with the *Tonnant*.[11]

The *Bellerophon* immediately ran into the French 36-gun *Aigle*. All the British ship's sails were backed to reduce the impact, but her starboard bow struck the Frenchman's port quarter with some force. Cooke sent his first lieutenant below decks to explain the situation to the officers there. *L'Aigle* had many men stationed in her rigging as sharpshooters, who, following the collision, began to wreak carnage on the upper deck. Edward Overton, the master, was one of the first to be hit, and Lieutenant Cumby, returning from his mission below, was shocked to see his friend being carried down with a shattered leg. He went to the quarterdeck ladder to meet a quartermaster who told him that the Captain had been killed by a musket shot. Cumby hurried on deck to take charge, the only unwounded man of the three who had read Nelson's memorandum that morning.

At once, Cumby saw that the position on deck was hopeless, as the musketeers of *L'Aigle* were picking off men one by one. The *Monarca* was still engaged on the port bow, though most of her guns had been put out of action, while two other ships were firing on the beleaguered *Bellerophon*, one nearly astern and the other on the port quarter. Cumby's first action in command was to order all the men, including Midshipman John Franklin, off the poop, the most exposed position of all, hoping that the gunfire of the 18- and 32-pounders below would be enough to win the uneven battle. Indeed *L'Aigle* soon closed all her lower deck

The Belleisle *enters the battle at 12.15 p.m. By E. Duncan, engraver.*

ports against the British gunfire, and abandoned the heavy artillery duel in favour of another tactic. Hand grenades were thrown on to the decks and through the open gunports, causing a great deal of injury to the crew. Cumby threw one overboard.[12] Another got as far as the gunner's storeroom where it exploded, setting the stores on fire. Fortunately, the blast also blew the magazine door shut, or both the *Bellerophon* and *L'Aigle* would have exploded together. The gunner, John Stevenson, calmly went up to Lieutenant George Saunders, in charge of the guns on the lower deck, and asked to borrow a few hands to deal with the fire. This was done and it was put out before the majority of the crew knew about it. Years of training in fire fighting had had some effect.

The battle continued, with fierce aggression on both sides. According to one officer,

> … *l'Aigle* twice attempted to board us, and hove several grenades into our lower deck, which burst and wounded several of our people most dreadfully: she likewise set fire to our fore chains: our fire was so hot, that we soon drove them from the lower deck, after which our people took their quoins out, and elevated their guns, so as to tear her decks and sides to pieces.

At 1.40 p.m., after more than an hour of this, *L'Aigle* began to drift away, with more than 400 of her men out of action and her starboard quarter beaten in. *Bellerophon* continued to fire and *L'Aigle* made no reply with her great guns.

But John Franklin became engaged in a duel of his own. He had spotted a man wearing a cocked hat on the foretop of *L'Aigle*, who had already killed several men with this rifle. Franklin was talking to a fellow midshipman who was struck down and fell at his feet. With a sergeant of marines he was helping to carry a wounded black seaman below decks, when another shot hit the wounded man in the breast. Franklin said to the sergeant, 'They'll have you next', but he responded by taking up a position below decks where he could bring his musket to bear on the Frenchman. Meanwhile Franklin had to dodge another shot by hiding behind the mast. Eventually, after seven shots from the sergeant below, Franklin saw the rifleman fall from his perch into the sea.[13]

At his guns on the lower deck, Midshipman Robert Patton was close to the after hatchway by which the wounded were carried down. He saw the 'melancholy procession' begin before the ship opened fire.[14] The cockpit became so crowded with the wounded that the surgeon asked Lieutenant Cumby for permission to use the great cabin instead. As there was a lull in the action, Cumby agreed to allow this for fifteen minutes, provided the men were taken below if any of the enemy's unengaged ships attempted to attack. Cumby met the wounded Captain of Marines, James Wemyss, and was told, ''tis only a mere scratch & I shall have to apologise to you for having left the deck on so trifling an occasion.' He was about to have his right arm amputated.[15] The *Bellerophon* went on to engage her first target, the *Monarca*, which had already been seriously damaged by the *Tonnant*, and she surrendered after a few shots. But the price was high.

> Our loss, as might be expected, was considerable, and fell chiefly on our prime seamen, who were foremost in distinguishing themselves; twenty-eight, including the Captain, Master, and a Midshipman, were killed outright; and 127, including the Captain of Marines, who had eight balls in his body and his right arm shot off, before he quitted the deck; Boatswain, and five midshipmen, were badly wounded, and about forty more slightly, so as not to be incapable of duty; nineteen of the wounded had already died before we left Gibraltar.[16]

The *Colossus* was a 'large class' 74-gun ship, almost as powerful as an 80. She had been completed only in April that year and was under the command of Captain Morris. As she approached the enemy a little before 1.00 p.m. she came under heavy fire. She headed for the bow of the French *Swiftsure* (captured from the British in 1801) but the enemy captain turned his ship in time so that the two ships were side by side, the *Colossus* to port, the

Swiftsure to starboard. Already the battle was intense and the view to starboard for the British gunners was obscured by smoke. In the confusion the *Colossus* ran into the Spanish *Argonauta* with her port side and for a while the two were locked together. British gunfire prevailed and the Spanish ship was almost silenced as the two ships came apart after about ten minutes, except for a few of the aftermost guns. Morris was wounded above the knee but stayed on deck as a tourniquet was applied. His ship fired a parting broadside into the *Argonauta*'s stern.

Meanwhile the *Swiftsure* came up on the *Colossus*'s port side and began to engage the after part of the ship, while the Spanish *Bahama* engaged her stern, firing across the bows of the *Swiftsure*. The French ship moved ahead and took the brunt of the British fire; she was soon defeated and fell back. The *Bahama* was now alone and lost all her masts in the ensuing gunfire. She surrendered by raising a union jack on some hen coops on the poop deck. The *Swiftsure* returned to the fray and tried to rake the *Colossus* by the stern. Morris was quick enough to see this and turned his ship just as the enemy attack began, so that the two were side by side again. The *Colossus* gave a broadside which brought down the French mizzenmast and the British *Orion* fired another broadside in passing, bringing down the mainmast; the *Swiftsure* finally surrendered. The *Colossus* lost forty men killed and 160 wounded, the highest number for any British ship in the battle.

*   *   *

As the *Victory* headed the other British line into battle, the largest object seen by the gunners of the *Bucentaure*, *Redoutable*, *Heros* and *Santisima Trinidad* was her fore topsail. It was the second biggest sail in the ship, 80 feet wide at the foot, 54 feet at the head and 54 feet deep, covering an area of 3618 square feet, made in the sail loft at Chatham Dockyard.[17] The main topsail was, of course, rather larger, but was hidden by the fore topsail. The next largest sails, the main and fore courses, were rather less deep and therefore smaller. Since the French tended to fire high, the fore topsail received a large proportion of their fire in the early stages of the battle. By the end of battle it had a great tear down the middle of the sail, probably caused by the accumulation of cannon shots, perhaps helped by wind damage late on. There were about twenty medium-sized holes, mostly made by individual cannon shots, and fifty or sixty smaller ones, probably the result of enemy musketry in close action. The sail survives today as the largest and most evocative single relic of the battle (as the *Victory*

A view of the battle, with Nelson's line beginning to engage in the centre of the picture, and Collingwood's line behind. Painted by Nicholas Pocock.

is largely reconstructed) and there are dozens of small square holes, undoubtedly made by souvenir hunters over the last 200 years.

Whereas the *Royal Sovereign* had entered the battle alone and well ahead of her supporters, the *Victory* was followed, almost too closely, by the *Temeraire*. The *Victory* began to slow down due to damage to her rigging and the *Temeraire* was less than a ship's length behind by the time Captain Harvey gave the order to cut away her studding sails, to slow her down, but even so she almost touched the flagship's stern.

On the poop of the *Victory*, Signal Midshipman John Pollard can lay claim to being the first officer injured. A round shot struck the ship beside him and a splinter hit his right arm. He dropped his telescope and Lieutenant Pasco asked if he was hurt. Pollard was slightly stunned and felt his right arm, which was not broken, so he answered no. He picked up his glass again and a few moments later a musket shot passed through it.

Nelson had identified the French flagship, *Bucentaure*, and headed to cross her stern. The *Victory* passed so close that her yardarms were over the poop of the Frenchman, who could only

> … bring some of the aftermost guns and the musketry fire from the poop and from the tops to bear on her; but all were very soon put out of action by the guns of her upper deck and works, and by the carronades on her poop, which rose considerably above us.[18]

Victory's guns fired an overwhelming raking broadside into the *Bucentaure*, dismounting up to twenty guns and killing and wounding nearly 400 men. The Frenchman was reduced to a defenceless state.

But as she passed away from the battered *Bucentaure*, the *Victory* was heading into trouble of her own. On her starboard bow was the French 74 *Redoutable*; to her port, slightly further away, was the 80-gun *Neptune*. Hardy tried to manoeuvre to avoid his bow being raked by one or the other, and ended up with his starboard side alongside the *Redoutable*, with the two ships locked together. The French captain, Lucas, was now in an ideal position to use his men's training in close-range battle. His men were skilled in grenades so that 'they had so acquired the habit of hurling them that … our topmen were throwing two at a time.' The British believed that the lower deck ports of the *Redoutable* were deliberately closed to prevent boarding, but Lucas denied this; they were simply held shut by the closeness of the two ships.

The *Temeraire* was not far behind and had to turn to avoid the *Victory* as she fired on the *Bucentaure*. She subsequently fired into the Spanish flagship, the unmistakable four-decker *Santisima Trinidad*, positioned just ahead of the *Bucentaure*. After about twenty minutes the scene was so obscured by smoke that Captain Harvey feared he might be firing into the *Victory*, and ceased fire to allow it to clear. Instead he saw the *Victory* closely engaged with the *Redoutable* and decided to come to her support.

Nelson, unlike other commanders, had not ordered the forty marines on the poop deck of the *Victory* to lie down on the approach to battle. Now they were under heavy fire from the decks and tops of the *Redoutable* and it was noted that none were wounded below the waist. Nelson remarked on their coolness but the two senior lieutenants were wounded and Captain Adair sent the most junior, Louis Roteley, below decks to get the remaining marines up from the gun crews, while those surviving were withdrawn from the poop to slightly more sheltered positions on the quarterdeck and gangway.

Below decks, Roteley found a scene of horror, with the ship engaged on both sides.

A man should witness a battle in a three-decker from the middle deck, for it beggars all description. It bewilders the senses of sight and hearing. There was fire from above, fire from below, besides the fire from the deck I was upon, the guns recoiling with violence reports louder than thunder, the deck heaving and the side straining. I fancied myself in the infernal regions, where every man appeared a devil. Lips might move, but orders and hearing were out of the question: everything was done by signs.

For all the chaos of the gundeck, the ship's marines were fully absorbed in their work with the guns and did not want to leave them. 'In the excitement of the action men had thrown their red jackets and appeared in check shirts and blue trousers. There was no distinguishing Marine from Seaman – they were all working like horses.' Roteley found four NCOs to help him, and they managed to get about two dozen men away from the guns, using force where necessary. Back on deck he found Captain Adair wounded but still firing, when another shot hit him fatally in the back of the neck.

At about the same time a shot struck the deck between Hardy and Nelson, who remarked, 'This is too warm work, Hardy, to last long.' Bourke the Purser was on deck although he should have been stationed in the cockpit to help with the wounded. Nelson said to him, 'Bourke, I expect every man to be at his station' and he went below. John Scott the Secretary, the father of three 'dear boys', was cut in two by a cannon shot. As his body was thrown overboard Nelson asked, 'Was that Scott? … Poor fellow!'[19]

At about 1.15 p.m., after about an hour of close action, Nelson was in the act of turning towards the enemy when a shot from *Redoutable*'s top hit him on the left shoulder. It fractured the scapula and then entered the thorax, broke the second and third ribs, penetrated the left lung, touched the pulmonary artery and broke the spine before lodging in the muscles of the back.[20] It is difficult to see how a single shot could have done more damage without killing its victim outright.

Nelson was lifted up by Sergeant Secker of the Royal Marines and two seamen, and carried the excruciating journey down four steep ladderways to the cockpit in the bowels of the ship. They were acting on the orders of Hardy, and probably it was instinctive reaction, because wounded men were always carried below. Yet it had two unfortunate consequences. It could only have worsened the spinal injury, and it denied Nelson the chance to die among his men, on the battlefield that was *Victory*'s quarterdeck. Nelson was in great agony, spurting blood, and his lungs were filling up with fluid. The famous words on his deathbed were issued in gasps, not articulated serenely as the written record seems to suggest.

Midshipman Pollard continued his duties as signal midshipman on the poop, and continued to be subjected to near misses.

After being engaged with the *Redoutable* some time I observed the officers and men

The Victory's *fore topsail,*
before it was damaged by
souvenir hunters in the
nineteenth century.

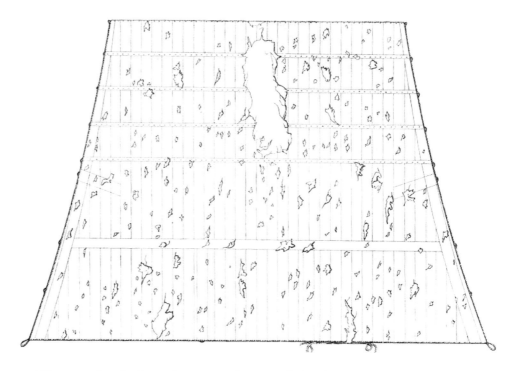

falling very fast, both on the poop and quarterdeck, when my attention was arrested by seeing in the tops of the *Redoutable* a number of soldiers in a crouching position, loading and directing their fire on the poop and quarterdeck of the *Victory*. The signal quartermaster called King was standing by me at this time. I pointed them out to him and there being a number of spare muskets on the signal chest for the use of the marines, I took one of them, King supplying me with ball cartridge from two barrels kept on the after part of the poop for the use of the marines. Captain Adair of the marines and the small arms party he had left (he after being either killed or wounded) was firing from the starboard gangway of the *Victory* into the *Redoutable*'s decks when Captain Adair was killed. The two lieutenants of marines was previously wounded by musket balls. As often as I saw the French soldiers rise breast high in the tops to fire on the *Victory*'s deck I continued firing until there was not one to be seen. King the quartermaster in the act of giving me the last parcel of ball cartridge was shot through the head and fell dead before me, this event gave me perhaps a great shock! I was the only officer left alive on the poop after the action ceased (that was stationed there), the others being either killed or wounded. Thus originated the claim that I was the person who shot the man that killed Lord Nelson.[21]

Lieutenant Roteley, however, believed that his marines, dragged up reluctantly from the middle deck to the quarterdeck, killed the man and many others.

The marines became exasperated. I was now in command, and the first order I gave was to clear the mizzen top, when every musket was levelled at that top, and in five minutes not a man was left alive in it. Some Frenchman has vaunted that he shot Nelson and survived the battle, and I have heard a book had been published so stating, but it must be a romance. I know the man was shot in five minutes after Nelson fell.[22]

The British ships were now at the second dangerous stage of the battle, with only some of them in action and likely to be overwhelmed by the enemy. In the *Euryalus*, Hercules Robinson could see nothing to worry about.

Anyone who has assisted in a naval battle must know how impossible it is for ships of the line to cluster round one intruder and swamp her; and even if they could assail a single one altogether, as twenty Irish caravants attack one obnoxious Shavanist at the fair, they obstruct each other and their sticks, instead of falling on the victim form a canopy over his head.[23]

Lieutenant Humphrey Senhouse had a good view of the battle from the decks of the *Conqueror*, three ships behind the *Temeraire*, and in retrospect he could see much danger at this moment.

> Instead of doubling on the enemy the British ships were on that day doubled and trebled on themselves. The *Victory, Temeraire, Royal Sovereign, Belleisle, Mars, Colossus* and *Bellerophon* were placed in such situations in the onset that nothing but the most heroic gallantry and practical skill at their guns could have extricated them. If the enemy's vessels had closed up as they ought to have done around these vessels from rear to rear, and had possessed a nearer equality in active courage and ability, it is my opinion that even British skill and British gallantry could not have availed.

The situation looked even worse for those who knew that Nelson was seriously wounded.

But no one believed that the British were going to lose. Less than a third of their ships were now engaged, and some of these were beginning to win in the skirmishes that were being fought. A score more ships were ready to join their comrades and to complete the attack on the French and Spanish line.

Nelson falls on the deck of Victory, *with gun crews and marines in action around him. By Denis Dighton.*

CHAPTER 19

The Later Battle

As the remaining British ships entered the action, each captain had to make his own choice about exactly how to engage the enemy. Since the leading ships were fully committed to their own fights, neither Nelson nor Collingwood had any more influence, which would have been the case even if the former had not been mortally wounded. Nelson's original plan had called for an 'advanced division' under 'an officer who, I am sure, will employ them in the manner I wish, if possible.' Such a squadron might well have been useful in the circumstances, particularly in relieving the first six ships of Collingwood's line. Blackwood in the *Euryalus* had orders to use Nelson's name in urging any ships forward as he thought fit, but there is no sign that he felt it necessary to use it.

Nelson had apparently planned to put the advanced division under Duff of the *Mars* – placing remarkable trust in a man he hardly knew. It is perhaps significant that he did not consider his third-in-command, Rear-Admiral the Earl of Northesk, for the honour. Northesk's ship, the 100-gun *Britannia*, was the oldest in the fleet, launched in 1762 and the last relic of the age of the establishments, which had constrained British ship design in the first part of that century. She had only joined Collingwood on the last day of September, from the blockade of Brest. Northesk did nothing to attract Nelson's attention after he took command and is only mentioned once in his correspondence, as 'the Earl' – for Nelson himself was only a viscount. In experience and character he was far inferior to the other rear-admiral, Thomas Louis, who was watering his squadron at Gibraltar. Louis might well have taken the initiative during the approach and rallied some of the remaining ships for a decisive blow, but Northesk did the opposite. Far from exercising the leadership due from his rank, Northesk showed signs of hesitation. Nothing was written down, but a strong tradition survived in the family of his flag captain, Charles Bullen, that the two had a dispute in the approach to battle. Northesk wanted to shorten sail and slow down, Bullen refused.[1] Captain Rotherham, Bullen's friend, wrote that Northesk 'behaved notoriously ill in the Trafalgar action.'[2]

As they sailed into action, the ships at the head of the line tended to look for worthy opponents, perhaps three-deckers or a flagship against whom, with total self-confidence, they expected to gain glory and fame by capturing a large ship or an admiral. Later arrivals, such as Captain Codrington in the *Orion*, tended to look for points where they could intervene with greatest effect in the developing battle, perhaps going to the aid of a ship that was heavily engaged.

In most battles, ships sailed into action with very few sails set – usually just the fore, main and mizzen topsails, allowing a maximum amount of sail area for a minimum amount of work in trimming them. The lower sails, the courses, were kept furled, for they needed a lot of attention and might interfere with the work of the gunners on the upper decks. At Trafalgar all ships carried considerably more sail than usual, in order to bring them into action in very light winds. They carried courses on the lower yards, and studding sails on booms, which projected beyond the yards of the topsails, topgallants and courses. As the ships approached the enemy line these became an encumbrance, because they restricted manoeuvrability. A large number of men would be needed to trim them in battle, or to take them in, but captains were reluctant to take men away from the gun crews in the circumstances, while the men themselves might have refused to go. The simple solution for some captains was to cut the studding sails and let them fall over the side. Captain Laforey did this in the *Spartiate* as the ship entered the battle just before 3.00 p.m.[3] Even the economical Collingwood did it in the *Royal Sovereign*, 'grieving, … no doubt, at the loss of so much beautiful canvas'.[4] If drawings are to be believed, some ships entered the battle with their studding sails still up. W. J. Huggins's painting of the *Belleisle* shows the remains of studding sails hanging from the booms as the ship entered the battle after the *Royal Sovereign*. In some cases the enemy completed the job. According to Lieutenant Hoffman of the *Tonnant*, 'We were saved the trouble of taking in our studding sails, as our opponents had the civility to effect it by shot before we got into their line.'[5]

Even without studding sails, it was not easy to manoeuvre ships in these circumstances, for the great majority of each ship's crew were needed to serve the guns. According to Captain Rotherham's quarter bill, a first-rate would have a crew of 738 'effective men', excluding officers and their servants: 224 of these would serve the 32-pounder guns on the lower deck, with 192 on the middle deck, 144 on the upper deck and fifty-three on the quarterdeck and forecastle, making a total of 613. A hundred and four men, mostly marines, were allocated to small arms fire from the decks and tops. There were twenty-two men in the magazines and twelve more were below decks to repair shot damage or help with the wounded. Five men were allocated to steer the ship and there were six signalmen, leaving only eight men in the rigging – two each for the fore and mizzen masts and four for the mainmast. They would probably be stationed in the tops, ready to carry out urgent repairs or free lines that became fouled. Major adjustments of the sails would require a far larger labour force.

The British had a clear advantage in the direction of the wind. In theory each ship could move in three major directions, to the east at right angles to the enemy line, to the north to run in parallel with it, or south to sail against it. There was no good reason for choosing the last course, to pass along the enemy line, which would have led each ship into to a series of brief engagements with several ships as they were passed. The first course brought the ships into action as fast as possible, and the second allowed them to engage with individual ships for as long as necessary. The French and Spanish, on the other hand, had only two reasonable courses. The wind prevented them from sailing west towards the approaching British fleet, and they could not go east without running into rocks and other dangers. They could either continue on their northerly course towards Cadiz, or turn round again if battle tactics dictated it.

On reaching the enemy line, each British ship would try to pass astern of an enemy ship, raking it through the stern windows. After that, it would turn to port to come alongside an enemy, so that the wind was now coming over the port side of the ship rather than over the stern. As well as the movement of the wheel and rudder, the sails of the ship would have to be adjusted by hauling on the braces – 'hauling up' as the sailors called it. Since most of the crew were devoted to the guns, this would have caused some difficulty, especially under strong enemy fire. Possibly, the men were got up from the lower gundecks, for large numbers were needed to haul on the braces to trim the sails of three masts. However, hauling up is much easier than tacking, in which all the sails have to be moved at exactly the right moment. Perhaps the crews of the upper deck guns were able to do it alone, moving the sails of each mast in turn, at the cost of a little speed. Perhaps it was done by calling up one man from each gun crew, allocated duty as a sail trimmer; but that could cause difficulties down below. However it was resolved, the ability to manoeuvre and fire at the same time was one of the keys to the British success.

For the French and Spanish resistance was strong, if unskilled. Lieutenant Senhouse of the *Conqueror* thought they fought with 'the greatest passive gallantry.'[6] Captain Rotherham of the *Royal Sovereign* found that 'the French fired with more vivacity at the commencement of the action than the Spaniards; but the Spanish showed more firmness and courage at the end than the French.'[7] Blackwood of the *Euryalus* concluded that 'the enemy have learnt to fight better than they ever did', and only Nelson's inspiration was enough to carry the British to victory.[8] But what the French and Spanish did not do well was to manoeuvre

A gun crew in action on the quarterdeck.

under sail. This was best illustrated by the conduct of the ten French and Spanish ships at the head of the line, cut off by Nelson's attack. At 1.15 p.m. Villeneuve signalled for all ships not engaged to 'take any such [action] which will bring them as speedily as possibly into action.' An hour or so later, in his last act of command, the Admiral signalled the van division to wear together to get into the action. Only six ships attempted to do so. Due to light winds the Spanish *Neptuno* had to tack with the aid of her boats so she became separated from the other five, but did manage to get into the main battle. The French *Intrepide* had a collision with another ship during the wearing, but nevertheless Captain Infernet took her independently into the main action to the relief of the *Bucentaure*. The other four ships – the *Formidable*, *Duguay-Trouin*, *Scipion* and *Mont-Blanc* – wore together and attempted a counterattack.[9]

The rest of the enemy van ships continued on their course. Nelson had originally planned that his division would form a line at right angles to the enemy, cutting off the leading ships. In fact this was never done, and each ship in the division simply chose an enemy ship to engage. Nor was it necessary, as the enemy van made no coherent attempt to get into the battle. How far this success was due to Nelson's tactical instinct and assessment of the enemy, how far to good luck, is very difficult to ascertain.

Below decks, the gun crews knew very little of the general battle. They could only look through the square opening of a gunport when it was not obstructed by the gun or obscured by smoke. In most cases, they could see the side of their target, an enemy hull, and very little else. They toiled hard at their duty, carrying out the task they had done many times before in practice or in action. On each shot the gun was allowed to recoil to the limit of the breech tackle and one man tightened the train tackle to prevent it from running out again. A man took a cartridge from its case and placed it in the gun; another rammed it home. Then someone placed a wad of old rope in the gun, a cannonball or other shot as required, and another wad to stop the ball from falling out and each was rammed home in turn. At the other end the captain of the gun reset the lock and secured a lanyard. Then most of the gun crew, except the captain of the gun who shouted orders, got hold of the two tackles to haul the gun out – a very heavy task if the ship was heeling away from the action. After the gun was run out, its captain waited till the enemy was in a suitable position, perhaps waiting for the upward roll of the ship, then pulled the lanyard to fire the gun again. In many of the individual encounters the enemy was too close to miss and gunnery took on a very pure form of simply loading and firing. But the seamen seem to have held their fire when the enemy was not in their sights. Lieutenant Senhouse of the *Conqueror* noted,

Our seamen, it is generally observed, fought not in their usual style, firing as fast as their guns could be wadded, and trusting to chance fore the result, but with the deter-

In the cockpit, a man is about to have his leg amputated, while others wait for treatment.

mined coolness and skilful management of artillery-men regularly bred to the exercise of great guns. Such valour nothing could withstand, and if our fleet had been six sail less than they were the victory would still have been ours.[10]

It was not pleasant below decks, as Lieutenant Rotely of the *Victory* discovered. The smoke, the darkness punctuated by numerous flashes, the noise of the gunfire and of the trucks of guns being run out, the cries of the wounded, all created an indescribable atmosphere. A seaman was in danger on a gundeck, from having his foot in the wrong place when a gun recoiled or was run out, or being hit by splinters of an enemy shot as it passed through the hull, but on the whole he was probably safer than his officers on the quarterdeck, or his comrades on the upper guns.

He became obsessed with his task to the exclusion of all else, perhaps seduced by this sublime form of teamwork, perhaps hypnotized by the rhythm of battle. Rotely described how difficult it was to get marines away from the guns and later told a naval audience, 'I need not inform a seaman of the difficulty of separating a man from his gun.'[11] Seven years previously at the Nile, Captain Hallowell of the *Swiftsure* had been 'aware of the difficulty of breaking the men off from their guns once they have begun to use them.'[12] It was this spirit, combined with years of training and total self-confidence, that made the British navy supreme. It allowed the British ships to fire at up to one round per minute, far faster than their opponents. It was this dedication which allowed the ships to prevail in each of the skirmishes now taking place all over the battlefield. The gun crews, as much as Nelson's tactical genius, would win the Battle of Trafalgar.

Further below decks in the ships' cockpits, the scene was horrific. In the *Leviathan*, the first casualty was Hugh Bambridge, a twenty-three-year-old seaman whose arm was shattered by a cannonball and had to be amputated near the shoulder joint. Thomas Main, aged thirty-nine, was hit in the arm by grape shot, also requiring amputation, while Andrew Moore, a quartermaster on duty at the ship's wheel, was slightly more fortunate. 'Was wounded by a grape shot passing into the upper and anterior part of his left thigh, about six inches below the groin, and taking a direction to the posterior part where it was extracted.' He suffered from fevers for some time afterwards, but survived. There were several wounds from splinters, and a few men had injured feet, apparently by guns running over them. The biggest single group of casualties came when one of the 32-pounder guns on the lower deck exploded. One man was wounded in the leg and face, another in the face, neck, breast and thighs, while Seaman David Morris 'was severely burnt over his forehead, face, neck and over the whole of his breast and belly … both eyes much injured, he is extremely weak'. He had been ill before the battle, but now faced a slow and painful death, taking more than two weeks.[13]

There were examples of almost fanatical bravery among the seamen. Purser Sam Rickards

Nelson lies dying in the cockpit, with Captain Hardy standing to his right. The height between decks is exaggerated in paintings. By Arthur Devis.

of the *Leviathan* records that 'One of our Brave fellows who lost an arm in the middle of the action, during the amputation sang "Rule Britannia" with a smile on his face.'[14] This was Thomas Main, captain of the foretop, who had his arm shot off by the Spanish *San Augustin*. When his comrades offered to assist him he said, 'I thank you, stay where you are; you will do more good there.' He went below by himself where he insisted on waiting his turn to be dealt with by the surgeon. In the *Victory*, a marine corporal also lost an arm and bound up the stump with a sash taken from a dead officer. A private was hit in the arm while in the act of firing. He completed the shot, then went to the cockpit unattended.[15] In the *Bellerophon*, Lieutenant Cumby records that Thomas Robinson, the boatswain, was wounded in both hands but went below alone and found the cockpit full of casualties. He declined the surgeon's services and had the purser's steward bind his hands before going back on deck. In the *Neptune*, Seaman Felix McCarthy was severely wounded in his left arm but gave up his place in the queue to be treated by the surgeon to a man who was severely wounded in the right thigh and arm. McCarthy, too, returned to his station after his arm was amputated.[16]

For all that, the seaman could be very squeamish when dealing with the dead. In the *Bellerophon*, Midshipman Robert Patton was at his guns on the lower deck when the assistant surgeon asked for help to clear corpses to make space in the cockpit. He detailed four men, 'who all begged to be excused from performing this duty', until Patton himself took hold of the first body to set an example. In all, nine bodies were dragged up to the lower deck and thrown overboard.[17]

In the *Victory*, the wounded Nelson was tended by Beatty the surgeon and Bourke the purser, and lay against a knee on the side of the ship, among the other wounded. Hardy visited Nelson after an hour or so and told the Admiral that twelve or fourteen ships had surrendered. Nelson had hoped for twenty. On his next visit Nelson's condition was far worse and he was in obvious pain and distress. He urged Hardy to anchor after the battle, sensing a storm was approaching. He was also concerned that he might be thrown overboard, as the dead often were in battle; but there was no question of that. He urged Hardy to take care of Lady Hamilton, and asked him to kiss him. After that, he said, 'Thank God I have done my duty.' Hardy went back on deck filled with emotion, and within fifteen minutes Nelson was unable to speak. He died at about 4.30 p.m., after two and three quarter hours of agony.

The death of Nelson had no material effect on the action, and little effect on morale while it was still unknown to the majority of officers and crews. In the mêlée of battle there was little more for an admiral to do once fight had been joined, especially in light winds and poor visibility caused by gunsmoke.

In Nelson's line the next three ships to enter the action after *Victory* and the *Temeraire*, were the 98-gun *Neptune* and the 74s *Leviathan* and *Conqueror*, who concentrated their attentions on the two most obvious targets – the fleet flagship *Bucentaure* and the four-decker *Santisima Trinidad*. The *Neptune* fired on both ships before becoming engaged with the Spanish *San Augustin*. The *Leviathan* fired into the flagship before going on to the larger Spanish ship, putting a broadside into her exposed stern and knocking down her main and mizzen masts. The Spaniard turned to bring the two ships side by side, but was soon defeated by the intense British gunfire.

The 64-gun *Africa* had become separated from the fleet during the night, and entered the action independently, almost abreast of the first ship in the Franco-Spanish van. She began to pass along the line, exchanging shots with several of the enemy and receiving very little damage in return. But Nelson's plan was to attack the enemy centre rather than the van, and after the signal to 'engage the enemy more closely', Captain Digby headed for the main battle which was developing in the centre, attacking the *Santisima Trinidad* as did several other ships.[18]

The *Conqueror* entered the action around 1.35 p.m. and engaged the *Bucentaure*, bringing some relief to the hard-pressed *Victory*. The fire from the enemy small arms was so intense after 2.00 p.m. that all men were withdrawn from the guns on the forecastle and quarter-deck.[19] Much of the *Conqueror*'s rigging was shot away, but the *Bucentaure* lost her three masts in quick succession and was defeated.

Several more ships joined the fray. The *Ajax*, under Acting-Lieutenant John Pilfold, claims to have been in action quite early, opening fire just after 1.00 p.m., and cutting the line a few minutes later. Nelson's old ship, the *Agamemnon*, opened fire at 1.30 p.m. Northesk's *Britannia* probably formed part of the same group during the approach, though the great naval historian, Sir Julian Corbett, deduced that Northesk's part in the battle was 'very obscure' and that he engaged mainly at long range.[20] She was fired on by three of the enemy just before 1.00 p.m., although an hour later she was still sailing to break their line, and she finally passed through at 3.00 p.m., engaging enemy ships on both sides.[21]

Captain Codrington of the *Orion* was determined to maintain a strict discipline on the entry to battle, 'not liking to waste our fire.' As the *Orion* approached he noted how the weather line was pressed close together so that the leading ships were forced to sail *en echelon*, rather than bow to stern. He was so impressed by the sight that he called the lieutenants up from the gundecks to witness it. One officer repeatedly questioned his decision to hold fire as enemy and friendly shot flew around them 'like hailstones', the men were 'as cool as if they had been used to such scenes'. The *Agamemnon*, two ships ahead of the *Orion*, was blazing away and wasting her ammunition, in Codrington's opinion. He sought out an unengaged enemy to attack, and sailed under the stern of the French *Swiftsure*. Her three masts were carried away in a single broadside and Codrington felt vindicated – 'Having repeatedly pointed out to my men the waste of shot from other ships, I now had a fine opportunity of convincing them of the benefit of cool reserve.'[22]

After that, Codrington began one of the most complex manoeuvres of any ship in the battle. He noticed that Captain Bayntum's *Leviathan* was trapped between the Spanish 74, *San Augustin*, and the French *Intrepide*, which had tacked round from the van to join the battle. He decided to give support, but first he had to get past a wall of ships of his own side.

> After several fruitless attempts to pass by one or two of our own ships, who kept up a distant cannonade on her, I managed, first to back all sail so as to get under 'Ajax's' stern, and then to make all sail so as to pass across 'Leviathan's' head, who hailed me and said he hoped I should make a better fist of it (if not elegant, still very cheering to meet so much confidence and good opinion); and then on to bear down sufficiently to

get our starboard guns to bear on 'L'Intrepide's' starboard quarter, and then to turn gradually round from thence under his stern, pass his broadside, and bring to on his larboard bow. [23]

Codrington's discipline must have been highly effective to bring off such manoeuvres. He was rewarded with a very low casualty rate, losing only one seaman killed and twenty-three men wounded.

The *Minotaur* and the *Spartiate* were the last ships in Nelson's line. Francis Whitney, master of the *Spartiate*, had time to record the early stages of the battle in some detail as his ship made slow progress in light winds.[24] His note-taking was interrupted around 3.00 p.m., when Rear-Admiral Dunamoir's division from the Franco-Spanish van approached – the four French ships that had worn, with the Spanish *Neptuno* a little astern of them. In passing they were already firing into British ships at the centre of the battle site, and a single cannonball killed two lieutenants on the *Conqueror*, just as one was congratulating the other on his impending promotion. Dunamoir did not hesitate to fire into some of the ships of his own navy, now prizes in the hands of the enemy. He was approaching the great knot of damaged ships, which included the *Victory*, *Royal Sovereign*, *Temeraire* and their disabled prizes. It was a dangerous moment, the only real threat of a counter attack during the battle.

Fortunately, the *Minotaur* and *Spartiate* were there to interpose themselves between the enemy and the British flagships. Captain Mansfield of the *Minotaur* allowed Captain Laforey of the *Spartiate* to lead, and both ships passed across the bows of Dunamoir's flagship, the *Formidable*. Then they hove to, with their sails pressed against the masts to hold them still in the water, and exchanged passing fire with the four Frenchmen, which were driven away from the mêlée. After that they engaged the Spanish *Neptuno*, shot down her mizzenmast and took her.

* * *

The rearmost ships in Collingwood's line still had some heavy fighting to do, though they were less damaged than the six that had preceded them. The *Achille*, under Captain King, followed the *Colossus* closely into action and soon fought off the Spanish *Montanes* before engaging the *Argonauta*, which surrendered after an hour of combat. But before she could take possession she was attacked by two of the enemy. The *Achille* had been built as a copy of the captured French *Pompee*, and named after another ship taken at the 'Glorious First of

The Belleisle *dismasted, with the undamaged frigate* Naiad *standing by. Published by G. Andrews.*

June' in 1794. She now engaged her namesake, the French *Achille*, and her compatriot the ex-British 74, *Berwick*. There was no time to think about the irony of the situation before the French *Achille* passed on to another target and the British ship pounded the *Berwick* into submission after an hour of fighting. For all her active role and two prizes, the *Achille* had only suffered about a third of the casualties of the *Colossus*, with thirteen men killed and fifty-nine wounded.

The *Revenge* was next in line. Captain Moorsom found the situation confusing. He stated that, because of the *Revenge*'s good sailing qualities, he had received a signal from Collingwood to form a 'line of bearing' on the *Royal Sovereign*, that is, to come abreast of him on a particular compass bearing. The result apparently, was that she came into the action rather quicker than would be expected from her formal position. But Moorsom soon gave up any attempt to rationalize the situation.

> I have seen several plans of the action, but none to answer my ideas of it – indeed scarce any plan can be given; it was irregular and the ships just got down as fast as they could, and into any space where they found the enemy without attending to their place in the line. A regular plan was laid down by Lord Nelson some time before the action, but not acted upon; his great anxiety seemed to be to get to leeward of them, lest they should make off for Cadiz before he could get near.[25]

Below decks on the *Revenge*, seamen William Robinson and John Powell stood by their respective guns. Moorsom, according to Robinson, maintained a strict fire discipline.

> … it fell our lot to cut off the five stern-most ships; and, while we were running down to them, of course we were favoured with several shots, and some of our men were wounded. Upon being thus hard pressed, many of our men thought it hard that the firing should be all on one side, and became impatient to return the compliment: but our captain had given orders not to fire until we got close in with them, so that all our shots might tell; – indeed these were his words: 'We shall want all of our shot when we get close in: never mind their firing: when I fire a carronade from the quarter-deck, that will be a signal for you to begin, and I know you will do your duty as Englishmen.'

The *Revenge* tried to sail between the fifth and sixth ships from the enemy rear, but they closed together and she found herself across the bows of *L'Aigle*, a French 74, whose jib-boom, the extreme point of her forward spars, got caught in the mizzen topsail of the *Revenge*. Two broadsides were fired carefully into the Frenchman before she got clear. *Revenge* had avoided the danger of being trapped between two enemy ships but, according to Moorsom, 'Perhaps it would have been better for me had he done so.' For the mighty *Principe de Asturias* came up on her quarter. According to Robinson,

> A Spanish three-decker ran her bowsprit over our poop, with a number of her crew on it, and in her fore rigging, two or three hundred men were ready to follow; but they caught a Tartar, for their design was discovered, and our marines with their small arms, and the carronades on the poop, loaded with canister shot, swept them off so fast, some of them into the water, that they were glad to sheer off.

The engagement with the three-decker continued, while three enemy ships came up, mainly from the unengaged part of the centre, and the *Revenge* was surrounded by four of the enemy.

Below decks, John Powell remained calm when enemy fire came close to him: '… a shot came in at the Porthole of the Gun to which I belong killed a midshipman & 5 other men besides cutting the foremast but I nor any of the men at my Quarters were hurt.' This was probably the same shot noted by Robinson. One of the gun's crew was the ship's cobbler and a fine dancer, 'a very merry little fellow, the very life of the ship's company, for he was ever the mirth of his mess, and on whatever duty he might be ordered, his spirits made light the labour.' He was knocked out when another man's head banged against his, and taken for dead. He was about to be thrown out of a gunport, like others killed in action, when his legs began to kick, and he was spared. 'It was well that I learned to dance; for if I had not shown you some of my steps, when you were about to throw me overboard, I should not be here now, but safe enough in Davy Jones's Locker.'

The intense action lasted an hour until the *Dreadnought* and *Thunderer* moved in against the *Principe de Asturias*, causing her to disengage. The *Revenge* began to repair some of her damage, particularly the shot holes near her waterline, 'between wind and water', which might cause her to sink. Her rigging was too damaged for her to re-enter the action of her own volition, and according to Robinson, 'In this condition we lay by the side of the enemy, firing away, and now and then we received a good raking from them, passing under our stern. This was a busy time for us, for we not only had to endeavour to repair our damage, but to keep to our duty.'

Captain Hope's *Defence* entered the fray around 2.20 p.m., when she engaged the French 74-gun, *Berwick*. The engagement lasted less than an hour, by which time, according to Midshipman Thomas Huskisson, 'her mizzen mast was over the side, her main and fore masts tottering, and her fire had become very languid.' The *Berwick* hauled off, only to be engaged by the British *Achille*. Meanwhile, the relatively undamaged *Defence* found another prey when the Spanish 74-gun, *San Idelfonso*, 'on our lee bow came whizzing over us.' The return fire was fierce and the *Defence*'s mainmast was hit in several places, her gaff had been cut in two, the lower and topmast rigging was much damaged and in the hull many chain plates and hanging knees had been carried away. One shot had gone through the knee of the head and there were several between wind and water. But just after 4.00, after less than an hour of fighting, the Spanish ship struck her flag and the *Defence*'s boat was sent over to her. A Spanish commodore, Jose de Vargas y Varaez, was brought on board wounded, but impressed Huskisson with his coolness when he took a lighted match out of one of the *Defence*'s match tubs to light his cigar. The ship had lost seven killed and twenty-seven wounded, while more than a third of *San Idelfonso*'s men were killed or wounded.

Some of the enemy ships had already surrendered when the *Thunderer* of 74 guns, under Acting-Lieutenant John Stockham, entered the action around 3.00 p.m. She went to assist the *Revenge* in her fight with the four enemy ships. She placed herself across the bows of the *Principe de Asturias* and this attracted the attention of the French *Neptune*, who attacked her briefly until both enemy ships sailed off. The *Thunderer* then sailed north to deal with Dunamoir's division, on Collingwood's instructions.

On the way into battle the 64-gun *Polyphemus* was hailed by the *Dreadnought*, and asked to give way to her, as her captain was anxious to get alongside the Spanish three-decker. She was delayed again when she had to haul the wind to avoid collison with the British *Swiftsure* and did not enter the action until after 3.00 p.m. The 98-gun *Dreadnought* did indeed find her Spanish three-decker, the *San Juan Nepomuceno*, although not before this ship had been attacked by several others. She surrendered to the *Dreadnought* after thirty-five minutes of close action, after which the British ship moved on to other targets. The British *Swiftsure*, went on to attack the French *Achille*.

The slow-sailing 98-gun *Prince* was one of the last to enter the action, but her heavy broadside was to do unique damage in what remained of the battle. Around 4.30 p.m. she was in action with the French *Achille*, which had already suffered at the hands of the British *Achille*, *Belleisle*, *Swiftsure* and *Polyphemus*. The Frenchman's foretop caught fire, perhaps due to fire from her own swivel guns or muskets. The crew prepared to cut away the mast and let it fall over the side to save the ship, when the *Prince* did the job for them. According to two surviving officers,

> Our situation was the more critical as our fire-engine [i.e. pump] having been rendered useless by a shot, there remained no means of arresting the progress of the fire. Several officers and midshipmen, accompanied by the few men that were left in the 18-pounder battery and part of those from the 36-pounder deck, went forward with the

carpenters to cut away the fore-mast; but the three decker fired into us at such close quarters that with her second broadside she succeeded in bringing down our masts and swept us as bare as a hulk. We had the misfortune to see our two masts fall amidships, an event that was the more calamitous as our flaming fore-top set fire to our boats. This cruel predicament did not deter us from redoubling our courage and from serving the 36-pounder battery with the greatest energy, whilst men who were left in the upper works and in the 18-pounder battery were employed in extinguishing the fire; but this was in vain, its progress continually increasing and the flaming debris of the boats falling on the 36-pounder gun-deck. At 4.30 the 18-pounder battery hardly showed more than one port. The *Prince* sheered off from us, doubtless from fear of an explosion. All hands then came on deck and losing all hope of extinguishing the fire, we no longer attended to anything except saving the ship's company, by throwing overboard all the debris that might offer them the means of escaping from almost certain death and awaiting the aid that the neighbouring ships might send them.[26]

The mêlée at the end of the battle, painted by Nicholas Pocock.

But destruction of this kind was not the British aim. Where possible they much preferred to capture ships rather than destroy them. As early as 2.00 p.m., according to the log of the *Thunderer*, 'the Enemy began to give way and strike' – that is lower their flags as a sign of surrender. The warships of the day had no weapons capable of sinking or destroying an enemy ship, and in general the attackers had no intention of doing so. A captured ship, however badly damaged, would bring prize money to the crew. It would be taken home in triumph to be shown off at anchor off Portsmouth or Plymouth, and it might attract the attention of painters or print-sellers. It might be added to one's own navy, such as the *Tonnant*, *Belleisle* and *Spartiate* in Nelson's fleet at Trafalgar, not to mention the *Berwick* and *Swiftsure* on the other side. It was generally accepted that eventually ships of one side or another would surrender in battle. The etiquette of this was never written down, on the British side at least, as it might legitimize the practice, so the rules were not absolutely clear. The more intensive warfare after the French Revolution had altered the rules to some extent, and fanatical officers, such as Captain du Petit Thouars of the *Tonnant*, at the Battle of the Nile, would resist to the very last.

But broadly speaking, it was agreed that a ship that had been dismasted, was surrounded by enemy ships of superior force, had put up a good fight and had suffered heavy casualties, should eventually surrender to prevent futile loss of life. The point at which this happened was left up to the commanders of the individual ships. Captain Infernet of the *Intrepide* decided that he would only surrender if his masts and rudder were shot away. Codrington of the *Orion* obliged; 'This we did for him in so handsome a way that he had no time to do us much injury.'[27]

Seamen were intense fighters and incredibly brave in the face of disaster, so there is no sign that any crews mutinied and forced their captains' hands. The decision was the captain's alone, or the officer who had succeeded him in the case of his death. Each officer stood alone on an embattled quarterdeck, with dead and wounded all around him, and tried to reconcile his patriotism, his pride in his service, his loyalty to his comrades and his fear of disgrace, with his natural humanity and the sense that any further resistance would be useless.

The usual way to indicate surrender was to haul down one's national ensign from the flagstaff at the stern. There were obvious possibilities for confusion here, which is why Nelson insisted that his ships carried at least three ensigns in different positions. Flags could be shot away, or could be taken down by junior officers without authority. The order to surrender might not reach every part of the ship simultaneously and guns might continue to fire from below decks after the quarterdeck had given up the fight. There were fanatics, especially in the ideologically driven French ships, who would not give up in any circumstances. The process of surrender was no more clean-cut than the battle itself had been.

All the same, it was still quite gentlemanly, especially between the British and the Spanish. Around 2.00 p.m. the *Africa* noticed that the *Santisima Trinidad* was dismasted and flew no colours and her guns had ceased firing, after an engagement with the *Neptune*. Lieutenant John Smith went across in a boat and climbed up to her quarterdeck, where the Spanish officers denied that they had surrendered, pointing out five French and Spanish ships passing close to them and capable of support. Smith was allowed to return to his ship. Not long afterwards the *Santisima Trinidad* really did surrender and removed any doubt by displaying the British flag hanging from her quarter.[28]

In practical terms it made no real difference which ship an enemy surrendered to, for all the victorious ships would share equally in the prize money. Yet there was a great deal of honour involved among the officers, and prestige among the seamen, especially when one ship felt it had done all the hard work and another moved in to strike the final blow. The *Defiance* was one of the last ships of Collingwood's line to enter the battle. After briefly engaging the Spanish three-decker, *Principe de Asturias*, she entered into a contest with the French *Aigle*, already seriously damaged in her intense fight with the *Bellerophon*. At about 3.00 p.m. the fire from the French ship began to peter out. Captain Durham ordered a ceasefire even though the tricolour was still flying. The ships were only a few yards apart, but there was a calm and it was impossible to manoeuvre any closer. The *Defiance*'s boats were all disabled, and a there was a deathly silence as *L'Aigle* awaited her fate. James Spratt took the opportunity to remind Durham of his promise on the approach to battle, that 'should we be boarded or have occasion to board he had no doubt that Mr Spratt would lead them to glory.' Spratt offered to swim over with his party and eventually the Captain agreed. Spratt called on all the boarders who could swim to follow him. He put his sword between his teeth in true Hollywood fashion, and a hatchet in his waistbelt. He was surprised to find himself alone in the water, for none had followed him. He attributed this to the 'general din' above which his orders could not be heard (though he refers to 'deathly silence' in another part of his account) or to a misunderstanding.

In any case he was undaunted. He climbed up the rudder chains of *L'Aigle* and entered through the stern ports. He made his way up through the decks amid the dead and wounded to reach the poop, putting his faith in 'a sweet little cherub that sits aloft to keep watch for the life of poor Jack'. He put his hat on top of his cutlass to rally the rest of the boarders, still in the *Defiance*. He tried to haul down the French colours but was attacked by three soldiers with fixed bayonets. He swung on the signal halyards to the top of an arms chest, injuring two of the Frenchman, and he threw the other on to the deck, breaking his neck. Spratt was dragged down, but was uninjured.

In the interim, a breeze had sprung up and the *Defiance* was able to come alongside. At last the boarding parties leapt on board *L'Aigle* and were about to kill an officer, who begged for mercy. He threw himself at Spratt's feet and was saved but he rose to find a musket levelled at his chest. He struck it downward but it went off, putting a bullet through a bone in his leg.

The officers of the *Bellerophon* were unimpressed with Spratt's heroics. They had done most of the work in defeating *L'Aigle*, and had suffered numerous casualties. One officer wrote that *L'Aigle* was 'an easy conquest for the *Defiance* a fresh ship.'[29]

The *Royal Sovereign* captured the Spanish *Santa Ana* after two hours, during which the Spanish ship's side was 'almost entirely beat in'. The *Royal Sovereign* suffered losses that were, in the ambiguous phrase of the historian, William James, 'tolerably severe'. Midshipman George Castle had begun the action wishing that his sister could have seen his guns 'thump into' the *Santa Ana*. He ended the battle in a different mood – 'it is shocking to see many brave seamen mangled so, some with their heads half shot away, other with their entrails mashed lying panting on the deck, the greatest slaughter was on the quarterdeck and Poop.'[30] The ship had lost five officers, twenty-nine seamen and thirteen marines, and ninety-four more were wounded, including Lieutenant Clavell; but the admiral's 'northern boys' were all alive. Before Collingwood had time to take stock of the situation, a boat from the *Victory* came alongside with news that would alter the whole mood of the battle. His beloved admiral, Lord Nelson, was mortally wounded.

Marine John Owen of the *Belleisle* was sent to take possession of the Spanish 80-gun ship *Argonauta* and was rowed over in the ship's pinnace.

The Master accompanied me with eight or ten seamen or marines who happened to be near us. On getting up the Argonauta's side, I found no living person on her deck, but on making my way, over numerous dead and a confusion of wreck, across the quarter-

The French Achille *burning at the end of the battle. From Jenkin's* Naval Achievements.

deck, was met by the second captain at the cabin door, who gave me his sword which I returned, desiring him to keep it for Captain Hargood to whom I should soon introduce him. With him I accordingly returned to the Belleisle, leaving the Master in charge of the prize, on board which I had seen only about six officers, the remainder (amongst whom was the captain, wounded) and all the men being below out of the way of the shot.[31]

Having set the French *Achille* on fire, the men of the *Prince* watched in horror as the conflagration spread. Though the ship pulled away from the blazing Frenchman to save herself, the men were not without compassion and lowered boats to rescue men in the water, with the assistance of the British cutter *Entreprenante* and the schooner *Pickle*. The end of the *Achille*, and indeed of the battle, came an hour later. According to the French account,

At 5.30 a part of the men in the water were saved; at the same hour the explosion occurred. It was not very violent seeing that we had taken the precaution of drowning the remainder of our powder. The ship disappeared with the tatters of her flag which had never been lowered, and very soon the rest of the crew, struggling for their lives, received prompt assistance, the boats being able to approach them in greater safety. We estimate our losses at 480 men killed, wounded and drowned.[32]

The log of the *Spartiate* describes the scene at the end of the afternoon.

At 5.20 the firing ceased – observed fourteen ships of the Enemy in our possession, including the *Santisima Trinidad*, and the *Santa Anna*, three deckers, two Admiral's ships, and the *Bucentaure*, Admiral Villeneuve … observed the *Belleisle* totally dismasted – the *Temeraire* between two Enemy's ships lashed alongside one of their their mainmasts, across the *Temeraire's* booms – the *Victory* and *Colossus* had lost their mizen masts – other ways much cut up – eight of the enemy's ships totally dismasted … damages we sustained, three men killed, three officers and eighteen men wounded; masts, rigging and sails very much cut up.[33]

If there was any feeling of triumph among the British, it was overcome by exhaustion. For many ships and crews, the worst was yet to come.

CHAPTER 20

The Storm

Captain Codrington had already predicted anticlimax. 'The battle after all, as I warned my officers, is nothing compared with the fatigue, the anxiety, the distress of mind which succeeds.'[1] Lieutenant Nicolas, the young marine officer of the *Belleisle*, noted the exhaustion as the battle ended.

> … four hours' exertion of body with the energies incessantly employed, occasioned a lassitude, both corporeally and mentally, from which the victorious termination now so near at hand could not arouse us; moreover there sat a melancholy on the brows of some who mourned their messmates who had shared their perils and their vicissitudes for many years. Then the merits of the departed heroes were repeated with a sigh, but their errors sunk with them to the deep. There were few who did not bear some marks of this sanguinary engagement, and those who had the good fortune to escape unhurt presented an appearance which testified the dangers they had encountered.[2]

Despite the magnitude of the triumph, there were some officers who thought that even more could have been done. Lieutenant Green, the amateur inventor of the *Conqueror*, was less than satisfied with the result.

> This action was most fortunate for the British fleet but in my opinion if the officers had done their duty in every ship, the action would have been over sooner and the whole of the enemy taken or destroyed. So great was the joy of all the people of England, and the remaining admirals, that all was hushed up.[3]

Unfortunately the next page is missing from his journal, so we have no way of knowing the cause of his dissatisfaction. Captain Moorsom of the *Revenge* was also dissatisfied. 'I am not certain that our mode of attack was the best; however it succeeded.'[4]

Codrington had no hesitation in criticizing his new commander-in-chief to Lord Garlies of the Admiralty.

> Lord Collingwood certainly went into action in the finest style possible, and is as brave a man as ever stepped on board a ship; I can also believe him to be a very good man in his way, but he has none of the dignity an admiral should have, and seems to have lost all the great outline of a chief command in his attention to minutiae. What he is now doing, God knows.[5]

Collingwood transferred his flag to the *Euryalus* frigate soon after the fighting ceased, 'That I might the better distribute my orders.'[6] Midshipman Joseph Moore was impressed with the pile of swords on the quarterdeck as dozens of officers came on board to surrender, but he felt sorry for the 'fine looking gallant fellows who had so bravely fought us the day before.' Collingwood stood aloof from all this, 'greedily drinking in the whole horizon

The Frenchwoman Jeanette is rescued after the battle. Published by Edward Orme.

which at that time was thickly dotted with dismal wrecks.'

The British sailors fished a young Frenchwoman called Jeanette out of the water; their amazement confirms that women were not common on warships at this time. She had disguised herself in order to follow her husband (a sergeant-major of infantry in one account, a main topman in another) into the *Achille*, only to see him killed in the battle. When the ship caught fire she had to strip, revealing her sex, and she jumped into the water where she was supported by one of her shipmates until they were picked up by the *Pickle*. She was transferred to the *Victory* on the evening of the 21st and dressed from clothes used for amateur dramatics on board. The officers gave her watch chains to tie up her hair.[7] Later, she was transferred to the *Revenge*, where Captain Moorsom 'ordered her two purser's shirts to make a petticoat; and most of the officers found something to clothe her. In a few hours Jeanette was perfectly happy and hard at work on her petticoat.'[8]

John Yule, a lieutenant of the *Victory*, was disappointed in his hopes of promotion. He wrote to his wife, 'Heaven spared me, my dear Eliza, but I return a lieutenant after all my golden dreams.' He admitted frankly to being traumatized by the affair.

> Although my ideas are now a little more collected that they were when I last wrote, they are by no means clear even now, the horrors of an action during the time it lasts and for a short time afterwards make everything around you appear in a different shape to what it did before and though a heart may for a moment be rendered callous by the dreadful carnage round him and tho' they may call us sea brutes for not feeling so acutely as they would do on shore, believe me my dearest girl we are not void of sympathy. The mind is made up to fall, before the conflict commences and each man when he sees his neighbour fall thanks God it was not himself.

> … the action will be by the nation conceived a very glorious one but when the devastation is considered how can we glory in it? How many orphans and fatherless has it made? How many has it made sad and how few (concerned) has it made glad? In the *Victory* we do not feel it a victory. The loss of our chief has thrown a gloom around that nothing but the society of our friends and families can dispel. That quarterdeck which was formally crowded is emptied. The happy scenes we formerly witness are now laid aside, the theatre, the music, the dancing which accompanied the dull part of

our time is now laid aside. We look to the seat of an old messmate and find he is gone – we ask for such and such a man – he was killed, sir, in the action, he lost a leg – we ask for no-one for fear of a similar reply one hundred and fifty killed and wounded. I am alive without a wound.[9]

Chaplain Scott of the *Victory* was shaken by the events in the cockpit, just as much as by the death of his beloved commander. 'Such was the horror that filled his mind at this scene of suffering, that it haunted him like a shocking dream for years afterwards.' He never talked of it except to say, 'it was like a butcher's shambles.'[10]

Norwich Duff of the *Mars* had the task of writing to break the news of his father's death to his mother, perhaps with the help of Captain Blackwood of the *Euryalus* who took his welfare in hand.

My Dear Mama,
You cannot possibly imagine how unwilling I am to begin this melancholy letter. However as you must unavoidably hear of the fate of dear Papa, I write these few lines to request you to bear it as patiently as you can. He died like a hero, having gallantly led his ship into action.[11]

All the same, the crew of the *Mars* were content with their new commander, Lieutenant Hennah. They got up a petition signed by the main warrant and petty officers, commending him on his 'humane and good conduct since your commencement in the ship', especially since the death of Duff. They offered to present him with a sword on arrival in port, but later settled for a tea service.[12]

Midshipman Aikenhead's final letters to his father and sister were duly sent off, for he had died on board the *Royal Sovereign*. A few weeks later they were published in the *Hampshire Telegraph*.[13]

Despite the exhaustion, grief and anticlimax, the sailors had no chance to relax after the battle. Their ships were badly smashed, some had difficulty in keeping afloat and many were incapable of sailing with their damaged rigging. The *Victory*, as described by Hardy, was by no means the worst damaged.

The hull is much damaged by shot in a number of different places, particularly in the wales, strings and spirketting, and between wind and water. Several beams, knees, and riders, shot through and broke; the starboard cathead shot away; the rails and timbers of the head and stem cut by shot; several of the ports damaged, and port timbers cut off; the channels and chainplates damaged by shot, and the falling of the mizzen mast; the principal part of the bulkheads, halfports, and portsashes thrown overboard in clearing the ship for action.

The mizzen mast shot away about 9 feet above the deck; the main mast shot through and sprung; the main yard gone; the main topmast and cap shot in different places and reefed; the main topsail yard shot away; the foremast shot through in a number of different places … ; the fore yard shot away; the bowsprit jibboom and cap shot, and the spritsail and spritsail topsail yards, and flying jibboom gone; the fore and main tops damaged; the whole of the spare topmast yards, handmast, and fishes shot in different places …

The ship in bad weather makes 12 inches water in an hour.[14]

To add to the men's hardship, many of their hammocks had been shot away in the rails during the action.[15] But there was no time to sleep. Each crew had two urgent priorities: to keep their ship afloat by pumping out water and blocking up the shot holes near the waterline, and to make temporary or 'jury' repairs to the rigging to give the ship some kind of mobility, in view of the winds which threatened to drive it on to the rocky and hostile coasts of southern Spain.

On top of that, there were the captured enemy ships to look after, all damaged in the rigging and often below the waterline. Eighteen had surrendered, although some were never fully taken possession of. Collingwood's journal describes the situation as he understood it on the morning of the 22nd.

> The Belleisle in tow of the Naiad to windward, the Colossus in tow of the Agamemnon, and the Tonnant in tow of the Spartiate. Passed the Prince towing the Trinidad, the Thunderer and the Santa Ana, and several other ships with prizes in tow, making in all 14 of the enemy's ships in tow …[16]

Prizes brought prisoners with them, who had to be guarded and their wounds tended. In general, senior officers were taken on board the victor's ships. The *Achille* took on board a substantial number of men from the captured *Berwick*, and had to clear sixty-seven water butts out of the hold to make room for them.[17] But in general the junior officers and seamen stayed on board their own ships, with a prize crew to guard them and sail the ship. This in itself might cause difficulties.

When sent on board one of the Spanish prizes, the men of the *Revenge* found her crew completely debilitated and demoralized.

> The slaughter and havoc our guns had made, rendered the scene of carnage horrid to behold: there were a number of their dead bodies piled up in the hold; many, in a wounded or mutilated state, were found lying amongst them; and those who were so fortunate as to escape our shot, were so dejected to crest-fallen, that they could not, or would not, work at the pumps, and of course the ship was in a sinking state.[18]

If this was not bad enough, the weather, which had helped Nelson's fleet during the battle, was to deliver a much crueller blow to the defeated and to the victorious fleets alike. The people of southern England were enjoying unseasonably bright weather, combined with frost and fogs, because an anticyclone had settled over the area. But a deep depression was tracking further south, towards the coasts of Spain and Portugal, bringing rain and gales.[19]

Nelson had predicted such a turn of events before the battle. He had noticed that the swell was building up despite the calm weather, and this indicated a storm out in the Atlantic. At midday, in his last signal to the fleet, he had ordered 'Prepare to anchor', although it is far from certain that every ship received the signal, at the very moment when the *Royal Sovereign* was beginning the engagement. Clearly he meant that each ship should get its anchors ready to drop as soon as the fight was over. Two and a half hours later, lying in agony and gasping for breath in the cockpit, he urged his flag captain,

> 'Anchor, Hardy, anchor … do you anchor, Hardy?' Captain Hardy then said: 'Shall we make the signal, Sir?' – 'Yes,' answered his Lordship, 'for if I live [i.e. long enough to see the end of the battle] I'll anchor.'[20]

But Nelson's orders were not executed and Captain Codrington thought he knew who was to blame. Regretting the death of Nelson he commented, 'He made the signal to prepare to anchor; and had Admiral Collingwood acted upon that hint we might now have secured all our prizes …'.[21] In a similar vein, Lieutenant Senhouse of the *Conqueror* commented,

> … if Lord Nelson had lived the fleet would have anchored immediately after the action, as we were only five leagues from the land and in shoal water where our anchors would have rode the ships securely, and having nothing else to attend to, we could have employed ourselves in rigging jury-masts and in securing the prizes; but this was neglected.[22]

Collingwood's defenders point out that the Admiral really had no choice, in view of the shat-

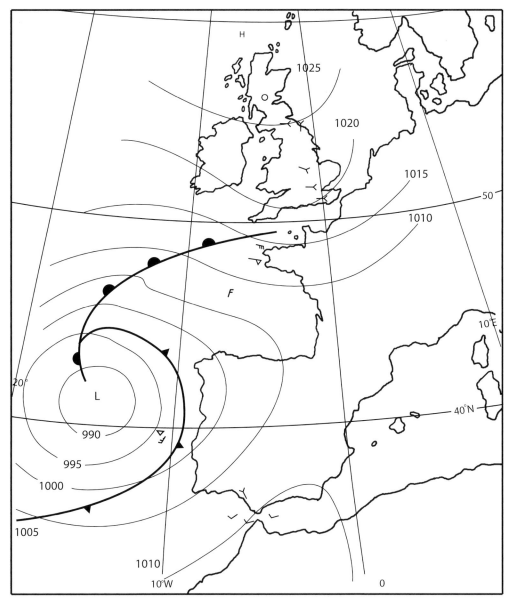

The weather after the battle, showing the approaching storm.

tered condition of the ships. His seamanship was just as good as Nelson's, if not better, and he, rather than the gravely wounded admiral below decks in the *Victory*, had to make the judgement. In any case, many of the ships and prizes did not have the means to anchor. Of the *Victory* herself it was reported, 'the starboard cat-head was shot away, the starboard bower and spare anchors broke, and the stock of the sheet anchor damaged by shot.' It was said of one of the prizes, the *Algeciras*, that of her anchors, the two at the bow were all that remained; one of them was broken in the shank, and the stock of the other was shot away and many other ships were in a similar plight.[23]

Yet the fact remains that Collingwood did not issue an order to anchor until about 9.00 in the evening after the battle, a delay of about four hours. Many ships had some kind of anchor and could probably have found a place to use it. Collingwood's seamanship was not at fault, but more energy in such an urgent matter might have saved a few ships and many lives. Collingwood was suffering from grief, exhaustion and the weight of responsibility. According to Joseph Moore, he stood on the deck of the *Euryalus* for hours after the battle, as was his custom in times of crisis. He was 'now and then tugging at the waistband of his

The day after Trafalgar, showing Victory *trying to clear the land, and the* Royal Sovereign *being towed by the* Euryalus. *By Nicholas Pocock.*

unmentionables [Moore was writing this in high Victorian times] ... his only food a few biscuits, an apple and a glass of wine every four hours.'[24] In Collingwood's own account, he was 'in a forlorn state; my servants are killed; and Clavell is wounded.'[25] With no effective staff, he did not find decision-making easy and he did not rise to the occasion.

It was still calm as the sun rose on the morning after the battle, when Captain Codrington's *Orion* spotted the Spanish 74 *Bahama* dismasted and drifting 10 or 12 miles south of Cape Trafalgar. Two hawsers of 8-inch circumference were joined together and passed to the Spaniard and she was taken in tow. At 11.00 the two ships headed south-east towards Gibraltar, but half an hour later the weather became squally and all sail had to be taken in except the topsails, which were close-reefed to present the minimum surface area. Even these had to be furled at midday and the storm continued for the rest of the day.

That night the *Belleisle*, the only completely dismasted British ship, was taken in tow by the frigate *Naiad*, in an attempt to keep her off the rocks of Trafalgar. Seamen struggled to erect jury, or temporary, masts to help prevent the ship being driven ashore. The tow rope parted several times, and the winds increased. Around midnight the Captain Hargood called all off-duty officers on deck, just as a 24-pounder gun broke loose to become the proverbial 'loose cannon', crashing around the deck and damaging everything it hit. According to Lieutenant Nicolas,

> With difficulty I got on deck. The ship rolled in the trough of the sea in such a manner that the water came in through the ports and over the waist hammock nettings, and the shot out of the racks were thrown about the decks, upon which the men, tired and exhausted, were lying. At one o'clock the roar of the elements continued; and every roll of the sea seemed to the affrighted imagination as the commencement of the breakers.[26]

In the captured French 74-gun *Algeciras*, Lieutenant Charles Bennett of the *Tonnant* was in charge of the prize crew. According to French accounts he treated the prisoners 'with the greatest consideration and with every sort of attention' but he was unable to provide the most important thing of all – safety. He had his men clearing the deck of debris and he hailed several passing ships with signals of distress, asking for a tow. But in the early stages he did nothing to rig jury masts which might have allowed some control over the ship's movements, perhaps because his prize crew of about fifty men would have had to enlist the support of the

The Belleisle, *with jury masts rigged, is towed by the* Naiad. *Published by G. Andrews.*

prisoners to do so. The night was 'very dark, foul weather and squalls, the wind a strong gale from the south-west. Next day Bennet fired distress signals every quarter of an hour, but still no one was able to come to his aid. By 5.00 p.m. the officer prisoners could see that the ship was drifting towards the Trafalgar shoal, 1½ miles away. They met and decided to reclaim the ship. They invited Bennett and two other officers into the great cabin and informed him,

> That after the noble defence of our ship we had a right to expect that assistance from the English fleet which they themselves had vainly demanded; that feeling ourselves released from the obligations that we had assumed when placing ourselves in their power, we had decided to retake our ship, but that they might be expected to be treated with consideration on our part, provided they did not compel us to employ force by a resistance after which they would still find themselves obliged to yield.

The British officers resisted the offer until they were promised to be set at liberty on arrival at a French or Spanish port. At 7.15 p.m., to cries of 'Vive L'Empereur', the French took back possession of the ship. They succeeded in getting her into Cadiz.[27]

There is some doubt as to whether the *Conqueror* had succeeded in passing a tow to the dismasted *Bucentaure* – the British claimed that they did so by 11.30 on the evening after the battle, the French are equally firm that they failed after several attempts. According to the *Conqueror*'s log, the tow had parted by midnight and was not re-established until daylight. In any case, the French officers became restive about the lack of protection offered by their captors. At 4.30 that afternoon the *Conqueror* 'went on the larboard tack and made off; nevertheless she remained within sight as well as another one, leaving a frigate to observe us within easy reach.' The French officers summoned the two British officers to their cabin and they agreed to hand over the ship peacefully. The French crew rigged jury masts and were able to make up to 5 knots, but despite the help of 'three men who called themselves coast pilots,' the ship was wrecked on the Puercas rocks at the entrance to Cadiz harbour.[28]

On the morning of the 23rd there was a calm and at 9.30 a.m. the *Orion* with the *Bahama* in tow was being driven towards land by the waves. Captain Codrington decided to anchor in 34 fathoms, close to the maximum depth at which anchors could be used. After that, he saw the remaining enemy ships in Cadiz making sail for a counter attack, for that morning Captain Cosmao of the French 74 *Pluton* had begun to rally a few ships, which had not gone to Cadiz, for a counter attack, by hoisting a senior officer's pennant and taking charge of the French *Neptune* and *Heros* and the Spanish *Rayo* and *San Francisco de Asis*. He picked up the Spanish *Santa Ana* and the *Neptuno*, plus a few frigates.

By this time the crew of the *Orion* were physically and mentally shattered and Codrington wrote of, 'my people so worn down as to be absolutely indifferent to my orders – neither my officers or myself able scarcely to produce more voice than a whisper.'[29] At midday Codrington decided to cut his cable and run with the prize. He headed towards the coast of neutral Portugal in the hope that his prize would not fall into enemy hands, but Cosmao's attack soon fizzled out. He reported,

> Twenty-five to twenty-eight sail were sighted at sea, of which 12 were dismasted, the others seeming to be in good condition; in view of this force I did not think it my duty to run the risk of a skirmish, seeing the bad state of the ships which composed the division. We re-entered [Cadiz] Bay, my ship in a sinking condition, and during the night a whole gale ... did not allow me to turn my attention to anything save the safety of my ship ...[30]

At 9.00 p.m. the stormy weather returned. The *Orion* was already carrying reduced sail, with the main topsail close-reefed and the fore topsail hauled up ready to be furled, when a gust blew both sails out. The ship was now carrying no sail and was 6 miles from a lee shore, and Codrington had to face up to the prospect of anchoring in a perilous position, and cutting his masts away. He appreciated the irony of the situation.

> I confess I thought it hard and grievous to be obliged to prepare for a watery grave, and to feed for some hours on bare hope, with all our sails blown from the yards and no possibility of setting others to claw off a lee shore, after having so well escaped the chances of the action.[31]

At 1.30 a.m. on the 24th the wind abated slightly and Codrington was able to set his main and fore sail close reefed. At the same time he decided to cut the tow rope to the *Bahama*, despite the entreaties of her crew. She was eventually taken to Gibraltar by the *Donegal*, which had joined from Gibraltar.

The *Revenge* had to abandon her tow of another prize at 10.00 a.m. on the 24th as the gale made it impossible for the pumps to keep up with the inflow of water, but there were not enough boats to take all the Spaniards off.

> On the last boat's load leaving the ship, the Spaniards who were left on board, appeared at the gangway and ship's side, displaying their bags of dollars and doubloons, and eagerly offering them as a reward for saving them from the expected and unavoidable wreck; but, however well inclined we were, it was not in our power to rescue them or it would have been affected without the proffered bribe.[32]

In battle the sailors at least had some control over their destiny and some hope of victory, and the whole affair had lasted only five hours, or much less for the ships that joined the action late. The storm was beyond anyone's control, and went on for days rather than hours, with no end in sight. As Codrington wrote,

> It is not fighting ... which is the severest part of our life, it is having to contend with the sudden changes of season, the war of elements, the dangers of a lee shore, and so forth, which produce no food for honour or glory beyond the internal satisfaction of doing a duty we know to be most important.

In the *Belleisle*,

> The hours dragged tediously on, and death appeared in each gust of the tempest. In

battle the chances were equal, and it was possible for many to escape; but shipwreck in such a hurricane was certain destruction to all, and the doubtful situation of the ship kept the mind in a perpetual state of terror. In this horrible suspense each stroke of the bell, as it proclaimed the hour, sounded as the knell of our approaching destiny, for none could expect to escape the impending danger…[33]

… when the welcome order to strike two bells (that is, five o'clock) was heard, it aroused our sinking energies, and every eye was directed towards the shore. In a few minutes 'Land on the lee bow! Put the helm up!' resounded through the ship, and all was again bustle and confusion.

When we got round, the breakers were distinctly seen about a mile to leeward, throwing the spray to such a terrific height that even in our security we could not behold them without shuddering. This was most assuredly a period of delight; but our intense dread had so long overpowered every other feeling, that our escape from destruction seemed like returning animation, producing a kind of torpor which rendered us insensible to our miraculous preservation.[34]

According to Captain Codrington, 'The Wednesday and the following night were to me severer times of trial than the day of battle.'[35] There was heartache as prizes were abandoned, not just for the loss of prize money and prestige, but also out of compassion for the men who might still be on board those ships, and every effort was made to rescue them in almost impossible conditions. *L'Aigle*, taken by James Spratt's daring, was still in the possession of the *Defiance* on the morning of the 22nd, but every attempt to get a tow rope on board failed. Boats were sent to take off the British prize crew, but one officer and twelve men had to be left behind as the *Defiance* was driven close to a lee shore.[36] Eventually, *L'Aigle* made her way into Cadiz.

The dismasted *Santisima Trinidad* was in tow of the almost undamaged *Prince* from the morning of the 22nd, but at 4.00 a.m. on the 24th, as the ship wore round to avoid running on to the shore, the tow rope broke. The *Prince*'s boats got the Spanish prize in tow again soon after daylight, but at 9.00 a.m. a signal was sent out from Collingwood to destroy the prizes. The Admiral noted, 'At 9, the weather having every appearance of blowing, a heavy sea from the westward, and no prospect of getting the captured ships on shore, made the signal to quit and destroy the prizes …'.[37]

The *Prince* cast off the tow and then hove to in order to stop in the water. With the assistance of the boats of the *Neptune* and *Ajax* they brought 500 men out of the prize, including many wounded. They then cut away the *Santisima Trinidad*'s anchors to prevent her being saved, and scuttled her by cutting holes in her decks to let the water in.

In the *Revenge*, William Robinson commented, 'It was a mortifying sight to witness the ships we had fought so hard for, and had taken as prizes, driven by the elements from our possession, with some of our own men on board as prize masters, and it was a great blight to our victorious success'.[38]

Rear-Admiral Louis's squadron, including the *Canopus* with Francis Austen as flag captain, was already at sea on 21 October, having taken on water at Gibraltar and Morocco. By the following day, reports were beginning to reach them that the enemy was out, but winds were light in the mouth of the Straits of Gibraltar, and progress was slow. On the 26th Captain Peter Parker of the sloop *Weazle* came on board with full details of the battle and the death of Nelson. Austen's private grief for the Admiral was mingled with disappointment at his own position and he wrote to his wife, 'Alas! my dearest Mary, all my fears are but too fully justified. The fleets have met and after a very severe contest, a most decisive Victory has been gained by the English 27 over the Enemy's 23.'[39] The death of Nelson cancelled all his promises and Austen gave up hope of a frigate. Furthermore, people would never say of him as they did of his sister's character, Admiral Croft, 'He was in the Trafalgar action'.[40]

Louis's squadron arrived on station on the 30th and surveyed the remains of the enemy, largely wrecked along the shores outside Cadiz. The French 74 *Algeciras* was still in the entrance to the harbour, warping her way in slowly by laying out a very long anchor cable and hauling it in by the capstan. Louis seriously considered the possibility of an attack on her. The temptation to put the final seal on the victory at Trafalgar must have been high, but it was not worth the risk. As Austen wrote, 'On standing in to reconnoitre the position of the enemy's ship, it was judged impossible to bring her out with the wind as it then was and it was not worth the risk of disabling one of the squadron in an attempt to destroy her.'[41] It was a 'melancholy satisfaction' to Lieutenant James Price of the *Queen*.[42] Even so, *The Times* reported guardedly on 9 November, 'It was said, that Admiral Louis had fallen in with the wreck of the enemy's fleet after the late action, and captured ten of them.'[43]

On 3 November another battle had taken place off Cape Ortegal in the north west of Spain. A British squadron of four ships of the line and two frigates under Sir John Strachan found five French ships of the line and five smaller ships, which had escaped from the action at Trafalgar. All of the enemy ships of the line were captured, providing a fine codicil to the battle itself, without any of the tragedy of the death of an admiral or the loss of prizes.

One by one, or in small groups, the damaged ships made their way to Gibraltar. The dismasted *Belleisle* was the first ship of the line to arrive, having been towed by the undamaged frigate *Naiad*; she dropped anchor at 1.20 p.m. on 24 October, almost exactly three days after she had lost the first of her masts. She was cheered by the crews of the other ships in the harbour. Four days later there was much greater activity, as the *Tonnant*, *Revenge*, *Colossus*, *Bellerophon* and *Thunderer* arrived, and the *Victory* herself dropped anchor at 7.00 that evening. A few more arrived on 2 November, including the *Royal Sovereign* (no longer flying Collingwood's flag); the *Temeraire* towed by the *Defiance*; the *Defence* with the *San Idelfonso*, the first of the prizes; and the *Orion*. British ships were anchored in the narrow space inside the mole or breakwater, the prizes were left outside.

Ashore at Gibraltar, the crews divided themselves into two classes.

> Some of the crews belonging to the different ships in the fleet would occasionally meet on shore, and one would say to another tauntingly, on enquiring to what ship he belonged; 'Oh! you belong to one of the ships that did not come up till the battle was

The Victory *approaching Gibraltar after the battle, by Clarkson Stanfield.*

nearly over;' and others would be heard to say, 'Oh! you belong to one of the Boxing Twelves, come and have some black strap and Malaga wine,' at the same time giving them a hearty shake by the hand. This was signifying that the heat of the battle was borne by the twelve ships which first engaged and broke the line.[44]

Collingwood arrived at Gibraltar in the 98-gun *Queen* on 13 November and stayed long enough to decide what to do with the damaged ships. Several of them, he knew, could not be repaired with the meagre facilities of the Rock and had to be sent home as soon as they could be fitted with some kind of jury rig to make them mobile. Eleven ships were fixed in this way – all those which had led the two lines into battle. The *Belleisle*, the most damaged of all in the rigging, was hauled alongside the sheer hulk at Gibraltar for the stumps of her old main, fore and mizzen masts and the bowsprit to be pulled out. She was fitted with a main topmast for a mainmast, a jib-boom for a mizzenmast, a fore topmast for a foremast and a spar and a jib-boom for a bowsprit. With much weaker and shorter rig than normal, she also needed smaller sails – a frigate's lower sail or course was used, and the *Belleisle*'s own topgallant sails were rigged at one level below normal, as topsails. On 3 November she was towed out from the mole and was ready to sail home two days later, in company with the *Victory*, *Bellerophon* and the frigate *Boadicea*. The small and fragile squadron met very unfavourable winds and it was 3 December before the *Belleisle* anchored off Plymouth.[45]

Collingwood planned to send the ships to England in batches of five or six as protection against enemy raiders at sea, but the reality was not quite as neat as that. Seven 74-gun ships left on 9 November, including the *Revenge*, *Mars* and *Defence*. A group of six, including the three-deckers *Royal Sovereign* and *Temeraire*, and the *Leviathan*, *Colossus*, *Tonnant* and *Spartiate*, left ten days later. The *Revenge* arrived at Portsmouth on 6 December and put into dock on the 14th, where she remained for over a year. She cost more than £10,000 to repair. The *Defence* was docked in April 1806 in the same yard and was out six months later, but at a cost of £23,000. The *Bellerophon* at Plymouth was repaired very quickly and spent less than a month in dock, but she cost £18,000, half of which was spent on rigging. The *Royal Sovereign* did not sail again from Plymouth until January 1807 and cost £53,000, easily enough for a new 74-gun ship.[46] At Portsmouth, the *Victory*'s repair was comparatively cheap. It cost less than £10,000 and took two months.[47]

Collingwood himself did not waste much time in port. He sailed from Gibraltar in the *Queen* on 22 November, to blockade the remaining Spanish fleet at Cartagena, just inside the Mediterranean, taking five of the least damaged ships – *Prince*, *Dreadnought*, *Orion*, *Swiftsure* and *Thunderer*. Despite the crushing victory the war was far from over. Just how far would only emerge in the course of years.

CHAPTER 21

The Aftermath

Apart from saving his own fleet from destruction, Collingwood's most immediate duty after the battle was to inform his superiors of what had happened. His dispatch, written on the *Euryalus* during the traumatic day after the battle, began with a masterly and memorable opening line – 'The ever-to-be-lamented death of Vice-Admiral Lord Nelson, who, in the late conflict with the enemy, fell in the hour of victory, leaves me with the duty of informing my Lords Commissioners of the Admiralty …'. After that he entered into a chronological account, beginning with the enemy leaving Cadiz. Like most correspondents of the age, Collingwood did not come directly to the point. If anyone was to read the letter from beginning to end, without any knowledge of the outcome of the battle, he would have been kept in suspense about the extent of the victory for more than 500 words before he learned that nineteen enemy ships had been taken or destroyed. With typical modesty, he said little about his own role in the battle.

On the same day Collingwood issued a general order to the ships of his fleet, repeating his phrase about 'The ever-to-be-lamented death' of Nelson. He praised the courage and skill of his men.

> But where can I find language to express my sentiments of the valour and skill which were displayed by the Officers, the Seamen, and Marines, in the battle with the enemy, where every individual appeared a hero on whom the glory of his Country depended? The attack was irresistible, and the issue of it adds to the page of naval annals a brilliant

The schooner Pickle, *the third vessel from the right.*

instance of what Britons can do, when their King and Country need their service.[1]

The schooner *Pickle* was a small vessel of 127 tons, about a sixteenth of the size of the *Royal Sovereign*. She was 73 feet long on the deck and carried a crew of thirty to thirty-five men, with an armament of six carronades. She was schooner rigged, that is, she had two masts, both rigged fore and aft, giving her a very good turn of speed in unfavourable winds. Such rigs were rare in Europe at the time, but much more common across the Atlantic; the *Pickle* had been built in Bermuda and taken into the navy in 1800.

She had taken little part in the battle, as was fitting for such a small vessel, but in the immediate aftermath she played a considerable role by rescuing 120–130 men, and one woman, from the water. Her commanding officer, Lieutenant John Lapenotière, was the great-grandson of a French nobleman and he had been brought up in Ilfracombe, North Devon. He first went to sea with his father, a naval lieutenant, at the age of ten in 1780. He attracted the patronage of Admiral Leveson Gower of the Admiralty and of Sir John Jervis in the 1790s, but he had no family or political 'interest'. Promoted lieutenant in 1794, he became a very successful commander of small craft such as schooners and cutters, in the way that Lieutenants John Quillam of the *Victory* and James Clavell of the *Royal Sovereign* were successful first lieutenants, but without much hope of promotion without a major fillip to his career.[2] Lapenotière knew this was about to happen at 9.00 a.m. on 26 October, when Collingwood summoned him on board the flagship. He was to take home the dispatches on the battle, and he knew that the bearer of good tidings would be promoted or honoured. The last of the enemy prisoners were sent on board the *Revenge* and the *Pickle* was ready to sail by noon. By 12.30, she was out of sight of the flagship.[3]

Lapenotière made a fast passage in strong and favourable winds, reaching the west country port of Falmouth in eight days. He took land transport for the 260 miles to London and got there in a day and a half, early in the morning of 5 November. According to tradition, Lord Barham was roused from his bed in the First Lord's house at the Admiralty, because he had complained four months earlier when he was not woken up with *Curieux*'s dispatch about the French fleet's movements. Soon the Admiralty clerks were at work making copies of Collingwood's dispatch to send to the King, members of the government and the press.

Seamen mourning the death of Nelson in a popular print.

Celebrations began as soon as the news of the victory was announced, though everyone was aware of their ambiguous nature. In London the Covent Garden Theatre produced 'a hasty, but elegant, compliment to the memory of Lord Nelson.'

> When the curtain drew up, we were surprised with the view of a superb naval scene. It consisted of columns in the foreground, decorated with medallions of the Naval Heroes of Britain. In the distance a number of ships were seen, and the front of the picture was filled by Mr Taylor and the principal singers of the theatre. They were grouped in an interesting manner, with their eyes turned towards the clouds from whence a half-length portrait of Lord Nelson descended ... [4]

This was only the beginning. The following night a 'general illumination' took place in the city.

> The principal streets from extremity of the metropolis to the other, presented a general blaze of refulgence, in which the Theatres, Public Buildings and those of the great Trading Companies, were eminently conspicuous. The India House, the Royal Exchange, the Mansion House, the Bank, the Excise Office, at the east end of the town, were peculiarly splendid; and at the West end, the Drury-Lane, Covent-Garden, Haymarket, and King's Theatres, were decorated with distinguished brilliancy. Drury-Lane presented the initials of the heroic NELSON, surmounted by an anchor, and enveloped in a wreath of palm and laurel, all formed by transparent lamps. Covent-Garden presented a brilliant N, surmounted by an anchor in gold coloured lamps, and decorated with runs, pillars and scrolls. The King's Theatre, and the Little Theatre, in the Haymarket, contributed most luminously to the testification of public joy; as did all the tradesmen of the ROYAL FAMILY in every part of the town. [5]

The news first reached Glasgow on Saturday, 9 November. In those days the city, which had benefited greatly from trade with the British Empire in tobacco and cotton, was strongly in favour of the union with England and the British government. The local volunteers and militia fired a *feu de joie* on Glasgow Green, and the City Council sent an address to the King, concluding that 'To this part of your Majesty's empire in particular, the annihilation of that proud fleet which so recently threatened the devastation of our colonial possessions in the West Indies is an event singularly interesting ...'.[6] The town was illuminated and most citizens put lights in their windows. Some went further and displayed 'transparencies', such as Cleland and Jack's upholstery warehouse and Mr Denholm's Academy in Argyll Street.

> In the east window was an urn, encircled with a wreath of laurel leaves referring to the death of the Hero. From the top of the urn arose a flame illustrative of his immortal fame with the words 'sacred to Nelson'. In another window were two figures of the crown and anchor, the nation's best hope; and in a third the letters GR surrounded with laurel.

The *Victory*, carrying Nelson's body, made slow progress back to England. She finally arrived at Spithead, off Portsmouth, on the morning of 4 December, but at first the weather was too rough to allow boats to communicate with the ship. After that she was visited by Hardy's friend, George Thompson, and by Captain Parker of the *Amazon*. On a previous occasion the two captains had discussed whether two British frigates could defeat a French ship of the line, but Hardy's respect for the enemy had increased during the battle. 'Now, after what I have seen at Trafalgar, I am satisfied it would be mere folly, and ought never to succeed.'[7]

Victory sailed on 10 December for the Thames but had to anchor off Dover for five days due to a north-easterly gale. She then sailed north to the anchorage at the Downs, where she was cheered by every ship that passed. She reached Long Reach near Chatham on Christmas Day, where the crew de-rigged her and took her guns out, in preparation for dry-docking. Seaman J— Brown wrote, 'We scarce have room to move, the ship is so full of

Nobility coming down from London to see the ship looking at shot holes.' The ship would be out of service for some time, and there was fierce competition for her experienced and battle-hardened crew, but they were allocated to Collingwood in his new ship, the *Ocean*. In the meantime 300 men were picked out to go up to London for Nelson's funeral. Each was issued with a blue jacket and trousers, a black armband and a black hat, as well as a gold medal with £7.[8]

Chaplain Scott's love for Nelson had increased over the months as his diplomatic secretary, and he admitted to being 'stupid with grief'. He took personal charge of the body, which had been preserved in brandy for the voyage home. He wrote urgently to Lady Hamilton's mother, telling her to break the news gently to her daughter, but fearing very much that the news sent by Collingwood would have reached her first, for the separation after the storm had preventing him communicating with the new commander-in-chief.[9] After seeing Nelson's body deposited in the Record Room in the Naval Hospital, Scott took up lodgings nearby in Park Row, Greenwich. He had adopted the principle of 'not leaving the place where he is until I lose sight of him for ever.'[10]

Nelson's funeral, in twentieth-century terms, might be seen as a combination of those of Sir Winston Churchill and Princess Diana – the warrior who had saved his country and the beloved but flawed popular icon. The body was borne into a barge for a procession up the Thames to London. On 10 January 1806 a great procession left the Admiralty Building in Whitehall, so long that its head had completed the journey before the tail had left. By his own request Nelson was buried in St Paul's Cathedral, for he believed that Westminster Abbey was built on marshy ground and would not survive.

As always, battle brought promotion, especially to those who had sufficient seniority, luck or ability. On 9 November 1805, four days after receiving news of the battle, the Palace announced that Nelson's brother, William, was to be made an Earl, and Collingwood was to be a Baron. All the active flag officers were promoted one grade. That was due to the creation of an extra rank of Admiral of the Red, but Collingwood went from Vice Admiral of the Blue to Vice Admiral of the Red, and Northesk from Rear Admiral of the White to Rear Admiral of the Red.

Much more significant were the promotions to junior officers. The two lieutenants who had been in acting command during the battle, John Pilfold of the *Ajax* and John Stockham of the *Thunderer*, were promoted straight to captain, without going through the intermediate rank of commander, on Christmas Day 1805, though neither ship had played a particularly decisive role in the battle. William Hennah of the *Mars* and William Pryce Cumby of the *Bellerophon* had both been in the thick of the fighting and had taken command in the most difficult circumstances, when the captain was killed in action. They were promoted to captain on the first day of 1806, and would always be behind Pilfold and Stockham in seniority.

Other lieutenants had slightly less dramatic rises. John Quillam, first lieutenant of the

The River Thames crowded with boats for Nelson's funeral.

Victory, was promoted commander then captain. As he had feared, John Pasco, the signal lieutenant, was promoted only to commander in the first instance, along with Edward Williams and John Yule of the same ship. Apart from that, the first lieutenants of all ships of the line and frigates present at the battle were promoted to commander, taking rank according to their seniority as lieutenants. Four midshipmen or masters mates from the *Victory* were to be commissioned as lieutenants, along with three from the *Royal Sovereign*, two from the *Britannia* and one from every other ship of the line or frigate. Their names were to be chosen by the captains of the ships. But such promotion had its problems. There were already more captains, lieutenants and especially commanders for the posts to be filled, and this wave of promotions made the situation worse, especially as the victory had not added a significant number of prize ships to the Royal Navy. The navy was creating a promotion block that would last for many years,

After the battle there was time to reflect on the hardships of a naval career. Rotherham's 'Growls of a Naval Life' ends on the sourest note of all. 'Having been some thirty years at sea setting down to reflect what sort of life you have spent and asking yourself whether you wish to pass such another.'[11] Jane Codrington tried to put her husband's regrets about the lack of family life into perspective.

> It is true, my very dearest, that the navy is a service that occasions many privations, exposes you to some hardships, and is the greatest enemy, for a time, to domestic comfort both to husband and wife; but you must also recollect how much both are occasionally rewarded for all their sufferings (as in our instance); not all my anxieties, not all the real misery of suspense, would induce me, if it were in my power, to give up your having been at Trafalgar; nor would any consideration, I am sure, purchase with you your absence on that glorious day.[12]

Nor did the victory at Trafalgar remove any of the hardships and uncertainties of a seaman's life. Edward Harrison, a seaman in the *Temeraire*, wrote to his mother soon after his ship arrived at Portsmouth.

> It is reported that our ship is going to be laid up and there is about 100 men drafted on board HM ship [illegible] from our ship [to]day and I expect that in the course of a week I shall be drafted also, but at present I cannot give any certain account of what ship will fall to my lot.[13]

William Robinson was a little luckier. While the *Revenge* was in dry-dock at Portsmouth he was allowed six days leave of absence, supported by a 'liberty ticket' signed by his officers. On the way he was pursued by the press gang in his home town of Fareham, but frustrated them by showing his ticket. Robinson resented being pursued by 'this detestable set ...[of] bloodhounds, who chase them with greater eagerness than a huntsman pursues the fox.'[14] Collingwood was loaded with honours after the battle – a baronetcy, the thanks of Parliament, a pension of £2000 for life, a testimonial from the Patriotic Fund, a gold medal and a sword from the Duke of Clarence. He took on Nelson's position as commander-in-chief in the Mediterranean Fleet, and this time the title was not a misnomer. With the main enemy force defeated he really did rule the inland sea, but that brought high expectations and much work. At first he was mainly concerned with the possibility of an enemy revival and spent much time blockading the Spanish at Cartagena. When the Spanish became allies in 1808, his ships helped the British under Sir Arthur Wellesley establish themselves in the peninsula. During this period he had to deal with the great variety of governments in the region – great powers such as Austria and Turkey, semi-piratical nations such as the North African states of Algiers and Tunisia, and weaker states such as Naples, which could easily fall under enemy domination. His operations were less auspicious than his diplomacy. In 1807 his subordinate, Sir John Duckworth, was unsuccessful at the Dardanelles, and in the following year Collingwood failed to intercept a French fleet for the relief of Corfu.

Collingwood's thoughts were constantly toward his homeland in the north of England, and he kept up an extensive correspondence with friends and family. He sought promotion for deserving officers, and regretted that there were few opportunities after the Trafalgar promotion filled up the lists. All this was done with the most meticulous care, and his advice to his daughter on letter-writing gives much insight to his character.

> To write a letter with negligence, without proper stops, with crooked lines and great flourishing dashes, is inelegant; it argues either great ignorance of what is proper, or great indifference towards the person to whom it is addressed, and is consequently disrespectful.[15]

This reflected his attitude to his diplomatic and naval correspondence, and after four years of this he was exhausted by his spartan but demanding existence. 'I, who enter into no pleasures, go to no feasts, or festivals, or midnight gambols, have no complaints but those arising from sheer fatigue of spirit.' In 1810 he wrote to his former first lieutenant, now Captain Clavell.

> I dare say you are very desirous of being employed again. If I had any influence with Lord Mulgrave, there is nobody on whose behalf I would use it in preference to you; and you may believe, that whenever I feel that I have any interest, I will exert it for you. I have been failing in my health very much for more than a year, and it is my constant occupation alone that keeps me alive. Lately I have had a very severe complaint in my stomach, which has almost prevented my eating. It is high time I should return to England, and I hope I shall be allowed to do so before long. It will, otherwise, be soon too late.[16]

On 3 March 1810 Collingwood was succeeded in the command of the Mediterranean Fleet at Port Mahon, Minorca, and prepared to go home in the Ville de Paris. For two days the wind prevented an exit, and two days out to sea his flag captain asked if the swell was disturbing him. 'No, Thomas, I am now in a state which nothing in this world can disturb me more. I am dying.' He passed away at 6.00 p.m. at the age of fifty-nine. A postmortem suggested that 'His death was occasioned by a contraction of the pylorus, brought on by confinement on board of ship, and by continually bending over a desk while engaged in his Correspondence.'[17]

Chaplain Scott of the *Victory* left the navy to become a typical provincial clergyman, if that was possible for a man of such peculiar experiences, appearance and personality. He was made a Doctor of Divinity by Royal mandate but failed to succeed Nelson's brother as Prebendary of Canterbury. He maintained correspondence with Nelson's circle, including Lady Hamilton, Hardy and the politicians Rose and Canning. He married a much younger woman in 1807 and settled in Essex. His wife bore three children, including one who died at the age of three due to the negligence of a nurse. Mrs Scott herself died in 1811 at the age of twenty-six. Six years later he became vicar of Catterick in Yorkshire. As well as bringing up his daughters, he campaigned to establish schools and wrote about the 'doctrinal errors' of the Roman Catholic Church. His book collection filled all the rooms of his house, but he made light of his role in history. According to his daughter, 'His neighbours were unaccustomed to regard him, except historically, as Nelson's chaplain.'[18] He died in 1840 at the age of seventy-two.

Captain Rotherham transferred from the *Royal Sovereign* to the *Bellerophon* immediately after the battle, to fill the vacancy left by the death of Cooke. He remained until 1808, making a meticulous and detailed list of the crew of great benefit to historians, but this was one of the least dramatic periods in the history of a great ship. Rotherham had no further service after that, and like many another veteran, he soon became embittered about the way he had been treated. In 1815 he was disappointed not to be made a Knight Commander of the Bath, although he 'had the honour to command the Royal Sovereign who led the British Fleet to Victory, a Victory! too well known by its splendour to require any comment.' After protest he was awarded the lesser honour of Companion of the Bath.

Nelson's Column in Trafalgar Square as first built, without Landseer's lions.

He was an inveterate writer to the newspapers complaining, among other things, about the organization of the Navy Board to *The Times* in 1817; the ennobling of certain mediocre naval officers to the *Morning Chronicle* in 1825; the fast promotion given to relatives of the Melville family to the *Morning Herald* in 1826; and the state of the naval administration to the *Sun* in the same year. Rotherham died of an apoplexy in 1830.[19]

Despite the shocking death of his father, Norwich Duff of the *Mars* remained in the navy. He saw much action in the Mediterranean over the next six years, including the Battle of Lissa in 1811, when Captain William Hoste led a squadron of frigates against a superior number of French and Venetian ships and defeated them. He was promoted lieutenant that year and became commander of the *Espoir* sloop in 1814. In that capacity he took part in the United States against Washington, Baltimore and New Orleans. He was promoted captain in 1822 but remained on half pay, slowly climbing up the ranks until he became a vice-admiral. He died in 1862 but the family naval connection continued into the twentieth century; one member was captain of a cruiser in World War I and another commanded a division of battleships at Jutland.

James Spratt, who had taken *L'Aigle* at Trafalgar with his sword between his teeth, was severely wounded in the battle. At Gibraltar his leg was sealed in a box to allow it to heal, but after some days it had to be opened because of the patient's extreme agony, and it was found that the leg was being eaten by maggots. Spratt was promoted lieutenant and given command of a shore signal station. After the war he was given a pension and promoted to commander in 1838. He settled into a rather boastful old age at Teignmouth in Devon. When the naval biographer, William O'Byrne, asked for a brief account of his life it ran to many pages, with sub-headings such as 'More work for Sprat.'[20]

The *Gibraltar Chronicle* of 2 November 1805 was probably the first to describe John Pollard in print as 'the man who shot the man who shot Nelson'[21], though he never made any such claim himself, and spent the rest of his life denying it.

Many of those who fought in the battle, especially the men without strong political influence, became increasingly disgruntled over the years. Peacetime promotion was rare, and even appointments to ships were few and far between. Peter Pickernell, second lieutenant of the *Revenge* in the battle, complained more than thirty years later that despite promotion to commander in 1810, 'for want of interest, never could obtain a command afloat'. Spencer Smyth, a midshipman of the *Defiance*, had seen more action than most. 'I have been engaged in three general battles and at the capture and destruction of 24 ships of the line, 23 frigates, 36 corvettes and brigs and three privateers, besides several more vessels.' He was promoted to commander after the victory against the Turks at Navarino in 1827 but then, being without interest, was placed on half pay. George Westphal, who as a midshipman had lain beside the dying Nelson in the cockpit of the *Victory*, complained that 'for all the distinguished services here detailed, I beg to observe that I have not so much to show by way of a decoration as a Waterloo drum boy.'[22] The old meritocratic navy of the wars became increasingly political and aristocratic as economic constraints began to bite, while middle-class expectations were raised in Victorian times.

Most of the figures from the lower deck disappear from view after their naval service was completed. William Robinson remained with the *Revenge* but strongly resented the appointment of her new captain, Charles Elphinstone Fleming, after the battle. As well as ordering the painting out of the *Revenge*'s 'Nelson chequer', he was 'cursed from stem to stern in the British navy' as an incompetent tyrant. As a literate seamen, Robinson became a purser's steward, a privileged member of the lower deck. He saw much blockade service and resented the nickname of 'Channel gropers' given to those who served in the vital but unglamorous blockade of Brest. He took part in the unsuccessful Walcheren expedition against the Netherlands in 1809 and even in his humble station he felt the disgrace of failure: '… disappointment was seen to hang upon every man's visage, and he was ashamed to own, whither he had been.' The *Revenge* took supplies to Wellington's army in Portugal in 1811, after which Robinson, as he put it, 'quitted, and took my leave of the naval service' – in other words, he deserted. He disappears from the records for the next twenty-five years, until 1836 when he took advantage of a boom in war writing to publish his memoirs as Jack Nastyface.

Benjamin Stevenson, pressed into the *Victory* in 1803, still regarded the naval seaman's lot as 'one of the most miserablest lives that a man ever led' in 1805. He served in Collingwood's flagship, *Ocean*, in 1806, and evidently became reconciled to the naval service. He was a warrant officer, gunner of the 16-gun brig *Halcyon* by 1809. He was quite lucky with prize money and by 1812 he had £273 in his account. In February 1815 he was released from the navy, having 'six orphan children to maintain'. He resumed his original name of Thompson and apparently affected the title of 'captain', but not for long; he died two days before Christmas 1815.[23]

Nelson's legacy to the British nation, apart from the immediate results of his great battles, is complex. He gave the Royal Navy an ideal of complete and uncompromising victory which has survived the centuries. The Royal Navy idolized him in World War I, but created an inflexible tactical system which he would have deplored, and failed to win victory at Jutland in 1916. In the second great war of the twentieth century Nelson was revived as a popular hero, and in the film *That Hamilton Woman*. It became Winston Churchill's favourite film, and he openly cried when he saw it for the fifth time on board the battleship *Prince of Wales*, on the way to a meeting with President Roosevelt. But it was probably the junior officers – submarine and destroyer captains and Fleet Air Arm pilots – who showed the Nelson spirit most effectively in that conflict.

Notes

Abbreviations
Addit Additional Manuscripts, British Library
BL British Library
NMM National Maritime Museum
NRS Navy Records Society
PRO National Archive
RNM Royal Naval Museum

Chapter 1 Mobilization
1 Vincente Tofino de San Miguel, *España Maritima or Spanish Coasting Pilot*, translated by John Dougall, London, 1812, pp. 130, 135, 136
2 T. C. Hansard, publisher, *Parliamentary History of England*, Vol. XXXVI, 1820, col. 1162
3 Roger Morriss, *St Vincent and Reform, 1801-04*, *Mariner's Mirror*, Vol. 69, 1983, pp. 269-90
4 PRO ADM 2/301
5 Navy Records Society, *A Narrative of My Professional Adventures*, William Dillon, ed. Michael Lewis, 1953. Vol. II p. 9
6 PRO ADM 1/689
7 C. S. Forester, ed., *The Adventures of John Wetherell*, London, 1954, pp. 31-4
8 NMM CHA/B/6
9 *Oxford Dictionary of Quotations*, Oxford, 1996, p. 178
10 Frederick Hoffman, *A Sailor of King George*, 1901, reprinted London, 1999, pp. 99-100
11 *Ibid.*, p 102
12 Based on *Naval Chronicle*, 1803, pp. 243-9, 328-37
13 Navy Records Society, *The Blockade of Brest*, ed. John Leyland, Vol. I, 1898, p. 8
14 Christopher Lloyd, *The British Seaman*, London, 1968, p. 289
15 NMM MS93/037
16 NMM BGY/T/1

Chapter 2 The *Victory*
1 NMM AGC/36/3
2 NMM CHA/B/4
3 *Mariner's Mirror*, Vol. 65, Feb. 1979, p. 64
4 Quoted in Navy Records Society, *Nelson's Letters to his Wife*, ed. George Naish, 1958, p. 381
5 Isle of Man Natural History and Antiquarian Society, Proceedings, New series, no. 1, Vol. VII, 1964-6, *Captain John Quillam RN*, by F. Cowin. Sent on by Wendy Thirkettle of Manx National Heritage
6 John Marshall, *Royal Naval Biography*,

London, 1823-35, Vol. ix, p. 430
7 *Ibid.*, Vol. vi, p. 344
8 *The Nelson Dispatch*, Vol. 5, part 11, July 1996, pp. 396-8
9 Portsmouth Record Series, *Records of the Portsmouth Division of Marines*, Portsmouth, 1990, pp. lii, 161
10 PRO ADM 11/66/1, 11/67/2
11 NMM AGC/36/3
12 Sir Nicholas Harris Nicolas, *The Dispatches and Letters of Lord Nelson*, London 1845-6, reprinted 1998, Vol. VI, p. 33
13 Alfred and Margaret Gatty, *The Life of A J Scott*, London, 1842, p. 235
14 *Ibid.*, pp. 163, 293
15 NMM AGC/S/16
16 Nicolas, *op. cit.*, Vol. VI, pp. 36, 41
17 Quoted in Christopher Lloyd, J. J. Keevil and J. L. S. Coulter, *Medicine and the Navy*, Vol. 3, p. 30
18 Nicolas, *op. cit.*, Vol. VI, p. 324
19 Royal Naval Museum, Rivers Papers, 1998/41 (1)
20 *The Nelson Dispatch*, Vol. 5, part 11, July 1996, p. 400
21 Nicolas, *op. cit.*, Vol. V, p. 65
22 Nicolas, *op. cit.*, Vol. V, p. 74
23 A. M. Broadley, *The Three Dorset Captains at Trafalgar*, London, 1906, *passim*
24 Kathrin Orth, *Crime and Punishment in the Royal Navy*, presented at the New Researchers in Maritime History Conference, 1995, p. 26

Chapter 3
The Threat from Boulogne
1 Edouard Desbriere, *Projets et Tentatives de Debarquement aux Iles Britanniques*, Vol. I, 1900, pp. 387-90
2 Navy Records Society, *The Keith Papers*, ed. Christopher Lloyd, 1955, Vol. III, p. 31
3 E. P. Thompson, *The Making of the English Working Class*, London, 1963, reprinted 1979, p. 495
4 PRO 30/149/1, f. 31
5 T. C. Hansard, *Parliamentary Debates from the Year 1803*, Vol. I, 1812, col. 892
6 NMM KEI/26/7
7 NRS Keith III, *op. cit.*, 79-81, 84-5, 53-4
8 Navy Records Society, *Letters of Admiral Markham*, 1904, p. 108
9 PRO ADM 1/629
10 NRS *Keith Papers* III, *op. cit.*, pp. 51, 56
11 NMM AUS/6
12 NMM MEL/7
13 A. Crawford, *Reminiscences of a Naval Officer during the Late War*, London, 1851, p. 148

14 Navy Records Society, *The Keith Papers*, Vol. I, ed. W. G. Perrin, 1927, pp. 7-8, 54, *passim*
15 NRS Keith III, *op. cit.*, pp. 133-47
16 NMM KEI/L/170
17 PRO WO 17/2786
18 National Army Museum manuscripts, 7805-72
19 BL Additional manuscripts 38358, f. 230
20 National Army Museum manuscripts 6807-367
21 PRO WO 30/70
22 Richard Glover, *Britain at Bay*, London, 1973, p. 195
23 Holland Rose, *Dumouriez and the Defence of England against Napoleon*, New York, 1909, pp. 285-6
24 NRS Keith Papers, *op. cit.*, Vol III, p. 49
25 *Ibid.*, Vol. III pp. 49-50
26 NMM KEI/L/170
27 *Sussex Militia List, Southern Division, Pevensey Rape*, 1803, Eastbourne, 1988, p. iii
28 *Parliamentary History*, Vol. 36 col. 1684
29 Rose, *op. cit.*, p. 242
30 B Lavery, *Nelson and the Nile*, London, 1998, p. 9
31 Phillip Ziegler, *A Life of Henry Addington*, London, 1965, p. 189
32 The History of Parliament, *The House of Commons 1790–1820*, Vol III, London, 1986, p. 636
33 *The Three Dorset Captains at Trafalgar*, *op. cit.*, p. 128
34 Navy Records Society, *Letters and Papers of Lord Barham*, ed. Sir J. K. Laughton, 1910, Vol III, pp. 67-8

Chapter 4 The *Bellerophon*
1 PRO ADM 35/1485
2 PRO ADM 51/1359
3 Navy Records Society, *The Channel Fleet and the Blockade of Brest*, ed. Roger Morriss, 2001, p. 641
4 ADL/L/B/56
5 NMM LBK/38
6 PRO ADM 101/90/1
7 Jedadiah Tucker, *Memoirs of the Earl of St Vincent*, London, 1844, Vol. 1, pp. 391-7
8 John Marshall, *Royal Naval Biography*, *op. cit.*, Vol. IV, pp. 966-69
9 NMM LBK/38
10 H. D. Traill, *The Life of Sir John Franklin*, London, 1896, p. 25
11 NMM BGY/P/3

Chapter 5 The Crews
1 John Nicol, *Life and Adventures*, p. 209

2 *The Three Dorset Captains at Trafalgar, op. cit.*, p. 126
3 Navy Records Society, *Shipboard Life and Organisation*, ed. B. Lavery, 1998, p. 354
4 Adam Smith, *Wealth of Nations*, Edinburgh, 1853, p. 49
5 G. L. Newnham Collingwood, *The Correspondence of Lord Collingwood*, London, 1828, p. 353
6 John Masefield, *Sea Life in Nelson's Time*, reprinted 1972, plate 15
7 W. H. Long, *Naval Yarns*, reprinted Wakefield, 1973, p. 151
8 *Mariner's Mirror*, Vol. x, pp. 89-90
9 John D. Clarke, *The Men of HMS Victory at Trafalgar*, Dallington, 1999, p. 17
10 NMM AGC/M/9
11 NMM RUSI/110a
12 NMM WEL/8
13 Navy Records Society, *Five Naval Journals*, ed. Thursfield, 1951, p. 10
14 William Robinson, *Jack Nastyface*, reprinted London, 1973, pp. 32-3
15 *Shipboard Life and Organisation, op. cit.*, p. 244
16 NMM WEL/8
17 *Shipboard Life and Organisation, op. cit.*, p. 355-6
18 *Ibid.*, p. 634
19 *Jack Nastyface, op. cit.*, p. 33
20 *Ibid.*, p. 38
21 NMM WEL/30
22 PRO ADM 12/24
23 *Shipboard Life and Organisation, op. cit.*, p. 627
24 *Ibid.*, p. 628
25 Navy Records Society, *The Health of Seamen*, ed. Christopher Lloyd, 1965, pp. 266-7
26 NMM BNY/2
27 PRO ADM 1/1931
28 PRO ADM 1/1534
29 *Shipboard Life and Organisation, op. cit.*, p. 264
30 *Ibid.*, p. 260
31 Phillip Patten, *The Natural Defence of an Insular Empire*, Southampton, 1810, p. 84
32 NMM AGC/M/9

Chapter 6 The *Defence*
1 PRO ADM 1/58, p. 32
2 PRO ADM 1/58, pp. 31-2
3 Thomas Huskisson, *Eyewitness to Trafalgar*, Royston, 1985, p. 66
4 Quoted in R. G. Thorne, *The History of Parliament, House of Commons, 1790-1820*, Vol. IV, 1986, p. 231
5 *Eyewitness to Trafalgar*, op cit, pp 55-7
6 Marshall, *Royal Naval Biography, op. cit.*, Vol. xi, p. 268
7 R. H. Mackenzie, *The Trafalgar Roll*, London, 1913, pp. 182-5
8 *Eyewitness to Trafalgar, op. cit.*, pp. 78, 52, 59
9 Quoted in B. Lavery, *Arming and Fitting*

the English Ship of War, London, 1967, p. 68
10 Admiralty Progress Books, Vol. 5 p. 50, Vol. 6 p. 82, photocopy in the NMM Library

Chapter 7 The Mediterranean Fleet
1 Nicolas, *Dispatches and Letters, op. cit.*, Vol. V, pp. 68-9
2 Alfred and Margaret Gatty, *The Life of A J Scott*, London, 1842, p. 105
3 Nicolas, *op. cit.*, Vol. V, p. 307
4 *Ibid.*, Vol. V, p. 272
5 *Ibid.*, Vol. VI , pp. 81-2
6 PRO ADM 8/86, 87, 88, 89
7 Nicolas, *op. cit.*, Vol. V, p. 107
8 *Ibid.*, Vol. V, p. 341
9 *Ibid.*, Vol. V, pp. 240, 274-5
10 Nicolas, *op. cit.*, Vol. V, pp. 317, 320
11 Augustus Phillimore, *The Life of Sir William Parker*, London, 1876, Vol. 1, p. 270
12 Nicolas, *op. cit.*, Vol. VI, p. 234
13 Navy Records Society, *The Keith Papers*, ed. Christopher Lloyd, 1955, Vol. III, p. 216
14 Nicolas, *op. cit.*, Vol. V, p. 403
15 *Ibid.*, Vol. V, p. 320
16 Phillimore, The *Life of Sir William Parker, op. cit.*, p. 271
17 Nicolas, *op. cit.*, Vol. V, p. 306
18 *Ibid.*, Vol. V, p. 319
19 *Ibid.*, Vol. V, p. 36
20 *Ibid.*, Vol. V, p. 425
21 *Ibid.*, Vol. VI, pp. 154-5
22 Ship histories, NMM Library
23 Nicolas, *op. cit.*, Vol. V, p. 461
24 *Ibid.*, Vol. VI, p. 50
25 William O'Byrne, *A Naval Biographical Dictionary*, 1849, reprinted Polstead, 1990, Vol. 1, p. 58
26 *The Nelson Dispatch* Vol. 5, 10 April 1996, p. 352
27 *Ibid.*, Vol. 6, January 1998, pp. 184-85
28 Nicolas, *op. cit.*, Vol. VI, p. 33
29 *Ibid.*, Vol. VI, p. 50
30 *Ibid.*, Vol. V, pp. 215, 371
31 *Ibid.*, Vol. V, p. 475
32 NMM BGY/T/1
33 Nicolas, *op. cit.*, Vol V, p 211
34 *Mariner's Mirror* Vol. 8, 1922, J. Holland Rose, *The State of Nelson's Fleet before Trafalgar*, p. 77
35 *Ibid.*, pp. 78-9
36 Nicolas, Vol. V, p. 320
37 *Ibid.*, Vol. V, pp. 352, 387, 433
38 *Ibid.*, Vol. V, p. 309
39 *Ibid.*, Vol. V, p. 480
40 *Ibid.*, Vol. V, pp. 276-77
41 *Ibid.*, Vol. V, pp. 208, 346
42 *Ibid.*, Vol. V, p. 375
43 *Ibid.*, Vol. VI, pp. 295-304, 391
44 Gatty, *op. cit.*, p. 252
45 *Ibid.*, pp. 137-41, 161
46 *Ibid.*, p. 195
47 Phillimore, *The Life of Sir William Parker, op.*

cit., p. 271
48 *Ibid.*, p. 271
49 *Nelson Dispatch*, Vol. 5, part 2, July 1996, p. 400
50 Gatty, *op. cit.*, p. 126
51 Nicolas, *op. cit.*, Vol. VI, p. 279
52 SLO, p. 518
53 *Nelson Dispatch*, 1995-6, pp. 340-1
54 Gatty, *op. cit.*, p 130-1
55 Nicolas, Vol. VI, p. 341
56 *Ibid.*, Vol. VI, p. 342
57 NMM AGC/11/5
58 Nicolas, *op. cit.*, Vol. VI, p. 349

Chapter 8 The *Mars*
1 Admiralty Progress Books, Vol. 5, f. 66
2 G. E. Mainwaring and Bonamy Dobree, *The Floating Republic*, London, 1935, pp. 90-3
3 A. N. and H. Tayler, *The Book of the Duffs*, Edinburgh, 1914, p. 260
4 *Ibid.*, p. 261
5 Navy Records Society, *A Narrative of my Professional Adventures*, William Dillon, ed. Michael Lewis, 1953, Vol. 1, p. 327
6 Nicholas Tracy, ed., *The Naval Chronicle, a Contemporary Record of the Royal Navy at War*, London, 1999, Vol. III, p. 185
7 PRO ADM 1/1727
8 Lady Jane Bourchier, *The Life of Sir Edward Codrington*, London, 1873, Vol. 1, pp. 44, 46

Chapter 9 The Chase
1 PRO ADM 95/45
2 Deirdre Le Faye, *Jane Austen's Letters*, Oxford, 1995, p. 176
3 Brian Southam, *Jane Austen and the Navy*, Hambledon and London, 2000, pp. 88-90
4 Nicolas, *Letters and Dispatches, op. cit.*, Vol. VI, p. 399
5 *Ibid.*, Vol. VI, p. 398
6 *Ibid.*, Vol. VI, pp. 397, 399, 401
7 Augustus Phillimore, *The Life of Sir William Parker*, London, 1876, Vol. 1, p. 284
8 NMM AUS/2b
9 Nicolas, *op. cit.*, Vol. VI, p. 410
10 Gatty, *The Life of A J Scott, op. cit.*, p. 170
11 Nicolas, *op. cit.*, Vol. VI, p. 440
12 Phillimore, *The Life of Sir William Parker, op. cit.*, pp. 283, 300
13 Nicolas, *op. cit.*, Vol. VI, pp. 421, 419
14 Joseph Allen, *The Life and Services of Sir William Hargood*, Greenwich, 1861, p. 110; Nicolas, *op. cit.*, Vol. VI, p. 431n
15 Gatty, *The Life of Scott, op. cit.*, p. 171
16 Phillimore, *The Life of Sir William Parker, op. cit.*, p. 292
17 Nicolas, *op. cit.*, Vol. VI, p. 431
18 *Ibid.*, Vol. V, p. 436
19 *Ibid.*, Vol. VI, p. 442
20 NMM WEL/30
21 Navy Records Society, Vol. XXVIII, 1904, *The Letters of Admiral Markham*, 19-4, p. 398

22 Sir Julian Corbett, *The Campaign of Trafalgar*, London, 1910, p. 155
23 Nicolas, *op. cit.*, Vol. VI, pp. 443-5
24 Phillimore, *The Life of Sir William Parker*, *op. cit.*, p. 289
25 NMM AUS/7, 2b
26 Gatty, *The Life of Scott, op. cit.*, p. 170
27 NMM AUS/2b
28 PRO CO 28/72
29 Phillimore, *The Life of Sir William Parker*, *op. cit.*, p. 292
30 Nicolas, *op. cit.*, Vol. VI, p. 446
31 Phillimore, *The Life of Sir William Parker*, *op. cit.*, p. 293
32 *Ibid.*, p. 293
33 Nicolas, Vol. VI, pp. 447-8n
34 PRO CO 295/11
35 Nicolas, *op. cit.*, Vol. VI, p. 455
36 *Ibid.*, pp. 451-5
37 Corbett, *Campaign of Trafalgar, op. cit.*, 169-70n
38 NMM AUS/2b
39 Nicolas, *op. cit.*, Vol. VI, pp. 467-8
40 Phillimore, *The Life of Sir William Parker*, *op. cit.*, p. 295-6
41 Nicolas, *op. cit.*, Vol. V, p. 471
42 *Ibid.*, Vol. VI, pp. 475
43 *Mariner's Mirror* Vol. 8, 1922, J. Holland Rose, *The State of Nelson's Fleet before Trafalgar*, p. 77
44 *The Three Dorset Captains at Trafalgar, op. cit.*, p. 131
45 Nicolas, *op. cit.*, Vol. VI, p. 478
46 *Ibid.*, Vol. VII, p. 5
47 Holland Rose, *op. cit.*, p. 77
48 NMM BGY/T/1
49 *The Dorset Captains at Trafalgar, op. cit.*, p. 133

Chapter 10 The *Euryalus*
1 A. J. Holland, *Bucklers Hard, a Rural Shipbuilding Centre*, Emsworth, Hampshire, 1985, *passim*
2 *Nelson's Watchdog*, 1805 Club Keepsake No. 4, 1998, pp. 1-7
3 Hercules Robinson, *Sea Drift*, Portsea, 1858, pp. 207-8, 221
4 PRO ADM 1/1532
5 NMM ADM/L/E/200
6 PRO ADM 1/1532, 1534
7 Navy Records Society, *Letters of Lord St Vincent*, ed. D. Bonner Smith, Vol. II, pp. 411, 352
8 Navy Records Society, *The Keith Papers, op. cit.*, Vol. III, pp. 87-93
9 PRO ADM 1/1534
10 Sir Julian Corbett, *The Campaign of Trafalgar*, London, 1910, pp. 265-6

Chapter 11 Barham at the Admiralty
1 Quoted in John Ehrman, *The Younger Pitt*, Vol. III, *The Consuming Struggle*, 1996, p. 765

2 Navy Records Society, *Letters and Papers of Lord Barham*, ed. Sir J. K. Laughton, 1910, Vol. III, p. 55
3 *Letters and Papers of Lord Barham, op. cit.*, Vol. III, pp. 76-8
4 *The History of Parliament, The House of Commons*, 1790-1820, Vol. V, p. 265
5 *Letters and Papers of Lord Barham, op. cit.*, Vol. II, pp. 165-6
6 R. G. Thorne, *The History of Parliament, The House of Commons 1790-1820*, Vol. V, London, 1986, p. 272
7 *Ibid.*, Vol. III, 1986, p. 597
8 *Letters and Papers of Lord Barham, op. cit.*, Vol. III, p. 95
9 *Ibid.*, p. 53-4
10 *Ibid.*, p. 307
11 Sir Julian Corbett, *The Campaign of Trafalgar*, London, 1910, pp. 178-9
12 *Letters and Papers of Lord Barham, op. cit.*, Vol. III, pp. 258-9
13 Navy Records Society, The Blockade of Brest 1803-5, ed. John Leyland, 1901, Vol. II, pp. 301-5
14 *Letters and Papers of Lord Barham, op. cit.*, Vol. III, pp. 259-60
15 *Ibid.*, p. 12
16 *Ibid.*, p. 98
17 Sir Nicholas Harris Nicolas, *The Dispatches and Letters of Lord Nelson*, London 1845-6, reprinted 1998, Vol. VII, p. 23
18 BL Additional Manuscripts 34936
19 Nicolas, *Dispatches and Letters, op. cit.*, Vol. VII, p. 16
20 *Ibid.*, p. 26
21 *Ibid.*, p. 28n
22 *Letters and Papers of Lord Barham, op. cit.*, Vol. III, p. 313
23 Nicolas, *Dispatches and Letters, op. cit.*, Vol. VII, pp. 26-7
24 BL Additional Manuscripts 34992, f. 3

Chapter 12 Cadiz
1 Edouard Desbriere, translated by Constance Eastwick, *The Naval Camapaign of 1805*, Oxford, 1933, Vol. 1, p. 132
2 J. Debrett, *The Little Sea Torch*, London, 1801, p. 83
3 *The Naval Campaign of 1805, op. cit.*, Vol. I, p. 133
4 *Ibid.*, Vo.l II, p. 90
5 *Ibid.*, pp. 93-4
6 *Ibid.*, p. 96
7 *Ibid.*, pp. 169-81
8 *Ibid.*, pp. 87-8, 102, 107
9 *Ibid.*, p. 215
10 *Ibid.*, p. 8
11 *Ibid.*, p. 21
12 *Ibid.*, p. 102
13 *Ibid.*, p. 33
14 *Ibid.*, pp. 111-2

Chapter 13 The *Revenge*
1 William Robinson, *Jack Nastyface*, reprinted London, 1973, pp. 87-8
2 *Ibid.*, p. 87
3 *Naval Chronicle*, Vol. 15, 1806, p. 69
4 PRO ADM 95/72
5 NMM WEL/8
6 Lady Jane Bourchier, *The Life of Sir Edward Codrington*, London, 1873, Vol. 1, p. 46

Chapter 14 Officers
1 NMM SPB/15
2 H. D. Traill, *The Life of Sir John Franklin*, London, 1896, pp. 6-8
3 Jane Austen, *Persuasion*, 1998 Penguin edition, p. 19
4 *The Life of Sir John Franklin, op. cit.*, p. 8
5 A. M. Broadley, *The Three Dorset Captains at Trafalgar*, London, 1906, pp. 111-12, 115
6 *Ibid.*, p. 128
7 Hercules Robinson, *Sea Drift*, Portsea, 1858, pp. 220-1
8 Frederick Hoffman, *A Sailor of King George*, 1901, reprinted London, 1999, pp. 4-10
9 William O'Byrne, *A Naval Biographical Dictionary*, 1849, reprinted Polstead, 1990, Vol. 2, p. 802
10 *The Three Dorset Captains at Trafalgar, op. cit.*, p. 128
11 NMM AGC/33/9
12 NMM WEL/8
13 Compiled from R. H. Mackenzie, *The Trafalgar Roll*, London, 1913, *passim*
14 NMM BNY/2
15 *The Trafalgar Roll, op. cit.*, p. 237
16 *Ibid.*, pp. 73, 164
17 Navy Records Society, *Shipboard Life and Organisation*, ed. B. Lavery, 1998, p. 567
18 PRO ADM 6/138
19 PRO ADM 6/166
20 PRO ADM 6/168, private papers, Mr Upton
21 PRO ADM 6/161
22 Christopher Lloyd, J. J. Keevil and J. L. S. Coulter, Medicine and the Navy, Vol. 3, pp. 29-35
23 William Burney, *New Universal Dictionary of the Marine*, reprinted New York, 1970, p. 513
24 PRO ADM 101/106/1
25 PRO Adm 101/115/1
26 Sir W. S. Laird Clowes, *The Royal Navy; a History*, London, 18897-1903, Vol. III, p. 518
27 *The Trafalgar Roll, op. cit.*, p. 109

Chapter 15 Collingwood and the Stick
1 Jeffrey Baron de Raigersfield, *The Life of a Sea Officer*, London, 1929, pp. 33, 35
2 Oliver Warner, *The Life and Letters of Vice-Admiral Lord Collingwood*, London, 1968, p. 123
3 M. D. Hay, ed., *Landsman Hay*, London, 1953, pp. 76-7
4 NMM LOG/L/C/246

5 *Landsman Hay, op. cit.*, pp. 75-6
6 *Ibid.*, p. 66
7 NMM/LOG/C/246
8 Navy Records Society, *Correspondence of Lord Collingwood*, ed. Edward Hughes, 1957, p. 155
9 *Ibid.*, p. 158
10 Hercules Robinson, *Sea Drift*, London 1863, p. 43
11 NMM SPB/15
12 NMM/LOG/R/303
13 G. L. Newnham Collingwood, *The Correspondence of Lord Collingwood*, London, 1828, pp. 124-5
14 *Ibid.*, p. 109
15 Lady Jane Bourchier, *The Life of Sir Edward Codrington*, London, 1873, Vol. 1, pp. 47-9
16 *Ibid.*, pp. 48-9
17 Nicolas, *Dispatches and Letters, op. cit.*, Vol. VII, p. 32
18 Navy Records Society, *Shipboard Life and Organisation*, ed. B. Lavery, 1998, p. 63

Chapter 16 The Fleet
1 Colin White, *Nelson's Last Walk, The Nelson Dispatch*, Vol. 5 part 11, July 1996, pp. 382-85
2 BL Additional Manuscripts 34930 f. 323
3 Nicolas, *Dispatches and Letters, op. cit.*, Vol. VII, pp. 36-54
4 Lady Jane Bourchier, *The Life of Sir Edward Codrington*, London, 1873, Vol. 1, p. 51
5 W. S. Lovell, *Personal Narrative of Events*, London, 1879, reprinted 1971, p. 45; *Letters and Papers of Lord Barham, op. cit.*, Vol. III, pp. 323-4
6 Sir Julian Corbett, *The Campaign of Trafalgar*, London, 1910, pp. 45-6
7 Frederick Hoffman, *A Sailor of King George*, 1901, reprinted London, 1999, p. 110
8 Thomas Huskisson, *Eyewitness to Trafalgar*, Royston, 1985, p. 66
9 PRO ADM 1/1727
10 John Marshall, *Royal Naval Biography*, London, 1823-35, Vol. II, p. 453
11 Brian Lavery, *The Ship of the Line*, Vol. 1, 1983, p. 126
12 Nicolas, *Dispatches and Letters, op. cit.*, Vol. VII, p. 117n
13 See Robert Gardiner, *Frigates of the Napoleonic Wars*, London, 2000, *passim*
14 *Ibid.*, pp. 153-79
15 Nicolas, *Dispatches and Letters, op. cit.*, Vol. VII, p. 63
16 *The Life of Sir Edward Codrington, op. cit.*, Vol. 1, p. 51
17 Nicolas, *Dispatches and Letters, op. cit.*, Vol. VII, p. 60
18 *Ibid.*, pp. 89-91
19 *The Life of Sir Edward Codrington, op. cit.*, Vol. 1, p. 52
20 *Nelson Dispatch*, Vol. 6, part 5, pp. 185-6
21 *The Life of Sir Edward Codrington, op. cit.*, Vol. 1, pp. 53-4

22 Navy Records Society, *Letters and Papers of Lord Barham*, ed. Sir J. K. Laughton, 1910, Vol. III, pp. 268-70
23 Nicolas, *Dispatches and Letters, op. cit.*, Vol. VII, p. 5
24 *The Life of Sir Edward Codrington, op. cit.*, Vol. 1, p. 55
25 BL Additional Manuscripts 34931
26 NRS Barham III, p. 323
27 *The Life of Sir Edward Codrington, op. cit.*, Vol. 1, p. 53
28 BL Addit 34992 f. 10
29 *Ibid.*
30 NMM ADL/D/6-
31 Warren R. Dawson, *The Nelson Collection at Lloyds*, London, 1952, p. 199
32 BL Addit 34992
33 *Nelson Dispatch*, Volume 6, part 6, pp. 237-8
34 *Nelson's Watchdog*, 1805 Club Keepsake No. 4, 1998, unnumbered page
35 *The Life of Sir Edward Codrington, op. cit.*, Vol. 1, p. 57
36 *The Campaign of Trafalgar, op. cit.*, pp. 333-5
37 *Ibid.*, p. 336
38 *The Life of Sir Edward Codrington*, Vol. 1, p. 58
39 *The Nelson Collection at Lloyds, op. cit.*, pp. 201-2
40 *Nelson's Watchdog*, 1805 Club Keepsake No. 4, 1998, p. 10

Chapter 17 Into Battle
1 Nicolas, *Dispatches and Letters, op. cit.*, Vol. VII, p. 137
2 G. L. Newnham Collingwood, *The Correspondence of Lord Collingwood*, London, 1828, p. 124
3 *Ibid.*, p. 75
4 *The Nelson Dispatch*, Vol. 6 part 6, pp. 238-9
5 Joseph Allen, *The Life and Services of Sir William Hargood*, Greenwich, 1861, pp. 278-9
6 *Ibid.*, p. 279
7 *Mariner's Mirror*, Volv XXIII, 1937, pv 374
8 NMM ADL/D/5, ADL/D/12, ADL/D/6
9 Hercules Robinson, *Sea Drift*, Portsea, 1858, pv 206
10 *The Nelson Dispatch*, Vol. 6, part 6, p. 239
11 BL Additional Manuscripts, 38052
12 NMM LBK/38
13 *The Life and Services of Sir William Hargood, op. cit.*, pp. 280-1
14 W. S. Lovell, *Personal Narrative of Events*, London, 1879, reprinted 1971, p. 50
15 NMM BGY/P/3
16 NMM LBK/38
17 *Mariner's Mirror*, Vol. XXII, 1936, p. 103
18 *Ibid.*
19 Royal Naval Museum, Rivers Papers, 1998/41(1)
20 Navy Records Society, *Logs of the Great Sea Fights*, Vol. II, p. 149, Edouard Desbriere, translated by Constance Eastwick, *The Naval Camaapign of 1805*, Oxford, 1933,

Vol. 2, pp. 138-39
21 Hercules Robinson, *Sea Drift, op. cit.*, pp. 205-6
22 *A Sailor of King George, op. cit.*, p. 114
23 *Jack Nastyface, op. cit.*, pp. 153-5
24 *A Sailor of King George, op. cit.*, p. 109
25 *Ibid.*, p. 114
26 *Mariner's Mirror*, Vol. XXII, 1936, p. 103
27 *Jack Nastyface, op. cit.*, p. 43
28 *The Nelson Dispatch*, Vol. 6, part 6, p. 239
29 Lady Jane Bourchier, *The Life of Sir Edward Codrington*, London, 1873, Vol. 1, p. 75
30 Frederick Hoffman, *A Sailor of King George*, 1901, reprinted London, 1999, p. 118
31 *Mariner's Mirror*, Vol. 69, May 1983, p. 164
32 *The Nelson Dispatch*, Vol. 6, no. 5, January 1998, p. 189
33 *Nelson's Watchdog*, 1805 Club Keepsake No. 4, 1998
34 Nicolas, *Dispatches and Letters, op. cit.*, Vol. VII, pp. 147-8
35 *Ibid.*, p. VII 140
36 *Ibid.*, p. 150
37 *Nelson's Watchdog, op. cit.*
38 *The Correspondence of Lord Collingwood, op. cit.*, p. 125
39 *Eyewitness*, pp. 71
40 *A Sailor of King George, op. cit.*, p. 114
41 *The Nelson Dispatch*, Vol. 6, part 6, p. 242
42 *Jack Nastyface, op. cit.*, p. 44
43 *The Correspondence of Lord Collingwood, op. cit.*, W. S. Lovell, *Personal Narrative of Events*, p. 50
44 *The Nelson Dispatch*, Vol. 6, part 9, p. 199
45 Sir Julian Corbett, *The Campaign of Trafalgar*, London, 1910, pp. 370-2, Brian Tunstall, ed. Nicholas Tracy, *Naval Warfare in the Age of Sail*, London, 1990, pp. 256-7
46 *The Correspondence of Lord Collingwood, op. cit.*, p. 126
47 Nicolas, *Dispatches and Letters, op. cit.*, Vol. VII, p. 146
48 Edouard Desbriere, translated by Constance Eastwick, *The Naval Camapaign of 1805*, Oxford, 1933, Vol. 2, p. 215

Chapter 18 The First Round
1 NNM WEL/30
2 Hercules Robinson, *Sea Drift*, Portsea, 1858, pp. 213-4
3 *The Nelson Dispatch*, Vol. 6, part 8, October 1998
4 *Naval Chronicle*, Vol. 15, 1806, p. 110
5 Compiled from Newnham, pp. 124-31, James, Vol. III, pp. 394-6, 405-8
6 Joseph Allen, *The Life and Services of Sir William Hargood*, Greenwich, 1861, pp. 122, 139-42, 146, 279-281
7 *The Life and Services of Sir William Hargood, op. cit.*, p. 283
8 William James, *A Naval History of Great Britain*, London, 1886, Vol. III, p. 408
9 *The Life and Services of Sir William Hargood, op. cit.*, p. 286

10 *Naval Chronicle*, Vol. III, p. 225
11 *The Nelson Dispatch*, Vol. 6, no. 11 April 1998, p. 242
12 NMM BGY/P/3
13 H. D. Traill, *The Life of Sir John Franklin*, London, 1896, pp. 27-8
14 NMM BGY/P/3
15 *The Nelson Dispatch*, Vol. 6, no. 6, p. 244
16 Nicolas, *Dispatches and Letters, op. cit.*, Vol. VII, p. 171n
17 Peter Goodwin, *Mariner's Mirror*, Vol. 83, 1997, p. 90
18 Edouard Desbriere, translated by Constance Eastwick, *The Naval Campaign of 1805*, Oxford, 1933, Vol. 2, p. 194
19 *Naval Chronicle*, Vol. XV, 1806, p. 38
20 Beatty's account in BL Additional Manuscripts 34992, f. 49
21 BL Additional Manuscripts 38050
22 *The Nelson Dispatch*, Vol. 6, part 9, January 1999
23 *Sea Drift, op. cit.*, p. 214

Chapter 19 The Later Battle
1 A. M. Broadley, *The Three Dorset Captains at Trafalgar*, London, 1906, p. 253n
2 NMM LBK/38
3 *Logs of the Great Sea Fights, op. cit.*, Vol. II, p. 250
4 Hercules Robinson, *Sea Drift*, Portsea, 1858, p. 206
5 Frederick Hoffman, *A Sailor of King George*, 1901, reprinted London, 1999, p. 114
6 *Macmillan's Magazine*, Vol. 81, April 1900, p. 425
7 NMM LBK/38
8 *Nelson's Watchdog*, 1805 Club Keepsake No. 4, 1998, p. 12
9 Edouard Desbriere, translated by Constance Eastwick, *The Naval Camapaign of 1805*, Oxford, 1933, Vol. 2, Oxford, 1933, Vol. 2, pp. 283-88
10 *Macmillan's Magazine*, Vol. 81, p. 419
11 *The Nelson Dispatch*, Vol. 6, part 9, January 1999, p. 384
12 Quoted in B. Lavery, *Nelson and the Nile*, London, 1998, p. 189
13 PRO ADM 101/106/1
14 *Mariner's Mirror*, Vol. XXX, 1944, p. 50
15 *Naval Chronicle*, Vol. 15, 1806, pp. 16-7, 109
16 Warren R. Dawson, *The Nelson Collection at Lloyds*, London, 1952, pp. 454-5, 391
17 NMM BGY/P/3
18 *The Three Dorset Captains at Trafalgar, op. cit.*, p. 268
19 NMM JOD/48
20 Sir Julian Corbett, *The Campaign of Trafalgar*, London, 1910, p. 391
21 Nicolas, *Dispatches and Letters, op. cit.*,Vol. 7, p. 196
22 Lady Jane Bourchier, *The Life of Sir Edward Codrington*, London, 1873, Vol. I, pp. 60, 64
23 *Ibid.*, p. 66
24 Navy Records Society, *Logs of the Great*

Sea Fights, Vol. II, pp. 249-50
25 NMM AGC/M/5
26 *The Naval Campaign of 1805, op. cit.*, Vol. 2, pp. 287-88
27 Lady Jane Bourchier, *The Life of Sir Edward Codrington*, London, 1873, Vol. I, p. 66
28 Nicolas, *Dispatches and Letters, op. cit.*,Vol. II, p. 186
29 *Ibid.*, p. 171
30 *Nelson Dispatch*, no. 6, part 8, October 1998, p. 346
31 Joseph Allen, *The Life and Services of Sir William Hargood*, Greenwich, 1861, p. 145
32 *The Naval Campaign of 1805, op. cit.*, Vol. 2, p. 289
33 Nicolas, *Dispatches and Letters, op. cit.*,Vol. VII, p. 168-9

Chapter 20 The Storm
1 Lady Jane Bourchier, *The Life of Sir Edward Codrington*, London, 1873, Vol. 1, pp. 72-3
2 Joseph Allen, *The Life and Services of Sir William Hargood*, Greenwich, 1861, p. 287
3 NMM JOD/48
4 Navy Records Society, *Logs of the Great Sea Fights*, Vol. II, p. 244
5 *The Life of Sir Edward Codrington, op. cit.*, p. 70
6 G. L. Newnham Collingwood, *The Correspondence of Lord Collingwood*, London, 1828, p. 137
7 *Jack Nastyface, op. cit.*, pp. 57-61, RNM Rivers papers, 1998/41(1)
8 *Logs of the Great Sea Fights, op. cit.*, Vol. II, p. 245
9 *The Nelson Dispatch*, Vol. 5, part 11, July 1996 p. 398
10 Gatty, *op. cit.*, p. 185
11 *Naval Chronicle*, Vol. XV, 1806, p. 293
12 NMM AGC/H/18
13 *Mariner's Mirror*, Vol. 69, May 1983, p. 164
14 *The Three Dorset Captains at Trafalgar, op. cit.*, p. 286
15 *Jack Nastyface, op. cit.*, p. 52
16 *Logs of the Great Sea Fights, op. cit.*, Vol II, p. 205
17 *Ibid.*, p. 270
18 *Jack Nastyface, op. cit.*, p. 61
19 Dennis Wheeler, *The Weather of the European Atlantic Seaboard during October 1805*, in *Climatic Change*, Vol. 48, 2001, pp. 361-85
20 Nicolas, *Dispatches and Letters, op. cit.*, Vol. VII, p. 251
21 *The Life of Sir Edward Codrington, op. cit.*, p. 71
22 *Macmillan's Magazine*, Vol. 81, April 1900, p. 120
23 *The Correspondence of Lord Collingwood, op. cit.*, pp. 141-2
24 BL Additional Manuscripts 38048
25 *The Correspondence of Lord Collingwood, op. cit.*, p. 138
26 *The Life and Services of Sir William Hargood*,

op. cit., p. 289
27 *The Naval Campaign of 1805*, Oxford, 1933, Vol. 2, pp. 256-58
28 *Ibid.*, p. 202
29 *The Life of Sir Edward Codrington, op. cit.*, p. 75
30 *The Naval Camapaign of 1805*, Oxford, 1933, Vol. 2, p. 238
31 *The Life of Sir Edward Codrington, op. cit.*, p. 73
32 *Jack Nastyface, op. cit.*, pp. 61-2
33 Joseph Allen, *The Life and Services of Sir William Hargood*, Greenwich, 1861, pp. 289
34 *Ibid.*, p. 290
35 *The Life of Sir Edward Codrington, op. cit.*, p. 75
36 *Logs of the Great Sea Fights, op. cit.*, Vol. II, p. 255
37 *Ibid.*, p. 206
38 *Jack Nastyface, op. cit.*, p. 51
39 Brian Southam, *Jane Austen and the Navy*, Hambledon and London, 2000, p. 95
40 *Persuasion*, Chapter 3
41 NMM AUS 2b
42 BL Additional Manuscripts 38050
43 9 November 1805
44 *Jack Nastyface, op. cit.*, p. 64
45 NMM ADM/L/B/54
46 Admiralty Progress Books, Vol. 6, f. 9
47 John Mackay, *Anatomy of the Ship – Victory*, London, 1987, p. 12

Chapter 21 The Aftermath
1 G. L. Newnham Collingwood, *The Correspondence of Lord Collingwood*, London, 1828, p. 131
2 John Marshall, *Royal Naval Biography*, London, 1823-35, Supplement Vol. ii, p. 384 ff
3 *Logs of the Great Sea Fights, op. cit.*, Vol. II, p. 319
4 *The Times*, 7 November 1805
5 *The Times*, 8 November 1805
6 *Extracts from the Records of the Burgh of Glasgow*, Vol. IX, 1796-1808, ed. Robert Renwick, Glasgow, 1914, p. 483
7 *The Dorset Captains at Trafalgar, op. cit.*, pp. 146-7
8 NMM AGC/B/11
9 BL Egerton Manuscripts 3782
10 *Ibid.*
11 NMM SPB/15
12 Lady Jane Bourchier, *The Life of Sir Edward Codrington*, London, 1873, Vol. 1, p. 98
13 NMM AGC/H/25
14 *Jack Nastyface, op. cit.*, p. 69
15 *The Correspondence of Lord Collingwood, op. cit.*, p. 494
16 *Ibid.*, p. 559
17 *Ibid.*, p. 564
18 Alfred and Margaret Gatty, *The Life of A J Scott*, London, 1842, p. 265
19 NMM SPB/15
20 BL Additional Manuscripts 38052
21 *The Times*, 9 November 1805
22 BL Additional Manuscripts 38052, 50, 54
23 NMM BGY/T/1

Index

Page numbers in italics refer to illustrations

Achille (Fr) *map 156*, *42*, 159, 175-7, *179*, 180, 182

Achille, HMS *map 156*, 121, 174-6, 184

Active, HMS 72

Adair, Captain William (RM) 21, 66, 165-6

Adams, Cicero 152

Addington, Henry 6-8, 38-40, 91

Africa, HMS 49, 55, 121, 138
    at Trafalgar *map 156*, 173, 178

Agamemnon, HMS *map 156*, 18, 88, 121, 138, 143, 145, 173, 184

Agincourt, HMS 64

Aigle (Fr) *map 156*, 103, 161-2, 175, 178-9, 189, 198

Aikenhead, Midshipman Thomas 153, 183

Ajax, HMS *map 156*, 93, 123, 134, 141-2, 173, 189, 195

Alexander, HMS 20

Algeciras (Fr) *map 156*, 103, 160-1, 185, 186-7, 190

Algiers 69, 196

Alonzo, HMS 59

Alva, R/A *map 156*, 158

Amazon, HMS 19-20, 65-6, 78-9, 82, *151*, 194

Ambuscade, HMS 77, 125-6

Amiens, Peace of 13, 26, 33, 35, 40, 43, 89

Amity, HMS 122

Amphion, HMS 19, 22, 24, 67, 79

Antigua 84, 127

Ape (GB) 69

Arbuthnott, Midshipman Alexander 160

Argonauta (Sp) *map 156*, 163, 174, 179-80

Argonaute (Fr) *map 156*, 102-3

Artois, HMS 88

Assistance, HMS 44

Astrea, HMS 44, 112

Atlas, HMS 124

Aurora, HMS 12, 75

Austen, Captain Francis 32, 38, 77, 77-8, 80, 82-3, 141, 189-90

Austria *map 7*, 75, 105

Badcock, Midshipman William 151

Badger, HMS 18, 158

Bahama (Sp) *map 156*, 163, 186-8

Ball, Captain Alexander 20, 63, 78-9

Bambridge, Hugh 171

Barbados 81-3, *83*, 84

Barfleur, HMS 23, 127

Barham, Admiral Lord 40, 85, *91*, 91-8, 105, 111, 136, 138, 143, 193

Basset Jones, Captain Christopher 56

Bastia, siege of 23, 131

Batavia (Neth) 107

Baynton, Midshipman Benjamin 67

Bayntum, Captain Henry William 53, 121-2, 148, 160, 173

Bayonaise (Fr) 125-6

Beatty, Surgeon William 23, 134, 147, 154, 172

Beaver, HMS 56

Bedford, HMS 49

Belleisle, HMS 67, 86, 135, 143, 145, 147-8, 177, 184, 186, *187*, 188-91
    at Trafalgar 151, 156, 158-60, *161*, *163*, 167, 169, *174*, 176, 180

Bellerophon, HMS 41, 41-5, *44*, 73-4, 119, 121, 144, 148, 152, 156, 179, 190-1, 195, 197
    at Trafalgar *map 156*, 149, 151, 161-2, *163*, 167, 172, 178

Bennett, Lt Charles 186-7

Berry, Captain Sir Edward 121, 138

Berwick (Fr) *map 156*, 22, 102-3, 135, 175-7, 184

Bettesworth, Captain George 84, 96

Bickerton, Admiral Sir Richard 79, 95

Bittern, HMS 78

Blackwood, Captain Henry 54, 88-90, *89*, 98, 121, 134, 143-6, 151, 153-4, 168-9, 183

Bligh, Admiral William 38, 67

Bligh, Captain George 20

blockade strategy 7, 24, 31, 33-4, 44-5, 60, 63-4, 67, 73-4, 79, 90, 95-6, 98-9, 104, 123, 132, 134, 196, 198

Blonde, HMS 21, 119

Boadicea, HMS 191

Boreas, HMS 18

Boulogne *map 7*, *map 28*, 19, 27-33, 28-30, 72, 90, 105

Bounty, HMS 19

Bradbury, Samuel Worthington 113

Brenton, Captain Edward 100-1

Brereton, Brigadier-General Robert 83-4, 86

Brest *map 61*, 20, 24, 27, 31, 44-5, 58, 62, 73-4, 84, 86, 95-6, 98-9, 120, 125, 168, 198

Brighton *34*, 37

Brilliant, HMS 89

Bristol, HMS 158

Britannia, HMS 111, 121, 137, 145, 196
    at Trafalgar *map 156*, 168, 173

Brook, Midshipman F 112

Brown, Captain William 141-2

Brunswick, HMS 73-4

Bucentaure (Fr) *map 156*, *101*, 102-3, 156, 163-5, 170, 173, 180, 187

Buckler's Hard 87, *87*

Bullen, Captain Charles 121, 168

Cadiz *map 61*, *map 100*, *map 145*, 5, 18, 21, 44-5, 60, 63, 70, 76, 79, 97-106, *100*, 111, 115, 132, 156, 187-9
    British fleet at 95, 98, 131-2, 134-46
    French fleet at 90, 98-100, 103-6, 131, 135

leaves for Trafalgar *map 145*, 143-6, 151

Nelson arrives at 98-9, 104

Calais 27, 32

Calder, Admiral Sir Robert 86, 96-7, 131-2, 143
    action off Finisterre 90, 96-7, 103, 123, 142
    court-martial 142-3, 153

Calvi, siege of 23, 131

Camperdown, battle of 19, 62, 128, *148*

Canning, George 10, 134, 197

Canning, William 40

Canopus, HMS 66-7, 77-8, *79*, 80, 82-3, 135, 141-2, 189

Cape Finisterre 86, 96
    see also under Calder

Cape St Vincent 24, 98
    battle of 7, 15, 19, 24-5, 46, 62, 74, 93, 103, 127

Capel, Captain Thomas Bladen 50, 114, 118, 121, 124

Captain, HMS 18, 124, 127

Carcass, HMS 17

Carslake, Midshipman John 24, 70

Cartagena 44, 191, 196

Cary, Midshipman Henry 24

Castle, Midshipman George 158-9, 179

Castlereagh, Lord 98

Cawsand Bay 26, 45, 128-9

Centaur, HMS *137*

Champion, HMS 124

Charlotte Dundas 33

Chaseman, Midshipman William 24

Chatham Dockyard *map 61*, 8-9, 11, *11*, 15-16, *16-17*, 19, 21, 24, 37, 163, 194

Clarke, Captain Robert 123

Clavell, Lt James 131, 147, 157-8, 179, 186, 193, 197

Clephan, Lt James 120

Clerk, John 81

Codrington, Captain Edward 76, 115, 118-19, 131-2, 135, 141-3, 145-7, 152, 168, 173-4, 178, 181, 184, 186-9, 196

Collingwood, Admiral Sir Cuthbert 18, 45, 47-8, 90, 94, 98, 115, 121, *127*, 127-34, 137-8, 140-1, 153, 155, 157, 181-2, 184-5, 190-3, 195-7, 199
    at Trafalgar *map 156*, 147-8, 156, 158-9, 168-9, 174-5, 176, 178-9
    order to anchor 184-6

Collingwood, Midshipman Francis Edward 134

Colossus, HMS *map 145*, 121, 143, 184, 190-1
    at Trafalgar *map 156*, 162-3, 167, 174-5, 180

Colpoys, Admiral Sir John 74

Conn, Captain John 77, 133

Conqueror, HMS 67, 82, 120-1, 169, 170-1, 181, 184, 187
    at Trafalgar *map 156*, 173-4

Cooke, Captain John 45, 121, 144, 148, 161, 197
Copenhagen, battle of (1801) 19-22, 25, 42, 58, 62
Cornwallis, Admiral Sir William 12-13, 24, 43, 73-4, 86, 96-9, 132
Corsica 18, 23, 37, 65, 69, 78
Cosmao, Captain 187-8
Cotton, Captain Charles 73
Courageux, HMS 135
crews *44*, 46-55, *52*
    conditions 46-55, *48-53*, 93, 183-4, 188-9, 196, 198-9
    numbers 6, 8-9, 13, 15, 73, 107-8, 112, 169
        at Trafalgar 143
    quality 12, 42, 45-8, 58, 97, 113-14, 150-1, 170-2
    and women *48*, 109-11, *110*, *112*, 130, 182, *182*
    see also desertions, discipline, officers, press gangs
Culloden, HMS 8, 128
Cumby, Lt William Pryce 44-5, 144, 147-9, 152, 156, 161-2, 172, 195
Curieux, HMS 84, 96, 193

Dalrymple, William 76
D'Auvergne, Captain 123
Defence, HMS *map 145*, 53-4, 56-60, *57*, 119, 121, 123, 138, 141, 143, 190-1
    at Trafalgar *map 156*, 149, 155-6, 176
Defiance, HMS 42, 118-19, 138, 142, 189-90, 198
    at Trafalgar *map 156*, 149, 178-9
Denmark *map 7*, 19, 22, 90, 101
Deptford Dockyard 73, 107
desertions 53-4, 104, 111-12
Dickinson, William 93-4
Digby, Captain Henry 93, 121, 138, 173
Dillon, Lt William 8, 75
discipline 7, 13, 21, 25, 44-5, 51, 53, 56, 68, 82, 113-15, *114-15*, 128-33
Donegal, HMS 67, 82, 188
Donnelly, Captain Ross 63-4
Dover *map 36*, 27, 37, 54
Downs station *map 32*, 26, 31-2, 37, 54, 113
Dreadnought, HMS 13, 42, 123, 129-33, 137, 145, 191
    at Trafalgar *map 156*, 176
Dublin class (GB) 15
Duff, Captain George 48, 59, *74*, 74-6, 138, 143, 152, 160, 168, 183, 198
Duff, Midshipman Norwich 74-6, 183, 198
Duguay-Trouin (Fr) *map 156*, 103, 170
Dumanoir-le-Pelley, Admiral *map 156*, 102, 174
Dumouriez, General Charles Francois 37, 39
Dundas, Henry *see* Melville, Viscount
Dungeness 26, 33, 37-8
Duquesne (Fr) 43
Durham, Captain Phillip 118-19, 138, 142-3, 149, 178

Earl Camden 45
East India Company 10, 40, 45, 108-9
East Indies 57, 60-1
Egypt 18, 34, 40, 62, 72, 96
    see also Nile, battle of the

Elephant, HMS 21
Ellis, 2/Lt Samuel 123
Emerald, HMS 21
Endymion, HMS 142
Entreprenante, HMS 180
Espoir, HMS 198
Euryalus, HMS *map 145*, 54, 87-90, 98, 121, 124, 134, 144, 146, 148, 151-2, 181, 183, 185, 192
    at Trafalgar *map 156*, 153, *154*, 166-7, 168-9
Excellent, HMS 18, 67, 127, 131

Falmouth 26, 193
Ferrol 95-7, 99, 134
Fleming, Captain Charles Elphinstone 112, 198
Flinders, Matthew 45
Flinn, Midshipman 70
Foley, Captain Thomas 19
Formidable (Fr) *map 156*, 102-3, 170, 174
Forrest, W/O Digory 120
Forte, HMS 60
Fortune, HMS 123
Fougeaux (Fr) *map 156*, 102, 158-9
France
    crews 103-4
    declarations of war 13, 15, 18, 26, 35
    fleet sizes *map 156*, 31, 140
    guns and gunnery 41, 100-2, 169
    shipbuilding and design 15, 26, *27*, 28-9, 41, 100-2, 135-6, 138
    transatlantic crossings *map 85*, 80-6, 90, 94, *94*, 98
Franklin, Midshipman John 45, *45*, 116, 161-2
frigates *map 145*, 24-5, 63-4, 72, 77-8, 85, 90, 102, 121, 132, 138-9, 143, 153, 194
Fullarton, Surgeon James 125

Gambier, Admiral Lord 58, 77, 92-3, 110-11
Ganges (GB) 76
Gardner, Admiral Lord 90-1
Garlies, Lord 76, 93, 181
George III, King of England 6, 26, 39, 194
Gibraltar *map 61*, *map 145*, 5, 15, 58, 60, 62, 64, 70, 74, 79, *80*, 85-6, 98, 106, 125, 138, 141-2, 144-5, 168, 186, 188-91, 198
Gibraltar, HMS 67
Gillespie, Dr Leonard 68-72, 134
Glatton, HMS 54
Glenmore, HMS 74-5
Glorious First of June, battle of the 42, 58, 62, 89, 127, 129, 132, 174-5
Gloucester, HMS 6, *51*
Goliath, HMS 19, 42
Gorgon, HMS 59
Graves, V/A Thomas 132
Green, Captain WP 82
Griffiths, Captain AJ 50-1
Grindall, Captain Richard 121
Grindall, Midshipman Festing Horatio 25
Guadeloupe 7, 84
Guillaume Tell (Fr) 89
guns and gun-handling 41, 54, 73-4, 88-9, 100-2, 108, 131, 133, 135-9, 149-52, *150-1*, 158, 160-1, 164, 167-71, *170*, 173, 175

Halcyon, HMS 199
Halloran, Lt 111
Hallowell, Captain Benjamin 78, 171
Hamilton, Emma, Lady 18-19, *19*, 25, 67, 70, 72, 86, 97-8, 154, 195, 197
Hammond, Captain Sir Andrew Snape 119
Hanover *map 7*, 26, 113
Hardy, Captain Thomas Masterman 19, *24*, 25, 40, 46, 69, 71, 81, 86, 117-19, 121, 124, 134, 164-5, 183, 194
    at Trafalgar 147, 153-4, 172, *172*, 184
Harford, Lt 108
Hargood, Captain 159, 180, 186
Harvey, Captain Eliab 121, 164-5
Harwich 9, *10*, 13, 33, 38
health and medicine 43-4, 67-9, 71, 85-6, 124-5, *125*, 130, 162, 171, *171*, 172
Hennah, Lt William 160, 183, 195
Henslow, Sir John 73
Hercule (Fr) 74
Hero, HMS 13
Heros (Fr) *map 156*, 163, 188
Hills, Lt Alexander 67
Hinchinbrooke, HMS 158
Hindustan, HMS 112
Hoffman, Lt Frederick 10-12, 117, 119, 153, 156, 169
Hole, Lt 108
Hood, Captain Alexander 25
Hope, Captain George Johnstone 53-4, 58-60, 121, 123, 141, 155-6, 176
Hope Watson, Charles 59
Hoste, Captain William 124, 198
Hotham, Admiral Sir William 18, 24, 58
Howe, Admiral Lord 15, 58, 132
Huskisson, Midshipman Thomas 56-60, 138, 149, 176
Huskisson, William 56-7
Hussar, HMS 9

Indomptable (Fr) *map 156*, 102, 159
Infernet, Captain 170, 178
Intrepide (Fr) *map 156*, 103, 170, 173-4, 178
Investigator, HMS 45
Invincible (Fr) 41
Invincible, HMS 89, 135
Ireland 33, 37-9, 45, 54, 67, 72, 90, 94, 152
Iris, HMS 90
Italy *map 7*, 6, 30, 62, 64, 138

Jamaica 22, 41, 43-5
Jervis, Admiral Sir John, Earl of St Vincent 6-9, *8*, 15, 18-19, 24, 33-4, 39-40, 42, 44, 63, 68, 70, 79, 89-91, 123-4, 131, 136, 193
Juno, HMS 64

Keats, Captain Richard 69, 80, *81*, 139
Keith, Admiral Lord 19, 24, 31-3, 37-8, 65-6, 90-1, 93
Kent, HMS 67
Keppel, Admiral Augustus 15, 136
King, Captain Richard 121, 174

Laforey, Captain Francis 121, 169, 174
Lapenotière, Lt John 193
Lapwing, HMS 129
Lechmere, Captain William 142
Leopard, HMS 77
Leviathan, HMS 53, 67, 121-2, 124, 148, 191
 at Trafalgar *map 156*, 154, 160, 171-3
Linois, Admiral 45
Lively, HMS 88
Loring, Captain John 43, 45
Louis, Admiral Thomas 77, 80, 85, 106,
 141-2, 145, 168, 189-90
Lowestoffe, HMS 127, 158
Lucas, Captain 104, 164
Lynx, HMS 124

Maddalena Islands *map 61*, *map 65*, 64-5, 69,
 72, 78, 110
Magrath, Surgeon George 22, 70
Majestic, HMS 107, 112-13
Malta *map 7*, *map 61*, 26, 62-7, 89, 138
Mangin, Chaplain Edward 50
Mansfield, Captain 174
Mansfield, Midshipman John 117-18
Mars, HMS *map 145*, 10, 13, 48, 59, *73*, 73-6,
 138, 143-4, 152, 183, 191, 195, 198
 at Trafalgar *map 156*, 160, 167-8
Marshall, James 45, 152
Martinique 7, 83-4
Mason, John 49, 55
McKerlie, Lt John 52, 120
Meleager, HMS 25
Melville, Viscount (Henry Dundas) 33, *38*,
 40, 58, 72, 74, 78-9, 91, 93
 replaced by Barham 79, 91
Merton 86, 97, *97*, 98, 134, 139
Middleton, Sir Charles *see* Barham, Admiral Lord
Miller, Captain Ralph 21
Minerve, HMS 25
Minorca *map 61*, 78, 197
Minotaur, HMS *map 156*, 10-11, 13, 152, 174
Monarca (Sp) *map 156*, 160, 160-1, 162
Montanes (Sp) *map 156*, *102*, 161, 174
Mont-Blanc (Fr) *map 156* 102-3, 170
Moore, Midshipman Joseph 181, 185-6
Moorsom, Captain Robert 107-8, 112-14,
 123, 141, 175, 181
Morocco 79, 189
Morris, Captain James Nicoll 121, 162-3
Mulgrave, Admiral Lord 44, 112, 197
Mullan, Matthew 103
Murray, William 125-6
Mutine, HMS 25
mutinies 7, 19, 24, 34, 42, 53, 58, 74, 93,
 133, 178

Nagle, Midshipman Archibald 119
Naiad, HMS 13, 121, *174*, 184, 186, 190
Naples *map 7*, 18-19, 25, 69, 78, 124, 196
Napoleon I, Emperor of the French 18, 23,
 26, 36, 40, *41*, 67, 95-6, 100, 104-6, *105*
 expedition to Egypt *map 63*, 18, 40, 72
 see also Nile, battle of the

plans for the invasion of England 6, 12,
 26-39, 72, 78, 94-5, 97, 99, 105
Narcissus, HMS 63-4
Nelson, Frances 18
Nelson, Horatia 154
Nelson, V/A Horatio Lord 10, 18, 117-18,
 120, 185
 'Band of Brothers' 19, 77, 118, 124, 143
 see also individual officers
 career 14, 17-19, 21, 23-5, 31, 40, 44, 58,
 61-4, 66-70, 103, 112, 122, 124, 127, 138
 see also Copenhagen, battle of, and
 Nile, battle of the
 character 19-20, 22, 25, 53, 70-1, 99, 130-2, 143
 death of 165-7, *167*, *172*, 172-3, 179, 184,
 189, 198
 letters 18, 20, 22, 24-5, 67-8, 70, 72, 78-80,
 84, 89, 132, 138-9, 142
 marriage 18, 76
 mourning and funeral 192-6, *193*, *195*, 198
 on Trafalgar campaign *map 156*, 98, 104, 106,
 121, 134-5, 147-8, 153-4, *154*, 158-9, 165,
 168, 178, 184
 pursuit of Villeneuve 78-86, 90, 96, 101, 141
 reputation 6, 60, 97, 141, 199
 tactics 63-4, 78-82, *81*, 105, 136, 139-40,
 139-41
 at Cadiz 98-9, 104, 108, 132-4, *134*, 138,
 142-4
 at Trafalgar *map 145*, *map 156*, 19, *139-40*,
 139-41, 143-9, 145, 151, 154, 156-8, 161,
 168, 170, 173, 175
Nepean, Sir Evan 93, 139
Neptune (Fr) *map 156*, 102, 159, 164, 176, 188
Neptune, HMS 13, 19, 119-20, 137, 189
 at Trafalgar *map 156*, 151, 154, 156, 172-3,
 178
Neptuno (Sp) *map 156*, 170, 174, 188
Netherlands 26-7, 31, 34, 37-8, 60, 101
Nicolas, Lt Paul (RM) 147-8, 159-60, 181,
 186
Nile, battle of the *map 63*, 6, 18-21, 25, 31,
 40, 42, 46, 56, 58, 62-3, 70, 77, 89, 97, 99,
 110, 124, 171, 177
Nore station 11, 111-12, 113
 Nore mutiny 7, 53
Northesk, R/A the Earl of *map 156*, 111, 121,
 168, 173, 195
Northumberland, HMS 83

Ocean, HMS 195, 199
officers 116-26
 conditions 71-2, 196
 entry and training 57-60, *116*, 116-20, *118*,
 120, 127
Orde, Admiral Sir John 60, 70, 79-80
Orient (Fr) 18
Orion, HMS 76, 115, 118-19, 125, 131, 135,
 141, 143, 145, 152, 168, 186-8, 190-1
 at Trafalgar *map 156*, 163
Ostend 27, 32
Overton, Edward 147-8, 161
Owen, Captain EWCR 31

Owen, Lt John (RM) 159, 179-80

Pakenham, Captain Thomas 89
Panther, HMS 74
Parker, Admiral Sir Peter 97
Parker, Captain Peter 189
Parker, Captain William 65, 70, 78-80, 82-4, 194
Pascoe, Lt John 70, 154, 196
Patten, Admiral Phillip 46-7, 51, 53-4, 93
Patton, Midshipman Robert 45, 162, 172
Paulet, Captain Lord Harry 44
Pellew, Captain Israel 121
Pellew, Captain Sir Edward 31, 129
Penelope, HMS 89
Phoebe, HMS *map 145*, *map 156*, 50, 78, 114,
 118, 121
Phoenix, HMS 90
Pickering, Lt Peter 108
Pickernell, Lt Peter 198
Pickle, HMS 144, 180, 182, *192*, 193
Pilfold, Lt John 173, 195
Pitt, William, the Younger 7, 10, 38-40, 93, 98
Plumridge, Lt James 149
Pluto, HMS 76
Pluton (Fr) *map 156*, 103, 160, 187-8
Plymouth Dockyard *map 61*, 8, 10-13, 22,
 24, 26, 37, 58, 74-5, 77, 96, 123, 128-9,
 132, 134, 191
Pollard, Midshipman John 164-6, 198
Polyphemus, HMS *map 145*, *map 156*, 45, 116,
 138, 176
Popham, Captain Sir Home 56-8, *57*, 123,
 144, 154
Portsmouth Dockyard *map 61*, 8, 9, 12, 26, 37,
 41, 56, 60, 75-6, 89, 98, 123-4, 132, 134,
 134, 191, 196
Portugal 7, 70, 79-80, 90, 134, 188, 198
Powell, John 108-11, 113, 175-6
press gangs and impressment 8-13, 9, 19, 43, 54,
 58, 86, 89, 113, *114*, 116, 120, 123, 152, 196
Price, Lt James 190
Prince George, HMS 93
Prince, HMS *map 156*, 12, 121, 125, 129,
 137, 145, 189, 191
 at Trafalgar *map 156*, 176-7, 180
Prince of Wales, HMS 131, 143
Principe de Asturias (Sp) *map 156*, 103, 175-6,
 178
Pringle, Captain 76
Prowse, Captain William 121
pursers 125-6, *126*
Pym, Captain Samuel 74

Queen, HMS 142, 190-1
Quiberon Bay, battle of 6, 15, 93, 101
Quillam, Lt John 19-20, 22, 154, 193, 195-6

Racehorse, HMS 70
Ram, Midshipman William 67, 141
Rambler, HMS 123
Ranger, HMS 21
Rattler, HMS 21
Rayo (Sp) *map 156*, 103, 188

Redmill, Captain Robert 138
Redoutable (Fr) *map 156*, 102-4, 157, 163-6
Renown, HMS 67
Resistance, HMS 24
Revenge, HMS 49-50, *107*, 107-15, 123, 141, 181-3, 188-91, 193, 196, 198
    at Trafalgar *map 156*, 152, 156, 175-6
Rhin (Fr) *map 156*
Rickards, Sam 171-2
Rivers, Midshipman William *23*, 24, 158
Rivers, William (gunner) 22-4, 151
Robinson, Captain Mark 133
Robinson, Midshipman Hercules 129, 151-2, 166-7
Robinson, Midshipman James 160
Robinson, William 49-52, 111-12, 114-15, 152, 156, 175-6, 189, 196, 198
Rochambeau, General 43
Rochefort *map 61*, 74, 95-6
Rodney, Admiral 58, 93
Romney, HMS 56-7, 59-60, 123
Rosily, V/A Francois 105-6, 156
Roteley, Lt Louis 156, 165-6, 171
Rotherham, Captain Edward 117, 121, *129*, 129-31, 133, 149, 157-9, 168-9, 196-8
Royal Dockyards 7-9, 101
    see also individual dockyards
Royal Marines 8, 11-13, 21, 49, *49*, 50, 53, 66, 70, 108, 113-14, 120, 123, 156, 160, 165, 169
    at Trafalgar 159, 162
Royal Sovereign, HMS 21-2, 64, 67, 80, 119, 121, *132*, 132-3, 137, 143, 153, 183, 190-1, 193, 196-7
    at Trafalgar *map 156*, 155-60, 164, 167, 169, 174-5, 179, 184
Royal William, HMS 42, 56
Ruby, HMS 59
Ruckert, Frederick 124, 144
Russell, HMS 12
Ryves, Captain George 64

Saintes, battle of the 6, 74
Salvador del Mundo, HMS 11-12, 13
San Augustin (Sp) *map 156*, 172-3
San Francisco de Asis (Sp) *map 156*, 188
San Idelfonso (Sp) *map 156*, 176, 190
San Josef, HMS 18, 21-2
San Juan Nepomuceno (Sp) *map 156*, 160, 176
San Justo (Sp) *map 156*
San Leandro (Sp) *map 156*, 159
San Nicolas (Sp) 18
Sane, Jacques-Noel 101-2
Santa Ana (Sp) *map 156*, 103, 158-9, 179-80, 188
Santisima Trinidad (Sp) *map 156*, 103, 136, 156, 163, 165, 173, 178, 180, 189
Sardinia *map 7*, *map 61*, 64-5, 66, 77-8
Saunders, Lt George 162
Scipion (Fr) *map 156*, 103, 170
Scott, John (purser) 14, 21-2, 140, 154, 165
Scott, Revd Alexander John 22, *22-3*, 63, 69-70, 72, 82, 154, 183, 195, 197
'Sea Fencibles' 33, 38, 45, 54, 77
Seaforth, Lord 83
Seahorse, HMS 17-18, 72
Secker, Sergeant (RM) *23*, 165

Senhouse, Lt Humphrey 167, 169, 170-1, 184
Serapis, HMS 108
Severn, HMS 123
Sheerness 11, 16, 32, 56
shipbuilding and design 41, *42*, 87-8, 100-1, 103, 132, 135, 168
Shoveller, Surgeon William 124
Sicily 69, 78
Sirius, HMS *map 145*, *map 156*, 121, 123, 144, 146
Slade, Sir Thomas 15, 132, 137-8
Smith, Cdre Sir Sidney 31
Smith, Lt John 178
Smith, Midshipman Robert 153
Smyth, Midshipman Spencer 198
Southampton class (GB) 15
Spain *map 7*, 5, 7, 15, 18-19, 25, 30, 44, 58, 60, 62-3, 64, 78-9, 83-4, 90, 96-9, *104*, 135, 143, 178, 188
    fleet at Trafalgar *map 156*, 140, 169-71
    see also individual ships
    shipbuilding and design 100-1, 103, 135-6
    at war with Britain 18, 62-4, 69-70
Spartiate, HMS 10, 13, 52, 83, 120-1, 137, 169, 177, 184, 191
    at Trafalgar *map 156*, 174, 180
Spear, Lt Richard 120
Spencer, HMS 67, 142
Spider, HMS 68
Spithead 7, 26, 53, 68, 74, 86, 89, 113, 119, 194
Spratt, Midshipman James 119, 149, 178-9, 189, 198
St Domingue 43
St George, HMS 21
St Lucia 83, 87
St Vincent, Earl of *see* Jervis, Admiral Sir John
Stevenson, Benjamin 13, 68, 86, 198-9
Stirling, R/A 96, 134
Stockham, Lt John 176, 195
Strachan, Captain Sir John 190
Suckling, Captain Maurice 17
Superb, HMS 67-8, 80, 86, 139
Sutton, Captain John 74-5
Sutton, Captain Samuel 19-20, 24, 79, 85
Swallow, HMS 42
Sweden *map 7*, 45, 101, 151-2
Swiftsure (Fr) *map 156*, 87, 102, 135, 162-3, 173, 177
Swiftsure, HMS 171, 191
    at Trafalgar 176

Taylor, William 151
Telford, Robert 113
Temeraire, HMS 121, 137, 164, 190-1, 196
    at Trafalgar *map 156*, 154, 165, 174, 180
Tenerife 18, 21, 89
Terror, HMS 74
Texel, HMS 123
Thalia, HMS 44
Theseus, HMS 21
Thomas, Lt Frederick 120
Thornborough, Admiral Edward 59, 74
Thunderer, HMS 13, 134, 142, 190-1, 195
    at Trafalgar *map 156*, 176-7

Tigre, HMS 78, 80, 142
Tonnant, HMS 10, 13, 135, 137, 177, 184, 186, 190-1
    at Trafalgar *map 156*, 152, 159-62
Torbay 13, 26, 43, 75
Toulon *map 61*, *map 63*, 6, 23-4, 31, 63-4, 67-8, 97, 99, 143
    French fleet breaks out from 68-9, 72
    for transatlantic crossing 78-9
Trafalgar, battle of *map 5*, *map 7*, *map 145*, *map 156*, 5-6, 126, 147-82
    engagement 147-80
    see also individual commanders and ships, and under Nelson
Triumph, HMS 19, 23, 67
Tunisia 69, 78
Tyler, Captain Charles 160-1

USA 33, 84, 134, 151-2
    War of Independence 7, 15, 18, 30, 45, 58, 74, 112, 127, 132
Utile, HMS 108
Utrecht, HMS 21

Valiant, HMS 15
Vanguard, HMS 18, 43, 56, 64
Venerable, HMS 127-8, 131, *148*
Victorious, HMS 54
Victory, HMS 13, *14*, 14-25, 48, 53, 64, 67-8, 70-1, *71*, 74, 79, 85-6, 90, 97-8, 110, 117, 121, 131, 134, 141, 143-4, 159, *166*, 171, 183, 185-6, 190-1, 193-6
    armament 17
    construction and design 14-15, 41, 137-8, 163
    guns 22-3, 41
    at Trafalgar *map 156*, 151-4, *154*, 156, 158, 163-7, 172-4, 180, 182, 182-3, 183
    victualling and supplies 68-71, 85, 113-14, 141-2, 148, 152
Ville de Paris, HMS 15, 124, 197
Villeneuve, Admiral Pierre Charles de *map 156*, 78, 83-5, 90, 94, 96, 98-100, *99*, 102-6, 131, 151, 156, 170, 180

warrant officers 21-3, *23*, 43, 120, 122, 123-6, 148, 199
Weazle, HMS 144, 189
Wellington, Duke of 34, 196, 198
West Indies 6-7, 12, 17-18, 21, 23, 34, 43-5, 61-2, 63, 74, 78-80, 83-4, 85, 90, 95-6, 99, 119, 127, 129, 148
    see also individual islands
Westphal, Midshipman George Augustus 25, 159, 198
Whitby, Captain John 63, 67
Whyte, Surgeon Alexander 43, 124
William Henry, Prince (Duke of Clarence) 18, 20, 97, 196
Williams, Lt Edward 196

Yule, Lt John 20, 24, 154, 182-3, 196

Zealand, HMS 108, 112-13
Zealous, HMS 142